MODELLING, PROGRAMMING AND SIMULATIONS USING LABVIEW™ SOFTWARE

Edited by **Riccardo de Asmundis**

Modelling, Programming and Simulations Using LabVIEW™ Software
Edited by Riccardo de Asmundis

Published by InTech
Janeza Trdine 9, 51000 Rijeka, Croatia

Publishing Process Manager Iva Lipovic

Technical Editor Teodora Smiljanic

Cover Designer InTech Design Team

Additional hard copies can be obtained from orders@intechopen.com

Modelling, Programming and Simulations Using LabVIEW™ Software,
Edited by Riccardo de Asmundis
p. cm.
ISBN 978-953-307-521-1

For EU product safety concerns:
IN TECH d.o.o., Prolaz Marije Krucifikse Kozulić 3, 51000 Rijeka, Croatia, info@intechopen.com or visit our website at intechopen.com.

Meet the editor

Riccardo de Asmundis has been a senior researcher at the "Istituto Nazionale di Fisica Nucleare" (INFN), Naples Section, since January 1st 2007, where he has been working since 1991. He taught computer architecture, automatic measurements and data acquisition systems at the Information Technology Department of the University "Federico II" of Naples from 2001 until 2004. He has been a Certified LabVIEW Developer (CLD) and Certified Professional Instructor (CPI) for the National Instruments Company (Austin, Texas) with continuity since 2004, frequently giving courses for National Instruments Italy, both in industries and universities.

Contents

Preface

Released by National Instruments (Austin, Texas) for the first time in 1986 for the Apple Macintosh, LabVIEW was conceived as a practical and original programming environment for hardware control and interfacing with host computer. The main aim was the introduction of an easy interface between a micro-computer and the instruments controlled by it, with a graphical interface which simulates the actual instrument on the computer screen: from this the derivation of the term "Virtual Instrument" and the more general "Virtual Instrumentation". The strong originality of LabVIEW as a programming language, instead, came from the innovative way of programming introduced since the beginning: a pure graphical way, in which the characters-based program lines are replaced with one or more graphical schemes which take the role of the human interface for the developer specialist. This way both "user interface" (the windows with which the final user will interact) as well as the "source code" (the actual program written by the developer) have high quality graphics aspects, carrying the two different contents and purposes. A meta-language is internally generated during development processes and is used as source for the LabVIEW Compiler for the generation of the final executive object. This object runs under a specific "run time engine" which is the real object handled by the Operating System and is automatically installed with the LabVIEW development system.

The development system has undergone an enormous evolution in the years, with an assessed regulation in terms of the new delivered versions today: a new version every year which carries in its name the reference to the year itself, and at least two releases in the same year. The latest version (LabVIEW 2010) represents the current evolution of a long improvement process which never stops: it includes, for instance, among many features, the straightforward control of NI-DAQ devices, several Protocols for Instruments controls and driving, Advanced automatic code generation as "Express Vis", direct Web integration, real time development environment for RT processing, FPGA code designing and integration, advanced graphical tools, high powerful mathematical processing tools, direct integration with Matlab and Mathematica, tools for modeling and industrial controls, and so on. The current philosophy related to the use of most of these tools is a strong reduction of the development time as well as the effective "designing time": many Virtual Instruments are already there and "ready to use".

"*For more than 20 years, NI LabVIEW graphical development has revolutionized the development of scalable test, measurement, and control applications. Regardless of experience, engineers and scientists can rapidly and cost-effectively interface with measurement and control hardware, analyze data, shared results, and distribute systems.*" This sentence was pronounced by Jeff Kodosky, one of National Instruments founder and the LabVIEW inventor, in the occasion of the 20th birthday of LabVIEW in 2006. Well, this should be the philosophy to be carried on by each single developer who, to be considered a good developer, should follow the product into its evolution along the years in order to be up to date for the new features and possibilities and to use it in an effective way.

We divided the book into four parts, based on the field of applications of the presented chapters.

The first Part is called "LabVIEW in Monitoring and Controls Domains" and includes four Chapters: it is dedicated to one of the canonical ways of utilization of LabVIEW, namely the control of instrumentation and experiments, even with distributed facilities in some cases. The Applications presented here are characterized by a general and common approach which is typical for LabVIEW in the control domain: this approach is based upon a set of instruments and/or sensors read out by the controlling PCs; data are then archived locally and optionally distributed to other control points over a network. Such an approach can be very powerful for the improvement of the quality of a laboratory, which can share resources and data, sometimes in a very flexible way.

The second Part, named "LabVIEW in Modeling" is dedicated to the Modeling performed in LabVIEW often compared with a different modeling system. Modeling, in general, is an approach to perform extended or complex calculations based on some physical model for different applications: the results of such calculations are used to fill tables or files and are susceptible to be presented in the appropriate graphical form in order to obtain practical responses on the simulated model. These responses are useful to continue the development of the research line involved from beginning. Three Chapters compose this Part: an application in biological field which involves Escherichia coli for protein production, a model for the hysteresis in magnetic materials and a third for the respiratory movements.

In the third Part, "LabVIEW for Specific Processes and Applications", we include Chapters characterized by very specific application fields. The purpose of these applications are similar to the ones presented in the first part, but with the main difference of being not so general as designing approach but strictly tuned for the application treated. Situations that lead to these solutions are the ones where the measures can be difficult or can involve specific hardware sometimes specifically developed for that. The development approach can be considered as limited to some kind of particular files (i.e. low current measurement, very low voltage or high voltage measurement, small dimensioned specimen, etc.). Four Chapters are included in semiconductor, spectroscopy and optical fields and in the health field.

The last Part, named "LabVIEW in the Educational Domain", includes two chapters whose content is somehow related to the education. They present general purpose applications for laboratory control but with an approach or a finality typical of the educational environment.

We hope this book dedicated to LabVIEW and its aspects can strongly evolve in the future, by including not only more Applications developed, but also by transmitting to the reader the likeness in the LabVIEW development without forgetting its power, flexibility and the universality intrinsically existing in it.

Riccardo de Asmundis
National Institute of Nuclear Physics, Napoli
European Organization for Nuclear Research (CERN), Geneva
Certified LabVIEW Developer and Instructor, National Instruments

Part 1

LabVIEW in Monitoring and Controls Domains

1

Advanced Total Lab Automation System (ATLAS)

Christoph Wagner, Andreas Genner, Georg Ramer and Bernhard Lendl
Vienna University of Technology
Austria

1. Introduction

In modern analytical chemistry not only do new measurement principles have to be investigated but newly found techniques also need to be developed into integrated and more and more automated analytical solutions. Exploring new techniques in research and development (R&D) environments mostly means designing different setups incorporating a huge variety of different equipment. Whether this hardware is a pump, a valve or more complex elements such as oscilloscopes, lasers or detectors, in one way or another they can be controlled by a computer or the acquired data is digitized and evaluated afterwards. Those setups, however, change frequently in R&D labs to evaluate new ideas or to improve a current setup. Inevitably whenever the setup chances, the software controlling it will also need adaptation. An ideal software platform, therefore, would reduce the time needed for making those changes to a minimum, giving the researcher the possibility to focus on the evaluation of new approaches and the characterization of new techniques. Especially for small startup companies it might also be of great interest that the needed software packages can be maintained and adopted by the scientist himself instead of the need to outsource it to a software company. This would not only reduce the cycle time from a new idea to the first prototype but also has the potential to decrease the associated costs.

One programming language ideally suited for such a software environment is LabVIEW from National Instruments. Due to its graphical programming language all data flow is visualized directly in the source code. This fact makes it easier to read and understand a given program, especially for beginners without programming experience in classical programming languages, such as C++ or Visual Basic. Another point where LabVIEW outperforms other programming languages is it's rich library of Graphical User Interface (GUI) elements, for example XY graphs are predefined as well as 3D graphs. Another advantage of LabVIEW is the very simple way to create parallel running tasks. In combination with LabVIEW's queues, which represent a "first in - first out" buffer system, separating the readout of data and its evaluation can be separated easily. Using National Instruments hardware for the data readout brings easy integration for the software developer. Secondly interfaces for RS-232, GPIB, USB etc. are also provided for communicating with third party hardware.

All these advantages make LabVIEW a good choice for developing software in R&D laboratories. Generally speaking, laboratories focus on the development of software for their current experimental setup ending up with a LabVIEW program built for this specialized task. Dominguez et al. designed a LabVIEW program to control a Sequential Injection Analysis (SIA) system (Dominguez et al., 2010) which consisted of a valve and a peristaltic pump. Jitmanee et al. used a more complex liquid handling system consisting of three valves and three pumps to automatically prepare samples for Inductive Coupled Plasma Mass Spectrometry (ICP-MS) measurements (Jitmanee et al., 2007). Barzin et al. proposed a spectrophotometric method for pH measurements in miniaturized systems where LabVIEW handles data acquisition from a flowmeter and a spectrometer and is linked to a Matlab feedback loop to calculate the appropriate flow rate which is sent to a syringe pump afterwards via LabVIEW (Barzin et al., 2010). In all these examples the program is limited to control the hardware it was designed for. In the first two examples automation tasks are carried out whereas in the latter one a complex control feedback loop is realized. When we started working with LabVIEW we wanted to create a software platform, which gives the operator the freedom to combine different hardware elements in any imaginable way without the need to make changes to the program code. Only adding new hardware to the software platform should require software changes, which would be easier using LabVIEW than any other programming language.

First we created a program that allowed the combination of valves, pumps and an high voltage supply for the sample preparation with an UV detector and infrared spectrometers from Bruker Optics to build different setups including SIA (Růzicka, 1992) and flow injection analysis (FIA) (Růzicka, 1981) systems as well as capillary electrophoreses systems (Wagner et al., 2010). To address all necessary components in a simple way we decided to use a scripting language containing commands representing tasks including switching a valve, applying voltages or starting measurements. The script was written manually and afterwards started sending commands to the connected hardware consecutively. This system allowed the easy combination of the integrated hardware into different analytical systems. However, after adding support for additional hardware and the need for more complex commands the GUI became too crowded with elements and writing the scripts became more and more difficult due to the number of available commands.

Our first program allowed the scientist to combine all integrated components with ease but adding new hardware components to the program became more and more sophisticated due to the growing source code. Therefore, we decided to create a new platform based on a client server approach, where every hardware component is controlled by a dedicated client which can be controlled remotely by a server application. A schematic of this software platform can be seen in figure 1. Each of the clients can be run in three different modes. The *local mode* directly interacts with the connected hardware upon user input, the *programming mode* sends commands to the server application and in the *server mode* the clients receive commands from the server and execute them on their hardware. In that manner adding new hardware is done by adding client specific program code to a provided client template, containing all necessary code to handle the communication with the server. Additionally the user doesn't need to remember client specific commands because the programming of a sequence can be done with the GUI of each client.

In the following we will describe our *Advanced Total Laboratory Automation System* (ATLAS), including a list of existing clients as well as two examples of experimental setups controlled by ATLAS.

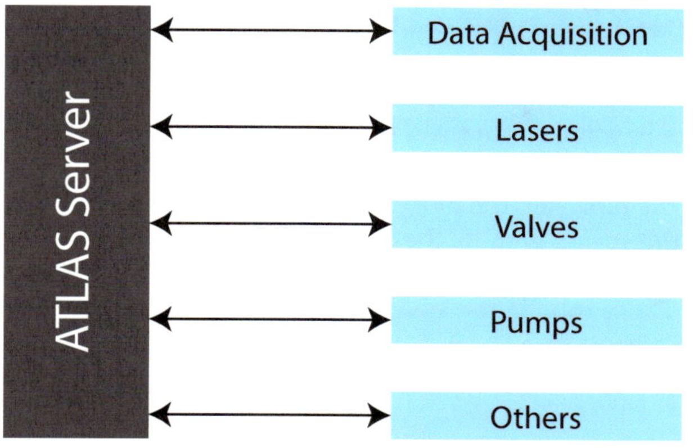

Fig. 1. Schematic of our *Advanced Total Laboratory Automation System* (ATLAS). Each hardware component is controlled by a dedicated client program which can communicate with the ATLAS server to be remote controlled.

2. The ATLAS platform

The ATLAS platform consists of one *server* application and numerous *client* applications. Each client controls connected hardware such as a pump, valves or a spectrometer. The *server* is used to remote control connected *clients* by sending script commands over a TCP/IP connection to the *clients*. Each *client* can be used in a *local* mode, as well, to control connected hardware directly. The *server* application was designed so that adding new *clients* can be done without modifying the *server* application.

2.1 Client server communication

2.1.1 Simple TCP/IP Messaging (STM)

The ATLAS software is based on the *Simple Messaging Reference Library (STM)*[1] maintained by National Instruments, which contains a set of VIs for developing server/client-based applications. Beside the *TCP Connection Manager VI*, which handles connection informations, the library contains also VIs for transporting data over TCP/IP connections.

First of all, a server, handling several clients, requires a *New Connection Monitor*[2], which creates a listener on a certain port (e.g. 8080) and waits until a client tries to establish a TCP network connection. In the next step the server defines meta data, which basically define data channels for data transportation. All information concerning a certain client connection is stored using the *TCP Connection Manager VI*, which represents a Functional Global Variable (FGV). All further communication between the server and the connected clients is handled in a seperate loop, called the server loop, by accessing this FGV.

The *TCP Connection Manager VI* offers also the functionality for listing all established connections. The resulting output is an array of connection-IDs which has to be indexed for sending or receiving data to a specific client. If the communication to a client breaks down due to hardware- (e.g. network cable is unplugged), or software problems (e.g. client program crashes) it is necessary to remove the connection information of this client from the

---

[1] http://zone.ni.com/devzone/cda/tut/p/id/4095

[2] http://zone.ni.com/devzone/cda/tut/p/id/3055

FGV. Otherwise the server may try to send data to an unreachable client which would lead to a timeout. All data between the server and the clients is transported by using the *STM Write Message* and *STM Read Message VIs*. Beside the string that has to be sent, a cluster, containing timeout settings, can be attached to the *STM Write Message VI*. At first, the meta data index, containing the data channel names is obtained, flattened to a string and concatenated with the data to send. In the next step the byte length of this data string is calculated and attached to the beginning of the string. Finally, the complete string is written to the TCP connection. The receiving program utilizes the *STM Read Message VI* to read the first four bytes of the transported string. These four bytes are converted to an integer representing the length of the remaining data string. In a second step this value is taken to read the residual data. Finally, the transported string can be accessed for further processing.

2.1.2 Communication principle

The communication between the server and the connected clients is controlled by the server only. This means that the server sends commands to the clients, which reply to the server afterwards (for a typical communication sequence see figure 2). Every 50 ms the server queries the status of the connected clients by sending the command *status*. Receiving the status request for the first time after establishing the connection to the server a client replies with *cmd:ID* identifying itself with its *client identifier*, where ID consists of two device depending alphanumerical characters. Upon the reception of a *cmd:ID* string the server stores the new client and the according STM connection ID. This data is accessed by the server to send client specific commands only to the according client in any further communication.

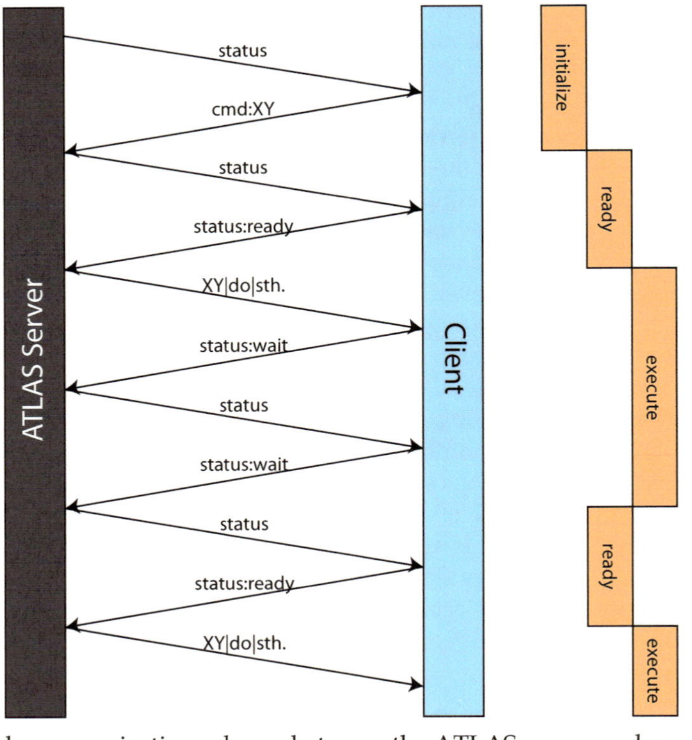

Fig. 2. Simplified communication scheme between the ATLAS server and one client.

Receiving further status queries from the server clients respond with either *status:ready*, *status:wait* or *status:error*. *status:ready* means that the client is ready to accept instructions from the server and that both, software and hardware, are working correctly. *status:wait* will be sent if the client is executing a command, such as measuring a voltage or recording a spectrum. In the case that a hardware failure occurred or an invalid command was sent to the client, it will respond with *status:error*.

After the user starts the execution of the sequence by clicking the corresponding button, the server checks whether all required clients are connected. If so, it will run the command interpreter, described in section 2.2.2. Afterwards the server begins distributing commands to the correct clients. After a command was sent the server goes on with polling the status of the connected clients. The addressed client starts executing the received command and answers *status:wait* to the server. The server will continue the execution of the script as soon as its status requests are answered with *status:ready* instead of *status:wait*.

In case a device failure occurs (e.g.: a tubing is plugged, a device becomes disconnected) or an invalid command was sent, the client controlling the according device will answer the status request from the server with *status:error*. As a result the server terminates the running sequence and executes the alias-command *AL|error*. As explained later in section 2.2.2 the server notifies all connected clients of the error event. The clients will execute a special protocol that contains commands for such an error case. Usually it is sufficient to abort the experiment, but some devices have to be shut down in a special way to avoid further problems.

2.2 Server application

2.2.1 Description

The central part of ATLAS server is a timed loop structure, further referred to as *server loop*, and can be seen in the middle of the plotted code in figure 3. As already mentioned in section 2.1.1 the *TCP Connection Manager VI* is used to list all connections established to clients. The resulting array of connection IDs of connected clients is treated in a for-loop structure. In this for-loop the server requests status information from the currently addressed client. It can respond with one of the following strings which is evaluated by the server in a case structure:

- *cmd:ID*: The client-ID is added to the list of *available client commands*.
- *programming*: The received string is added to the *commands_list*.
- *status:ready*: In that case the corresponding LED in the *available client commands*-list turns green.
- *status:wait*: A variable is set to prevent sending the next command. In addition, the LED next to the client-ID turns red, indicating that the client is currently executing a task.
- *status:error*: The command queue is flushed and therefore the command `AL|error` is interpreted. As the software should also display an error message, the client-ID is inserted into a queue. Outside of the communication loop is a while loop which is only used for displaying error messages. This makes it possible, to go on with sending the error information immediately to all clients instead of waiting for an user interaction.

If a time-out occurs while the server awaits the answer from the client because the connection was interrupted, the *TCP Check Connection VI* removes the connection from the *Connection Manager VI* and the client-ID is removed from the list of *available clients*. This client list is displayed on the GUI to visualize the status of the connected clients. Finally, the received string from the client is logged together with a timestamp for debugging purposes.

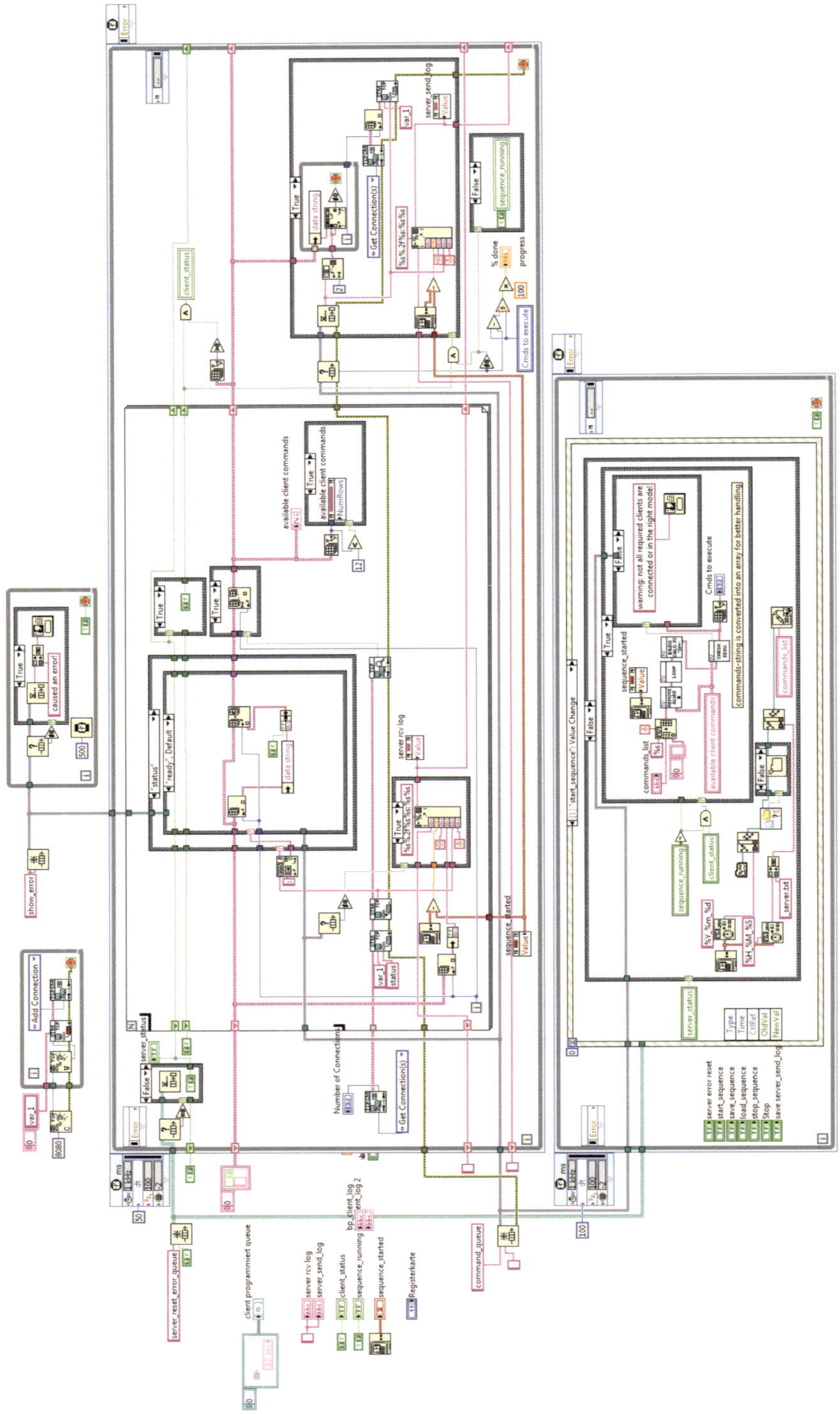

Fig. 3. Code of the ATLAS server application.

This procedure is repeated in the for-loop for each client and after each client responds *status:ready* the server takes the next available command from the script. The corresponding client is identified by its client ID and the command is sent over the corresponding TCP connection. In addition the timestamp and the sent string are logged and the progress of the script execution is visualized.
User input such as loading, saving, starting and canceling of sequences, as well as saving the server-send-log, is treated by an additional event handler structure. Whenever a script is executed the server automatically saves the script sequence to be able to connect recorded measurement data unambiguously with the used sequence.

2.2.2 Additional server features

Before the ATLAS server starts distributing the commands to the corresponding clients, the sequence has to pass an interpreter. It enables three useful features which are a for-loop, a mathematical formula solver and the use of aliases. Moreover, the software supports the usage of comments, which have to start with a hash key. These features can be used to program complex script sequences and are summarized in table 1.

feature	code	result
comment	`#this is a comment`	

loop	`loop($i=5|9|1)`
	`WA|$i|sec`
	`loop_end`
		`WA|5|sec`
		`WA|6|sec`
		`WA|7|sec`
		`WA|8|sec`
		`WA|9|sec`

mathematics	`loop($i=0|2|1)`
	`WA|(5^$i+2^2-exp(0.5)+sin(1.5))`
	`loop_end`
		`WA|4.349|sec`
		`WA|8.349|sec`
		`WA|28.349|sec`

alias	`AL|name|sample_001`	`AA|name|sample_001`
		`AB|name|sample_001`
		`AC|name|sample_001`
		`AD|name|sample_001`

Table 1. Examples for the script-interpreter features. It is able to handle loops, formulas and aliases.

2.2.2.1 Loop constructions in the script sequence

Often a part of a sequence has to be executed many times. For example, a scientist wants to measure a large number of liquid samples by using valves and pumps. One way to solve this problem is to enter every line of the sequence manually, which means that every change of the valve-position and every operation of the pump has to be written down in the sequence. As this way is inefficient and hard to adopt to further experiments, the ATLAS server implements a function that is similar to a for-loop in conventional programming. In C++, for example, a for-loop begins with `for(int i=5; i<13; i++){` and ends with `}` whereas the repeated code is located between the braces. Scientists, who want to use such a function in their ATLAS sequence, have to write the repeated section between the lines `loop($i=5|13|1)` and `loop_end`. The opening bracket is followed by `$`, a variablename, `=` and the starting point for the variable. The next number is the last variable value and the third number represents the increment. Nested loops are also allowed whereas different variable names have to be used.

2.2.2.2 Solving mathematic formulas

It is important to mention that the loop-feature only allows for a constant increment. To overcome this limitation the ATLAS server can solve formulas based on *NI_Gmath.lvlib:Eval Formula String.vi*[3]. The mathematical expressions are defined by writing them between brackets and the result will have a precision of 3 digits after the decimal separator. As the loop-function is interpreted before any formula is solved, it is also possible to use loop-variables in these mathematical expressions.

2.2.2.3 Aliases

Another feature in the ATLAS scripting language are aliases. These are abbreviations for longer program sequences which are used frequently. For example, a cleaning procedure in a liquid handling system, consisting of many single instructions, can be saved in the file `<ATLAS directory>\Server\alias\cleaning.txt`. After that the cleaning procedure is inserted in the script sequence by using the command `AL|cleaning.txt`, which shortens the script sequence and makes it easier to comprehend the whole sequence.
Aside from custom built aliases, the ATLAS server can access the aliases `AL|name|measurement_name` and `AL|error`. Their special characteristics are that the server replaces the alias-indicator `AL` by all available client-identifiers. Using `AL|name|measurement_name` will distribute a measurement filename to all connected clients which will save their measurement data by this name. `AL|error` is used to distribute the information, that an error has occurred, to all connected clients immediately.

2.3 Client applications

Each client can be operated in 3 different modes: The *server* mode, the *programming* mode and the *local* mode. If a client is switched to the *server* mode, it tries to connect to the ATLAS server over TCP/IP and after the connection has been established the device can be remote controlled by the server. The *programming* mode offers a comfortable way to create a script sequence on the server since every user event will be sent to the ATLAS server as the according script command instead of executing it. In *local* mode the connected device is controlled directly and user input is executed immediately.
The code structure is based on a state-machine[4] and a simplified scheme of the state-machine used is shown in figure 4. It consists of three states called *init*, *state changed* and *running*. The *init* state is used for initializing the user interface, setting constants, configuring a RS-232 connection etc. The *state changed* state is called if the user changes the client mode. Depending on the selected mode the network connection to the ATLAS server is established. If the connection initialization fails, the client automatically switches back to the *local* mode. All other functionality of the client is located in the *running* case of the state-machine.
The *running* state contains code elements for communicating with the ATLAS server, handling user inputs and controlling the connected device. An overview of the code can be found in figure 5. To simplify the block diagram all client specific hardware functionalities have been removed. The code inside the *running* state is based on a *producer consumer architecture*[5] consisting of three loops in our case. The first loop contains an event handler for user interactions whereas a second loop receives script commands from the ATLAS server

[3] http://zone.ni.com/reference/en-XX/help/371361G-01/gmath/advanced_formula_vis/
[4] http://zone.ni.com/devzone/cda/tut/p/id/2926
[5] http://zone.ni.com/devzone/cda/tut/p/id/3023

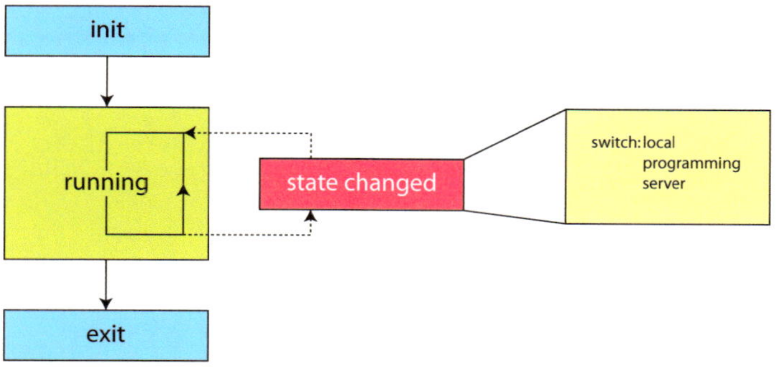

Fig. 4. Scheme of the client's architecture, which consists of a state-machine. It enables the software to switch between the different operating modes "client", "server" and local".

in *server* mode and passes them on to the third loop functioning as the consumer loop. In *programming* mode, however, the second loop is used to send script commands to the ATLAS server upon user interaction. The consumer loop interprets the script commands and translates them into hardware interactions. The exchange of commands between these three loops is realized by a queue (referred to as command queue) code structure. A second queue (referred to as status queue), which can also be seen in figure 5 is used to transport the status of the client from the consumer loop to the server loop and on to the ATLAS server if the client is in *server* mode. The differences in program execution for the three different states are explained in further detail below.

- **local** mode: The communication between the server and the client is deactivated. User interaction on the front panel triggers the event handler which assembles a script command, representing the user input from the GUI, and adds this script command to the command queue triggering the consumer loop execution.
- **programming** mode: The server loop is used to send script commands received via the command queue to the ATLAS server after receiving a status request from the server. The consumer loop, however, does not pass on any command to the connected hardware.
- **server** mode: The server loop is used to receive script commands from the ATLAS server and adds them to the command queue. The event handler structure, however, can still add commands to the command queue on user input to enable the user to interrupt automated script execution. The server loop is also used to reply to status requests from the ATLAS server according to the current state of the client, which is transported over the status queue as described above.

2.3.1 Available clients

At the moment 16 different clients are available and listed below. The list contains the client identifiers and a short description of the client functionality.

AC: Self-developed 230V AC power socket.

The AC client can switch a power socket and is connected to the PC via a RS-232-port.

BC: Self-developed Boxcar-Integrator.

This client reads the data, whereas the gating- and trigger-delay have to be set manually at the device.

BP: Beep client.

If the ATLAS server has to alert the user, the BP client can be used. It produces an audible tone with a certain frequency for 100 ms and is already included in the ATLAS server.

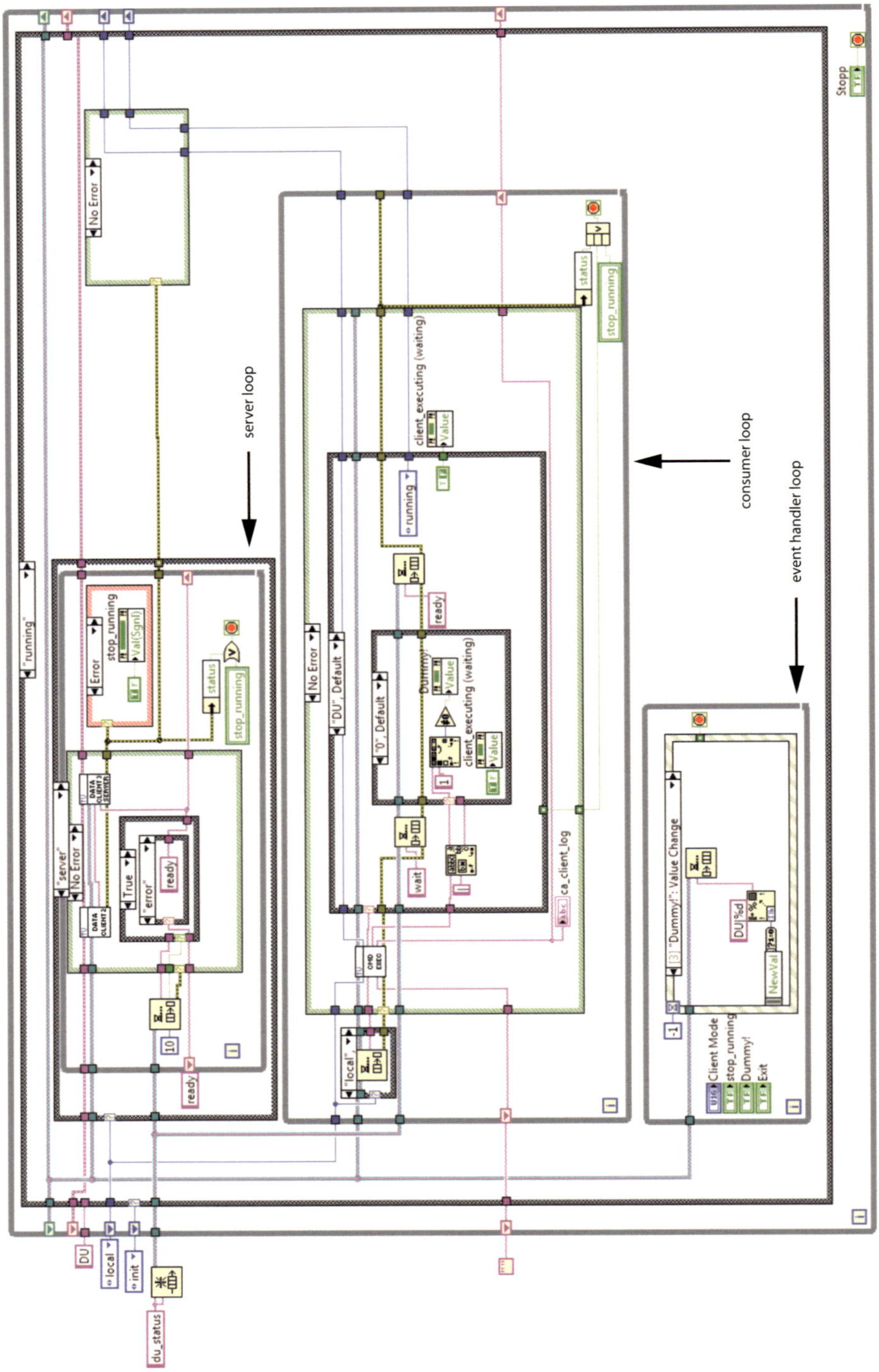

Fig. 5. Block diagram of a simplified ATLAS client, showing the *running* state. See the text for further information.

CA: Syringe pumps by Cavro Scientific Instruments (Sunnyvale, CA, USA).
Liquids can be aspired and dispensed from two liquid connections at different speeds. The ramping up and down to the programmed speed can also be programed.

DB: A digital board from TVE Elektronische Systeme GmbH (Vienna, Austria).
This board is a combination of a 16-bit-AD converter for a thermoelectrical cooled infrared detector. The integrated CPU supports features such as trigger delay, internal averaging and base line correction and is connected to the PC via USB.

DI: Micro dispenser from Picology AB (Sweden).
The piezo-element of the dispenser is controlled by burst signals from an Agilent 33120A function generator. The size of the dispensed drops and the number of drops per second can be adjusted.

DL: External Cavity Quantum Cascade Laser from Daylight Solutions Inc. (CA, USA).
The wavenumber and the intensity of the emitted light can be set among other laser parameters. The DL client also supports a scanning mode, where the emission wavenumber of the laser is tuned automatically.

GI: Miniplus 3 peristaltic pump from Gilson Inc. (Middleton, WI, USA).
The speed as well as the pumping direction can be controlled.

HV: CZE 1000R high voltage supply from Spellman (NY, USA).
It is supported via an DAC module from National Instruments. The output voltage of the module is transformed into high voltage output (10 V equal 30 kV).

LC: Waverunner 64-Xi oscilloscope from LeCroy Corp. (NY, USA).
Only the most important features such as setting V/div, timebase and trigger-parameters are implemented. Single pulses can be read and stored.

OP: FTIR spectrometers from Bruker Optik GmbH (Ettlingen, Germany).
This client connects to OPUS over a DDE connection and can trigger measurements utilizing predefined experiment files. Single and repeated measurements are supported.

TE: TDS 220 oscilloscope by Tektronix (OR, USA).
Only the most important features such as setting V/div, timebase and trigger-parameters are implemented. Single pulses can be read and stored.

UV: Capillary UV-Detector from Dionex (Sunnyvale, CA, USA).
The client allows to set four wavelengths for absorption measurements. It can autozero the absorbance values and record the absorbance over time.

VI: Valves from Vici AG (Switzerland).
Injection and selection valves are supported by this client.

WA: Wait client
The wait client allows a delay of the execution of the next command by a defined time period. It is also included in the ATLAS server as the BP client.

XY: Custom-built XY stage.
The XY stage is operated by a Trinamic TMCM-610 stepper motor control, which is controlled by the XY client. This client allows the user to move the stage for a certain distance by a predefined speed.

3. Sample applications

3.1 Example I: Quantification of lactate in aqueous solution using an External Cavity Quantum Cascade Laser

In clinical diagnostics numerous parameters, such as glucose, phosphate and lactate in blood have to be measured with high precision and accuracy in short time intervals. One measurement principle suitable for such requirements is infrared spectroscopy. Using classical Fourier transform infrared spectrometry (Griffiths & Haseth, 2007) two approaches can be chosen. Measuring the solution in transmission requires low path lengths typically below 25 μm in the spectral region of 1000 - 1250 cm^{-1} due to the high absorbance of water in the region of interest. The measurement cell can suffer from bio-fouling on the window materials when biological samples are measured. Additionally, particles in the sample solution can cause cell-clogging in such small path lengths. The second suitable measurement method overcoming the clogging problem is attenuated total reflection (ATR). Using the ATR technique the light doesn't transmit through the sample solution but is coupled into an IR transparent crystal (e.g. Germanium). At the surface between the crystal and the sample total reflection of the light occurs and the evanescent field of the propagating light is reaching into the sample. This evanescent field interacts with the sample and is absorbed by the target molecules. Applying the ATR technique allows the use of flow cells on top of the crystal with bigger dimensions since the light doesn't need to penetrate the whole sample thickness. This advantage comes with the tradeoff that the penetration depth of the light into the sample is small compared to the transmission measurement. Therefore, one must expect higher limits of detection limits of detection and less sensitivity according to Lambert Beer's law (1). Additionally bio fouling on the crystal surface is an even bigger issue due to the low penetration depth.

$$A(\mathrm{cm}^{-1}) = -\log\left(\frac{I(\mathrm{cm}^{-1})}{I_0(\mathrm{cm}^{-1})}\right) = \varepsilon \cdot c \cdot l \qquad (1)$$

In this formula I_0 denotes the measured intensity of the light reaching the detector without sample whereas I gives the intensity after the light was absorbed by the sample. ε[L/cm] is the molar absorption coefficient at a given wavenumber. c[mol/L] denotes the concentration of the analyte and l[cm] gives the path length of the measurement cell.

Increasing the optical path length of the measurement cell would solve both drawbacks, described above, at the same time. Larger cell dimensions would make the cleaning of the cell easier, accompanied by better sensitivity because of the increased interaction length. Replacing the IR spectrometer with a Quantum Cascade Laser (QCL) (Faist et al., 1994) enables the penetration of higher path lengths at one wavenumber due to the higher energy output of the laser compared to the light source of an IR spectrometer. Applying an External Cavity Quantum Cascade Laser (EC-QCL), which can shift its emission wavenumber over a range of 200 cm^{-1} gives a spectrum instead of a single absorbance value at a given wavenumber.

Using an EC-QCL enabled us to use an optical path length of 130 μm for the measurement of physiological relevant compounds in Ringer solution. Using ATLAS we realized an experimental setup for the measurement of liquid samples and tested it on lactate samples in Ringer solution.

3.1.1 Experiment

For our studies we combined an EC-QCL (tuning range: 1030 - 1230 cm^{-1}) from Daylight Solutions Inc. with a thermoelectrically cooled Mercury Cadmium Telluride (MCT) detector and a Sequential Injection Analysis (SIA) system for sample preparation (Brandstetter et al., 2010). The detector signal was digitized by a specially designed analogue to digital

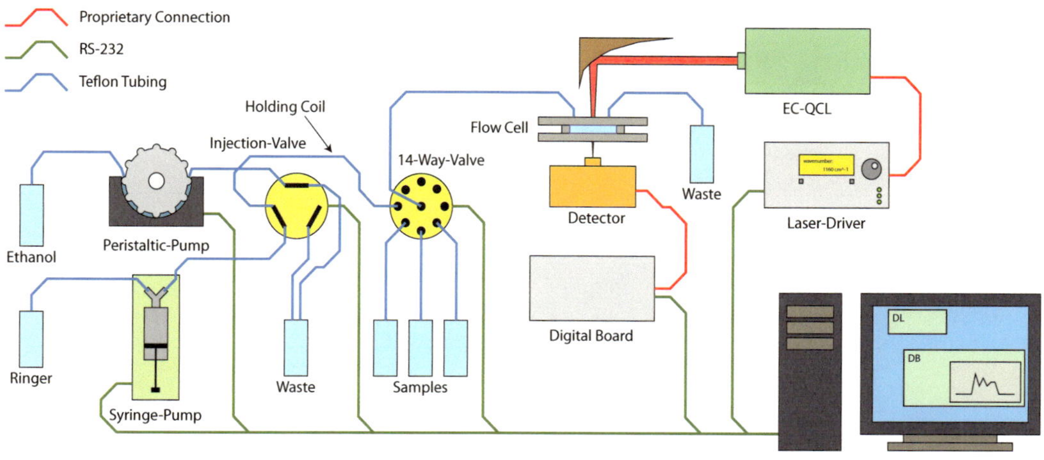

Fig. 6. Experimental setup for the measurement of lactate in Ringer solution using an External Cavity Quantum Cascade Laser.

converter (ADC) board which was read out by the *digital board* ATLAS client. Using a SIA system improves on manual sample injection by means of reproducibility and repeatability. Applying the SIA system also helps to reduce sample contaminations since the system can be cleaned automatically before a new sample is injected for the next measurement.

For this setup, shown in figure 6, the ATLAS clients for the digital board, the EC-QCL from Daylight Solutions Inc., the syringe pump from Cavro Inc., valves by Vici Inc. and the client for the Gilson Miniplus 3 peristaltic pump were connected to the ATLAS server. All hardware parts were connected to a notebook by RS-232 connections over USB-to-RS-232 converters. The peristaltic pump in the setup was only used if air bubbles were found in the tubings. In that case the system was purged with ethanol first to drive the bubbles out of the system and afterwards the ethanol flask was exchanged with Ringer solution manually and the tubings were filled with Ringer solution again.

In a first experiment lactate in Ringer matrix was pumped through the measurement spot repeatedly to examine the achieved flow profiles. Therefore, the whole system was filled with Ringer solution first. The laser parameters were sent by the client to the laser control unit and the emission wavenumber was tuned to 1130 cm^{-1}. After initiating the emission of light the data acquisition was started and the intensity of the detected signal was streamed onto the hard drive continuously. In the meantime the syringe pump picked up the lactate sample through the 14-way-valve into the holding coil. After switching the 14-way-valve back to connect the holding coil with the measurement cell the syringe pump dispensed the lactate sample through the measurement cell. The pickup and dispense procedure was repeated while the data acquisition continued. In figure 7 the obtained flow profile for two repetitions is plotted against time. Whenever the sample solution passes the measurement cell the measured intensity on the detector decreases due to absorption taking place in the cell. The obtained flow profiles are in good agreement with theory. Optimization of the pumped lactate volume and the used flow rates allowed adjustments of the system in such a way that, at the maximum of the absorption, undiluted sample was measured. Knowing the exact time when this maximum reached the flow cell was crucial for the following experiment.

To obtain a calibration curve for lactate in Ringer solution a second command sequence was programmed. Firstly Ringer solution was pumped through the measurement cell utilizing a

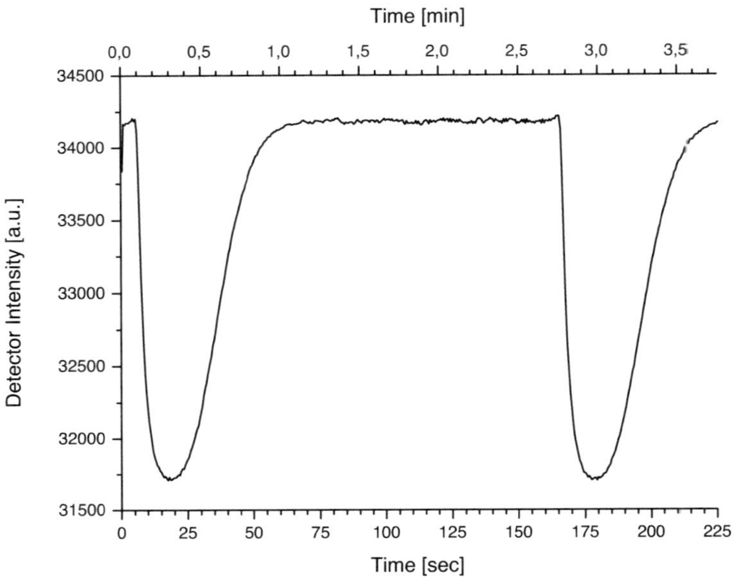

Fig. 7. Lactate solution was pumped through the measurement cell twice while the EC-QCL emitted light at 1130 cm^{-1} and the digital board read out the detector values.

Cavro syringe pump. After the cell was purged the flow was stopped and the ATLAS server sent a signal to the digital board to start recording. Afterwards the EC-QCL was started by the server to scan over a wavenumber region ranging from 1030 to 1230 cm^{-1}. This measurement served as I_0(cm^{-1}) in equation (1). Then the valves switched positions allowing the syringe pump to pick up a sample of lactate into the holding coil. After the 14-way-valve was switched to connect the holding coil with the flow cell the sample was pumped into the measurement spot. Subsequently, the flow was stopped at the absorption maximum determined earlier. Now the EC-QCL received a trigger signal from the server to start another measurement, which gave I(cm^{-1}) in equation (1). Then the valve of the syringe pump was switched to the opposite direction and picked up Ringer solution from the storage flask. After switching the valve back the whole system was purged again. This step was repeated twice to flush any possible remaining lactate out of the measurement spot.

The sequence described above was automatically repeated for all five sample concentrations by changing the 14-way-valve to the appropriate position in each of the measurement runs. Afterwards the absorbance spectra were calculated manually and the data shown in figure 8 were plotted in Origin. Calculating a linear calibration function for the measured absorbances at the band maxima gave a R^2 value of 0.996.

In conclusion we can report that setting up a SIA system using ATLAS can by achieved easily. The integration of the EC-QCL and the data acquisition electronics into the SIA sequences was simple too after the ATLAS clients for the laser and the ADC board had been developed.

3.2 Example II: Using IR spectroscopy as a detector for liquid chromatography

Liquid chromatography (LC) is a widely used technique in analytical chemistry to separate mixtures of substances before detecting and quantifying them. The sample is injected onto a

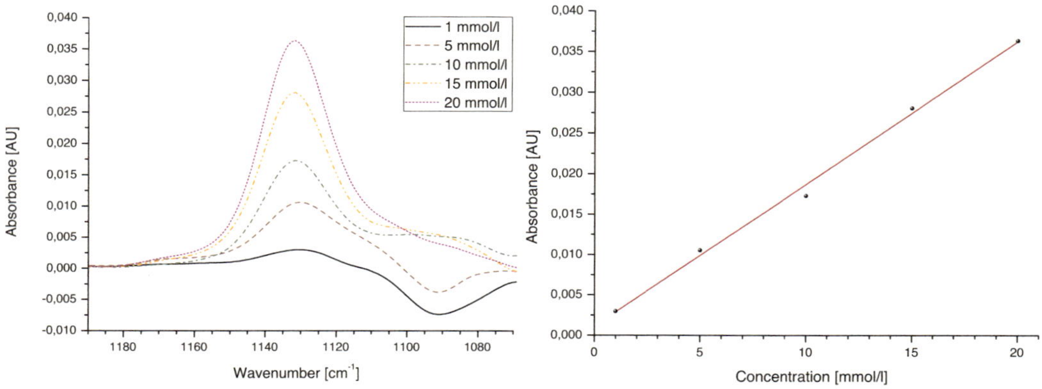

(a) Recorded spectra (b) Calibration line

Fig. 8. 5 different concentrations of lactate in Ringer solution were measured and the absorbance values at 1131. 7 cm^{-1} are plotted as a calibration curve giving a R^2 value of 0.996.

separation column where different molecules in the analyte mixture are retained for a varying time dependent on the nature of the column and the analyte itself. The analytes are driven through the column by a single solvent mixture, called isocratic mode, or the composition of the solvent mixture is changed during the elution, which is called gradient mode. Classical detectors used for detection in LC are mass spectrometry (MS) and UV-VIS spectroscopy. IR spectroscopy was not commercialized until today as a detection principle for LC because the solvents used cause high absorption in the infrared spectral region and overlap with the very small absorptions of the analyte molecules. However IR spectroscopy has some advantages as detection principle. First it is a non destructive detection principle, compared to MS. Second, the IR spectrum can be seen as a fingerprint of a target molecule which simplifies the identification of target molecules compared to UV-VIS spectroscopy.

Using IR spectroscopy as the detection principle in LC can be done in two ways. In the online method the exit of the separation column is connected to a flow cell and IR spectra are recorded during the elution of the analytes. Since the time resolution of the chromatogram depends mainly on the time needed to record a spectrum a tradeoff has to be made here. Increasing the spectral averaging will give better signal to noise levels and therefore better sensitivity. However, the time resolution of the chromatogram will decrease and two peaks, which are eluted shortly after each other, might be not detected separately. The strong absorption of the solvent can be easily subtracted in an isocratic eluation whereas background correction algorithms have to be used in gradient elution (Quintás et al., 2009a;b).

The second possible method is based on physically eliminating the solvent from the sample and the IR spectra are measured afterwards as traces on an IR transparent substrate. This method enables averaging of as many spectra as needed without decreasing the time resolution of the chromatogram because the time resolution is mainly determined by the deposition method of the eluents on the measurement substrate.

Using ATLAS we have coupled a Dionex Ultimate 3000 capillary LC system to a micro dispenser (Laurell et al., 1999), which was used for eluate deposition on CaF_2 windows followed by subsequent IR detection. The setup described below was already used by manually controlling all components before ATLAS became available and proved capable of measuring pesticides down to concentrations of 2 μg/mL (Armenta & Lendl, 2010).

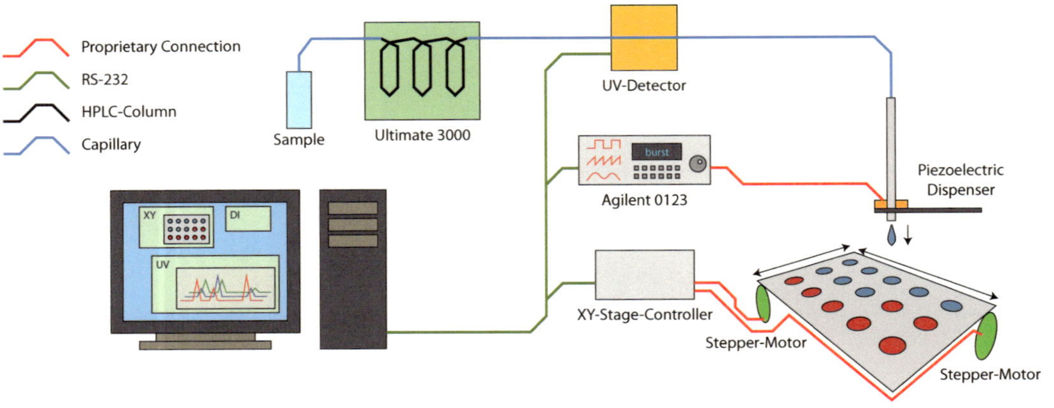

Fig. 9. Experimental setup for the coupling of a liquid chromatography system with offline IR detection utilizing a micro dispenser for sample deposition.

3.2.1 Experiment

Our system, as shown in figure 9, was built combining an Ultimate 3000 capillary LC system (Dionex, Sunnyvale, CA, USA), which is not implemented in ATLAS yet, a Dionex UV detector, a home built XY stage and a micro dispenser from Picology AB (Bjaerred, Sweden). The UV detector was configured and read out via a RS-232 connection by an ATLAS client. The stepping motors of the XY stage were connected to a controller board (Trinamic TMCM-610) which was controlled by another ATLAS client. The piezo crystal of the micro dispenser was actuated by a specially designed electronics board which amplified a burst signal generated by an Agilent 33120A function generator. The burst period, giving the number of droplets dispensed each second, and the burst amplitude, giving the volume of each dispensed drop, were set by a dedicated dispenser ATLAS client. The droplets of the eluent were dispensed onto a heated plate of IR transparent CaF_2 mounted on the XY stage moving the plate constantly during the deposition.

A typical experiment consisted of the following steps. First the injection of the sample onto the LC column was initiated manually since the LC system is not implemented into the ATLAS system yet. Immediately afterwards a preprogrammed ATLAS control sequence was started containing the following steps:

- The desired wavelengths for the UV measurement are set
- The absorbance signal of the UV detector is set to zero
- The dispenser parameters are set
- The movement of the XY stage is initiated at a certain speed and a programmed distance to travel
- The UV measurement is started
- The dispensing of the droplets is triggered

After the elution of the injected substances was completed the CaF_2 plate was removed from the XY stage and was analyzed on a Hyperion 3000 IR microscope from Bruker Optics (Ettlingen, Germany). The plate was measured in transmission mode applying a line scan along the deposited material.

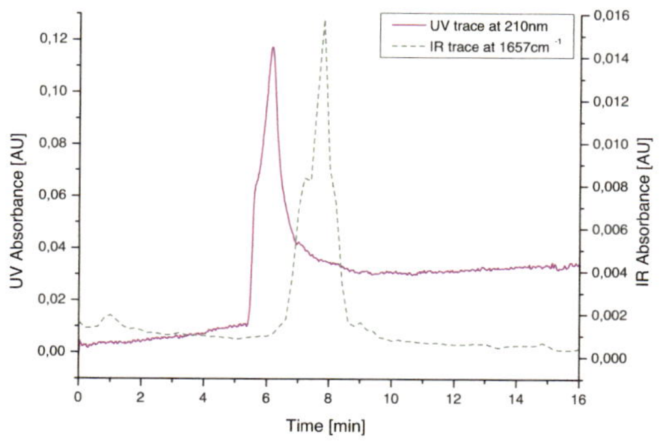

(a) Traces of the eluted caffeine sample

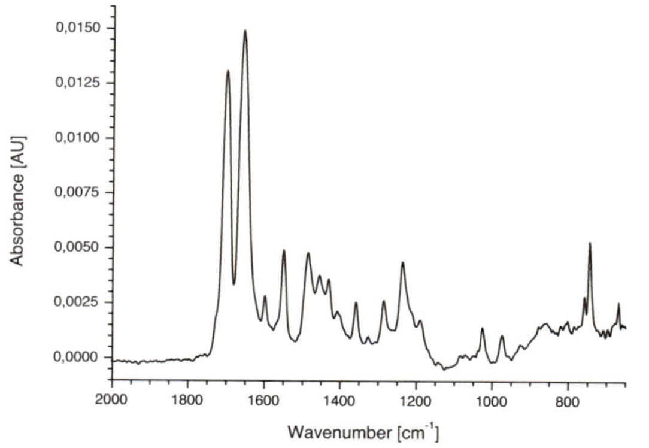

(b) IR spectrum of caffeine at the maximum of the eluted peak

Fig. 10. Measurement results from the coupling of a liquid chromatography system with offline IR detection.

First results testing the ATLAS system were obtained by injecting 1 μL of a 60 ppm solution of caffeine onto a C18 separation column. A mixture of water and acetonitrile (50:50 % v/v) with 0.1% acetic acid served as the mobile phase flowing at a speed of 2 μL/min. The UV detector was set to measure at 200, 210, 250 and 350 nm wavelengths every 500 ms for 15 min and the XY stage was moved with 25 μm/s for a distance of 3 cm. The dispense rate was set to 25 drops/s.

The obtained chromatogram of caffeine is plotted in figure 10. The time delay between the UV and IR measurement can be explained by the distance between the UV measurement cell and the micro dispenser. The IR trace was obtained by integration of the caffeine band located at 1657 cm^{-1}. The plotted IR spectrum of caffeine represents the maximum of the IR trace.

Concluding we can state that using ATLAS enabled us to setup a measurement system coupling a LC system with online UV detection and offline IR detection. Inclusion of the Dionex Ultimate 3000 chromatograph would allow for fully automated measurements with this system eliminating the manual injection of the sample.

4. Conclusion and Outlook

In this chapter we introduced ATLAS, our LabVIEW programmed lab automation system. While LabVIEW is routinely used in many labs to control laboratory equipment, usually these programs are ad-hoc solutions which are used for one type of experiment only and are never published. What sets our system apart from previously reported works are its expandability and flexibility. Through its Server-Client layout the ATLAS system can easily be expanded to be able to control a wide range of lab equipment - any instrument, that can be controlled by LabVIEW, can be controlled by our program - and experiment parameters can be easily changed.

To give the reader an idea of possible applications of ATLAS we described two ATLAS controlled experiments, which would have been very inconvenient to do manually, but were easily implemented with the help of the presented lab automation system.

In the future we plan to extend our program by the ability to send measurement data from clients to the server and have the server make decisions based on this data. Furthermore, the final version and the source code of ATLAS will be made available on our website (http://www.cta.tuwien.ac.at/cavs), to allow other users to use and improve it.

5. Acknowledgment

The authors want to thank Eva Aguilera Herrador, Julia Kuligowski and Markus Brandstetter for supplying us with their measurement data which are presented in section 3.

6. References

Armenta, S. & Lendl, B. (2010). Capillary liquid chromatography with off-line mid-ir and raman micro-spectroscopic detection: Analysis of chlorinated pesticides at ppb levels, *Anal Bioanal Chem* 397(1): 297–308.

Barzin, R., Shukor, S. & Ahmad, A. (2010). New spectrophotometric measurement method for process control of miniaturized intensified systems, *Sensors and Actuators, B: Chemical* 146(1): 403–409.

Brandstetter, M., Genner, A., Anic, K., Lendl, B. (2010). Tunable external cavity quantum cascade laser for the simultaneous determination of glucose and lactate in aqueous phase, Analyst, available online, doi: 10.1039/c0an00532k.

Dominguez, R., Muñoz, R. & Araiza, H. (2010). Automated analytical system based on the sia technique, *Pan American Health Care Exchanges, PAHCE 2010* pp. 117–119.

Faist, J., Capasso, F., Sivco, D., Sirtori, C., Hutchinson, A. & Cho, A. (1994). Quantum cascade laser, *Science* 264(5158): 553–556.

Griffiths, P. R. & Haseth, J. A. D. (2007). *Fourier Transform Infrared Spectrometry*, Wiley-Interscience.

Jitmanee, K., Teshima, N., Sakai, T. & Grudpan, K. (2007). Drc™ icp-ms coupled with automated flow injection system with anion exchange minicolumns for determination of selenium compounds in water samples, *Talanta* 73(2): 352–357.

Laurell, T., Wallman, L. & Nilsson, J. (1999). Design and development of a silicon microfabricated flow-through dispenser for on-line picolitre sample handling, *J. Micromech. Microeng* 9(4): 369–376.

Quintás, G., Kuligowski, J. & Lendl, B. (2009a). On-line fourier transform infrared spectrometric detection in gradient capillary liquid chromatography using nanoliter-flow cells, *Analytical Chemistry* 81(10): 3746–3753.

Quintás, G., Kuligowski, J. & Lendl, B. (2009b). Procedure for automated background correction in flow systems with infrared spectroscopic detection and changing liquid-phase composition, *Appl Spec* 63(12): 1363–1369.

Růzicka, J. (1981). *Flow Injection Analysis*, Vol. 62 of *Chemical Analysis*, Wiley, John & Sons, Incorporated.

Růzicka, J. (1992). The second coming of flow-injection analysis, *Analytica Chimica Acta* 261(1- 2): 3–10.

Wagner, C., Armenta, S. & Lendl, B. (2010). Developing automated analytical methods for scientific environments using labview, *Talanta* 80(3): 1081–1087.

2

In-House Control System for Medium Size Research Facility

Hideaki Ohgaki and Yoshitaka Iwasaki
Kyoto University, SAGA Light Source
Japan

1. Introduction

A medium size research facility has a difficulties to develop control systems for their own special equipments, especially for accelerator facilities, because there is only few experts for constructing the control system and the control objects are not mass-product ones in most case. We have experienced such situation and we found a solution for a development in a medium size accelerator complex, SAGA Light Source (SAGA-LS) by using distributed MS-PC control system which is connected with a standard Internet protocol and is developed by Labview.

The SAGA Light Source (SAGA-LS) (Tomimasu, et al., 2003), (Iwasaki, et al., 2003) is a medium size synchrotron light research facility located at Kyusyu-Island, Japan. The accelerator control programs have been developed in-house from the beginning of the machine commissioning using Labview. At this stage almost all of the components of the accelerator, for instance, magnet power supplies, radio frequency (RF) system, vacuum monitoring and beam position monitoring system, are controlled and monitored by server and client model with LabView. During the commissioning period integrated sub-systems such as a feed-forward orbit correction system for insertion devices, a feedback power supply control system, a beam based beam position monitor (BPM) calibration and the other control applications have also been developed with Labview. E-mail services for alarm information and Web server that delivers accelerator status for entire facility are also developed by Labview. External codes are available to help the accelerator operation. For example TRACY2 (Nishimura, 1988) is used for accelerator modelling to establish the machine parameters in cooperate with Labview control system. In this chapter we describe the SAGA-LS accelerator control system as an example of developments of the control system for a medium size research facility using Labview.

2. Design

SAGA-LS accelerator consists of 255 MeV injector linac and 1.4 GeV electron storage ring. The circumference of the storage ring is 75.6 m. Figure 1 shows the geometrical layout of SAGA-LS facility. At this stage 10 beam lines are offered to user experiments.

The control system for the SAGA-LS accelerator, which consists of magnet power supplies, a radio frequency, and a vacuum monitoring system, should be implemented with communication interfaces, because those are distributed in wide area of the facility, and operators have to manipulate these components from the control room. The Ethernet LAN is standard communication interfaces and we can easily use it with MS-PCs and LabView system with server and client model. We adopted Ethernet LAN as communication interfaces with each accelerator devices and PCs, because of its high cost performance. For the connectivity to the accelerator hardware, we selected commercial base off-the-shelf distributed input output devices (I/O devices) such as PLC (FA-M3; YOKOGAWA), and Fieldpoint (National Instruments). A serious issue on SAGA-LS facility is its tightly restricted budget and, hence, the limited number of staff in the facility. Thus, the control system for SAGA-LS should be simple and robust, while inexpensive, easy to develop, to maintain and to be expandable. The solution of this problem in the view point of hardware is the usage of the PC and the off-the-shelf products. On the other hand for the application developments we use the Labview environment, because a few number of staff have to develop the control applications with in-house efforts toward variety of demands from the construction period to the use operation period. Other reasons of using Labview and its merits are discussed in chapter 5.

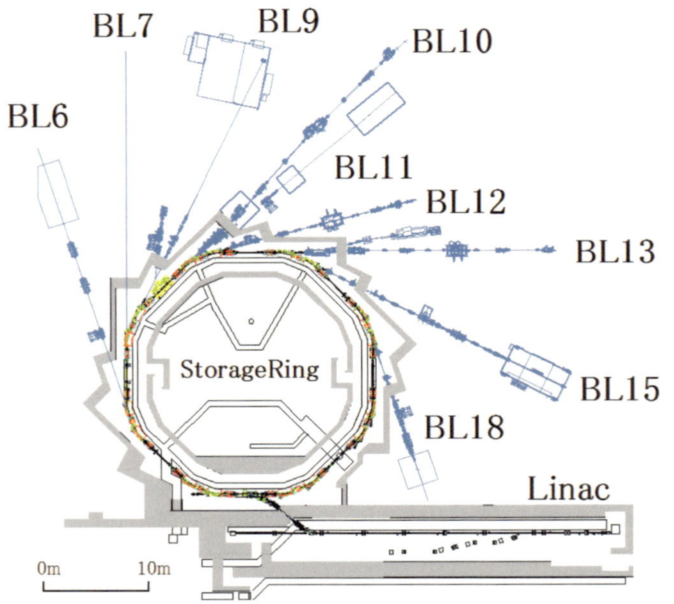

Fig. 1. Geometrical Layout of SAGA Light Source.

The PC control system is widely used in many facilities because of a very high cost performance of PC. On the other side, there are sophisticated and well-established control systems based on workstations, such as EPICS. It is an efficient way to use those resources to design a control system, because a many of hardware drivers and utility software specialized for accelerator control are available in EPICS system. PC-based EPICS system with the PC-UNIX operating system could also be an efficient way to design a control system, because we can use plenty of the existing resources. However, it is difficult to modify and expand the EPICS system with the limited number of accelerator staff, especially in the case without EPICS specialists. Fortunately, the number of the control items of the SAGA-LS is about 600 and there are very few demands for a real-time control. Only

exception is synchronous operation for power supplies for a quick energy ramping in the storage ring. In this case a PLC with preloaded ramping pattern is available. Hence, we have designed a MS-Windows PC-based control system, which uses the EPICS channel access (CA) only for the purpose of utilization of the general EPICS utility code, and off-the-shelf I/O devices. There are several manners to communicate with server PCs and client PCs. The DataSocket, Shared Variables, which in built-in protocol in the Labview system, are one of the methods for this purposes. But we use not only Labview, but also other programming tools for accelerator control system such as Delphi. ActiveX CA can be used under the any developing environment of MS-Windows OS. Thus we decide to use ActiveX CA as communication protocol for accelerator control system. There are several excellent works to develop CA components for the MS-Windows environment. ActiveX CA (Kay-Uwe Kasemir, 2000) is one of such component. The PC running the ActiveX CA server with I/O devices works as a standalone PC I/O controller which can communicate with the EPICS CA through the Labview interface.
Figure 2 shows the schematic view of the architecture of the SAGA-LS accelerator control system including beam line and office LAN. In figure 2, the RF powe supplies of linac, electron gun and the many kinds of beam diagnostic equipments are omitted.

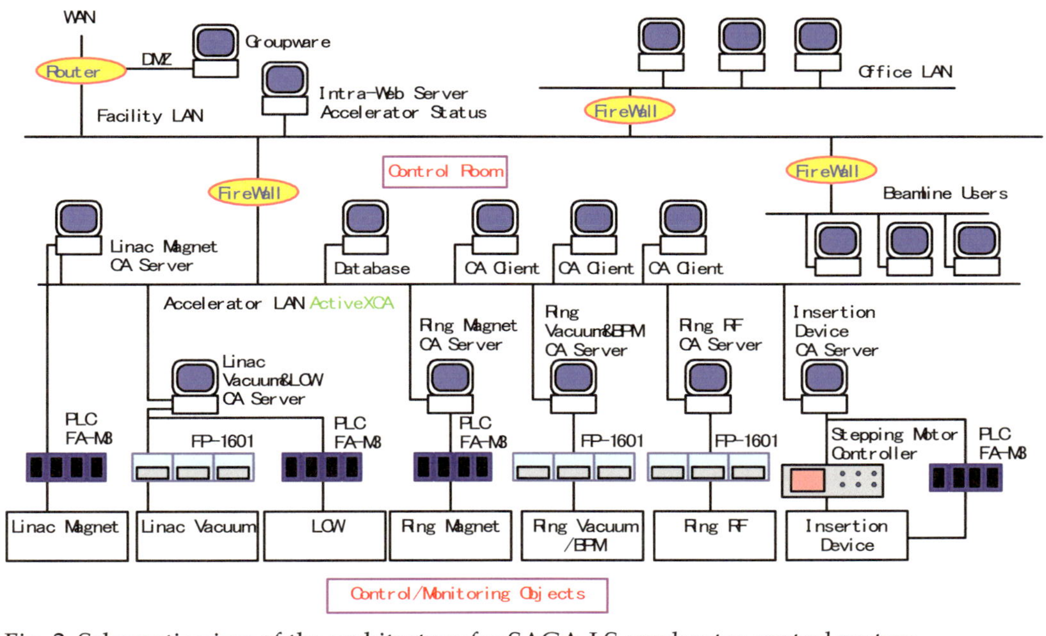

Fig. 2. Schematic view of the architecture for SAGA-LS accelerator control system.

The accelerator, beam line and office LAN are separated by firewalls to secure the accelerator cotrol network. To control the insertion devices from the beam line users, for instance the operation of undulators, an exception of security policy is added in accelerator firewall. Simple TCP/IP protocol is used for control method of insertion devices from the beam line users. An intra-web server is placed in middle zone of facility LAN to deliver the machine parameter in any location of the SAGA-LS facility. The intra-web server delivers the status of the accelerator for the beam line users. The details of web system and E-mail system are described in section 5.7.

3. System Implementation

3.1 Console PC

The machine commissioning of SAGA-LS accelerator was begun on 2004, and we selected Window 2000 as operating system of server and client PCs because of its stability, and MS-Windows OS is familiar environment for the facility staff. The cost performance of Windows PC is one of the reasons for the choice. At the present stage the higher version of MS-Windows OS, i.e., Windows XP, Windows Vista and Windows 7 is also used for new control components of the accelerator.

Console applications are developed using Labview with ActiveX CA. The client PC communicates with not only one server PC but also several servers for the purposes of cross sectional applications: COD correction program, measurement of response matrix (R-matrix), beam based BPM calibration and so on. A few example of console programs will be described in section 5.2, 5.3 and 5.4.

The data archive system (Database; MySQL), which records accelerator parameters is installed in the system. The logger programs and the trend viewers are constructed using Delphi and Labview respectively. ODBC is used for connecting MySQL with Labview.

3.2 PC-IOC

Recent industrial IO devices are reliable and high-speed access via built-in Ethernet modules can be available. Thus we construct the IOC only with such off-the-shelf industrial I/O devices. We put PCs between the console computers and the I/O devices, because:

I. Industrial I/O device itself cannot directly communicate with consol PC with ActiveX CA.
II. Server PC can be used as a local controller during installation and maintenance.
III. Server PC works as IOC for GPIB and non-Ethernet devices such as digital voltage meter.
IV. The device LAN should be separated from the facility LAN to secure the network.

FieldPoints are a candidate for the I/O devices, because of its reliability and hot plug and play operation, and good connectivity to the software environment of Labview. FA-M3s (Yokogawa; PLCs) are used for the I/O devices for magnet power supplies, cooling water system and insertion devices. Digital voltage meter, which monitors the beam current in electron storage ring, is connected to a beam current monitor PC with GPIB. As the PC-IOC works as a local control machine for the maintenance, i.e. repairing or conditioning, the PC-IOCs should be located close to their control objects.

There are over 10 Windows 2000 or Windows XP PCs for PC-IOC that equipped with ActeveX CA servers. The server applications have been also developed with Labview. Almost all of the control applications have been developed in the facility. The only exception is PLC program for magnet power supplies those are developed by Techno-AP (Ibaraki, Japan) at first stage of installation. The PLC program has been modified by the facility staff.

3.3 Performance

The data communications between the PC-IOCs (servers) and the consol PCs (clients) are done via 100 Mbps LAN, which is isolated from the facility LAN and from the beam-line users by firewall.

As the ActiveX CA only supports the polling data transfer method, the communication rate between client and server is mainly limited by number of the process variable (PV). Further more, we must combat with the data-synchronous problem in the multi-client system. To resolve the problem we use "SET VALUE" and "READBACK VALUE" for "CA put." In figure 3, the method using "SET VALUE" and "READBACK VALUE" is illustrated. Nominal communication rate for 144 variables of magnet power supply for storage ring are about 5 Hz in the present system. Further improvement in the communication rate can be expected by using the block data transfer method in the ActiveX CA. Feasible studies on the block data transfer to the magnet power supply in the storage ring shows that the communication rate can be achieved 9.5 ms/144 data. However, the block data transfer method looses simplicity and flexibility in the development of the client applications. Therefore we use block data transfer method only for the client PC which is required for a synchronous operation between many power supplies, such as COD correction client. The Windows PCs and ActiveX CA satisfy our demand with the communication rate of 1 to 10 Hz. The details of design, implementation, performance of the control system of SAGA-LS are summarized in references (Ohgaki et al., 2003), (Ohgaki et al., 2005).

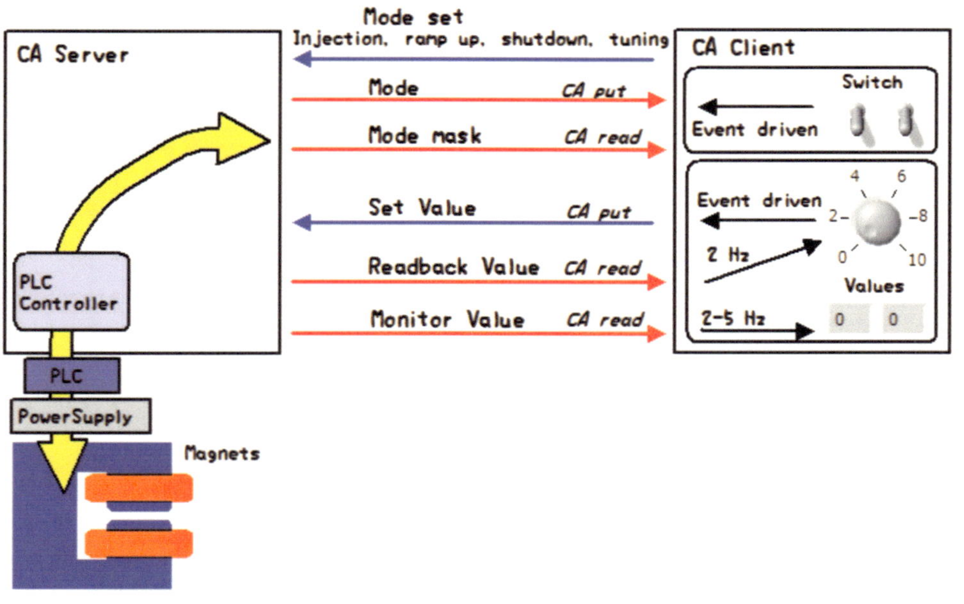

Fig. 3. PV configuration of the magnet control system using ActiveX CA.

4. Example of application programs

4.1 Magnet power supply

The purpose of control system for magnet power supply is simple: to switch on/off the power supply; to change and monitor the output current; to indicate interlock alarms; to inform the status: However there are 144 magnet power supplies in SAGA-LS electron storage ring, and these must be controlled synchronously during the energy ramping operation, otherwise, a large orbit shit of electron beam or a serious beam instability will be occurred, and in worse case the stored beam will be lost.

To fulfil the requirement for the magnet power supply control sub-system, we adopted PLC as a control device. PLC is used to guarantee the synchronous and rapid operation. The synchronization accuracy of PLC is sufficient for our requirement (within 10ms coincidence). For the energy ramping up, the ramping pattern whose step size are 10,000 points per each magnets are pre-loaded in the file registry of the PLC.

PC program, which is developed by Labivew, thus, have two main routines. One is for connection to the PLC to control and to receive status from the power supplies. And the other routine is to accept demands from the external client PC for the orbit correction, for instance. As described before, the communication between server PC and client PC is done by ActiveX CA. In Figure 4, front panel of control application for magnet power supply and block diagram are shown.

Typical feature of this application program is that we use “Queue with Type Definition File” so that many series of tasks are not conflicted each other. By using “Queue with Type Definition File”, the drawn area of block diagram becomes to be compact compared to using the other syntax. The scalability of “Queue” for new procedure is quite simple. Basically this magnet program and ladder program of PLC is developed by Techno-AP (Ibaraki, Japan), and modified by SAGA-LS staff for further development of machine operation. The functions of the feed-forward control of power supply for insertion devices and feedback control for stabilisation of power supply have implemented in the program as well. The details of feed-forward and feedback system will be mentioned in section 5.5 and 5.6 respectively.

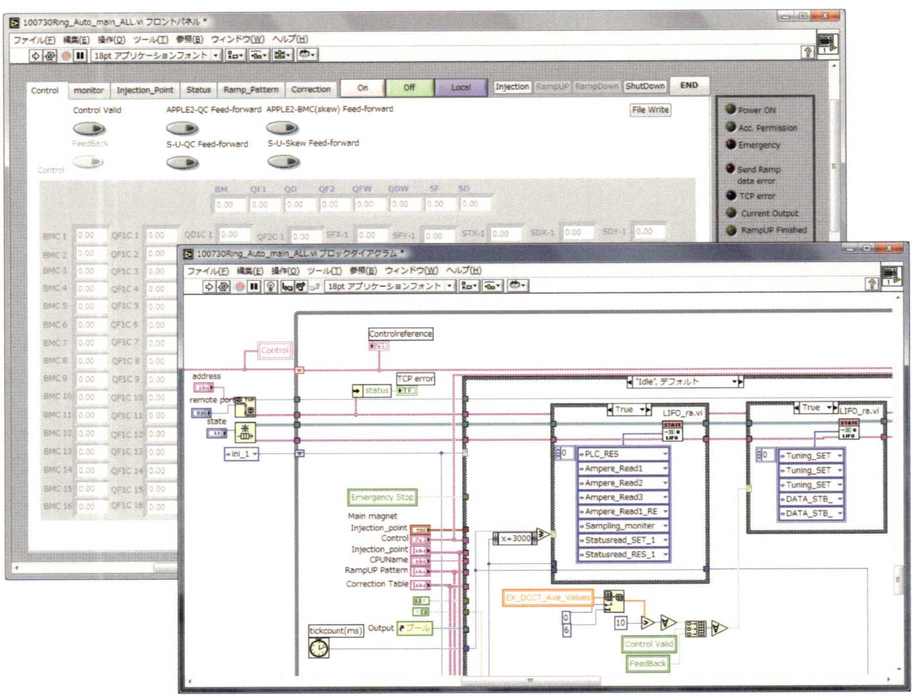

Fig. 4. Front panel and block diagram of the storage ring power supply control application. We are sorry that some words are written in Japanese, because we use Japanese version of Labview.

4.2 Vacuum monitoring

The electron beams circulating in the storage ring is scattered by residual molecules and stored current is gradually degreasing. To maintain a long lifetime of the electron beam, the pressure level of the accelerator must keep in an ultra-high vacuum. Hence the monitoring of the vacuum level is important for a stable accelerator operation. The vacuum level is measured by the vacuum gauge, and the analogue signal from the gauge controller is collected using a Fieldpoint 16bit ADC. The vacuum server PC translates the analogue signals to physical values and put the value as Process Variables (PVs). The sever PC and Fieldpoint configured PC-IOC. There are 24 vacuum gauges in the storage ring and 3 gauges in front end of beam lines where the beam profiles are measured. In the beam transport line near the injection septum magnet there is a vacuum gauge as well. All of the vacuum levels are

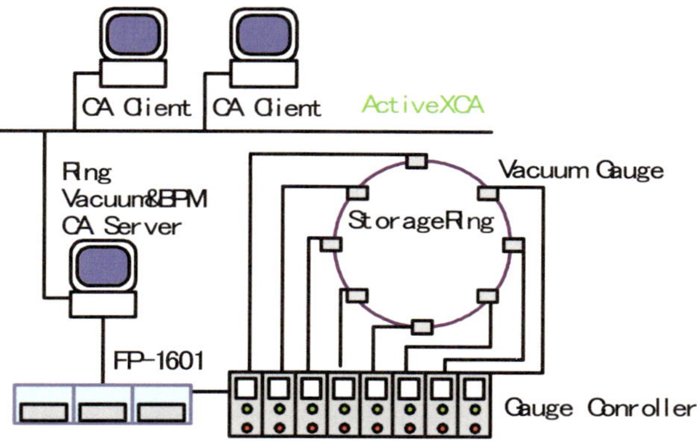

Fig. 5. Schematic view of vacuum monitoring system of SAGA-LS accelerator.

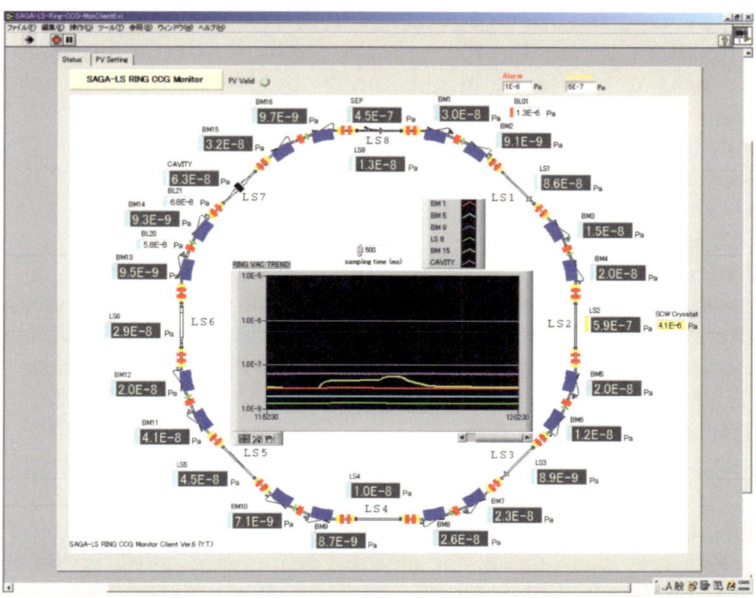

Fig. 6. Front panel of vacuum monitoring system. The vacuum is indicated not only as digital numbers but also trend graph. Vacuum levels of the ring are alarmed using colored indicator.

monitored from the control room and recorded into the database. Figure 5 shows the schematic view of the vacuum monitoring system of SAGA-LS accelerator. The vacuum server PC also serves the beam position to reduce the number of server PC. The trend of the vacuum level is graphically indicated in the front panel of the client PC as illustrated in figure 6. The easiness of construction of front panel and adequate graphical interfaces are superior points of Labview environment.

4.3 Beam position monitoring and closed orbit distortion correction

Beam line users use the synchrotron light emitted from the bending magnet or from the insertion devices. If the beam positions are not well defined, the path of the light would be changed, and it causes the fluctuation of the exposure light on the sample specimen. Thus the beam orbit should be corrected. Furthermore if the electron beams pass though the peripheral part of the quadrupole magnet, the electrons are affected by the multipole magnetic field, and it makes the accelerator parameter (such as twiss function) distorted, and a beam instability would be arose. Therefore the beam orbit is fixed to the center of magnetic field of the quadrupole magnets. The beam positions are measured using pick-up electrode and the signals are processed using BPM electrical circuit. DC voltage signals are read with Fieldpoint 16bit ADC, and the DC signals are translated to the physical values in the BPM server PC.

Here we briefly describe the principle of closed orbit distortion (COD) correction. If the $\vec{x}$ and $\vec{\theta}$ are the vector of beam positions measured by BPMs and the vector of kicks by the quadrupole magnets respectively, there is a linear relation with these quantities, $\vec{x} = \mathbf{R}\vec{\theta}$. $\mathbf{R}$ is called orbit response matrix. The matrix element of matrix $\mathbf{R}$ is the single kick response to a BPM. If the inverse matrix of $\mathbf{R}$ is obtained, the kick angles to correct the orbit distortions are represented as $\vec{\theta} = \mathbf{R}^{-1}\vec{x}$. Although the response matrix can be calculated with a simulation code by using the machine parameters (strengths of the quadrupole magnets and kick angle of steering magnet), but the response matrix is directly measured by the beam behaviour with kicks of the steering magnets and with monitoring by the beam positions in our case. We obtained measured orbit response matrix as follows:

I. Measure the beam orbit without kicks
II. Excite a steering magnet;
III. Measure the orbit shift
IV. Turn off the steering magnet
V. Repeat these procedures until all of the steering magnets are excited.

After the measurement of orbit response matrix, the orbit distortions are corrected with the corresponding steering kicks. The inverse of matrix **R** is driven using the method of Singular Value Decomposition (SVD), of which procedure is included in Labview mathematical library. This is also the great advantage to use Labview. The accuracy of correcting the COD against the reference orbit is less than 20μm in both directions with 24 BPMs at SAGA-LS storage ring. Figure 7 shows the front panel of COD correction program.

4.4 Beam based beam position monitor calibration

As is described in previous section, the electron beams circulating in the storage ring is measured by BPMs. Usually BPMs are aligned to the center of the quadrupole magnet, but the electric center of the BPM does not correspond to the center of the quadrupole magnetic field by the initial setting of the installations. If the beams pass through the off-center of the

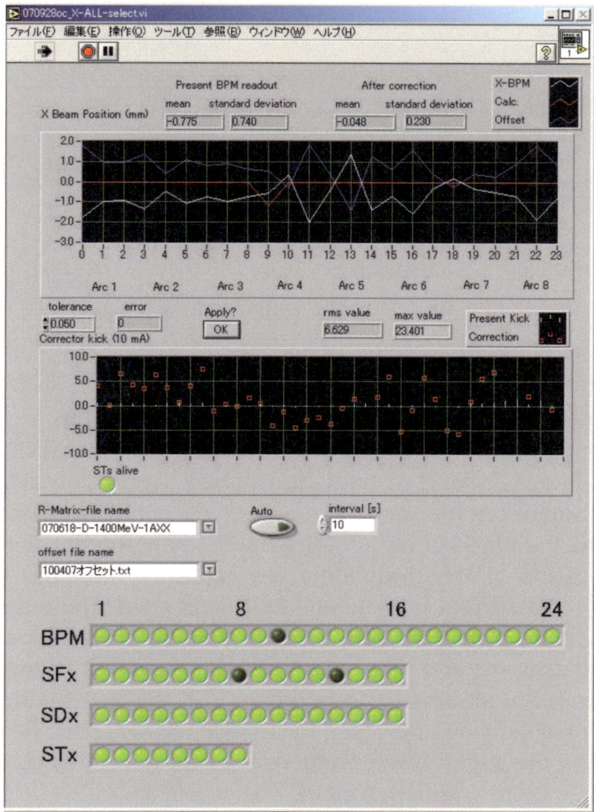

Fig. 7. Front panel of COD correction program. Any BPM and steering magnet can be selected (or masked) for the correction.

quadrupole magnet, the beam is kicked with the multipole magnetic field. Such multipole field causes the orbit shift and decreases the dynamic aperture, which limits beam lifetime. Thus the calibration of the BPM to the magnetic center of the quadrupole magnet is significantly important.

The method of beam based BPM calibration is follows;

I. Generate bump orbit near the BPM to be calibrated.

II. Change the excited current of quadrupole magnet close to the calibrated BPM.

III. Measure the orbit shift by the other BPMs in the storage ring.

IV. If the beam passes though the center of quadrupole, might become to be zero.

On these procedures, the steering and quadrupole magnets are sequentially exited and beam positions are measured. The BPM offset is analysed using Labview on line. In the analysis linear fitting routine included in Labview mathematical library is used. The application of the beam based BPM calibration automatically change the value of the steering and the quadrupole magnets, and monitors the beam position. Such complex and multi-task application is performed by networking and multi-client architecture with ActiveX CA data communication. Figure 8 illustrates the method of BPM calibration. By using the beam based BPM calibration, it was found that over 1mm offset in maximum are existed in the SAGA-LS storage ring.

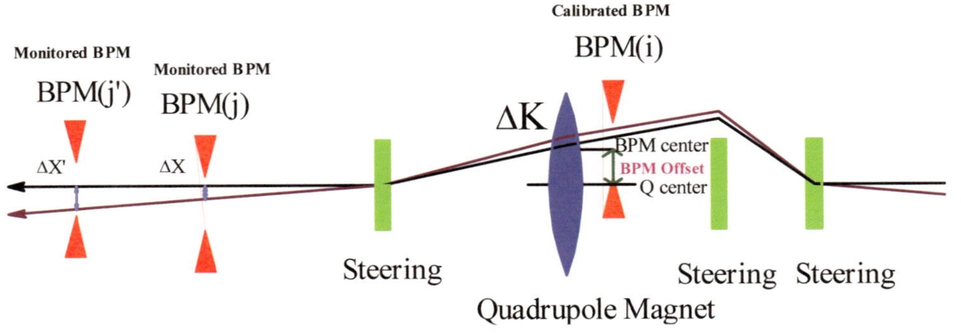

Fig. 8. Method of beam based BPM calibration.

4.5 Feed-forward correction of orbit, tune shift, skew correction

In SAGA-LS storage ring, there is a planner undulator and an APPLE-II undulator. The APPLE-II type undulator is a kind of undulator, which varies not only the photon energy but also the polarization of photon beams. Therefore, the control system should be prepared to control the gap and the phase of undulator without changing the electron beam orbit and size. The magnetic fields of the undulators are carefully measure and adjusted before installation, but the residual dipole magnetic field and quadrupole and skew quadrupole magnetic field are not completely compensated in general. The residual dipole field causes the orbit shift and quadrupole and skew quadrupole component change the beam size. For the free operation from the undulator users during the machine operation, these magnetic fields should be automatically compensated by an external magnetic field. The residual field is a unique function to the gap and the phase of the undulator, hence we have constructed feed-forward magnetic compensation system. The server PC of the magnet power supply reads the gap and the phase in the interval of 0.1 sec, and automatically produces the corresponding exciting current to the dipole magnet, the quadrupole and the skew

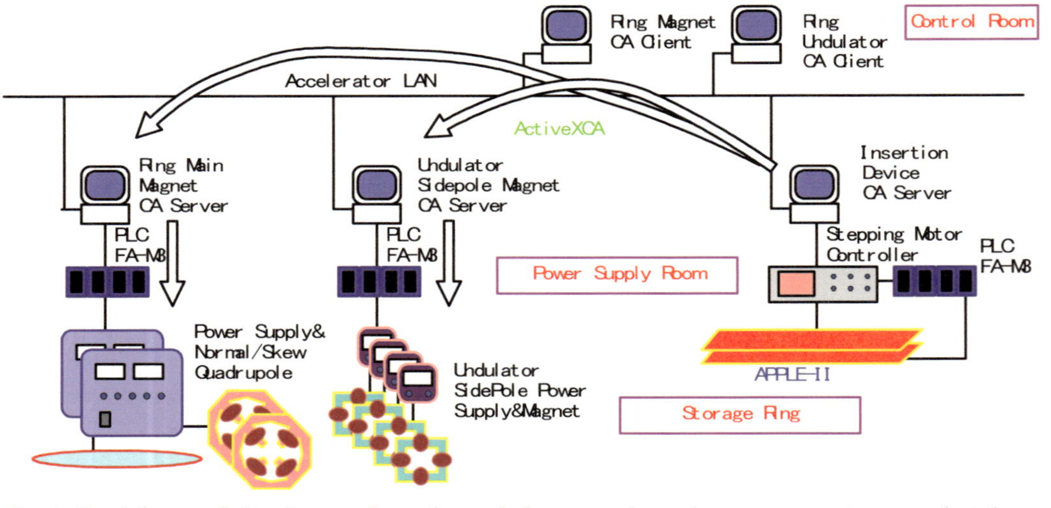

Fig. 9. Feed-forward dipole, quadrupole, and skew quadrupole magnet against gap height and phase position of the APPLE2.

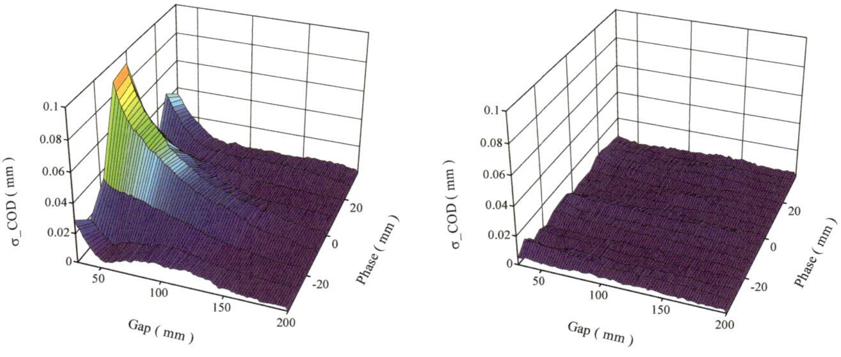

Fig. 10. Result of feed-forward dipole correction. The figure shows the horizontal COD: before; right, after; left. The COD have been reduced less than 10 μm by feed-forward correction system, and this result confirms the free operation of the undulator from the beam line users.

quadrupole magnets. In that case, the magnet server PC acts as a client PC for undulators. The magnet currents have been determined from the experimentally measured values. However the experimental data are the discrete set against the gap and the phase, the feed-forward correction application program calculates the exciting current with an arbitrary point by the linear and the polynomial interpolation of the measured data. Figure 9 shows the schematic view of the feed-forward system, and figure 10 is the correction result of the horizontal orbit shift. Before the correction, the standard division of the COD against the reference orbit is larger than 100 μm. After the correction it was reduced to be less than 10 μm.

4.6 Feedback system of magnet power supply

Magnet power supplies excite the magnets to produce required magnetic field. When the exciting current of the power supplies are drifting, we observe the tune shift and it causes, variation of the beam size and the beam lifetime. Although the output current is monitored through Digital Analogue converter (DAC) in the power supplies and PLC, the accuracy of the DAC is not sufficient for the beam diagnostics at the early stage of the user operation. To prevent these fluctuation we have installed an external DC current transformer (DCCT) to monitor the current with an accuracy of $\pm 1\times 10^{-4}$, whose uncertainty dominantly comes from the accuracy of the Fieldpoint 16bit ADC. By measuring the output currents of the power supplies, we clearly found the source of the tune shift.

After constructed the monitoring system of the output current of power supplies, we developed a slow feedback system of the magnet power supply. The output currents are measured external DCCT, and the signals are processed by DCCT electric circuit. The output voltages from the DCCT electric circuits are collected by the Fieldpoint ADC in 1Hz. Figure 11 shows the configuration of the slow feedback system for the magnet power supply. With this system the accuracy of the set point and the drift is $\pm 2\times 10^{-4}$. In figure 12 measured fluctuations of the output currents of the quadurapoles are shown. There still exist unexpected tune shifts in SAGA-LS storage ring. The fluctuation of the cooling water temperature of the magnets and the room temperature of the storage ring could be a possible source of the unexpected tune shift.

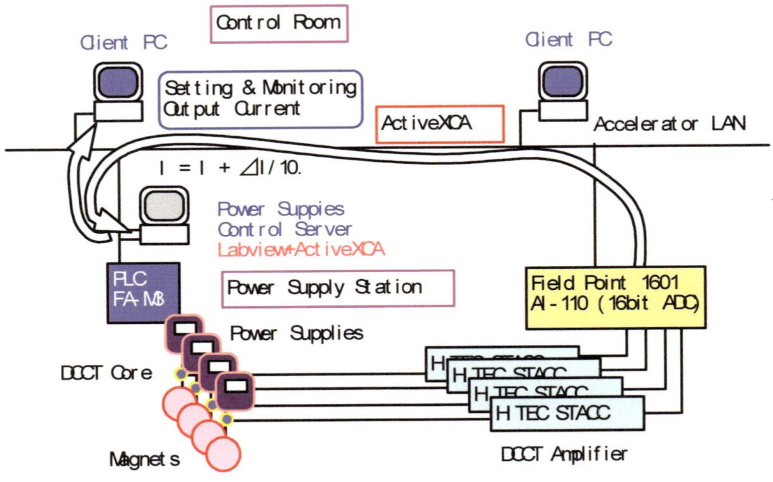

Fig. 11. Schematic view of slow feedback system of magnet power supplies. .

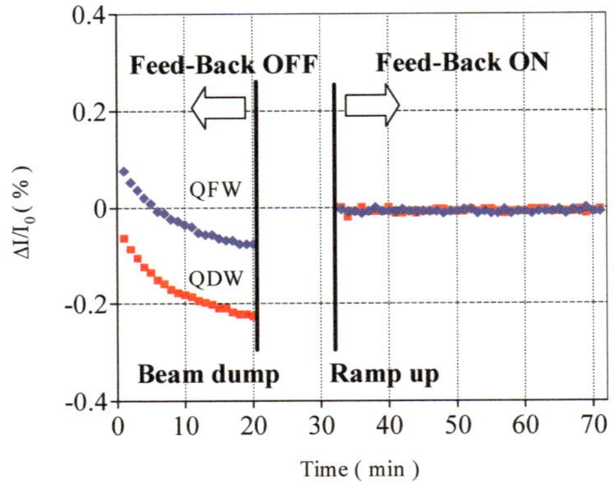

Fig. 12. The trend graph of output current of magnet power supplies (QFW and QDW). With the feedback system, the drifts of the power supplies are clearly reduced.

4.7 Web system, FTP, and E-mail system

In the present system we offer the accelerator status, such as the stored current, the electron energy, the position of the insertion devices, the mode of operation and so on, by using an inter-web server installed in the intermediate zone of the facility LAN. We use "APACHE" server as the web server, and Labview is used for generating the html file with NI Report Libraries. The trend of the stored current is drawn by the MySQL database. Figure 13 illustrates the web image of the intra-web.

The inter-web server also produces quasi-real time (1Hz) status services within our facility for the beam line experiments and alarm monitors. An exception of firewall policy is added to the accelerator firewall. Simple TCP/IP protocol is used for such application programs, because ActiveX CA uses several ports and it might be dangerous for the accelerator LAN.

For delivering the major parameter of the accelerator to the public via World Wide Web, we are prepared the external web server with the global IP address. To send the front panel image (jpeg image), we use an FTP client program, which was downloaded from the NI

Developer Zone (National Instruments) and was modified for our demands. A lot of sample programs are bundled in the Labview package and further sample programs are stored in the NI Developer Zone where we can discuss about our problems in the Labview developing environment and the development of applications.

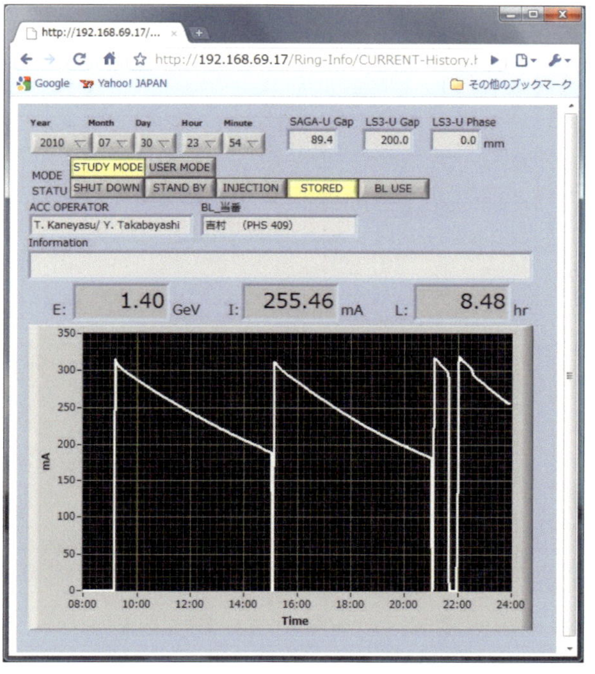

Fig. 13. Image of intra-web service at the machine study mode.

At present day, almost all people have their own mobile phone. The E-mail system also is developed for users to get the details of the accelerator status, for instance, the vacuum levels, the temperature of cooling water, etc. The procedures of the E-mail application are follows: when users send the message to the E-mail server, the E-mail client quickly receives the mssage from the E-mail server and resolves the mail subject, and replies to the address with required accelerator parameter as a message. Figure 13 is the block diagram of the E-mail application and sub VI. Basic program of the E-mail receiver and sender are also downloaded from the NI Developer Zone. In our E-mail sending the authentication method of MD5 is required from the E-mail server. Thus, we implement the function to the E-mail sender via RFC configuration scheme. Alarm system of the accelerator is also implemented in the E-mail application program.

5. Accelerator model calibration with external code TRACY2

The method of accelerator modelling by fitting the measured response matrix with calculated orbit response matrix is well known and widely adopted to many light sources for stable operations (Safranek, 1997), we also examined the procedure to diagnose the machine optics and to restore the periodicity of the twiss functions. In the analysis we use the tracking code TRACY2, and Labview can call this code as an external code in the application programs.

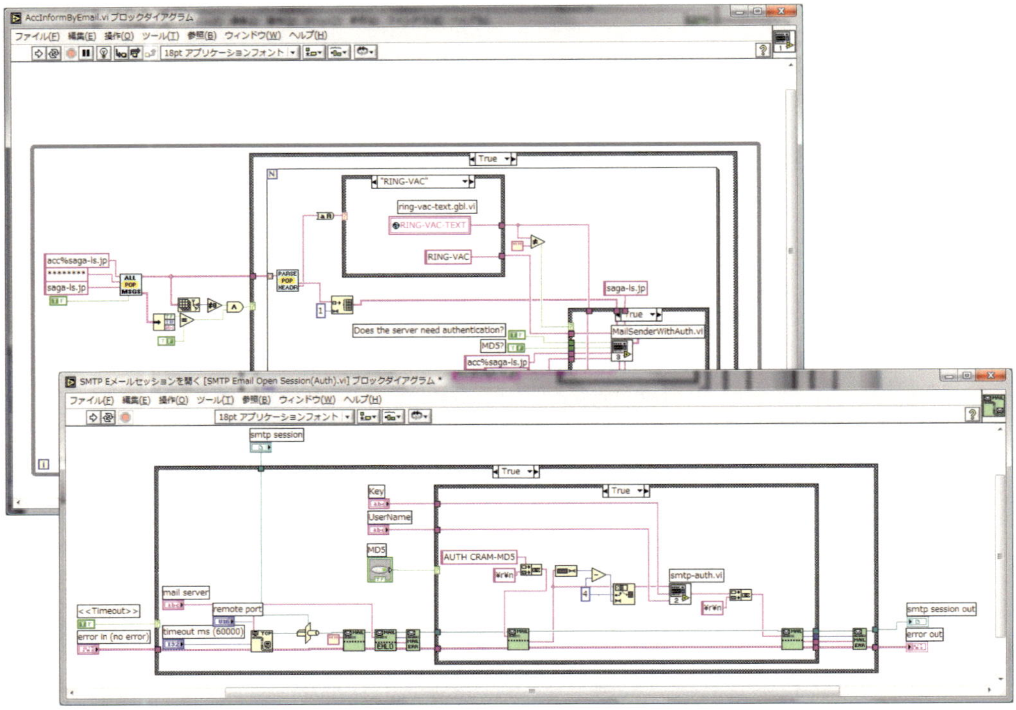

Fig. 14. Block diagrams of the E-mail application and its sub VI.

The orbit response matrix is defined by a variation of COD, which results from unit kick by a steering magnet. The matrix element R_{ij} represents the orbit shift at the i-th BPM caused by a unit kick from the j-th steering magnet. The subject is finding best-fit parameters of which maximum likelihood reproduce the experimentally obtained data. Such parameters could be found by minimizing the quantity χ^2. In our problems χ^2 is defined as follows,

$$\chi^2 \equiv \sum_{i,j} \frac{\left(R_{[\mathrm{model}]i,j} - R_{[\mathrm{measu}]i,j}\right)^2}{{\sigma_{ij}}^2} \qquad (1)$$
$$i = 1, 2, \cdots, M, j = 1, 2, \cdots, N$$

where $R_{[\mathrm{model}]i,j}$, $R_{[\mathrm{measu}]i,j}$ and ${\sigma_{ij}}^2$ are the calculated and the measured response matrix elements and the standard deviation of the measurement errors in the beam position, respectively. M and N denote the numbers of the BPMs and the steering magnets. In such fitting problems the SVD method is a standard solving technique (William, et al.,). SVD is also used to resolve the COD as already mentioned in section 5.3. Here, we will resolve 168 parameters with 1872 conditions.

Although it is not mathematically clear that the all parameters can be exactly resolved or have unique solution in principle, because the response matrix is not a linear function of the quadrupole strength. To confirm whether the fitting procedure could derive a unique solution or not, and exactly reproduce the parameters under the condition of the SAGA-LS lattice formation, firstly we simulated the ideal case in which the measurement errors are neglected. At the simulation, we prepared the calculated response matrix with randomly distributed parameter sets. Then we adopted the fitting to the calculated response matrix. Figure 15 shows the result of the simulation of the fitting for the quadrupole strength of QF1. After 5 iterations all parameters of QF1 was completely converged to originally setting values.

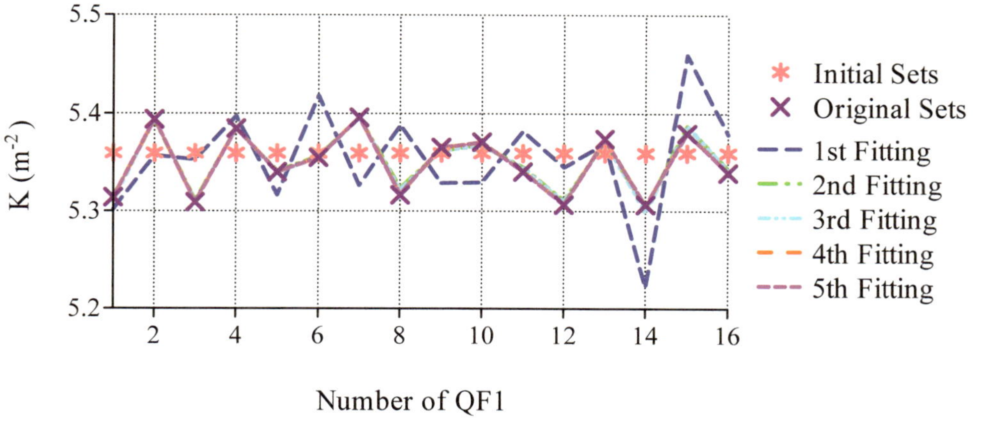

Fig. 15. Fitting transition of the QF1 K-values. After 5th iteration the fitting procedure completely reproduce the original set points.

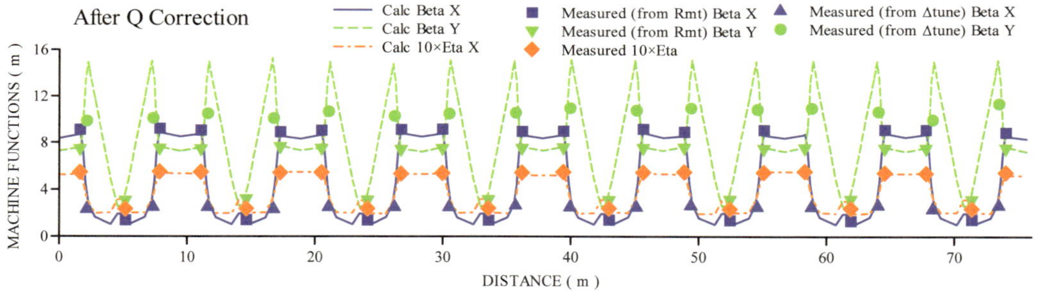

Fig. 16. Calculated and measured twiss functions after the quadrupole correction.

Figure 16 is the correction result of twiss function after the parameter fitting. We confirmed that there was no significant distortion in the twiss function in the storage ring and a good periodicity in the twiss function was observed. This method is useful for the accelerator diagnostic, because if one of the quadrupole magnet the irregularity of the twiss function is observed, and this response matrix fitting procedure can indicate the wrong component.

6. Future plan

6.1 Present status of the control system and its problems

The in-house Labview based control system stably works. The communication speed of the control parameter is about 10 Hz which is high enough for daily operation of the facility. Almost all accelerator components are integrated into the present system except for timing system which will be included in 2011.

Partially we use Labview8.5 running on Windows 7 and there is no problem between the old version of Labview (7.1) and the Windows XP including ActiveX CA communication. However, we still have problems, as;

1. client PCs for the data communication between the MySQL database and Labview sometimes hung up.
2. AD conversion speed of the Fieldpoint 16-bit ADC (1 Hz) is the bottleneck of the system performance of BPMs and vacuum monitor.
3. The number of the control PCs (server PCs and client PCs) are increased rapidly and this causes heavy maintenance load for operator. This also causes human errors in operation.

Therefore we are going to improve our system in the following cares.

I. Selection of database system including Labview DSC system
II. Replacement of the Fieldpoint to CompactRIO
III. Development of integrated client program
IV. Integration of server PCs to reduce the number of the control PC.

6.2 Improvement of user interfaces

In this section we will describe our recent improvement concerning to the III listed in the previous section.

From the commissioning period the number of the accelerator components has been increased rapidly. Especially the increasing the number of the client PC makes the operation complex. At the present stage we have to do 20 steps to offering the synchrotron radiation light to the experimental users. The complexity of machine operation sometimes causes human errors. Therefore we intend to improve the interface of the machine operation.

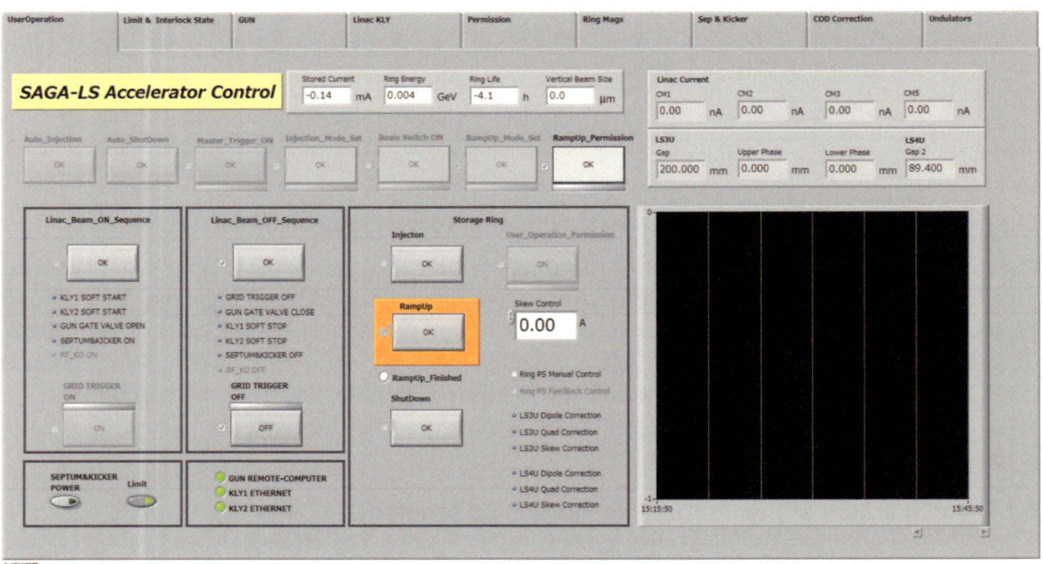

Fig. 17. Front panel of multi-purpose client PC. The program is running on Windows 7 and touch panel display. User can access each button intuitively without using a mouse.

We are developing a multi-purpose client program to integrate the client PCs to avoid human errors based on the operation complexity. The multi-purpose client program also adopted sequential programming which automatically sets accelerator parameters. We employed a touch panel display for an intuitive manipulation of operation of the accelerator as well. Figure 17 is the front panel of the newly developed multi-purpose client PC running on Windows 7. In this program "Tab button" is used for the individual programs. To reduce the operation procedure, the radiation interlock system is also integrated into this system. Although some parts of component concerning to the interlock system, such as master trigger, is not included in the system at this stage, the operation is significantly improved. After the all accelerator components are integrated into one, we expect that we can offer the synchrotron light to beam line users with only one-touch. The shutdown process will be also simplified. Sequential programming is done with Labview "stuck sequence structure" and with local variables. The easiness of multi-threads programming and sequential programming is also one of advantage of Labview.

6.3 Model based control system

The idea of model based control system is that operator controls accelerator with desired physical values calculated from a simulation code. At the beginning of the machine commissioning the first purpose of the control system is to put on/off the switch, change the machine parameters from remote location (control room). The machine parameters are manipulated so that the accelerator working as the desired manners. But we have mentioned in chapter 6 the measurement parameters of the accelerator are sometimes different from the designed values. The reasons of differences are, the measurement errors, calibration error of the power supplies of magnets, the non-linearity of the BPM gain, rotation of the BPM, misalignment of the magnets, the coupling of magnetic field that is caused by the adjoining magnet, and so on, that varies the accelerator parameter. Thus the beam based accelerator calibration is important to estimate the actual machine parameters and thus to estimate the machine status.

After the machine parameters are fixed and the machine works stably, usually the machine parameters do not need to be changed in daily operation at light source facilities. However, when the new operating point of the accelerator is required, the model based control system is useful. Because corresponding new machine parameter can be derived with the model calculation. We will develop the model based control system with Labview, which can execute external code and dynamic link library for beam behavior simulations in the accelerator. GOEMON (Nishimura) is the dynamic link library for the simulation code of storage ring, and ELEGANT (Borland) is for linac.

7. Conclusion

We have been developed in-house PC based control system for the medium size accelerator facility, SAGA-LS. The control program has been developed by Labview with ActiveX CA for distributed client-server system. With the easiness and flexibility environment of PC-Labview, daily control tools for the facility have been rapidly constructed by in-house resources. The successful improvements of the Labview application programs are helped by the sophisticated sample program bundled with Labview and also sample programs in the NI Developer Zone. Multi-thread and sequentially procedure, mathematical library, report generation library greatly reduces the development time. Multi-purpose CA client program has been developed with touch panel display on Windows 7 to improve the user operation interfaces. In the model calibration of the accelerator program the external code TRACY2 is also implemented. We are intending to implement the accelerator code GOEMON, which is the DLL version of TRACY2, to our control system.

8. References

Tomimasu, et al., (2003). The SAGA Synchrotron Light Source in 2003, *Proceedings of particle accelerator*, pp. 902-904, Portlrand, May 2003.

Iwasaki, et al., (2003). Lattice Design of SAGA Synchrotron Light Source, *Proceedings of particle accelerator*, pp. 3270-3272, Portlrand, May 2003.

Nishimura, (1988). TRACY, A Tool for Accelerator Design and Analysis, *Proceedings of European particle accelerator*, pp. 803-805, 1988.

Kay-Uwe Kasemir, (2003). http://ics-web.sns.ornl.gov/kasemir/axca/index.html.

Ohgaki, et al., (2003). Design of Control System for SAGA Synchrotron Light Source, *Proceedings of particle accelerator*, pp. 2387-2389, Portlrand, May 2003.

Ohgaki, et al., (2005). PC-LabView BASED CONTROL SYSTEM IN SAGA-LS, *Proceedings of particle accelerator*, pp. 3976-3978, Knoxville, 2005.

William H. Press, Saul A. Teukolsky, William T. Vetterling, and Brian P. Flannery, *Numerical Recipes in C,* The Art of Scientific Computing Second Edition, Cambridge University Press, ISBN 0-521-43108-5, Cambridge.

Safranek, (1997). Experimental determination of storage ring optics using orbit response measurements, *Nucl. Instr. and Meth.,* Vol.A388, pp. 27-36 (1997).

NI Developer Zone. http://zone.ni.com/devzone/cda/tut/p/id/5053.

Nishimura, (2001). GOEMON, A C++ LIBRARY FOR ACCELERATOR MODELING AND ANALYSIS, *Proceedings of particle accelerator*, pp. 3066-3068, Chicago, 2001.

ELEGANT, (2000). Borland, APS LS-287 (2000).

3

Electric and Nonelectric Quantities Measurement in Power Engineering using LabVIEW

Jan Machacek[1], Jan Slezingr[2] and Jiri Drapela[3]
Brno University of Technology
Czech Republic

1. Introduction

We need to measure both electric and nonelectric quantities solving the series of problems in power engineering. Graphical programming environment of the program LabVIEW seems to be useful helper and provides good tool for measuring both an automatic independent measurements of specific tasks, using measuring cards and instruments. The LabVIEW belongs to widely used measuring tools at Department of Electrical Power Engineering, Faculty of Electrical Engineering and Communication power engineering, Brno University of Technology. Since the LabVIEW is used to solve a number of projects at our department and there is only limited space in this article, we decided to mention only the most interesting ones. The first project deals with measuring operating characteristics of the photovoltaic cell. It consists of standard interconnection of measuring devices (producer Metex), which measure data that are transferred by program LabVIEW to the computer. Next, the data are mathematically and graphically processed. Different projects in LabVIEW offer a wide spectrum of front panels in the framework of this program allowing to connect each measuring device by its specific way. Some of them are listed here.

Another of the many tasks developed at our department is an autonomous measurement of electric and non-electric quantities of photovoltaic and wind power installation. A specific part of this project included the connection of meteorological station VIASALA which required a particular set of control interfaces created by LabVIEW. The LabVIEW environment has also created a comprehensive measurement system for detection of resistance of modern light sources to interference in the voltage supply, as well as a system to test and develop devices to measure the flickering of light sources. The system is implemented on the PXI platform.

First describes control of serial communication in LabVIEW software here, because serial communication is a popular means of transmitting data between a computer and a peripheral device such as a programmable instrument or even another computer. Serial communication uses a transmitter to send data, one bit at a time, over a single communication line to a receiver. You can use this method when data transfer rates are low or you must transfer data over long distances. Serial communication is popular because most computers have one or more serial ports, so no extra hardware is needed other than a cable to connect your instrument to the computer (or two computers together). In many applications, the electronics takes advantage of the LabVIEW program provides. It is mainly the fact that LabVIEW is a graphical programming language that uses icons instead of lines of text to create applications. In contrast to text-based programming languages, where instructions determine program execution, LabVIEW uses dataflow programming, where the flow of data determines execution. In LabVIEW, you build a user interface with a set of tools and objects. The user interface is known as the front panel. You then add code using graphical representations of functions to control the front panel objects. The block diagram contains this code. In some ways, the block diagram resembles a flowchart.

2. Serial communication between LabVIEW and simple meter

Serial communication requires that you specify four parameters: the *baud rate* of the transmission, the number of *data bits* encoding a character, the sense of the optional *parity bit*, and the number of *stop bits*. Each transmitted character is packaged in a character frame that consists of a single start bit followed by the data bits the optional parity bit, and the stop bit or bits. A typical character frame encoding the letter "m"is shown here Lab (2006).

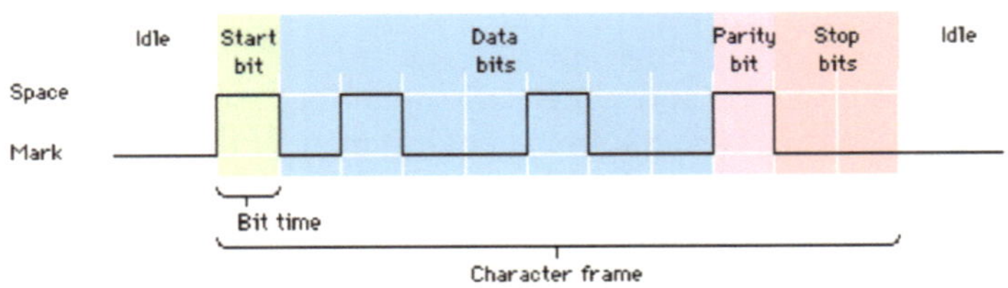

Fig. 1. Typical character frame encoding the letter "m"Lab (2006).

Baud rate is a measure of how fast data is moving between instruments that use serial communication. RS-232 uses only two voltage states, called MARK and SPACE. In such a two-state coding scheme, the baud rate is identical to the maximum number of bits of information, including "control"bits, that are transmitted per second.
MARK is a negative voltage and SPACE is positive; the previous figure shows how the idealized signal looks on an oscilloscope. The truth table for RS-232 is:

Signal $> +3$ V = 0
Signal < -3 V = 1

The output signal level usually swings between +12 V and -12 V. The "area dead"between +3 V and -3 V is designed to absorb line noise.
A start bit signals the beginning of each character frame. It is a transition from negative (MARK) to positive (SPACE) voltage; its duration in seconds is the reciprocal of the baud rate. If the instrument is transmitting at 9600 baud, the duration of the start bit and each subsequent bit will be about 0.104 ms. The entire character frame of eleven bits would be transmitted in about 1.146 ms.
"Data bits"are transmitted "upside down and backwards". That is, inverted logic is used and the order of transmission is from least significant bit (LSB) to most significant bit (MSB). To interpret the data bits in a character frame, you must read from right to left, and read 1 for negative voltage and 0 for positive voltage. For the figure above, this yields 1101101 (binary) or 6D (hex). An ASCII conversion table shows that this is the letter "m".
An optional *parity bit* follows the data bits in the character frame. The parity bit, if present, also follows inverted logic (1 for negative voltage and 0 for positive voltage.) This bit is included as a simple means of error checking. You specify ahead of time whether the parity of the transmission is to be even or odd. If the parity is chosen to be odd, the transmitter will then

set the parity bit in such a way as to make an odd number of 1's among the data bits and the parity bit. The transmission in the figure above uses odd parity. There are five 1's among the data bits, already an odd number, so the parity bit is set to 0.
The last part of a character frame consists of 1, 1.5, or 2 *stop bits*. These bits are always represented by a negative voltage. If no further characters are transmitted, the line stays in the negative (MARK) condition. The transmission of the next character frame, if any, is heralded by a start bit of positive (SPACE) voltage.

2.1 Serial port (RS-232)

The RS-232 is a standard developed by the Electronic Industries Association (EIA) and other interested parties, specifying the serial interface between Data Terminal Equipment (DTE) and Data Communications Equipment (DCE). The RS-232 standard includes electrical signal characteristics (voltage levels), interface mechanical characteristics (connectors), functional description of interchange circuits (the function of each electrical signal), and some recipes for common kinds of terminal to modem connections. The most frequently encountered revision of this standard is called RS-232C. Parts of this standard have been "adopted"(with various degrees of fidelity) for use in serial communications between computers and printers, modems, and other equipment. The serial ports on standard IBM compatible personal computers follow RS-232 Lab (2003).
Devices that use serial cables for their communication are split into two categories. These are DCE (Data Communications Equipment) and DTE (Data Terminal Equipment.) DCE are devices such as your modem, TA adapter, plotter, etc., while DTE is your computer or terminal. RS-232 serial ports come in two "sizes", the D-Type 25-pin connector and the D-Type 9-pin connector. Both of these connectors are male on the back of the PC; thus, you will require a female connector on your device. Below is a table of pin connections for the 9-pin and 25-pin D-Type connectors Lab (2006).

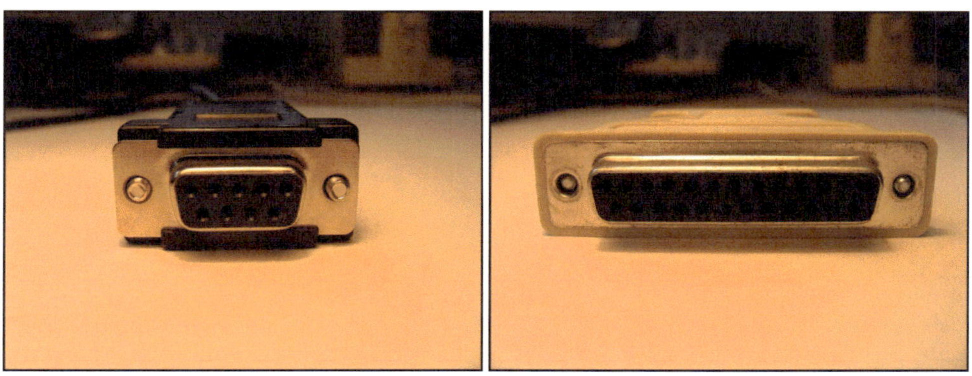

(a) DB-9 connector and pinouts. (b) DB-25 connector and pinouts.

Fig. 2. Serial connectors

The 9 pin's connector is occasionally found on smaller RS-232 lab equipment. It is compact, yet has enough pins for the "core"set of serial pins (with one pin extra). Important: The DB-9 pin numbers for transmit and receive (3 and 2) are opposite of those on the DB-25 connector (2 and 3). Be careful of this difference when you are determining if a device is DTE or DCE. The 29 pin's connector is "standard"RS-232 connector, with enough pins to cover all the signals

Function	signal	9 pin	25 pin	DTE	DCE
Data	TxD	3	2	Output	Input
	RxD	2	3	Input	Output
Handshake	RTS	7	4	Output	Input
	CTS	8	5	Input	Output
	DSR	6	6	Input	Output
	DCD	1	8	Input	Output
	DRT	4	20	Output	Input
Common	Com	5	7	-	-
Other	RI	9	22	Input	Output

Table 1. Lines of serial interface Lab (2006).

specified in the standard. The table shows only the "core"set of pins that are used for most RS-232 interfaces Lab (2003).

2.2 Control of serial port in LabVIEW

The LabVIEW **Instrument I/O Serial** subpalette contains functions and VIs used for serial port communication. You should notice that some of the functions in this subpalette are the VISA functions you used previously for GPIB communication. The VISA Write and VISA Read functions will work with any type of instrument communication and are the same whether you are doing GPIB or serial communication. However, because serial communication requires you to configure extra parameters, you must start the serial port communication with the VISA Configure Serial Port VI.

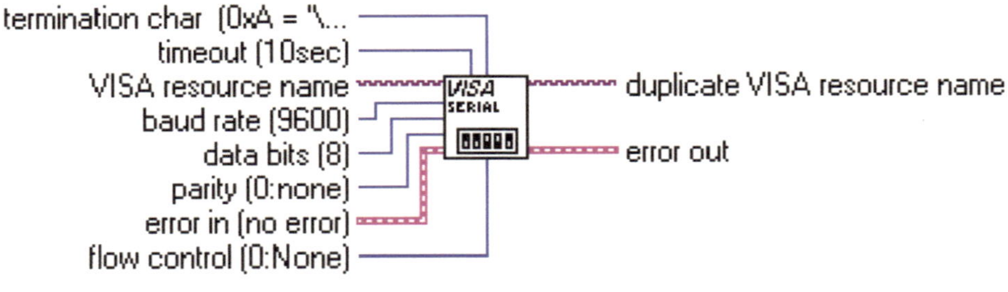

Fig. 3. VISA configure serial port Lab (2006).

The VISA Configure Serial Port VI initializes the port identified by **VISA resource name** to the specified settings. **Timeout** sets the timeout value for the serial communication. **Baud rate, data bits, parity**, and **flow control** specify those specific serial port parameters. The **error in** and **error out** clusters maintain the error conditions for this VI Lab (2003).

The example above shows how to send the identification query command *IDN? to the instrument connected to the COM2 serial port. The VISA Configure Serial Port VI opens communication with COM2 and sets it to 9600 baud, 8 data bits, odd parity, one stop bit, and XON/XOFF software handshaking. Then the VISAWrite function sends the command. The VISA Read function reads back up to 200 bytes into the read buffer, and the error condition is checked by the Simple Error Handler VI.

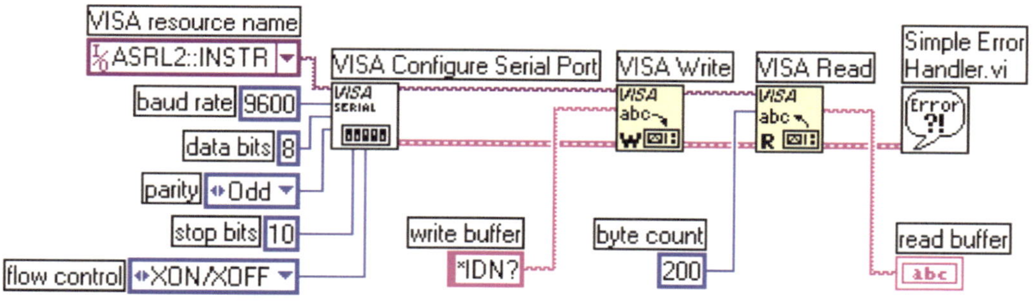

Fig. 4. The example of configuration. Lab (2006).

2.3 Specific application of serial communication in LabVIEW

The aim of the study was to create a measurement programme within a Lab VIEW programming environment for a laboratory task of "efficiency measurement of photovoltaic conversion". The use of the programme has brought the following benefits:

- digitalization of measurement,
- automation of measurement,
- archiving of measured values,
- easy further processability of values,
- immediate graphic processing,
- speed of measurement,
- and others.

2.3.1 Analysis of laboratory task

The programme should read the values of current and voltage on a photovoltaic cell. This is done with two Metex multimeters, one connected as a Voltmeter, the other as a Amperemeter. The values measured by the devices should be displayed on the computer. A good solution is to connect the measuring devices to the computer by means of a serial port. As there was not a computer available equipped with two RS-232 serial ports, it was necessary to use a Delock converter from a RS-232 interface to a USB for one device. Although the communication via the RS-232 interface compared to the more advanced USB is rather slow, it is wholly sufficient for this task.

The value from the measurement devices is displayed on the computer screen at once, without delay, and that is why the programme meets another requirement for the measurement, namely the recency of the values displayed. Data should further be processed in the structure of tables and simple charts. This requirement has been met by using appropriate blocks in the programme which as a result saves data in three columns of a table and then plots the current dependency charts: P = f(I), U = f(1) and P,U = f(I).

Another requirement for the programme function was to provide a option of saving or exporting the measured data into a different programme. The measured data programme. This is enabled by one block that asks the user to enter the file name and path to the file. The data is saved in the way as shown in the table. The LabVIEW programme creates files with a LVM suffix (LabVIEW Measurement), that can be opened in any text editor, e.g. NotePad, MS Word.

2.3.2 Programme analysis

As mentioned above, programmes are created within Lab VIEW through merging blocks. In the programme for measurement only some of the great amount of those prepared in advance were used. Serial communication surely belongs to the essential parts of the programme. There is more than one way within Lab VIEW to effecting serial communication within the measuring device and the computer. Within the Functions -> Instrument I/O -> Serial palette we will find nodes for communication with a serial port. These are now referred to as "old-fashioned". Their use is no longer recommended at present. They are included in the palette to provide compatibility with the earlier applications. The author had difficulty operating the control lines of the serial port using these functions. The other possibility of operating the port is to use e.g. library .dll which exports the relevant functions. The author, though, has not used the mentioned procedure either.
The National Instruments company has developed a higher level comprehensive interface for the control of peripheries, named NI-VISA. This is basically a set of what is called "API functions", that can be generally called from almost any programmable language and that can use a wide range of differing instruments, i.e. by far not just the serial port. There is also a VISA interface for LabVIEW, i.e. for the language G. National Instruments recommends using the latter interface for the new applications.

2.3.3 Communication with the measuring device

The serial port is a system means. In order to be able to use it, we need to designate it for use in our application. This phase of the port use is called "opening"of the port and in the block diagram it will be realized by the Functions ->Instrument I/O -> VISA -> VISA Advanced -> Visa Open node.
VISA Open (see Fig. 5) - opens sessions for equipment specification and returns a session identifier which can be used to call some other operations of this equipment.

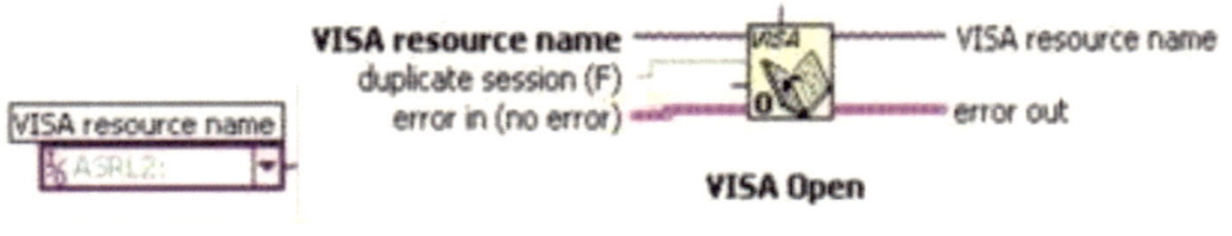

Fig. 5. VISA Open with VISA Resource Name constant.

Relevant input parameters:
A VISA resource name - indicates category and source of the open VISA sessions. The session does not have to be the correct one. Only the category of sessions and the resource name are relevant.
The relevant output parameters:
A VISA resource name - is the source where a session and its category are opened. The category has to match the input VISA resource name.
A VISA Resource Name constant will be created through right-mouse clicking on the node and selecting the Create Constant option on the menu that will appear. Then we will define the value of the constant in the pulldown menu. We will be able to choose from several options, depending on what interfaces are installed in the system at that moment. ASRL1::INSTR is the code for the first serial port, and similarly ASRL2::INSTR codes the other serial port.
Next the communication parameters will need to be set, i.e. the Baud Rate (speed of communication) to 1200, the number of Data Bits to 7, the number of Stop Bits to 2.0, and the level of RTS State control line to Unasserted. We will set the parameters for the open port using the Functions - Instrument I/O -> VISA - VISA Advanced -> Property Node.
The Property Node (see Fig. 6) - This node has an adjustable number of input and output terminals. In the individual Property Node arrays the required property can be set up. Each array is either designed for reading or for entry. We will set this property in the menu by the right - mouse clicking ("Change to Read", resp. "Change to Write"items). To summarize, we will choose the needed properties, set them for writing and assign values to them using the constants.

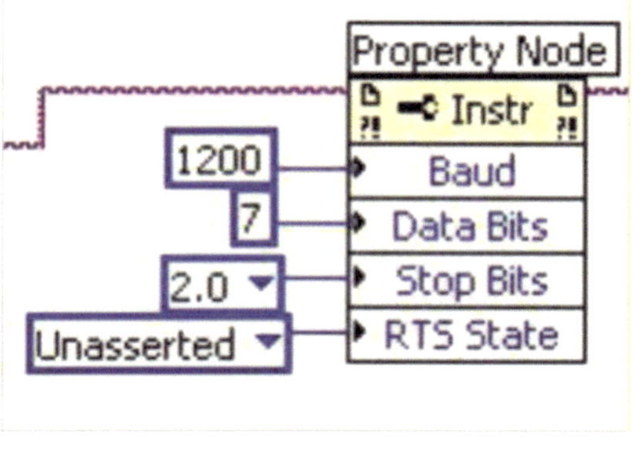

Fig. 6. Property Node with the set transmission parameters.

After that we will use the WHILE cycle and repeatedly execute entering of the CD command to the port and reading of the string (fourteen symbols for the Metex multimeters) from the port. The Functions -> Instrument I/O -> VISA -> VISA Read node is used for reading and the Functions -> Instrument I/O -> VISA -> VISA Write node for writing.
VISA Read (see Fig. 7) - the function is reading the prescribed number of bytes from the designated device or interface.

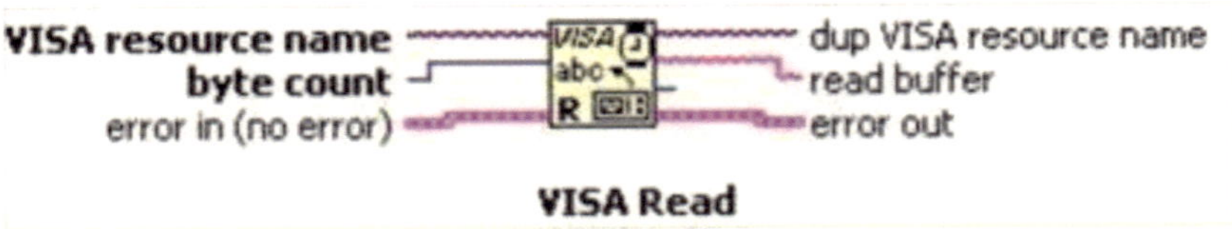

Fig. 7. VISA Read.

Relevant input parameters:
A VISA resource name - determines which interface will be opened. This parameter has the defined values of the ports named COM1, COM2 and LPT1.
Byte count - is the amount of bytes to be loaded to the buffer - 14 in our case.
Dup VISA resource name is a copy of the VISA resource name and is transmitted to the next VISA function.
Relevant input parameters:
Read buffer - transmits the symbols read from the entered interface.
VISA Write (see Fig. 8). Enters data from the "write buffer"to the device or interface specified in the VISA resource name.

Fig. 8. VISA Write.

Relevant input parameters:
write buffer - contains data to be entered in the device.
Dup VISA resource name is a copy of the VISA resource name and is transmitted to the next VISA function.
The WHILE cycle ends once the user has clicked the Stop button which is a representation of the terminal of the same name in the block diagram. The node D is responded by the Controls -> String & Path -> String Indicator (see Fig. 9) on the front panel, where the received string is displayed.

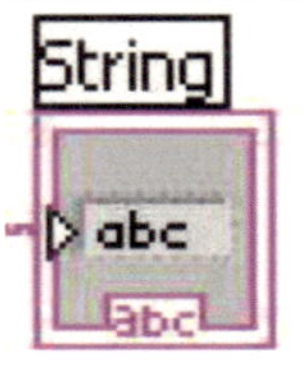

Fig. 9. String Indicator.

When using the port is at an end, it should closed for other applications to be able to gain access to it if they request to. The closing of the port is done through the Functions -> Instrument I/O -> VISA ->VISA Advanced -> Visa Close node.
VISA Close (see Fig. 10) closes the specified session of the device or the resulting object. VISA Close accepts all the available categories.

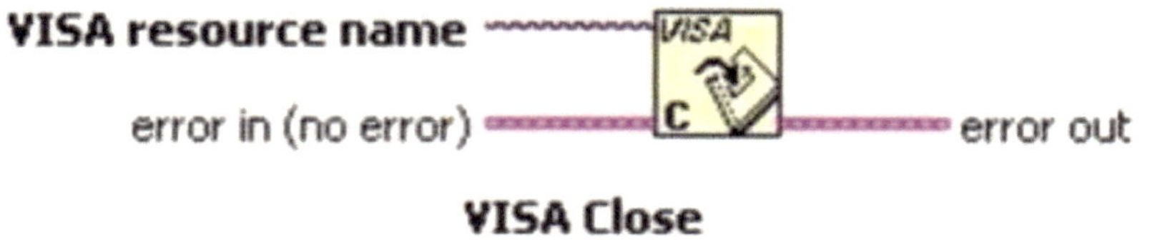

Fig. 10. Visa Close.

The general view of the serial port operation:
We have two measuring devices connected to the computer over two serial ports. Within the programme the serial port operation has to be executed twice. The simplest serial communication will be activated by just connecting of all the aforementioned blocks in a row. The block connection of the serial port operation for the COM2 port is shown below (see Fig. 11):

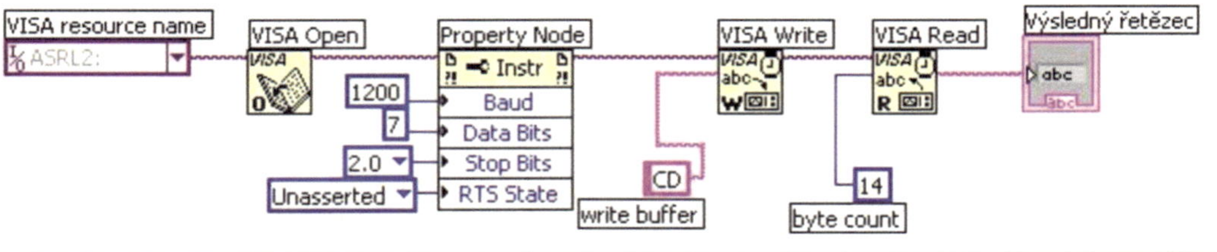

Fig. 11. Operation of Serial Port.

2.3.4 Data processing, calculations

We have activated the serial port in the Lab VIEW environment and the measuring devices have already been sending data to the programme in regular intervals. The data is, however, of the String data type which cannot be used for calculations and so the data type needs to be changed. Moreover, the string sent by the multimeter also contains an abbreviation relating to the measured quantity and a unit of the given quantity, blocks for the transmission of the data type would not be able to convert the values and it is therefore necessary to remove all symbols except for digits from the string.
Match Pattern (see Fig. 12) is an appropriate block for removing of selected symbols from the *string*. The input parameters of the block include a string, where a string is loaded for filtering, and a *regular expression* that contains symbols that will be retained in the string. In our case we wish to leave all the digits and a sign in place, the regular expression therefore contains a

string of the necessary symbols. The resulting output is a *match substring* which only contains digits and a sign.

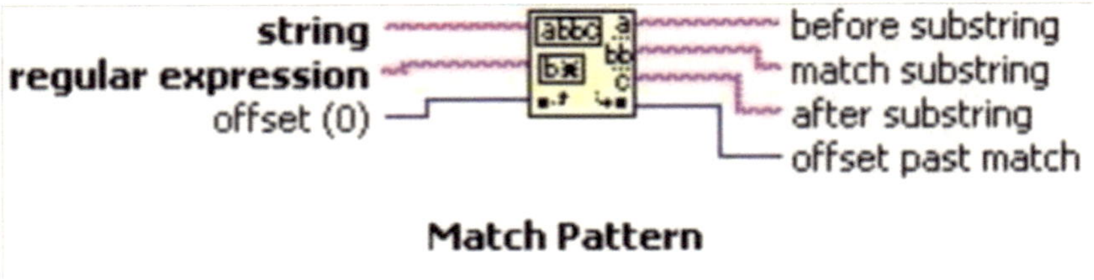

Fig. 12. Match Pattern.

In order to convert a string to a "double"data type used by all the computing blocks, we will use the Fract!Exp String To Number block (see Fig. 13). We will send a string to the *string* input and on the *number* output we will obtain a value of the measured quantity in the numerical form that we can already use for calculations.

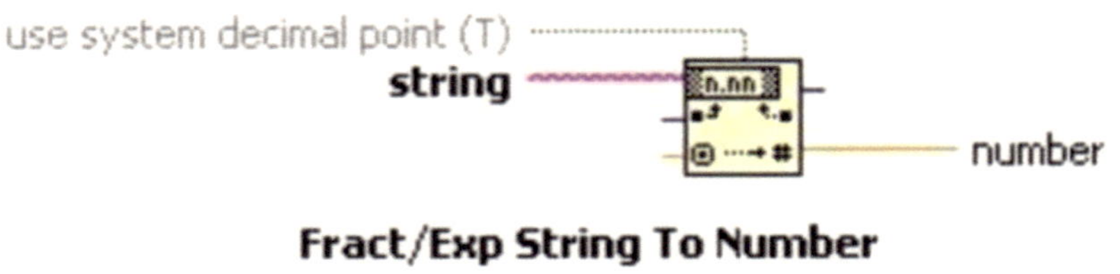

Fig. 13. Fract/Exp String to Number.

From the serial ports' outputs we have obtained the Voltage U and Current I values, flowing through the FV (photovoltaic) cell. We will calculate the Performance P value by using the Multiply block (see Fig. 14) which can perform multiplication between the numbers brought to the input x and y, and their product then appears on the output.

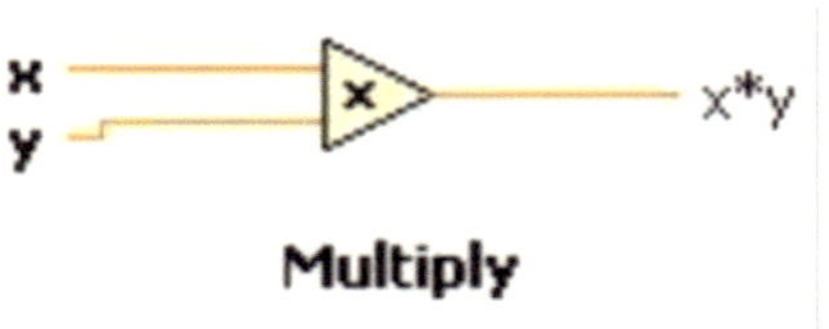

Fig. 14. Blok Multiply.

We will set the value of an impact performance P_{dopad}, to be calculated based on pyranometer sensitivity and pyranometer output voltage, using the Numeric Control (see Fig. 15) block. This we will find within Controls - Numeric Controls - Numeric Control on the Front Panel. Similarly, we will also set the size of area S.
Before calculating efficiency a maximum performance Pmax of a FV cell yet needs to be determined. We will obtain the maximum value by using a Max&Min block (see Fig. 16). The

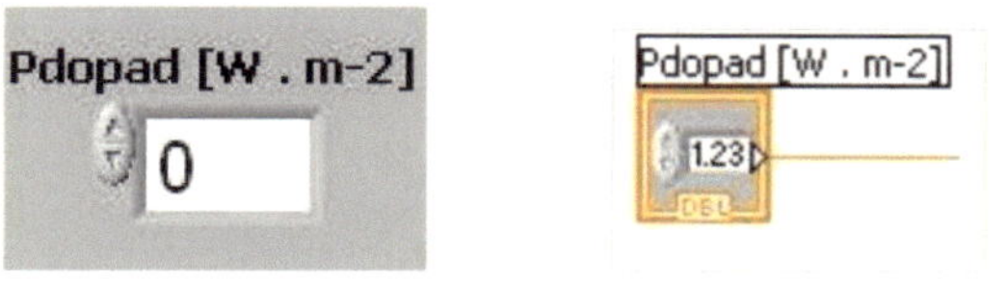

Fig. 15. Numeric Control on the Front Panel and Block Diagram.

Fig. 16. Max&Min.

Max&Min block downloads the values transferred to its inputs, which results in the value on the Max output.
Using the Multiply block (see Fig. 14) we will determine the area capacity rating P_{plon} as the product of a maximum performance P_{max} and a cell area S.
The values P_{dopad} and P_{plon} are known to us, and using the Divide block we can determine the efficiency of a FV cell. The Divide block (see Fig. 17) executes the quotient of two values transferred to its inputs, and the output shows the quotient as the result. The quotient and the product could also be determined using the Formula block, but the Multiply and Divide blocks are sufficient for calculations this simple.

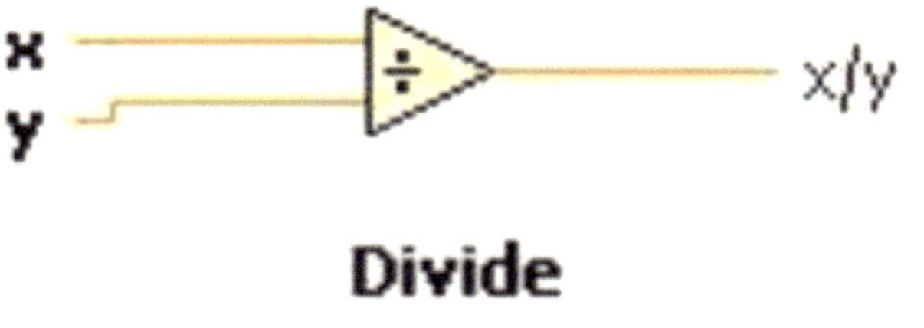

Fig. 17. Blok Divide.

The immediate value of efficiency η, along with the values of Current I, Voltage U, Performance P, Cell Area S and Impact Performance P_{dopad} can be displayed on the front panel (see Fig. 18).
The front panel further consists of a table to which we enter the measured values. The block for the table is placed in Controls -> Text indicators -> Table (see Fig. 19). In order to be able to write at the same time the values of current, voltage and performance to the table, we need to use the Merge Signals (see Fig. 19) block which will merge the signals into a single one which we will bring to the single input of the table. We can set the number of columns and rows in the table, in our case 3 columns and 20 rows. The options further provide for the display of headings for columns and rows and of a scroll-bar.

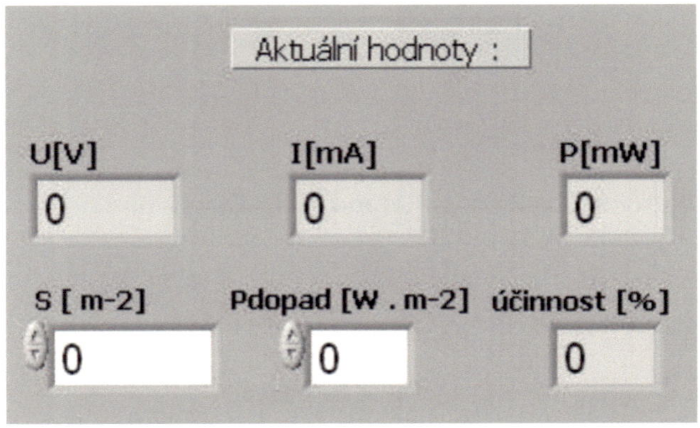

Fig. 18. Current values on the Front panel.

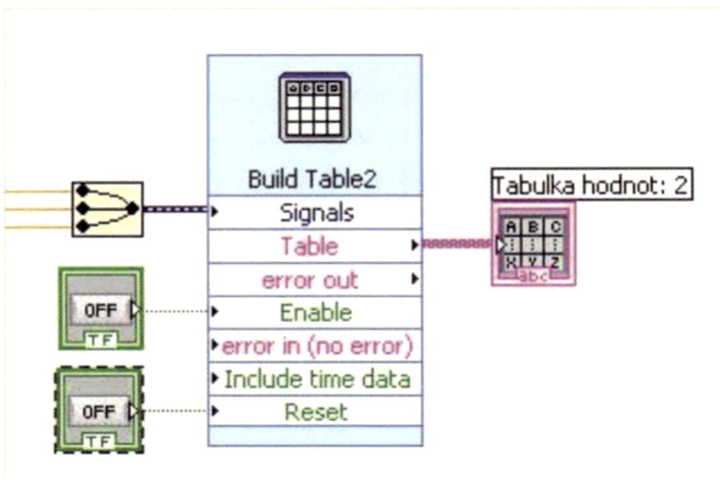

Fig. 19. Table of values with Merge Signals block and tabs for entry and deletion.

On the front panel of the table we can see the values of current, voltage and performance in the columns (see Fig. 20). We will enter values into the table by bringing Log 1 to the Enable input, and perform the table deletion by bringing Log 1 to the Reset input. These operations are executed by means of two tabs on the Front panel, to be found in the Controls -> Buttons & Switches -> Text Button (see Fig. 20).

We can plot the measured values in charts; there were three dependence charts needed for this task, specifically VA - characteristic U = f(I), Performance characteristic P = f(I) and Performance as well as VA characteristics in a single chart U,P = f(I). To create the charts we chose three Build XY Graph blocks (see Fig. 21), to be found in the Controls -> Graph Indicators ->XY Graph. Each block of the chart has two inputs for the values x and y on the axis and further inputs for enabling Entry and Deletion, that we will connect similarly as for the block of the table, to the tabs ENTER and DELETE.

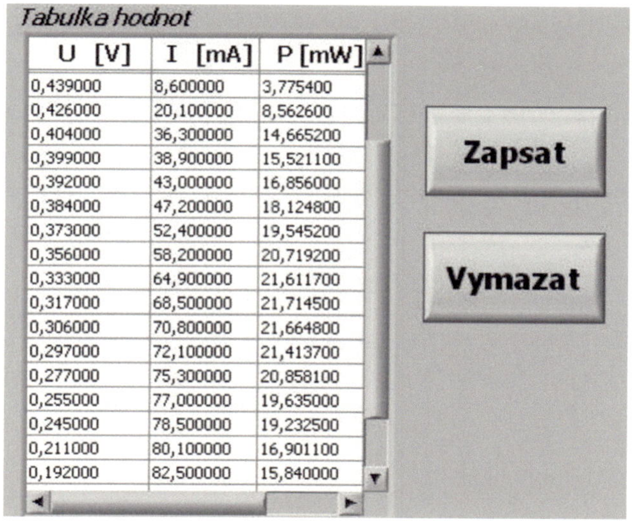

Tabulka hodnot

U [V]	I [mA]	P [mW]
0,439000	8,600000	3,775400
0,426000	20,100000	8,562600
0,404000	36,300000	14,665200
0,399000	38,900000	15,521100
0,392000	43,000000	16,856000
0,384000	47,200000	18,124800
0,373000	52,400000	19,545200
0,356000	58,200000	20,719200
0,333000	64,900000	21,611700
0,317000	68,500000	21,714500
0,306000	70,800000	21,664800
0,297000	72,100000	21,413700
0,277000	75,300000	20,858100
0,255000	77,000000	19,635000
0,245000	78,500000	19,232500
0,211000	80,100000	16,901100
0,192000	82,500000	15,840000

Fig. 20. Table with measured values, tabs for entering values and deletion on the right.

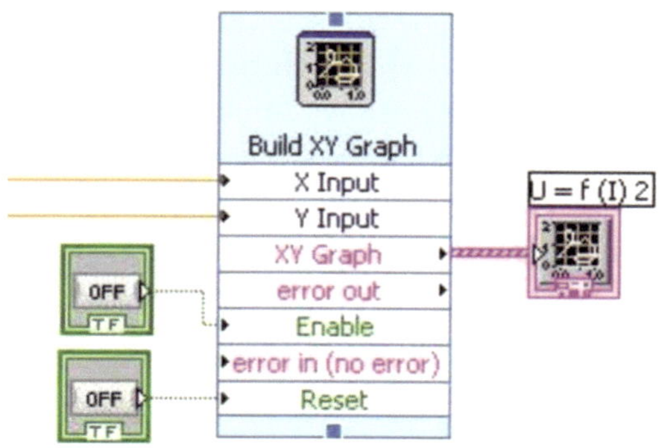

Fig. 21. Build XY Graph block with entry and deletion tabs.

The window of the chart on the front panel is displayed as shown (see Fig. 22). In order to be able to display multiple courses on the chart U,P = f(I), we need to again use the Merge Signals block and select two axes and two courses in the chart setup. The chart options include the setting of the cursor and further the setting of colours of the courses/curves and the cursor. The chart can connect points (values) in several ways, though any connecting line of a trend (linear, logarithmic) cannot unfortunately be used here, as provided e.g. within the MS Excel programme.

After the measurement of data the next step involves its saving. The Write LabVIEW Measurernent File block (see Fig. 23) was used to save the data in a file. This block is located in the Function -> Output -> Write LabVIEW Measurement File in the Block diagram. I have connected the writing to the table, to the charts and the file to a single tab, since these operations should be started at the same point in time. The programme should save data

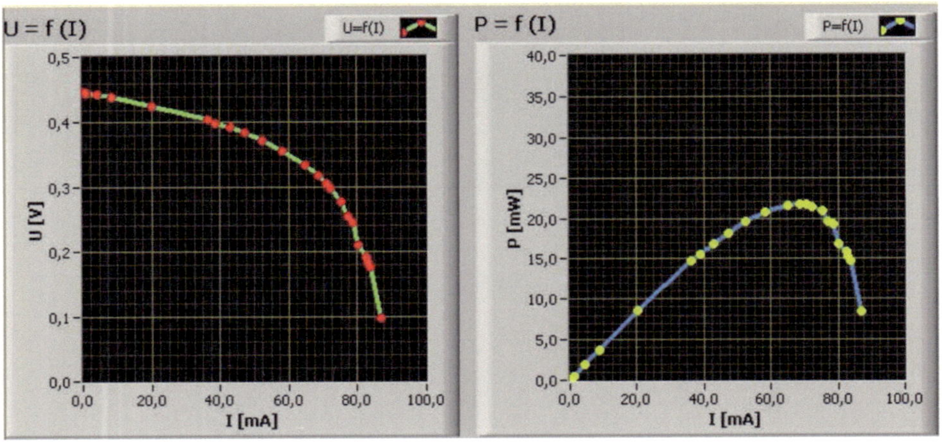

Fig. 22. Grafy na pøedním panelu.

to a single file, give the user a possibility of choosing a path to the file and the file name, and that is why I have chosen to use t'Action -> Save to one file -> Ask user to choose file -> Ask only onet' in the block setting. During the first measurement a dialog box appears to save a file (see Fig. 23). Within the block setting you can further select display of a heading for a file and time of measurement. To delete the content of a file we use the DELETE tab, which is common for the table and the chart. The LabVIEW programme creates files with a LVM suffix (LabVIEW Measurement), that can be opened in any text editor.

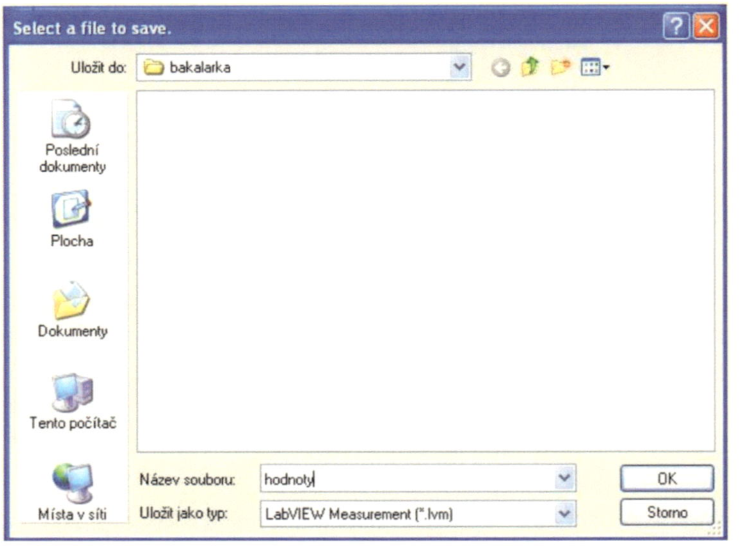

Fig. 23. Dialog box for writing to a file.

Overall view of the front panel and the block diagram is shown below.

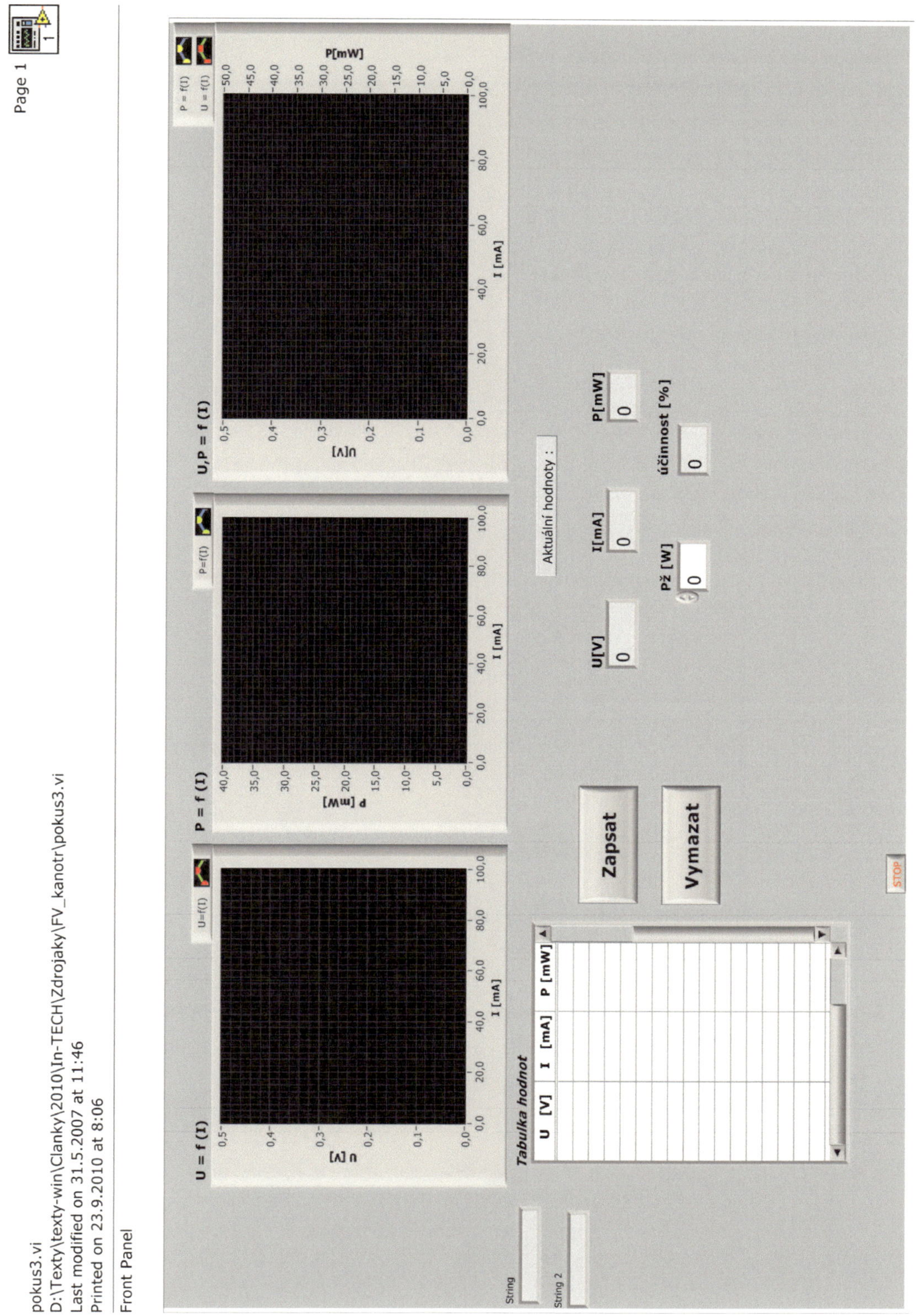

Fig. 24. General view of the front panel of a virtual device.

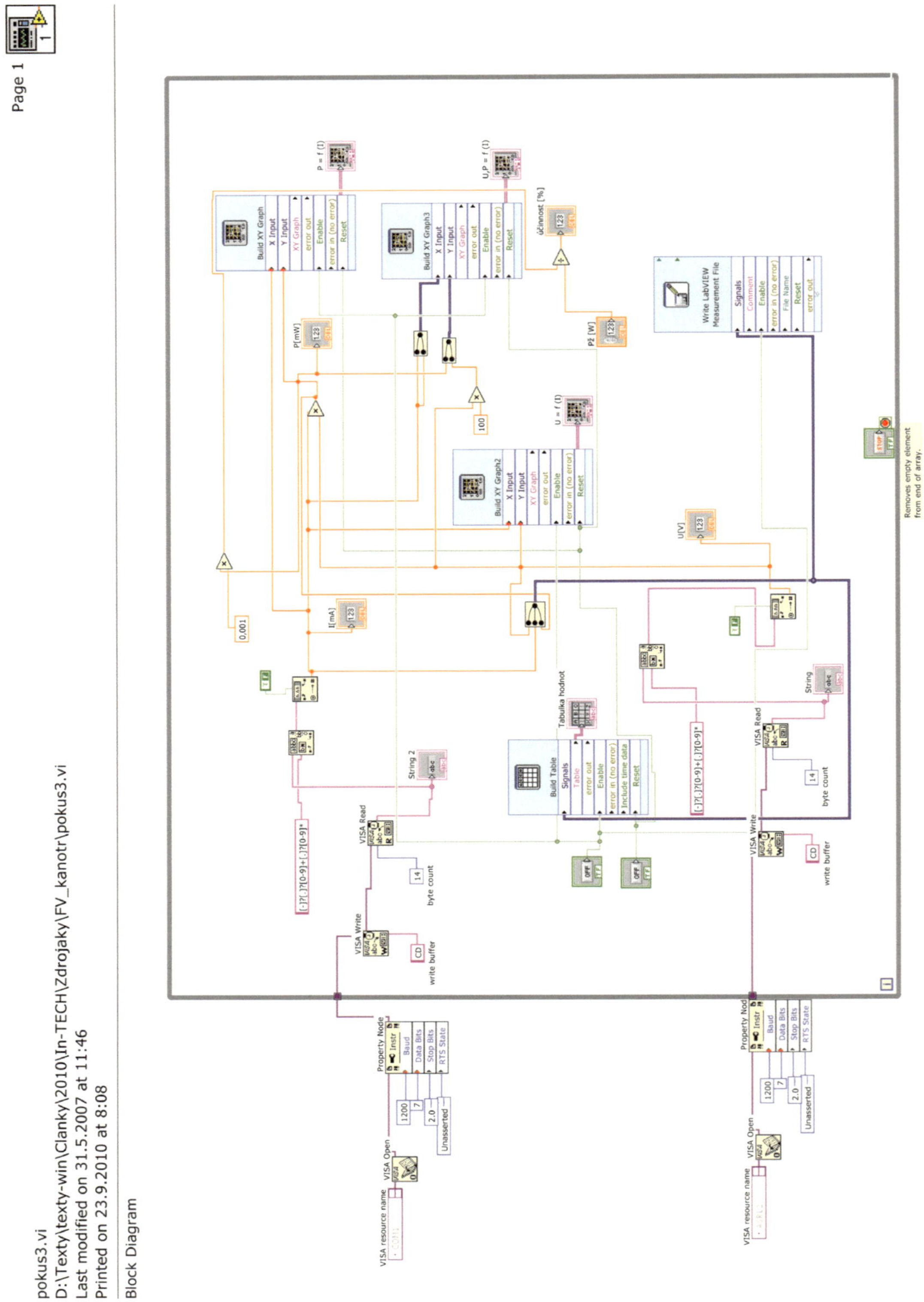

Fig. 25. Block diagram of a virtual device.

This is an example of a functioning virtual device which communicates through a serial line with a real measuring device, visualizes the measured values and further processes them. This is one of the basic uses of Lab VIEW for the construction of a practical application. A device constructed in this way, or a source code, can be further compiled to form a separate application independent of the LabVIEW programming environment.

The following picture is just a sample design of Metex, a simple virtual device communicating through a serial port.

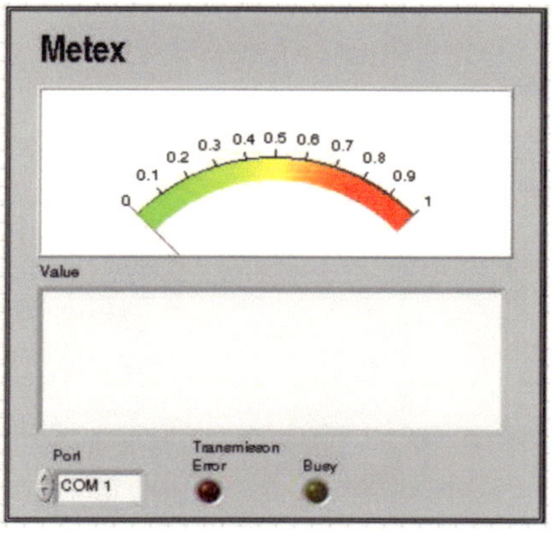

Fig. 26. Block diagram of a Metex 4560 cr. virtual device.

VISA configurator module is used again for communication via a serial port, which is, however, part of a "sub vi"application. The other blocks are just the means to process, control and display data. A detailed analysis of this application, however, is not the focus of this paper.

3. Flickermeter in the LabVIEW environment

3.1 Introduction

One of the major problems in regard to the quality of electric power involves quick changes in the voltage, i.e. its fluctuation, causing flickering of the light flow from the light sources. The light flow flickering may subsequently create an undesired perception of flickering which adversely impacts visual performance. This is a subjective visual impression initiated by a light stimuli, whose brightness or spectral distribution changes in time. The flickering of light sources may cause mental or physical fatigue or major physiological discomfort in people.

Voltage fluctuation may be caused by interference during the generation, transmission, distribution and consumption of electricity. The voltage fluctuation in the grid may be due especially to the fluctuation of active and reactive power of some appliances.

In order to measure the degree of perception of flickering was developed a UIE/IEC flickermeter which based on the measurement of voltage fluctuations evaluates the corresponding level of perception of flickering. The flickermeter models the transmission

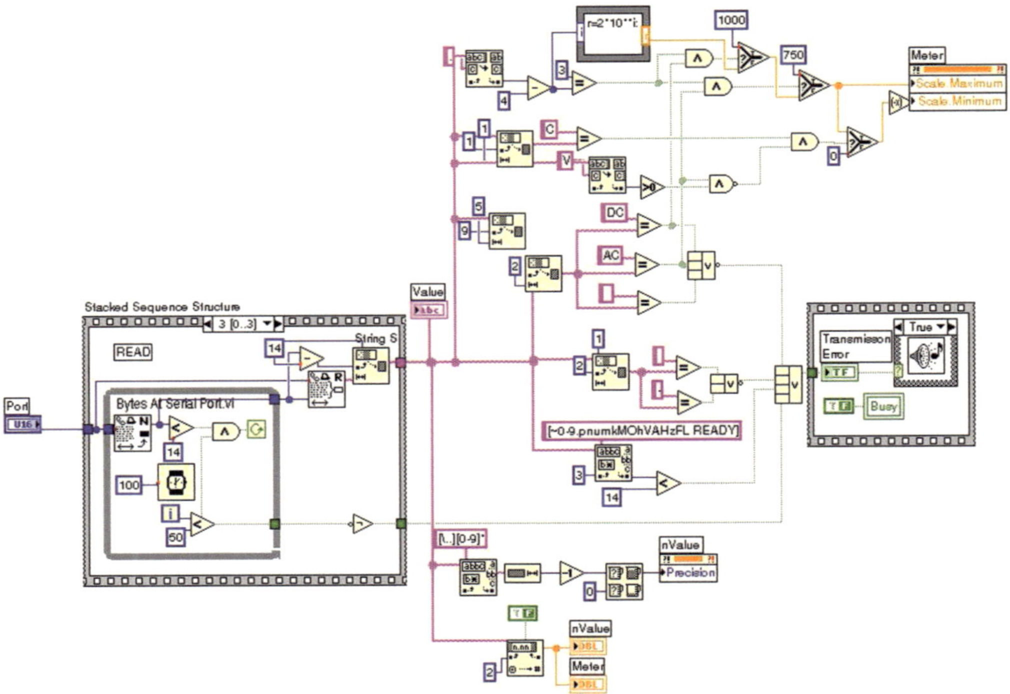

Fig. 27. Block diagram of a virtual device.

function of the light source and eye and the memory effect on the brain. The function of flickermeter is based on two critical activities: simulation of the light source - eye - brain chain and the statistical analysis of the output signal in real time. The light source modelled within the construction of flickermeter is a light bulb with a 60 W power and double coiled filament, rated for 230 or 120 V voltages.

The flickermeter is typically implemented as a function in the measuring devices designed for monitoring of the quality of electricity in the electrical networks. For the research purposes regarding the development of new types of flickermeter, a standard flickermeter has been implemented in the Labview environment at the Department of Electrical Power Engineering. The meter is used as a reference instrument for the new development constructions of flickermeter.

3.2 Implementation of the flickermeter in the LabView environment

The flickermeter construction is based on the study of human brain reaction to flickering light. The description of a flickermeter function and its detailed specification is included in the EN 61000 - 4 - 15 standard, see IEC (1997). The flickermeter function has been described in the introduction. It evaluates the course of voltage and provides a Pst value for the output, which expresses the degree of flicker perception by the normalized observer.

The flickermeter described in the standard is an analogue measuring device. The present-day digital measuring devices use a modified version of the standard flickermeter. S-transmission functions of analogue filters, used for describing the device in the standard, have been transformed into a digital form using bilinear Z-transformation.
UIE / IEC flickering-meter model was constructed as a virtual device within LabView. It is made up of the following basic blocks:

- voltage measurement,
- input signal normalization,
- filtration and weighting,
- statistical analysis.

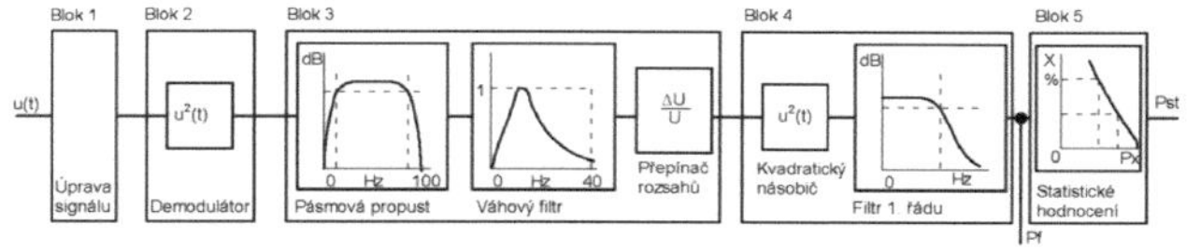

Fig. 28. Block diagram of a virtual device.

3.3 Voltage measurement

The voltage measurement uses the NI-PXI 4472 measurement card which is able to measure voltage in the range +-1OV. To measure the mains voltage it is necessary a ballast that will modify the magnitude of voltage; Slezingr et al. (2009).
The card's inputs are galvanically separated and properly isolated so it is possible to bring the mains voltage potential to the input terminals. This allow for using the voltage modification with a resistance voltage divider proven to provide the highest accuracy and linearity in the broad frequency range.
Voltage measurement for the flickermeter in the LabView block diagram is taken by means of express VI DAQ Assistant from the Input palette. The assistant automatically finds the measurement cards connected to the computer and mediates their configuration by the user. The measurement card is then represented by a single block in the block diagram, whose output is a data flow with an excessive quantity.
The measurement card connection is detailed in the LabView Help. For the purpose of flickermeter operation it was necessary to set an "Acquire Continuously"option in the Task Timing tab. A sampling frequency is set for the required 3200 S/s. The sampling frequency selection has to be made right at the start of flickermeter designing as all the filters used are specified using constants that depend on the sampling frequency.

3.4 Simulation of the light source - eye - brain chain

The block of signal normalization includes the measurement of input voltage effective value and calculates a maximum value. The input signal is normalized to a unit-amplitude signal.

The simulation of the light source -ėye - brain chain is performed as a cascade of filters. The filters used in the flickermeter are designed as a cascade of digital filters. There is IIR Filter used from the Signal Processing -> Filters -> Advanced IIR Filtering menu. The transmission function of this filter is specified using Forward Coefficients and Reverse Coefficients in the form of array of coefficients. The array is set up using the Build Array block.

A "TRUE"signal to the init/cont input is also transferred to the input of the TIR Filter block, for the signal filtering to go on continually for the whole period of the programme run, Hanzelka & Bien (2000).

The complete solution of one of the filters is shown in (see Fig. 29).

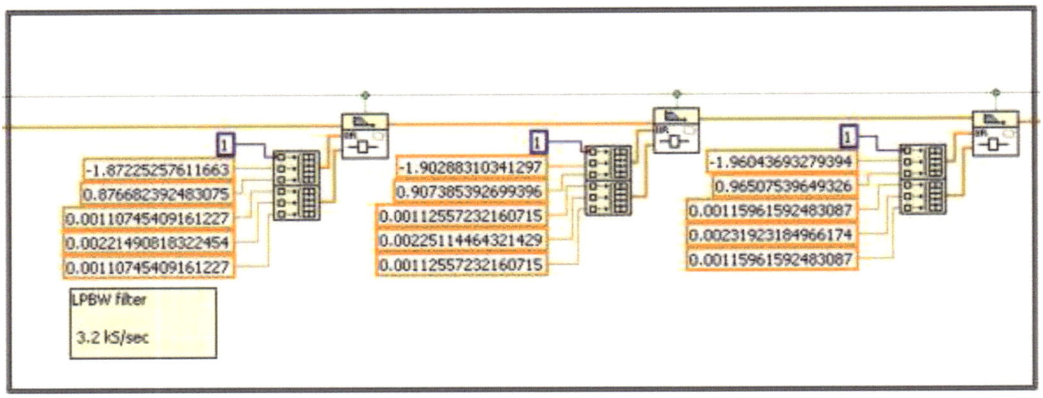

Fig. 29. Block diagram of the constructed filter.

3.4.1 Problems relating to filter stability

The practical implementation of the digital filters within LabView has indicated an increased likelihood of filters becoming unstable if the transmission function of the filter is higher than the second order of magnitude. It is therefore useful to transform transmission functions of the higher orders to a product of transmission functions of the lower orders of magnitude.

3.4.2 The programme run

The complete flickermeter is created as a programme loop named WhileLoop with 1 s programme delay using the TimeDelay block. Within each step of the loop a block of 3200 samples is read from the measurement card and data is transformed from the DynamicData type to the Array data type which is processed by individual filters. The filters' output is a single value for each block, denoted as Pf, of immediate degree of perception of flickering. Pf values are saved in an accumulator designed as Express VI Collector, during each individual passage of the loop. It accumulates values for a period of time required for calculation of the PST value (typically 10 minutes, though the programme allows for different times of accumulation. too).

3.4.3 Statistical signal analysis

An array of values is again placed on the accumulator output, administered in a statistical classifier whose block diagram is represented here below. The classifier function is consistent with the description within the standard. The number of classes required by the standard is minimally 64, the constructed algorithm uses 10000 of them.

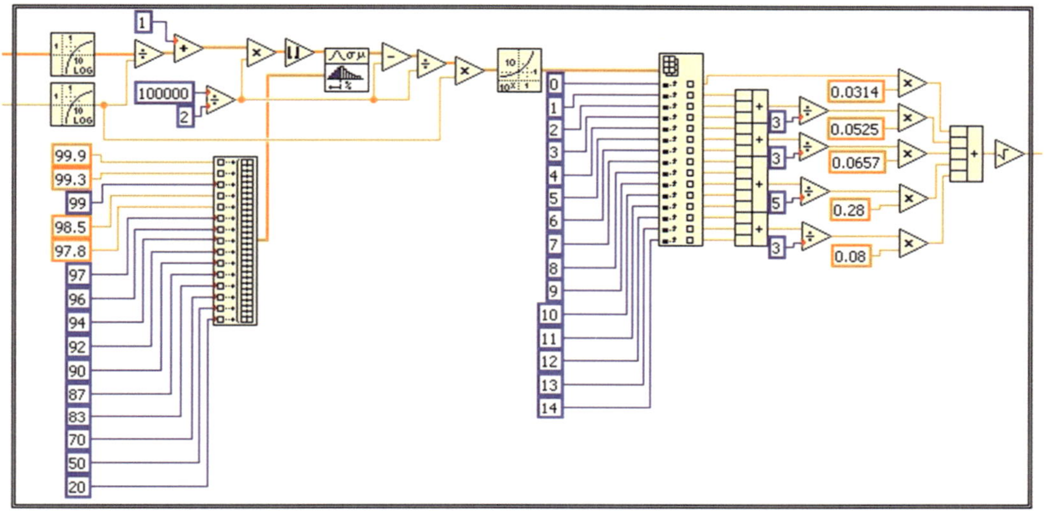

Fig. 30. Statistical evaluation of data.

3.4.4 The flickermeter control

START and STOP pressbuttons and Pf and Pst indicators are placed on the front panel. The input voltage curve, Pf current value and Pst measured results are displayed on the graphic displays.

The text indicator displays information about the current status of the meter. Three possible states may take place:

- starting the meter with counting-down the time-period for which it has to wait for the initial transient performance to pass,
- "Wait"status when the flickermeter stands by and waits for the START button to be pressed. This status takes place after the set time for the meter's starting lapsed, or after the STOP button is pressed,
- status of data accumulation for subsequent calculation of Pst value while counting down the remaining time of accumulation. This state stays active after pressing the START button until the STOP button is pressed, or the time of accumulation has lapsed, and the Pst calculation is made. The Pst value will always be overriden with the latest value on the display after the time of accumulation lapsed.

The flickermeter is programmed so as to enable using of the measured values also as a data source for further VI running on the same computer. The flickermeter is part of a comprehensive measurement system that can remote start the flickermeter and read the measured results using global variables.

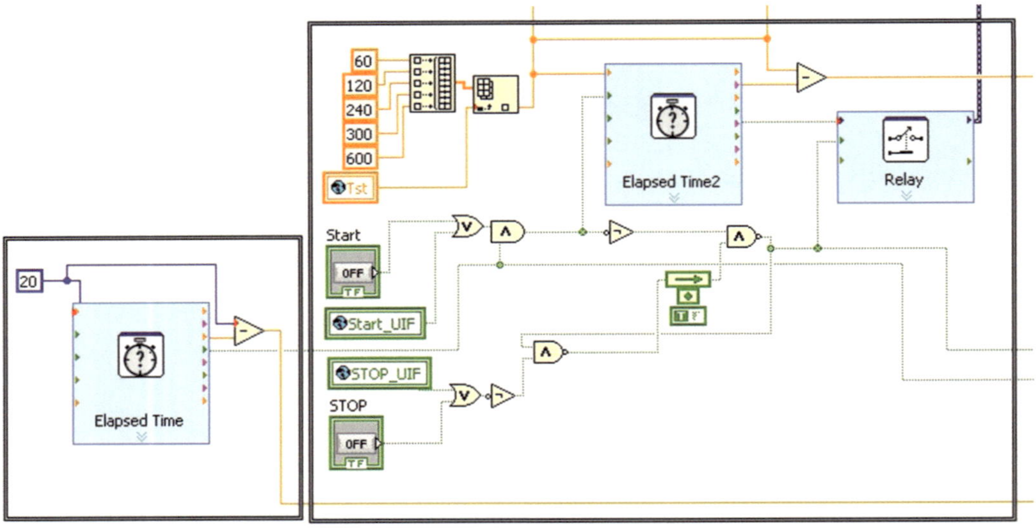

Fig. 31. Block diagram of the timer.

The general view of the user interface of the flickermeter is as shown on the following page.

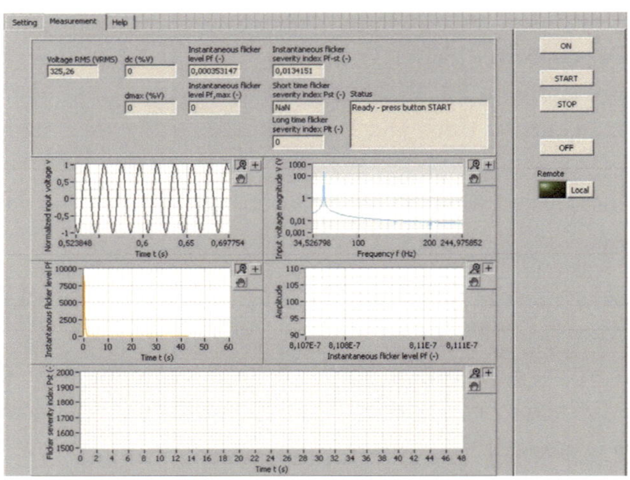

Fig. 32. Block diagram of the timer.

The flickermeter has been verified by the tests required by the standard. Its response to the test signals is fully compliant with its requirements and it now used within the development of the new types of the meter.

The described meter is now used as a reference device in the research of new constructional solutions of the flickermeter and in the development of a generator of different kinds of disturbance voltage fluctuations. It can be operated on any kind of computer with a measurement card connected. It can be built into comprehensive systems focusing on the area of electric power quality, based on virtual instrumentation.

4. Communication and control of Viasala WXT520 meteostation in LabVIEW environment

Finally the communication of LabView and a Viasala WXT520 meteostation is described. The meteostation is part of an extensive measurement system which on a long-term basis monitors electrical and physical quantities of the system of solar panels. A picture of a meteostation is shown in 33.

The meteostation delivery also included configuration software which, though, can only be used for meteostation configuration and testing of meteostation. With regard to the needs of the considered system of long-term online monitoring of data from solar panels the delivered software was inadequate as it did not enable digital access to the measured data. It was therefore needed to define and create our own application that would allow for integrating the WXT52O meteostation into the measurement system.

The core of the problem thus was to create an application within LabVIEW, that would be able to communicate with the meteostation using the RS-232 serial interface and would transfer the measured data further on, making it available for further processes within the measurement system that has also been programmed in the LabVIEW development programme environment.

The unique feature of this application is that it enables connection of a device to LabVIEW which does not have a primary support within LabVIEW in the form of measurement card, proving universality of the LabVIEW software environment. The only supported common communication standard is the serial port RS-232 interface.

The meteostation includes numerous detectors and sensors (see Fig. 33) measuring temperature, pressure, speed of wind, rainfall etc.

where:

1 wind transducers (3 pcs)

2 precipitation sensos

3 pressure sensor inside PTU module

4 Humidity and temperature sensors inside the PTU module

The basis for the communication configuration is the table of wiring of screw terminal pins on the meteostation terminal block, based on which the VISA block was set in the block diagram of the measurement application.

Fig. 33. Meteostanice WXT520 Viasala VIA (2008).

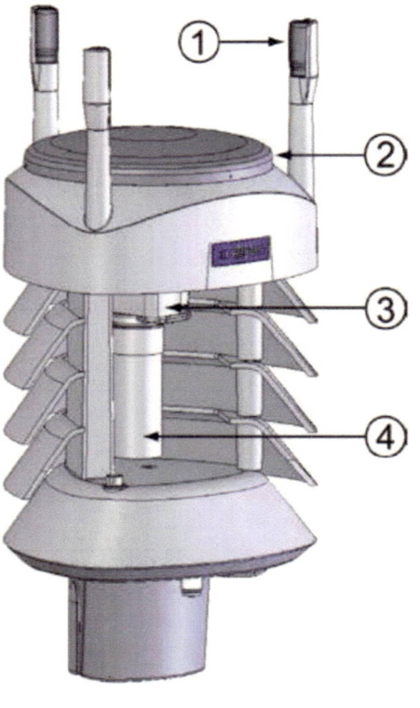

Fig. 34. Cut away view VIA (2008).

Screw Terminal Pin	RS-232	SDI-12	RS-485	RS-422
1 RX-	-	-	Data-	Data in (RX-)
2 RX+	-	-	Data+	Data in (RX+)
3 TX-	Data out (TxD)	Data in/out (Tx)	Data-	Data out (TX-)
4 TX+	-	-	Data+	Data out (TX+)
5 RXD	Data in (RxD)	Data in/out (Rx)	-	-
6 SGND	GND for data	GND for data	-	-
17 HTG-	GND for Vh+	GND for Vh+	GND for Vh+	GND for Vh+
18 HTG+	Vh+ (heating)	Vh+ (heating)	Vh+ (heating)	Vh+ (heating)
19 VIN-	GND for Vin+	GND for Vin+	GND for Vin+	GND for Vin+
20 VIN+	Vin+ (operating)	Vin+ (operating)	Vin+ (operating)	Vin+ (operating)

Fig. 35. Connection of pins for different VIA communication interfaces VIA (2008).

As can be seen from the block diagram of the application (see Fig. 37), it was necessary to configure a number of further variables to ensure the correct function, such as the following:

- channel selection,
- measurement interval,
- input port,
- communication protocol.

Subsequently the complete programme was created, whose user interface is shown below (see Fig. 36). The logic of the programme is roughly outlined by the following:

- setting of inputs
  - on/off measurements
  - definition of channels, ports etc.
- definition and configuration of individual sensors,
- repeated reading of data from the meteo-station in set intervals,
- display and entry of values.

5. Conclusion

The paper describes a few examples of using LabVIEW for the measurement of electric and non-electric quantities in electro-energy applications. The most frequently involved is evidently the LabVIEW communication with a measuring device using a serial port, but there are also applications putting it to good use, such as the described flickermeter which is constructed directly on the NIPXI platform, distributed by the National Instruments company. Through virtual instrumentation and launching of LabVIEW the simplification and greater effectiveness of the design have been achieved, and the same has in turn been applied in the construction of new laboratory tasks and research measurements. The described examples

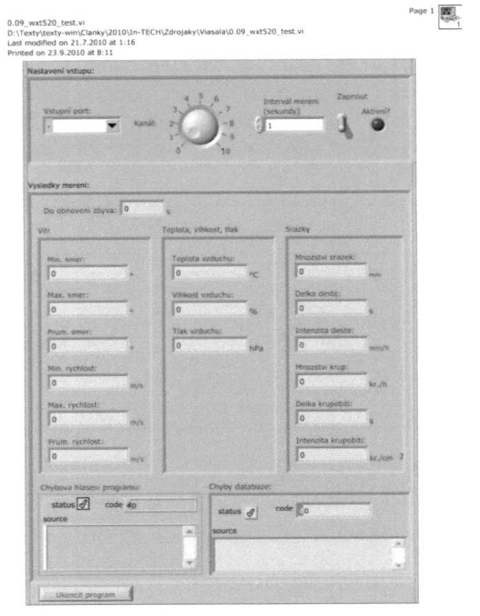

Fig. 36. User interface.

indicate possible use of LabVIEW as a concentrator of individual measuring devices and peripheries, which can be customized based on user requirements. Its operation is based on a single measurement interface which combines all the varied instruments used, and visualizes, archives and processes the measured data and if necessary also transmits it to another part of the measurement system. An integral part of the programme is the possibility of creating an effective user interface, from which the system can be administered as a whole. The final part of the paper also deals with a possibility of connecting LabVIEW to and its communication with a non-standard instrument which is not primarily designed for the communication with LabVIEW. As it has turned out, provided that standards of the communication interface are complied with, in our case the RS 232 protocol, the connection can be basically made without difficulty. This makes LabVIEW a universal software in the sphere of virtual instrumentation.

6. Acknowledgment

This paper includes the results of research funded by the Ministry of Education, Youth and Sports of the Czech Republic as part of project No.MSM 0021630516 and project No. CZ.1.05 /2.1.00/01.0014 Centre for Research and Utilization of Renewable Energy.

7. References

Hanzelka, Z. & Bien, A. (2000). Guide to quality of electrical supply for industrial installations, part 5, flicker and voltage fluctuations, *Technical report*, Power Quality - Working Group WG2, Tomsk.

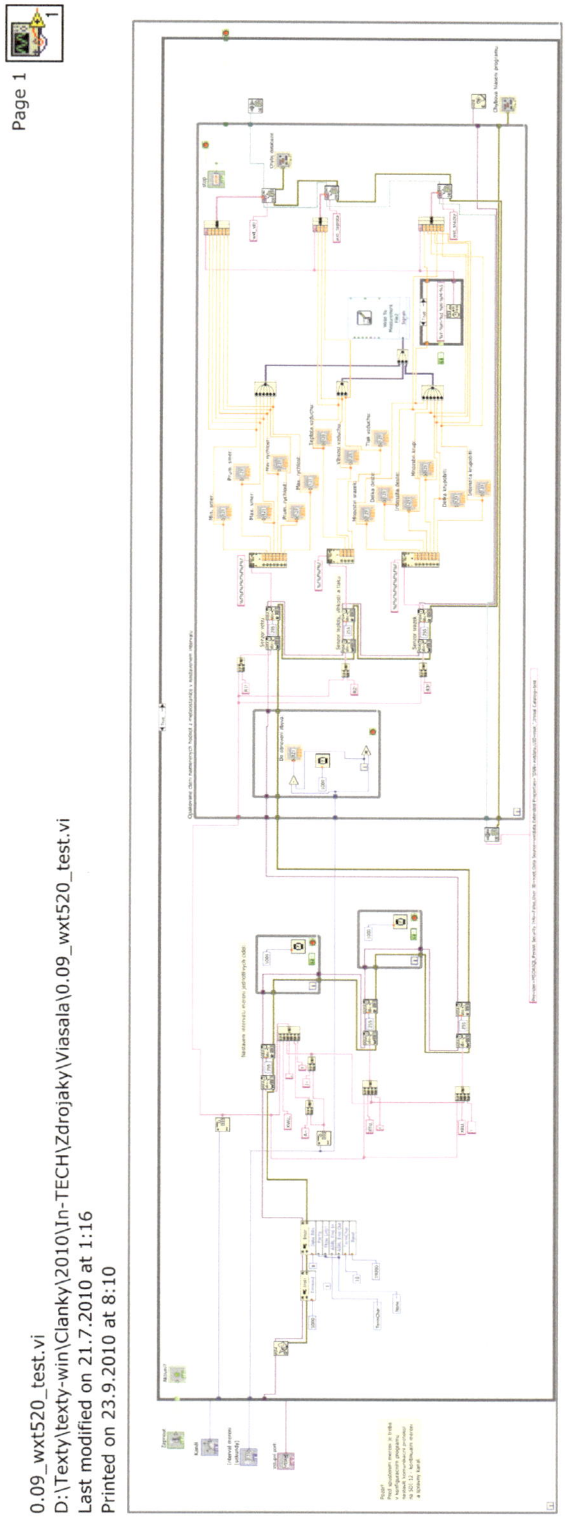

Fig. 37. Block diagram of the communication and control programme .

IEC (1997). 61000-4-15 - cem - part 4: Testing and measurement techniques - section 15: Flickermeter - functional and design specifications, International Electrotechnical Commission.

Lab (2003). *LabVIEW User Manual*, edition - part number 320999e-01 edn.

Lab (2006). *LabVIEW™Basic I Introduction Course Manual*, edition edn.

Slezingr, J., Drapela, J. & Tezky, J. (2009). Flickermeter implementation in labview, *Proceedings of the 15^{t}h International Scientific and Practical Conference of Students, Post- graduates and Young Scientists MODERN TECHNIQUE AND TECHNOLOGIES MTT 2009*, Tomsk, pp. 11–13.

VIA (2008). *User's Guide*, edition - m210906en-a edn.

4

Distance Process Monitoring using LabVIEW Environment

Valentin Sgârciu and Grigore Stamatescu
University POLITEHNICA of Bucharest
Romania

1. Introduction

Technological process supervision assumes acquisition, processing and returning the commands for a big number of parameters. At the same time, it is necessary to monitor the investigated parameters, because the history is needed in guaranteeing the performances, but also establishing the causes which lead to malfunctions.
Communication technologies and we refer here to Internet, which is mainly spread, allow data, acquired from long distances, to be concentrated in high performance servers. In the same time, following the temporal evolution of acquired parameters can be done from any computer, connected to Internet. This issue is suited both in technological processes, but also in education process, where a laboratory with high performance acquisition equipments and an Internet connection can be used by other laboratories less equipped. We have focused on a solution of data acquisition/distribution, using Lab VIEW framework, designated for remote process control and long distance learning.
The chapter is organised as follows: Section 2 presents arguments in favor of remote data aquisition and ways it can benefit the industrial operator. Section 3 shows our general view on such a system and a laboratory implementation of a simulation environment. Section 4 is dedicated to the client applications, each running on a dedicated network-connected workstation. Section 5 describes the main server application, the communication technologies we have used and an analysis of network performance in the current scenario. Section 6 presents the conclusion we can draw from our work, further developments and improvements.

2. Why remote data aquisition?

In many of industrial processes, the control at a distance of the equipments based on the received parameters is preferred. Sometimes, this process is absolutely necessary because of some high risk elements, or because of the conditions that do not allow the user to access it. As an example, one can mention the atomic piles where because of the high degree of radiations, the watch and control of the parameters must be done at a distance. Another example can be the watch of the furnaces, especially in the foundry works where because of the high temperatures, the user cannot physically stay in those areas.
More than this, an advantage of the watch/ control at a distance is the possibility to watch more over than one equipment with a single acquisition server. This aspect allows the

taking over of the data from more sensors connected to various industrial equipments and also the transmission of the controls to them. The process can be developed from more than one host in the same time. Thus, there can be a client host that commands through Internet the parameters modification of an installation, relying on a pressure sensor, while another client modifies the working characteristics of a thermal system, both sensors being connected to the same server. To sum up, one can say that the advantages of control at a distance of the industrial equipment, relying on the watch/control of the parameters are:

- people should not have to work in the risk areas;
- the possibility to control more than one equipment in the same time from different hosts;
- the possibility to watch from a larger number of stations, without extra investments.. It should be mentioned that the control of a sensor can be done by a single terminal, while the watch can be developed from many such terminals;
- the possibility of making some statistics in real time of the functioning of the equipment. This can be done even by the management department of a company.

3. Distributed system architecture

This section describes the distributed system, set up in an laboratory environment. It includes the following components:

- 3 workstations: PCs running Windows XP Professional SP3 and different versions of LabVIEW (higher than 8.2). Common hardware configuration Pentium 4 processor 3.06 GHz, 512MB RAM, 80GB HDD.
- 1 workstation acting as application server: PC running Windows XP Professional SP3 and LabVIEW 2009. Superior hardware configuration Pentium DualCore processor, 2GB RAM, 250GB HDD.
- network infrastructure: network server, routers, ethernet cables;
- always-on internet connection: required by the application server to share information with the outside world.

A diagram of the proposed system is shown in Figure 1.

In order to prove the feasability of the distance monitoring application, we have used multiple processes - developed in LabVIEW and running on the corresponding workstations. For this chapter, three applications have been chosen:

- **Temperature Monitoring and Control**: based on the plug-in data aquisition board NI PCI-6014E (produced by National Instruments), which focuses both on the continous aquisition of analog temeperature samples and on the generation of digital commands for a heating element with the possibility of dynamic adjusting of the temperature limits (lower and upper limit) for the desired operation of the system;
- **Acquisition/Generation of Digital Signals**: based on the plug-in KPCI-3102 (produced by Keithley) board which targets mainly the acquisition of digital signals and the generation of numeric commands to the exterior;
- **Environmental Monitoring throughWireless Sensor Networks**: based on IRIS 2,4GHz wireless sensor nodes (produced by Memsic Inc.) forming a self-organizing, self-healing wireless mesh network and a MIB520 USB gateway as a data sink. The gateway is then connected with LabVIEW thorugh appropiate drivers and the environment data (temperature, humidity, pressure, light, acceleration) is passed on to the server for processing, analyisis and storage.

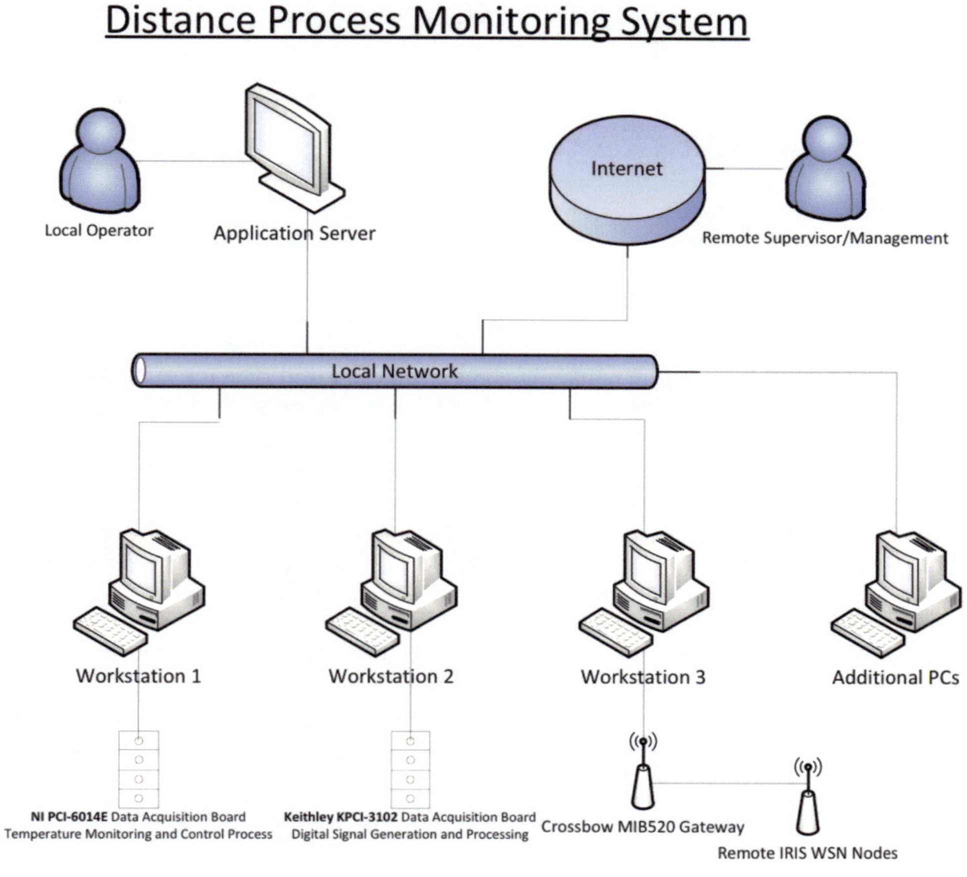

Fig. 1. Proposed Diagram of the Distributed System

For the chosen applications, the data acquisition boards/serial gateway represent the core of the local hardware system. The selection of hardware components was made in order to demonstrate the good integration with LabVIEW and the remote communication in the local network or Internet even if we are dealing with products from different manufacturers.

The principle scheme of the NI PCI-6014E is shown in Figure 2 and we then make short comments on the different blocks:

- **I/O Connector**: the connector to which the inputs and outputs from real world are brought up; the connector is prolonged through a ribbon cable next to a connection board where, through screw terminals, electrical links with real world are made;
- **Analog Input**: analogical inputs block; its components are: the analogical multiplexer MUX, the instrumental amplifier NI-PGIA with programmable amplification factor, the numerical-analogical converter ADC, the temporary memory for numerical equivalents of input signals AI FIFO and the trigger modes for input signals Analog Trigger;
- **Analog Output**: the analogical outputs block; its components are: two numerical-analogical converters (DAC0 and DAC1) and a memory (AO FIFO) where the numerical equivalents of analogical output signals are brought, as well as the necessary controls for choosing the working domain and the polarity of the output tension;

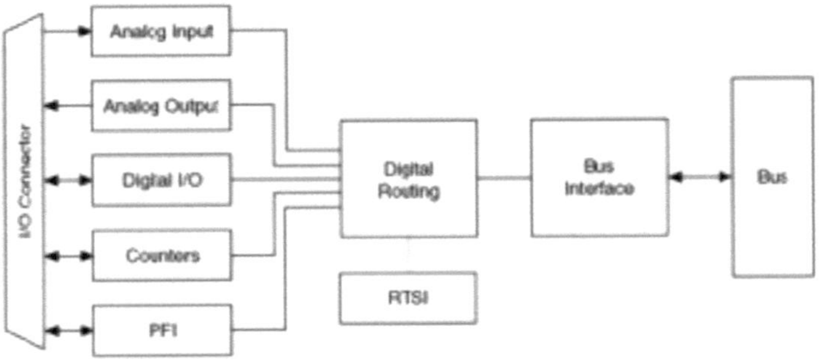

Fig. 2. Principle scheme of National Instruments PCI-6014E

- **Digital I/O**: numerical inputs/outputs block composed of 8 pins for general usage that can be individually configured, through software, as numerical inputs, respective numerical outputs;
- **Counters**: contains two counters of 24 bits, each one having two inputs (Source and Gate), one output (Out) and two software registers capable of different operations;
- **PFI (Programmable Function Interface)**: contains 10 connections with the outside of the board through which one can collect temporary signals from outside and can generate different kinds of internal board signals, inclusively the signals in relation with the operation mod for the two counters of 24 bits;
- **Digital Routing**: contains all the circuits which manage the data flow between PCs pipe-line and the acquisition subsystems (analog and digital inputs/outputs, counters). The numeric routing circuits use FIFO memory in each subsystem to ensure an efficient flow of data. Also, through these circuits pass temporal and control signals which synchronize the acquisition;
- **RTSI (Real-Time System Integration Bus)**: an additional pipe-line through which you can achieve synchronization for specific measuring functions, when there are more than one acquisition board installed on the same PC, making use of the same time events;
- **Bus Interface**: contains the hardware components through which the acquisition board connects to the PCs pipe-line, also it requires a driver which is included with the product.

The multifunction plug-in KPCI-3102 board, produced by Keithley Instruments, has the block diagram described in Figure 3, where:

- **16 Channel Mux**: represents the 16 analog inputs fed into the Gain Amp through an analog multiplexer;
- **ADC**: analog to digital converter which allows for the control of the conversion clock;
- **Tristate Buffers**: tristate memory units with the possibility of selection for the corresponding analog inputs or their digital equivalents on two 8bit ports;
- **1 kSample Input FIFO**: temporary FIFO memory of 1k of memory on each input sample;
- **Bidirectional 8bit Latch**: programmable bidirectional memory units for the digital input/ outputs (DIO), ports A and B;
- **4 User Counter/Timers 16bit each**: four 16bit counter/timers, available to the user;
- **Multiplying DAC**: digital to analog converters with multiplication (two);
- **Trigger Clock Logic; A/D Counter 24bits; TScan Counter 24bits**: logical circuits for external synchronization of the acquired analog channels;

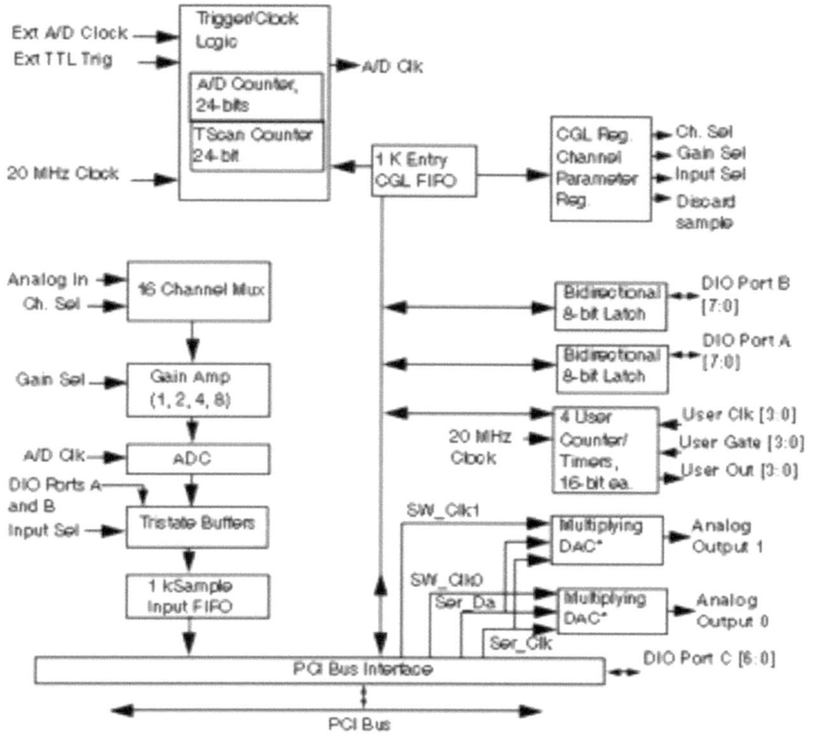

Fig. 3. Block Diagram of the Multifunction Digital Analog I/O Board KPCI-3102

- **CGL Reg., Channel Parameter Reg.**: registries for external configuration;
- **PCI Bus Interface**: connection to the computer PCI Bus.

Connecting the workstation with the installed KPCI-3102 board to the physical process, a wide ribbon cable is used 1:1 and a screw terminal board (see Figure 4).

Fig. 4. Connecting the Data Acquisition Boards through 1:1 Cable to the Screw Terminal

Finally, we use the MIB520CB USB Interface board for USB connectivity to the IRIS wireless sensor network we have deployed throughout the laboratory. This provides communication capabilities as well as in-system programming for the processor/radio boards of the nodes. It is supplied with power via USB bus. Our model CB employs a female connector. The board uses a FTDI FT2232C chip to use USB ports as virtual COM ports which are later used for data acquisition. Therefore the appropiate drivers have to be installed on first use. It will install two COM ports. The lower one is used for mote programming which we will not handle in this paper and the higher number one for data communication via USB. A top view photo of the MIB520CB is shown in Figure 5.

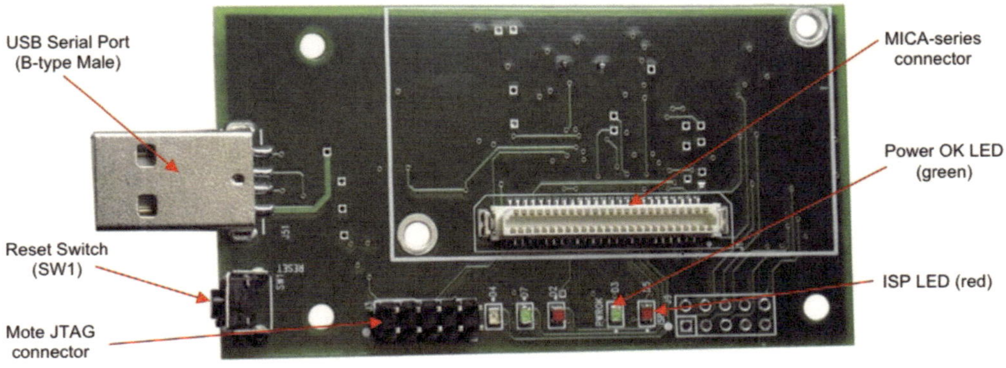

Fig. 5. Photo of top view of an MIB520CB

4. Client applications

4.1 Temperature monitoring and control

Many real applications, often encountered in process automation practice, require maintaining the process variables between certain limits, realising therefore a bipositional control of the investigated parameters. For example, an air conditioning unit for a HVAC application should maintain room temperature around 24°C ± 0.1°C. This means that, during winter, the heater is switched on until the room temperature reaches the upper limit of 24.1°C, turning it off until the temperature reaches the lower limit of 23.9°C and repeating the sequence. This happens also in summer conditions (heat) when the system controls the cooling element of the unit. This simple example can be accompanied by many others such as: keeping the liquid level in a tank between certaing values using level sensors, mantaining the pressure in a container using pressostats, which prove the variety of applications which employ bipositional control. Electronic control units can use signal from analog transducers with unified current output (4mA ÷ 20mA) and there are also models which allow connection directly to the sensitive element for the investigated variable.

The goal of this application is to demonstrate the usefullness of multifunction data acquisition boards for monitoting and bipositional control. This is achieved by using the LabVIEW environment to acquire and process signals, generating commands and displaying the progress of the process variables to the user.

For the monitoring and bipositional temperature control, we employ the laboratory set-up shown in Figure 6:

- Thermostatic Bath: metallic enclosure with lid, thermoresistance Pt100 and water heater, filled with water;
- SA: power supply;
- ATr: Pt100 thermoresistance adapter, calibrated for the 0°C ÷ 100°C range;
- INTr: numeric measured temperature indicator (000 for 0°C to 999 for 100°C);
- Heater control unit (top-right corner): relay block, REED intermediate relay and power relay type RI33, used for controlling the water heater element;
- Connector block: external connection terminal board CB-68LP shipped with the PCI-6014 board;
- C: 220μF capacitor;
- K: single pole switch;

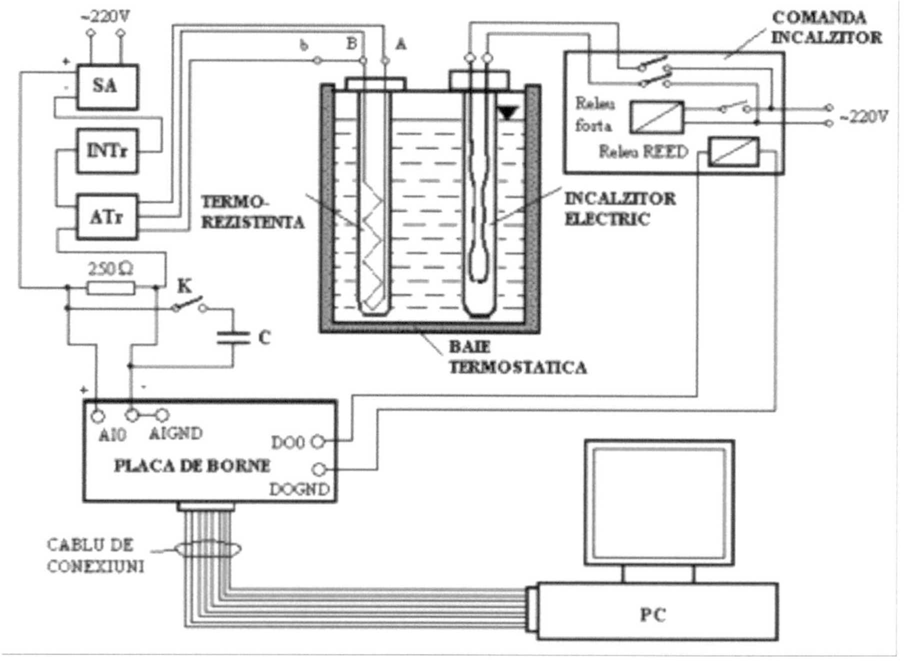

Fig. 6. Laboratory Set-Up for Temperature Monitoring and Control Application using NI PCI- 6014E Board

- PC: personal computer workstation with appropiate data aquisition board drivers for the NI PCI-6014E and software for application development according to the requirements: monitoiring and bipositional control of the temperature in a thermostatic bath by aquiring the analog voltage value on a 250 Ω resistance inserted in the current loop of a temperature transducer with thermoresistance and the numeric control of the electric heater including the analysis of passive filtration (capacitive) and software filtration on the quality of the control system.

Operating within the LabVIEW environment, we first have to install appropiate drivers for the NI PCI-6014E board, following the procedure described by the user manual. This being performed, we go on to the actual programming of the LabVIEW virtual instrument. This application has been initially developed under LabVIEW 6.1 but has been kept up-to-date and the current version is compatible with the LabVIEW 2009 version to accomodate the reader with the benefits brought upon by newer versions of the software.

Figure 7 shows the block diagram and Figure 8 shows the front panel/user interface of the monitoring and bipositional control application using the multifunction data aquisition board NI PCI-6014E.

Before starting with deploying the LabVIEW code, the following clarfications have to be made:

- the top section of the block diagram implements the data acquisition on the ai0 analog input channel, using DIFF configuration mode of the NI PCI-6014E board and generating the digital command on the 0 digital output port; It should be mentioned that the newest versions of the DAQmx drivers for National Instruments hardware components include a configuration wizard which reduces the complexity of the written code to a single block, however the configuration steps decribed at this stage remain valid.

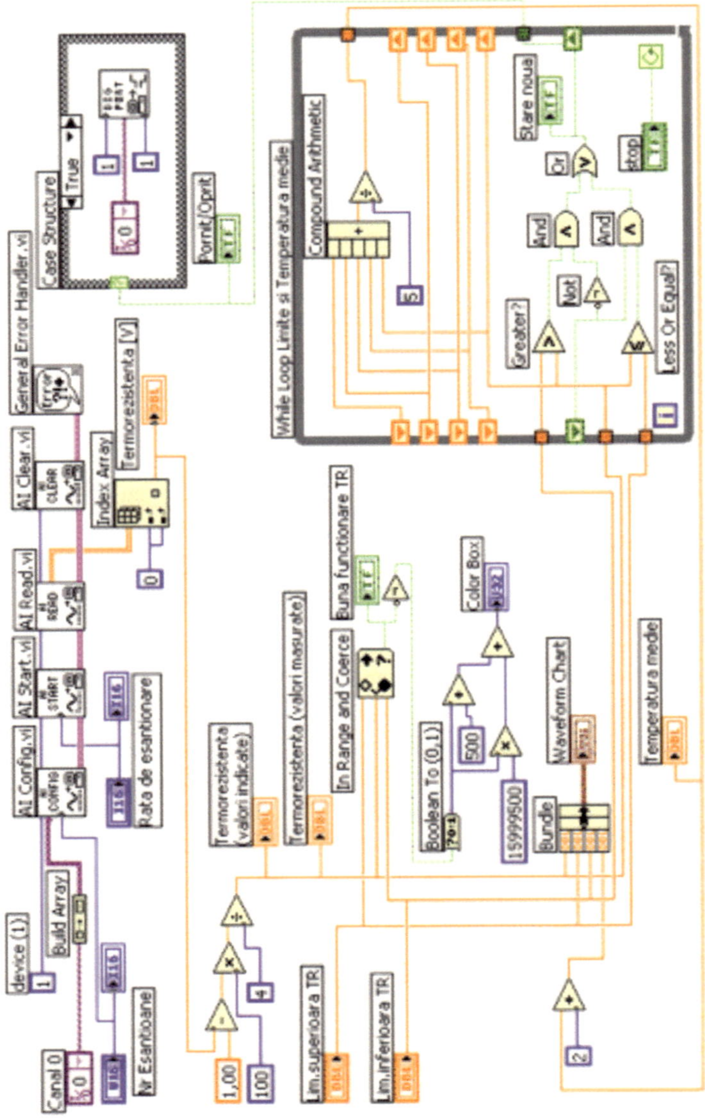

Fig. 7. Block Diagram for Temperature Monitoring and Control Application using NI PCI-6014E Board

- the acquired values represent voltage samples in the 1 ± 5 V range, considering the fact that we are measuring the voltage on a 250Ω resistance in a 4mA ÷ 20mA current loop, we show this values to the user as voltage and as degrees on the front panel;
- to better symbolize to the operator the state of the process (between or outside the lower/upper limit interval) the dedicated temeperature indicator turns blue when the temperature is between the limits and red when it is outside this interval; also when the temperature value is detected to enter the interval a LED indicator signals the good functioning of the installation;

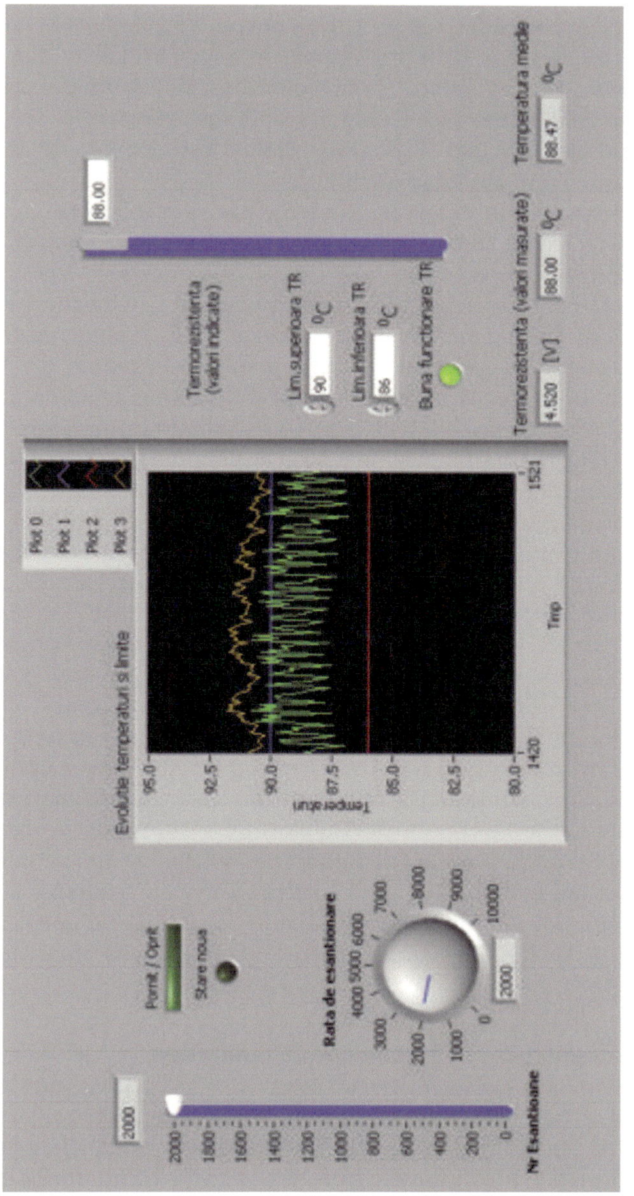

Fig. 8. Front Panel for Temperature Monitoring and Control Application using NI PCI-6014E Board

- the limits, the current temperature value and the median temperature value are illustrated on a Waveform Chart indicator; the median temperature value for the chart representation is reduced by 2 units in order not to be overwritten on the current value (the code implementing this is shown in the lower left corner of the block diagram);
- the While loop in the lower right corner of the block diagram plays a double role: it implements a logical hysteresis comparator, that means a LED indicator changes value

when the temperature value is out of the interval set by the two limits, and calculates the mean over the last 5 temperature values in a recursive way; the mean temperature indicator will offer a correct reading only after the first 5 samples have been acquired.

In order to rapidly delpoy the block diagram and the front panel the user can reffer to Figures 7 and 8 and also the LabVIEW User Manual can provide valuable references and therefore we will not go into any more details.

The virtual instrument operates when pressing the Run control on the upper toolbar and the application should be saved in the appropiate folder using a relevant name. The system operation will be described next.

After deploying the laboratory set-up according to Figure 6, with the switch K opened, the power supply SA is turned on and the heater control block is powered. We then launch the application into execution by pressing the Run continuosly button on the toolbar. Correct values for the lower and upper temperature limits should be entered on the front panel (with regard to at least a 3°C difference between the two in order to insure a smooth operation of the system) and the Waveform Chart indicator should be adapted to clearly notice the evolution of the values on the chart. The sample rate and sample number should be set to a 1:1 relation. If the Chart rate is too fast, the user should modify the Time scale of the chart.

Because, upon the first running of the application, the temperature in the thermostatic bath is low (according to the room temperature), the ON/OFF and New State LEDs will be on and the temperature color indicator will be red. Upon first reaching of the inferior temperature value, the LED indicating the good operation of the system will be switched on, the temperature indicator will become blue and the ON/OFF and New State LEDs will continue to be on. They will switch off upon reaching the upper limit.

During the operation of the application, the influence on the reaching of the upper limit with increasing temperature and on the reaching of the lower limit with decreasing temperature of the time constant of the thermoresistance will be noticed. Also, when modifiying the scale of the Y-Axis of theWaveform Chart in order to have a better view of the signals, the user will be able to quantitatively determine the acquisition noise on the analog channel and the impact of digital filtering through recursive software mediation. While running the application, the K switch should be closed and one can notice the impact of passive filtering on the analog signal. When the exepriments are over, the application is stopped using the Abort Execution control on the toolbar.

4.2 Digital signal acquisition, processing and generation

Many real-world situation present us with signals, which carry information, in a digital form. They come from physical measures with two stable states, indicating the presence/absence of the studied measure. There are also many transducers which act as detectors for the presence of the investigated measure, which supply an output signal in binary logic (absence means 0, presence means 1).

Another important category of measures commonly associated with binary signals are switches which offer two states (for example a push button closes a contact which can bring a constant voltage to a circuit, equivalent to a "1" logic state and when it is left loose the circuit is open and the corresponding state is "0"). Classic and modern automation systems often employ digital signals because many applications require mantaining the controlled parameters between certain limits and not their continuos measurement. There are also situations when the transducers generate series of impulses proportional to the investigated measure (for example, in the case of rotation speed transducers) which requires digital data acquisition. In conclusion, the data acquisition systems are realized in such way that they allow the acquisition of binary logic voltages, compatible to the standardized voltage levels type TTL or CMOS.

Our application aims at acquiring digital TTL signals coming from a reversible counter, processing them internally in the PC and generating numeric signals which are displayed on a 7-segment display using functionality offered by the LabVIEW environment.

The laboratory set-up is described in Figure 9 which includes the following components:

- **GS**: rectangular TTL signal generator;
- **PCL**: logic circuit board which includes the counter, decoder for the 7 segments and the 7 segments display;
- **SA**: power supply 5V, 1A;
- **K**: monopolar switch for applying the TTL input to ND (direct counter) or NI (reverse counter);
- **STP-68**: external connector board, connected to the KPCI-3102 PCI Board through the 1:1 CAB-305 cable;
- **PC**: workstation with software suite installed.

The producer of the plug-in board provides appropiate drivers for the use with Windows and LabVIEW and by installing the drivers a additional user library shows up in the Functions palette of the LabVIEW interface. This allows the developers to access the specific blocks for programming application with this data acquisition board. It includes blocks such as analog input/output, digital input/output etc. We will assume that all the steps necessary for installing of the Keithley board have been followed according to the user manual provided by the manufacturer.

The first step to be taken before writing the application is the configuration of the board through the DriverLINX Configuration Panel (Start>Programs>DriverLINX). Here the user has to create a new device, Device 0, and using the configuration option setting port0 as digital input and port1 and port2 as digital outputs. The first use case is acquiring digital signals from the SN74190 reversible counter on port A (0) of the KPCI-3102.

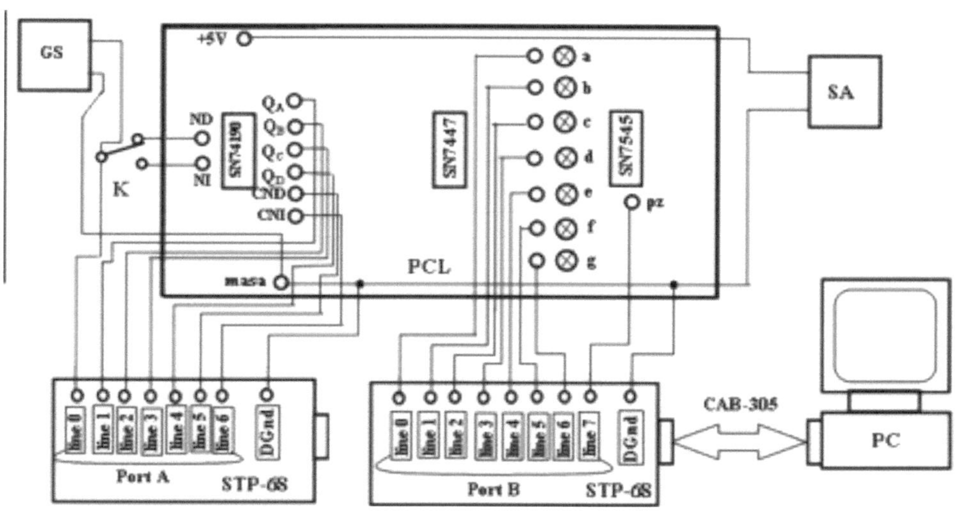

Fig. 9. Set-Up for Digital TTL Signals Acquisition, Processing and Generation using KPCI-3102 Board

Figure 10 shows the block diagram for the applicatin for direct/reverse counter and Figure 11 illustrates the front panel in the case of direct counting.

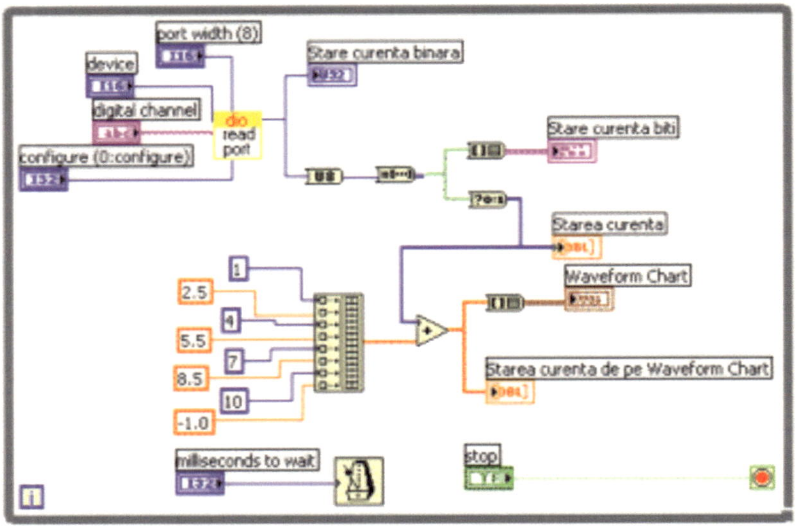

Fig. 10. Block Diagram for Direct/Reverse Counter

In order to quickly realize the front panel and block diagram, indications from the LabVIEW user manual can be used. The most important element is this case is the Keithley "dio read port" subVI which can be found in the Functions>User Libraries>Keithley DAQ VIs palette. After the correct wiring of all the elements of the block diagram, the structural integrity of the application is confirmed by the transformation of the Run indicator on the top toolbar into a continuos arrow.

Performing the experiment takes place as follows. The K switch is set in the ND position and the power supply SA and the GS TTL signal generator are turned on. After running the application the user observes 7 binary signals on the Waveform Chart of amplitude 0V and 1V, which have been modified with the constant values shown before the Build Array element in the block diagram. The signal generator frequency should be set at 10Hz and the sampling rate, modified via the milliseconds to wait control, must be chosen such as the Waveform Chart should clearly illustrate all waveforms.

Running the application will show that there is a relation between the counter input and the state of the four bistables of which the counter consists of (Qa, Qb, Qc, Qd) and the transport command CND. If K is switched, the chart will show plot 7 - CNI and plot 6 -CND will be permanently set to "1" according to the operating mode of the reversible counter NT. The application is aborted via the Stop button and can be saved under a relevant name.

In order to complete the second part of the experiment we have to realize the virtual instrument as shown in Figure 12 (block diagram) and Figure 13 (front panel).

Upon the carefull analysis of the block diagram it can be seen that it uses standard LabVIEW blocks, two subVI's built specifically by the authors (a binary counter and a 7 segment decoder) and an external control component built around the Keithley provided DAQ VI dio write port. After wiring the blocks together and placing all the elements on the front panel, the application should present no compile errors and be saved.

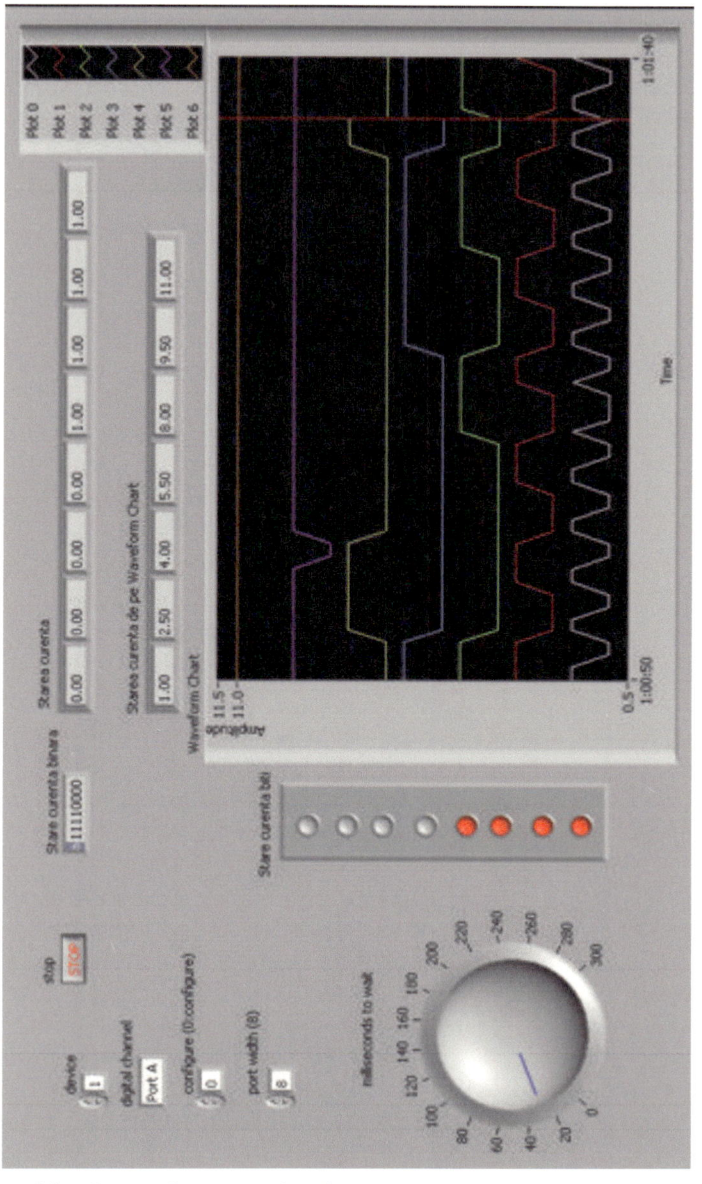

Fig. 11. Front Panel for Direct Counting Application

Having the set-up described in Figure 9, the user sets port B(1) for the digital output in the digital channel front panel control by giving it the value 1. The power supply SA is then switched on and the application is started and the single impulse operating mode is selected. The binary counter is set to 0 by pushing the boolean controls Reset and J-K in 0 and then in 1. At this moment all the 4 LEDs corresponding to the NB outputs (Qa, Qb, Qc, Qd) are inactive which represent an initial 0 stage as well as the segments of the SN7545 display. By each activation of the single impulse ("Monoimpuls") button the user can see that one binary unit is added to the counter and in the display. The coherence between the simulated display in LabVIEW and the real 7 segment display SN7545 is checked. The switch is then moved to the Generator position with an amplitude of 8 and a frequency of around 0.0020. That will result in an automatic operation of the counter in one second increments. The Waveform Chart will show small disruptions of the waveform corresponding to the modification of the values of the NB counter. The application can be aborted by pressing the Stop button on the front panel toolbar.

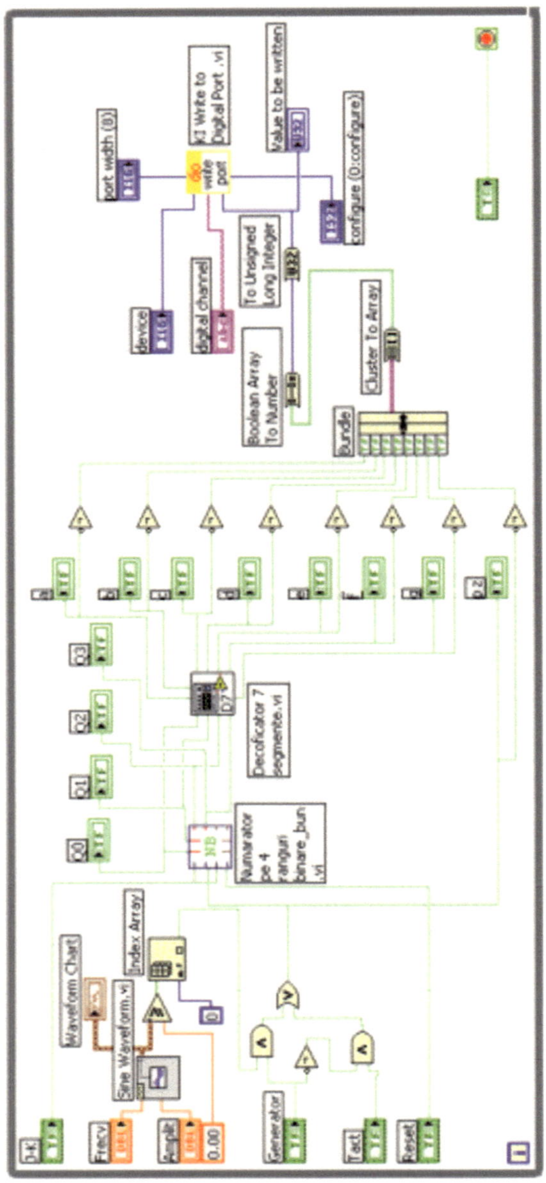

Fig. 12. Block Diagram for Controlling the Numeric Display SN7545 thorugh Port B(1) of the KPCI-3102 Board

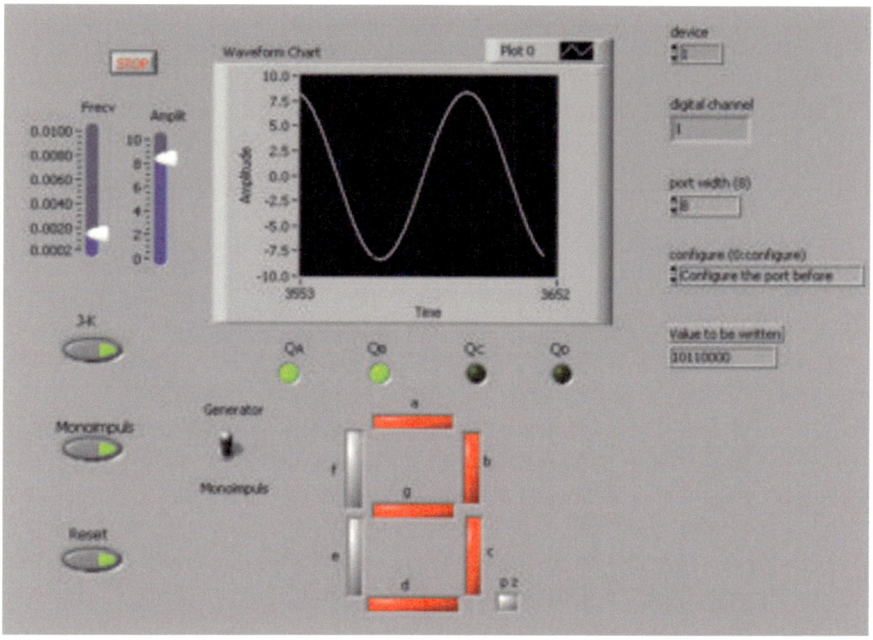

Fig. 13. Front Panel for Controlling the Numeric Display SN7545 thorugh Port B(1) of the KPCI-3102 Board

4.3 Environmental monitoring through wireless sensor network

Wireless sensor networks have represented, especially in the last decade a booming field of study and represent an interdisciplinary research area for the academic community. Although that wireless sensor networks are facing slower than expected adoption in the industry due to concerns regarding reliable communication protocols and standardization, they are a viable solution for environmental monitoring applications. In this kind of scenarios many small sized nodes should be able to provide accurate data about the investigated environmental parameters. The nodes would be powered from batteries or energy harvesting techniques and would have a lifespan ranging from months to even years.

For our experiments, we have used wireless sensor nodes produced by Memsic Inc. (former Crossbow). The experimental scenario consists of 3-4 IRIS 2.4GHz nodes deployed in the laboratory which feed data to a MIB520 USB gateway connected to the PC. The nodes consist of XM2110 radio/processing modules with MTS400 sensor boards and are battery powered from 2 x AA batteries. They are able to offer data for the following environmental parameters: temperature, humidity, pressure, light, 2-way acceleration along with health information about the network and battery voltage. The nodes run a proprietary firmware on top of TinyOS (a small scale open-source operating system for such resource constrained devices) and they form a self-organizing, self-healing wireless mesh network. MoteView and MoteConfig are the Windows applications with the help of which data is read from the gateway which finally receives all packets from the nodes and commands such as configuration information are send to the nodes.

Fig. 14. MIB520 USB Gateway and IRIS Sensor Node

The application we are describing in this section is based on a LabVIEW driver developed for this wireless sensor network product by the manufacturer. This is available at ni.com as a free download and after being installed in the system it offers all the necessary subVIs which allow the developer to read data from the MIB520 USB Gateway. Our customized application with block diagram (Figure 15) and front panel (Figure 16) is shown below.

The block diagram includes elements to configure the data acquisition from the USB gateway such as COM port, data buffer size and resource access. The main while loop performs the actual read of the packets and parses them acording to the known message format for the corresponding sensor board (MTS400). Data is then available for further processing. In this case we create arrays of enivronmental measurements for the parameters mentioned above and they are linked to the shared variables which are pushed through the network, displayed and stored on the server. This application includes also a boolean shared variable which controls the data acquisition, meaning that the server operator has the possibility of remotely starting/ pausing the process. The front panel of this application is a simple representation of the list of nodes identified in the network, the parsed numeric data from the on-board sensors and simple graphical representations for two of the parameters (humidity and light).

Our main goal is to replicate and extend the functionality of the original MoteView application, this not being supported on newer operating systems such as Windows Vista or Windows 7 under the form of a stand-alone LabVIEW executable application which would enable easy distribution. This should include the virtual instrument and variable library but also the Crossbow XMesh drivers an the necessary run-time for computers without any installation of the development environment. The main functions should be database storage, custom graphs, node configuration and mapping the sensor network. The first steps have been described in this section.

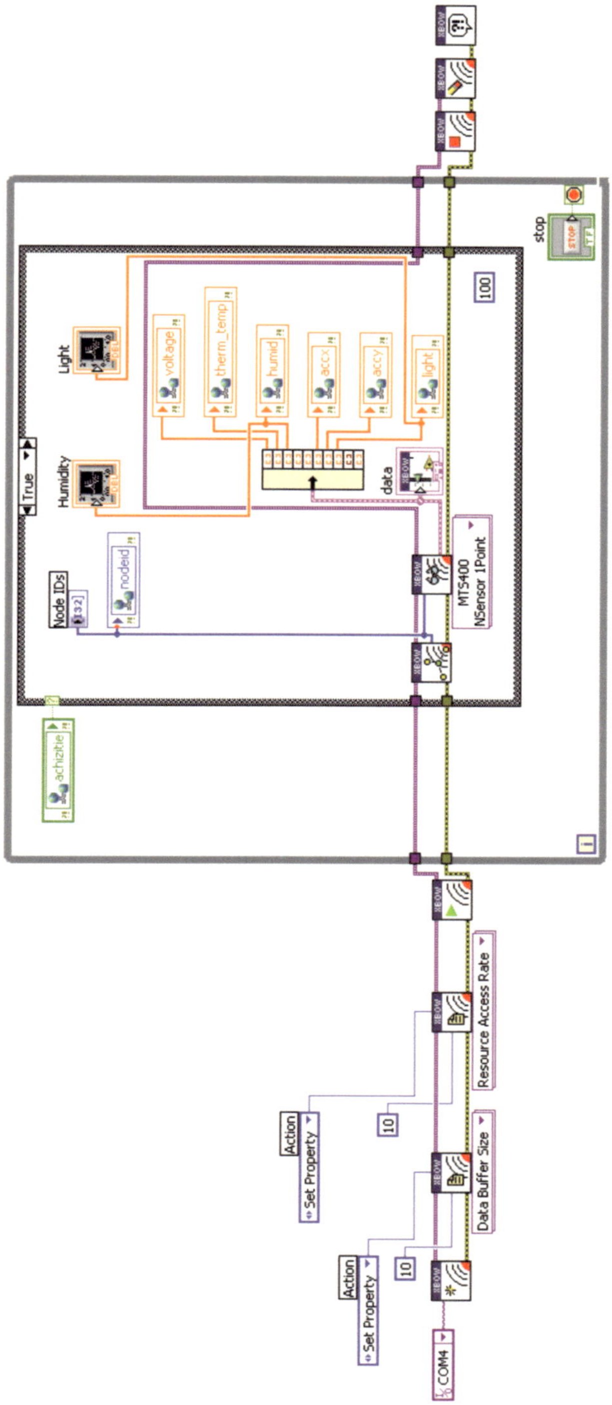

Fig. 15. Block Diagram of WSN Monitoring Application

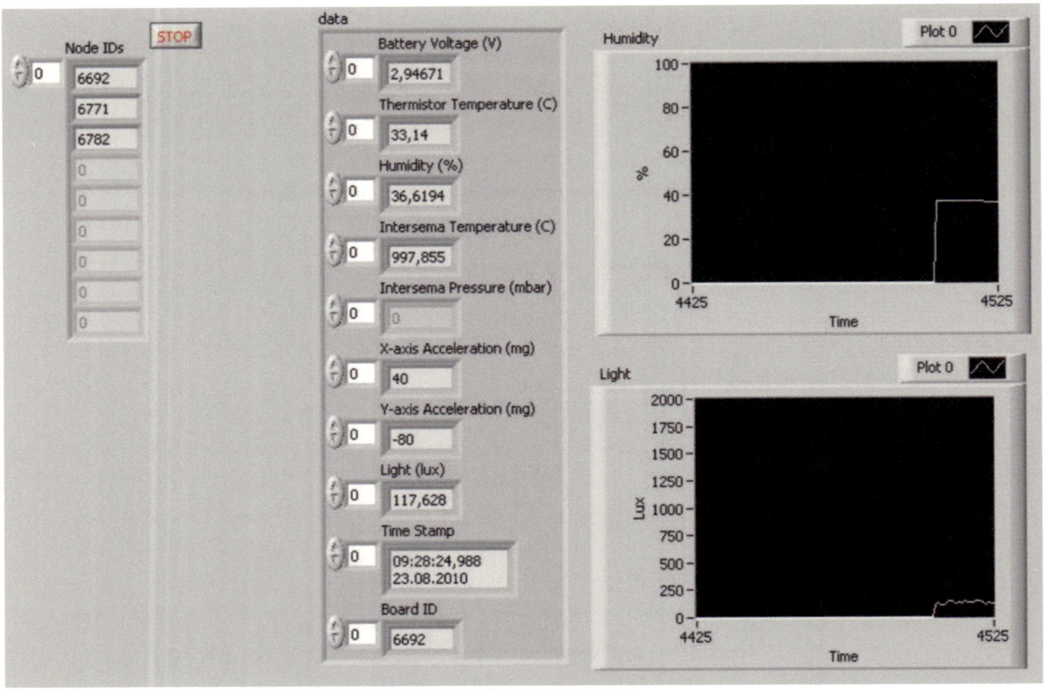

Fig. 16. Front Panel of WSN Monitoring Application

5. Server application

5.1 Communication technologies

The applications described until now in this chapter were initially designed to function as stand alone experiments on dedicated workstations. The main idea behind this chapter is to link them together under the umbrella of a single network server which collects all the data. The advantages of this distributed approach comes from the fact that the system can use dedicated workstations, each with their on specific hardware and software which are connected by a network. The server represents a more capable hardware configuration for data processing, storage and can also act as a gateway between the process and the Internet. The technology chosen to implement this concept of sharing data between tasks running on different systems is that of LabVIEW Shared Variables. The shared variables are a feature which appeared in LabVIEW since version 8 was released and have been steadily improving since. The shared variable abstracts network communication from the LabVIEW block diagram and makes it easy to share data between networked systems. The type of shared variables we are using for our deployment is networked-published shared variables of different types such as double, arrays of doubles, booleans or integers. After being added to the project library of a certain LabVIEW application, the shared variables take the form of a terminal which can be dropped onto the block diagram to be written or read from. They also offer error input and output terminals to notify the user of communication errors and a timestamp output that informs about when the value read was written. Behind all this is a custom UDP protocol to send data to a server called the shared variable engine, which then publishes the data to all clients on the network reading the shared variable. Because a publish-subscribe architecture is used to transfer data, many clients can read and write to the same variable without writing additional code. An important feature is buffering, which can be used for accounting for temporary fluctuations between read/write rates of a variable. Readers that occasionally read a variable slower than the writer can miss some updates. If the application can tolerate missing data points occasionally, the slower read rate does not affect the application and you do not need to enable buffering. However, if the reader must receive every update, enable buffering. The SVE (Shared Variable Engine) can be hosted on Windows PCs and real time targets. In our practical experiments we found out that the custom UDP protocol needed specific ports to be opened (depeding on the implementation of the Logos architecture of LabVIEW) in order for the data to pass through the Windows firewall.

For our system the following table for shared variables was employed. The three client applications feed data into the network in the form of the shared variables. These are the read by the server which displays them on a local monitoring panel. The server also publishes its own shared variable, a boolean variable which controls the data acquisition from the wireless sensor network connected to workstation 3.

No.	Name	Type	Data	Published By
1	temp	double	Current temperature	Application 1
2	tempmed	double	Median temperature	Application 1
3	tempv	double	Acquired voltage value	Application 1
4	comanda	boolean	Digital output state	Application 1
5	limsup	double	Upper limit	Application 1
6	liminf	double	Lower limit	Application 1
7	obiectiv	boolean	Functioning between limits	Application 1
8-15	channel8_15	boolean	Digital input states	Application 2
16	nodeid	array of integer	List of detected nodes	Application 3
17	voltage	array of double	Battery voltage	Application 3
18	therm_temp	array of double	Thermistor temperatures	Application 3
19	humid	array of double	Humidity values	Application 3
20	light	array of double	Ambiental light values	Application 3
21	accx	array of double	X Axis acceleration	Application 3
22	accy	array of double	Y Axis acceleration	Application 3
23	achizitie	boolean	Start/Pause WSN monitoring	Server

Table 1. List of Shared Variables

During our experiments, the network traffic was not affected by the 23 shared variables being transmitted at high sample rates between the workstations and the server. However LabView offers several customization options in order to insure a reliable data stream between stations with very large numbers of shared variables (buffering, variable sample rate).

5.2 Description

The remote monitoring server application is made up of the block diagram and the front panel, like it can be seen in Figure 17 and Figure 18. The project for this application includes the virtual instrumes and the library which contains references to all the shared variables being read through the network. The values are being read in a while loop which ensures continous operation fron the push of the Run button on the toolbar until the Stop button on the front panel or the Abort execution button on the toolbar have been pressed. The loop is timed at 200ms, a value which we considered insures maximum performance of the system and doesn't load the network with unnecessary samples. The shared variable read blocks are wired to the corresponding indicators in order to show the data on the front panel. The front panel represents the user interface and the most important part of this application. It is divided into three parts, each corresponding to a certain application: temperature monitoring and control, digital signal acqusition system and wireless sensor network monitoring application. The operator can view the data in near real-time, control the aqusition for the wireless sensor network through the switch button. The application can be expanded by creating a local database to store the data, generate reports and also by linking it to even more different systems. The server can also act, using the functionality provided by the LabVIEW web server as a gateway between the local network and the internet.

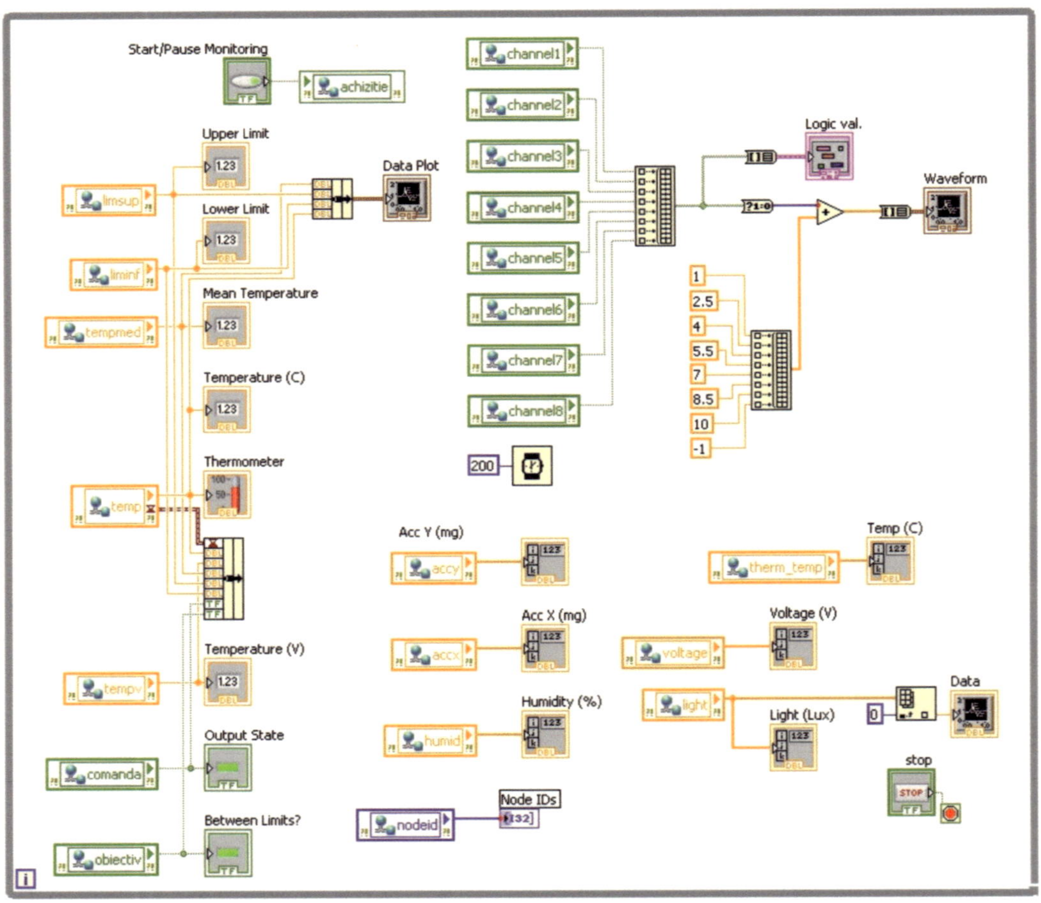

Fig. 17. Block Diagram of the Server Application

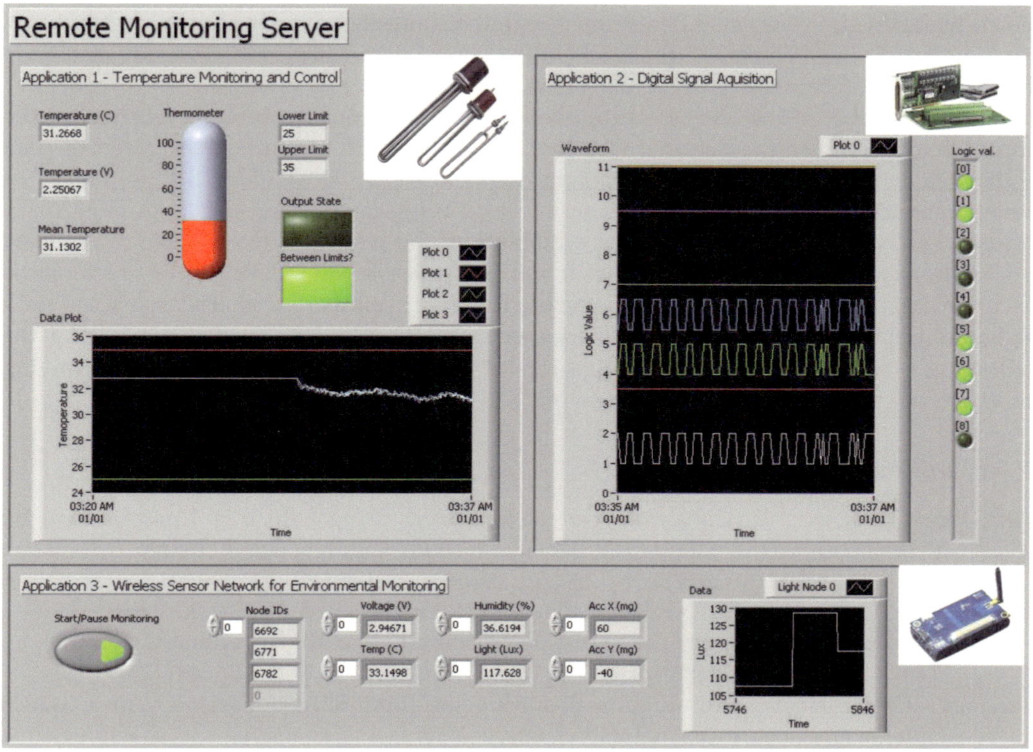

Fig. 18. Front Panel of the Server Application

6. Conclusion

The application was designed and developed to prove a couple of concepts about the data acquisition in general and some notions about the possibility of adding remote controlling/monitoring. This has a teaching purpose: it is being used for a series of experiments between several laboratories, at the moment. From one point of view one can process the experimental data gathered from a real process, but one can also see the result of one remote command sent to industrial equipment in the real time. The main part is, as we mentioned earlier, the server with the data acquisition board. The first application presented in this paper handled the process of remote controlling of the temperature of a precinct, the workstation can deal with more than one application in the same time. Thus it can monitor parameters provided by 16 sensors and it can lead till four industrial equipments in the same time, using the data acquisition board NI PCI 6014E.
The second application we have described concerns the handling of digital signals which can be found in large numbers in today's discrete automation systems. We have used a Keithley Instruments KPCI-3102 PCI board to acquire, process and generate numeric signal from/to the outside world. The integration with the LabVIEW environment has been done through appropiate drivers offered by the manufacturer which appear under the form of blocks in the instrument library, ready to be placed and wired on the block diagram.
The third application realised connectivity between the PC (with LabVIEW) and a wireless sensor network gateway. The gateway received packets from all the nodes of the network

which included environmental data from integrated sensors such as temperature, humidity, light, pressure. Our VI parsed the packets for useful data, displayed it locally and then forwarded the information to the application server.
Finally, the application server is acting like a data sink in our scenario. It receives all the process variables from the distributed system under the form of shared variables. The data is displayed, process or stored all also through LabVIEW WebServer the possibility of remote monitoring via the Internet.
Future developments will highlight the scalability of the system as we are able to add new workstations handling various processes to the network. We will focus more on reaching the communication limits of the network through a high number of shared variables with higher sample rates. The results of the experiments should give insight concerning the deployment of the LabVIEW Shared Variables for large industrial processes involving hundreds or even thousands of such network values.

7. References

Vlad, M. S. & Sgârciu V. Distance Process Monitoring using LabVIEW Environment, In: Proceedings of the IEEE AQTR 2006 Conference, Cluj-Napoca, Romania.

National Instruments LabVIEW 2009 User Manual, Available online at: http://www.ni.com/pdf/manuals/371361f.zip, checked August 2010.

National Instruments Using the LabVIEW Shared Variable, Available online at: http://zone.ni.com/devzone/cda/tut/p/id/4679, checked August 2010.

Garcia, G. Create Distributed Applications with LabVIEW Shared Variables, In: Q2 2006 issue of the Instrumentation Newsletter.

Luis Felipe Herrera-Quintero et al. Wireless Smart Sensors Networks, systems, trends and its impact in environmental monitoring, In: Proceedings of the IEEE LATINCOM 2009 Conference, Medelin, Columbia.

Rancea I. & Sgârciu V. & Stamatescu G. Remote Acquisition Processing and Generation of Digital Signals for a Reversible Counter through LabVIEW Environment, In: Proceedings of the DAAAM 2009 Conference, Vienna, Austria.

Stamatescu G. & Sgârciu V. & Stamatescu S. PC-Based System for Level Transducer Interfacing, In: Proceedings of the SENSORDEVICES 2010 Conference, Venice, Italy.

Part 2

LabVIEW in Modeling

5

Modeling and Simulation of Production of Metallothionein and Red Fluorescent Fusion Protein by Recombinant *Escherichia Coli* Using Graphical Programming

Ling Gao[1], Yilin Ren[2], Yao Ma[3], Jianqun Lin[3] and Jianqiang Lin[3]
[1]*School of Information Science and Engineering, Shandong Normal University, Jinan 250014*
[2]*School of Life Science, Shandong Normal University, Jinan 250014*
[3]*State Key Lab of Microbial Technology, Shandong University, Jinan 250100*
China

1. Introduction

Metallothioneins (MTs) are a family of low molecular weight, cysteine rich, metal binding proteins, and exist in a variety of organisms ranging from bacteria to mammals (Moffatt & Denizeau, 1997). MTs play significant roles in clearance of free radical against oxidative damage (Masters et al., 1994), trace element metabolism and heavy metal detoxification (Feldman & Cousins, 1976), cell metabolism (Cherian & Apostolova, 2000), disease processes (Sens et al., 2001; Velázquez et al., 1999), rare metal accumulation (Nordberg, 1998), heavy metal removal and environment protection *et al.* (Nordberg, 1998; Elinder et al., 1981). The important applications stimulate the interest of large scale production of MT. Compared with the conventional method by extraction from animal organs, MT production by using recombinant *E. coli* has obvious advantages in reducing cost, increasing efficiency and product quality. However, recombinant MT is easily hydrolyzed and unstable for the thiol group of cysteine when produced by recombinant microorganism (Saito & Hunziker, 1996). By integrating the MT gene with fusion tags, MT was successfully expressed in *E. coli* (Hong et al., 2001; Yang et al., 2007). On the other hand, rapid measurement of MT production is important for optimization of fermentation process. MT was reported to have light absorption at the wave length of 250 nm after binding with Cd (Onosaka & Cherian, 1982), which could be used for MT measurement. But, according to our experience, this method has low accuracy and poor reproducibility. In order to detect MT production in an easy and rapid way during fermentation process, in this study, MT gene is fused with red fluorescent protein (RFP) gene and coexpressed in recombinant *E. coli*. Modeling and simulation is a powerful tool for the analysis of the mechanism and dynamic responses of the fermentation process, and for process optimization and automatic control. The production of recombinant protein using recombinant *E. coli* involves the regulations of aimed gene transcription and translation, which process can be well described by using the white box structured model involing operon regulation and is done in this research. But, the structured model has the disadvantage of extreme complex not suitable for the purpose of process optimization.

Therefore, a grey box unstructured model is also constructured, which model is simple enough for process variable prediction in real applications but still sufficient for modeling the major regulation effects on the aimed genes of the recombinant strain. LabView is a data driven and graphical programming software tool, widely used in process simulation, data acquisition and automatic control. The MT production mathematical model developed using LabView is easily incorporated into the model based on-line optimization and automatic control system of MT fermentation process developed using LabView in the future. In this research, the structured and unstructured mathematical models and computer simulation of MT production and RFP fluorescence are made. The final developed mathematical model includes substrate consumption, the growth of the recombinant *E. coli* cells, the repression and induction of the aimed genes, the production of the aimed protein, and the maturation of the expressed RFP. The mathematical model consists of two levels: the intracellular level for the expression and induction of the aimed genes and the reactor level for the dynamic changes of substrate and cell concentrations as well as the fluorescence. This research shows the advantages and the usefulness of the data driven and graphical programming software of LabView in modeling and simulation of biological phenomena.

2. Experimental production of MT fusion protein

The human MT (hMT-1A) gene sequence was obtained from Genebank. Some rare codons for *E. coli* were modified, and the sequence was synthesized chemically (Su et al., 2009). The plasmid pGHM-RFP was used for MT production (Fig. 1). DsRed2 gene was cloned and ligated with hMT-1A gene to construct the fusion protein expression vector. In order to minimize the conformational change and final clearence of RFP, a Gly-Gly-Gly tri-peptide and thrombin restriction site were designed and inserted between DsRed2 and hMT-1A genes in pGHM-RFP construction. *E. coli* BL21(DE3) (Novagen, Germany) was used as the host cell to construct *E. coli*(pGHM-RFP). The plasmid pGHM-RFP has a *tac* promotor (Ptac), which is a combination of -10 reagion of *lac* promotor and -35 reagion of *trp* promotor (DE Boer et al., 1983).

Cultivations of *E. coli*(pGHM-RFP) were made at 37°C, shaken at 180 r/min. The volume of 250 μl of seed culture was inoculated into 40 ml of flask containing 300 ml of LB medium (10 g/l tryptone, 5 g/l yeast extract, 10 g/l NaCl, pH 7.0) and 100 μg/ml of ampicillin. Isopropyl-β-D-thiogalactoside (IPTG) was added to the final concentration of 0.2 mM when OD_{600} reached 0.9~1.1. Samples were made every hour and the cells were harvested by centrifugation at 7000×g for 10 min at 4°C. Proteins were analyzed using 12% SDS_page, and stained by 0.25% Coomassie brilliant blue R250. The amount of MT produced was analyzed by ImageQuant TL (GE Healthcare, USA) using BSA (bovine serum albumin) as the standard. Fluorescence intensity was measured using RF-5301PC (Shimadzu, Japan). The results were shown in Fig. 2. The results showed that the fusion protein of GST-MT-RFP expressed immediately after IPTG induction, but the fluorescence was detected about 6 hours after the induction (Fig. 2). The fluorescence was detected about one hour after MT production reached the maximum, and then increased. It indicated that RFP fluorescence could be used as the suboptimal indicator for termination of MT fermentation process. In addition, the fluorescence intensity of RFP was quite strong, which ensured the accuracy of the detection. The possible reason for the delay of the appearence of RFP fluorescence should be that the maturation of red chromophore undergoes a period of oxidation, which costs some time (Verkhusha et al., 2004). The time delay of the RFP fluorescence made it unsuitable for online monitoring and optimization of MT fermentation process, but could be used as the suboptimal indicator for termination of the MT fermentation process.

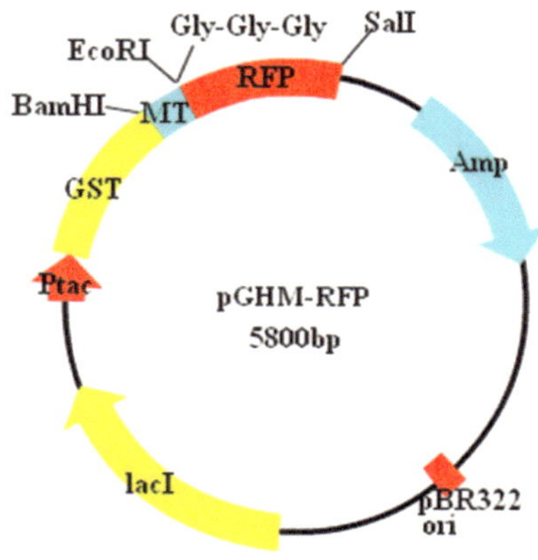

Fig. 1. The structure of plasmid pGHM-RFP.

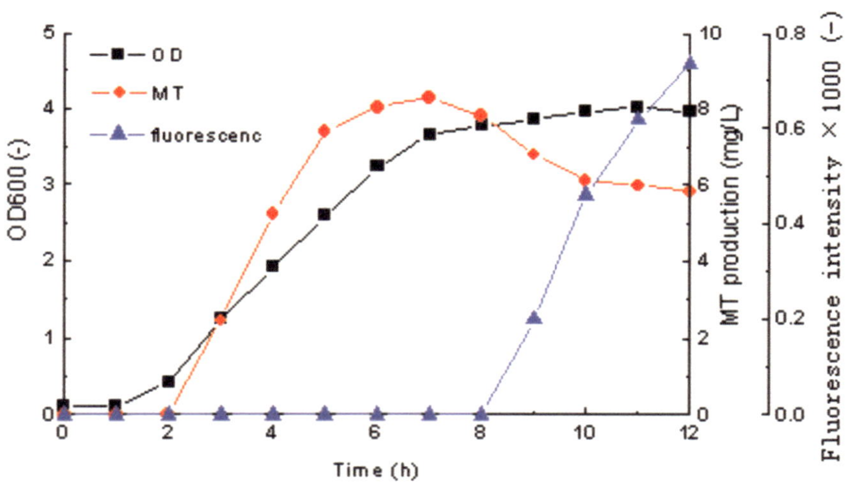

Fig. 2. The time courses of cell growth, MT fusion protein production and RFP fluorescence.

3. Structured model for plasmid based MT production

3.1 Modeling of operon regulation

The detailed structure and regulation mechanism of *tac* promotor-operon was shown in Fig. 3. From Fig. 3 for the control mechanism, it shows that the operon is coordinately controlled by two regulatory sites positioned upstream of the aimed genes, which are the regulatory sites of cAMP-CAP complex and the lacI repressor protein (Fig. 3). For the lacI repressor mechanism, when the active lacI repressor protein is binding to the operator gene, mRNA polymerase can not pass through the operator gene to transcribe the aimed gene. When the inducer molecules (lactose or its structure analogue IPTG) binds to lacI to inactivate the lacI repressor and make it get off from the operator, the mRNA polymerase can pass through the operator gene to transcribe the aimed gene. On the other hand, the operon is also controlled by the mechanism of carbon catabolite repression. The binding of mRNA polymerase to the promotor gene (at the -10 and -35 reagions) is loose, needs to be strengthened by the cAMP-CAP complex. The catabolite activator (CAP) protein is activated when it binds to cAMP to form the complex. When glucose concentration is high in the medium, the intracellular cAMP concentration is low, as a result, the concentration of cAMP-CAP complex decreases, and the binding of mRNA polymerase to the promotor becomes loose and the aimed gene is untranscribed (Fig. 3).

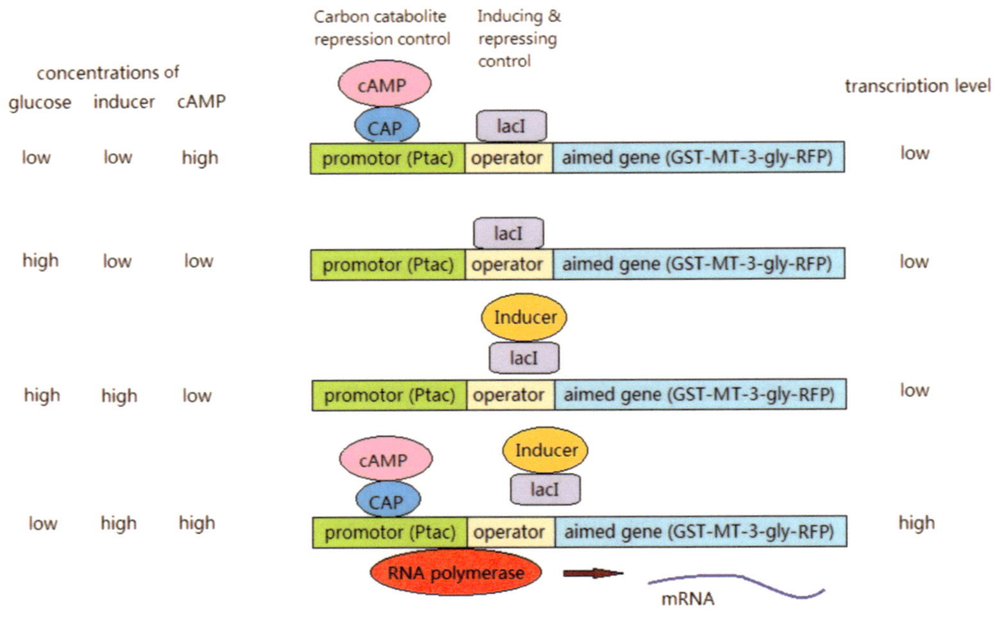

Fig. 3. The structure and regulation mechanism of the operon of pGHM-RFP (adapted from Abeles et al., 1992).

The induction and repression control mechanism of the operon ensures that the genes under control will not be transcribed without induction by the inducers. The binding of the repressor protein (lacI) to the inducer (lactose) or to the operator gene is described by Eqs. (1-2). The binding of the inducer to the repressor-operator complex is described by Eq. (3).

$$X_r + nS_{lac} \underset{k_{-1}}{\overset{k_1}{\longleftrightarrow}} X_r nS_{lac} \tag{1}$$

$$X_o + X_r \underset{k_{-2}}{\overset{k_2}{\longleftrightarrow}} X_o X_r \tag{2}$$

$$X_o X_r + nS_{lac} \underset{k_{-3}}{\overset{k_3}{\longleftrightarrow}} X_o X_r nS_{lac} \overset{k_4}{\rightarrow} X_o + X_r nS_{lac} \tag{3}$$

Where, X_r, the repressor protein; S_{lac}, lactose; X_o, the operator gene; n, the number of the lactose binding sites of the repressor protein. Eq. (3) shows that the inducer-repressor complex of X_rnS_{lac} has low binding affinity to the operator X_o, quickly falls off. Therefore, $[X_oX_rnS_{lac}]$ can be neglected in the following balances. Balances for the repressor, operator, and inducer are

$$[X_r]_t = [X_r] + [X_rnS_{lac}] + [X_oX_r] \tag{4}$$

$$[X_o]_t = [X_o] + [X_oX_r] \tag{5}$$

$$[S_{lac}]_t = [S_{lac}] + n[X_rnS_{lac}] \tag{6}$$

Where, the index t refers to the total concentration. As there are more free lactose molecules than that combined in the complex, the last term in Eq. (6) can be neglected:

$$[X_{lac}]_t = [S_{lac}] \tag{7}$$

From above equations, the following equations can be obtained:

$$\frac{dX_r}{dt} = k_{-1} \cdot X_rnS_{lac} - k_1 \cdot X_r \cdot nS_{lac} - k_2 \cdot X_o \cdot X_r + k_{-2} \cdot X_oX_r \tag{8}$$

$$\frac{dX_rnS_{lac}}{dt} = k_1 \cdot X_r \cdot nS_{lac} - k_{-1} \cdot X_rnS_{lac} + k_4 \cdot X_oX_rnS_{lac} \tag{9}$$

$$\frac{dX_o}{dt} = k_{-2} \cdot X_oX_r - k_2 \cdot X_o \cdot X_r + k_4 \cdot X_oX_rnS_{lac} \tag{10}$$

$$\frac{dX_oX_r}{dt} = k_2 \cdot X_o \cdot X_r - k_{-2} \cdot X_oX_r - k_3 \cdot X_oX_r \cdot nS_{lac} + k_{-3} \cdot X_oX_rnS_{lac} \tag{11}$$

$$\frac{dX_oX_rnS_{lac}}{dt} = k_3 \cdot X_oX_r \cdot nS_{lac} - k_{-3} \cdot X_oX_rnS_{lac} - k_4 \cdot X_oX_rnS_{lac} \tag{12}$$

As there are more repressor molecules than there are operators, and in this case the last term in Eqs. (4) and (8) can be neglected. The fraction of repressor-free operators,*Q1*, is obtained:

$$Q_1 = \frac{[X_o]}{[X_o]_t} = \frac{X_o}{X_o + X_r} \tag{13}$$

The carbon catabolite repression control mechanism of the operon ensures that the genes under control will not be transcribed when a preferred substrate is available, e.g., glucose. The mechanism of operator activation by CAP-cAMP complex can be described by reactions of (14) and (15):

$$X_{CAP} + mX_{cAMP} \underset{k_{-5}}{\overset{k_5}{\leftrightarrow}} X_{CAP}mX_{cAMP} \tag{14}$$

$$X_p + X_{CAP}mX_{cAMP} \overset{k_6}{\underset{k_{-6}}{\leftrightarrow}} X_pX_{CAP}mX_{cAMP} \tag{15}$$

The balances for CAP and promotor are

$$\left[X_{CAP}\right]_t = \left[X_{CAP}\right] + \left[X_{CAP}mX_{cAMP}\right] + \left[X_pX_{CAP}mX_{cAMP}\right] \tag{16}$$

$$\left[X_p\right]_t = \left[X_p\right] + \left[X_pX_{CAP}mX_{cAMP}\right] \tag{17}$$

From Eq. (14) to (17), Eq. (18) to (21) can be obtained.

$$\frac{dX_{CAP}}{dt} = k_{-5} \cdot X_{CAP}mX_{cAMP} - k_5 \cdot X_{CAP} \cdot mX_{cAMP} \tag{18}$$

$$\frac{dX_{CAP}mX_{cAMP}}{dt} = k_5 \cdot X_{CAP} \cdot mX_{cAMP} - k_{-5} \cdot X_{CAP}mX_{cAMP}$$

$$-k_6 \cdot X_P \cdot X_{CAP}mX_{cAMP} + k_{-6} \cdot X_PX_{CAP}mX_{cAMP} \tag{19}$$

$$\frac{dX_p}{dt} = k_{-6} \cdot X_pX_{CAP}mX_{cAMP} - k_6 \cdot X_p \cdot X_{CAP}mX_{cAMP} \tag{20}$$

$$\frac{dX_pX_{CAP}mX_{cAMP}}{dt} = k_6 \cdot X_p \cdot X_{CAP}mX_{cAMP} - k_{-6} \cdot X_pX_{CAP}mX_{cAMP} \tag{21}$$

From the above equations, the fraction of promoters being activated can be obtained:

$$Q_2 = \frac{\left[X_pX_{CAP}mX_{cAMP}\right]}{\left[X_p\right]_t} = \frac{X_pX_{CAP}mX_{cAMP}}{X_p + X_pX_{CAP}mX_{cAMP}} \tag{22}$$

The intracellular level of cAMP in Eq. (22) can be described by the empirical equation correlating X_{cAMP} and the extracellular concentration of the preferred energy source (S), eg. glucose:

$$X_{cAMP} = \frac{K}{K+S} \tag{23}$$

3.2 Modeling of plasmid copy number and mRNA polymerase limiting effect

The plasmid copy number (N_P) in the host cell is variant, which is reversely corelated with the specific growth rate (μ). The more plasmids it contains the slower it grows. The cell grows fastest ($\mu = \mu_{max}$) when it contains no plasmid. On the other hand, it is regarded that when N_P increases towards its maximum value of $N_{P.\max}$, the plasmid replication rate decreases. Then, the plasmid replication rate can be described by Eq. (24), which is decreased with the increases of the plasmid copy number and the specific growth rate.

$$r_P = k_{P.\max} \cdot N_P \cdot \left(1 - \frac{N_P}{N_{P.\max}}\right) \cdot \left(1 - \frac{\mu}{\mu_{\max}}\right) - \mu \cdot N_P \tag{24}$$

Where, $k_{P.\max}$, the maximum plasmid replication rate; μ, the specific growth rate; $\mu_{\max}$, the maximum specific growth rate.

In the recombinant srtain that contains multicopy plasmid, the promotors in the plasmids and in the chromosome will compete for the mRNA polymerase. Therefore, the transcription rate is not increased linearly with the increase of gene copy number but in a decreased manner. The mRNA polymerase competing effect can be described by Eq. (25) (Lee & Bailey, 1984).

$$Q_3 = \left(1 - \frac{N_P}{N_{P.\max}}\right)^{\alpha} \tag{25}$$

3.3 Modeling of mRNA transcription and aimed protein synthesis

The intracellular aimed mRNA synthetic rate and degradation rate can be described by Eq. (26):

$$r_{mRNA} = k_{+mRNA} \cdot Q_1 \cdot Q_2 \cdot Q_3 \cdot N_P - \left(k_{-mRNA} + \mu\right) \cdot X_{mRNA} \tag{26}$$

Where, X_{mRNA}, the intracellular aimed mRNA; k_{+mRNA}, the constant for aimed mRNA synthesis; k_{-mRNA}, the constant for aimed mRNA degradation. The last term of Eq. (26) describes the degradation and cell growth dilution effects on intracellular mRNA. Then, the intracellular plasmid based MT fusion protein synthesis rate can be described by Eq. (27):

$$r_{MT} = k_{+MT} \cdot X_{mRNAk} - \left(k_{-MT} + \mu\right) \cdot X_{MT} \tag{27}$$

Where, X_{MT}, the intracellular MT fusion protein concentration; k_{+MT}, the intracellular MT fusion protein synthesis rate; k_{-MT}, the intracellular MT fusion protein degradation rate.

The structured model developed above is based on the mechanism of biological reactions and signal transductions, and is useful in analysis of the molecular and physiological dynamics and mechanisms. But, the structured model involved too many model parameters of intracellular reactions and signal transductions that are difficult to measure, which makes the model difficult for practical uses.

4. Unstructured model and simulation of MT production

As discussed in last section, the structured model is too sophisticated for bioprocess modelling and simulation in practical applications. In contrast, unstructured models without detailed intracellular mechanisms are convenient and widely used in this field. But, one major drawback of the unstructured model is that the unstructured black box model sometimes can not reflect the real dynamics of the bioprocess. For example, the Monod model and the Luedeking-Piret model are most often used unstructured models for the cell growth and product production, which are not sufficient to model the gene induction and repression effects. In this section, an unstructured model will be constructed for recombinant MT fusion protein production, and improvements are made in this model so that it can describes the induction and repression effects on the aimed genes exerted by the bioreactor level process variables of the concentrations of related substrates in the culture medium.

In last section, the inducer and repressor control mechanism of the operon is summarized into Q_1, and the carbon catabolite repression control mechanism is summarized into Q_2 by using several intracellular reactions and signal transductions. Hear, unstructured model will be constructed for Q_1 and Q_2. In the experiments described in section 2, IPTG is used in replace of lactose as the inducer, which is unable to be degraded and has strong inducing effect than lactose. Therefore, the induction effect exerted by IPTG is in the extremes, which can be regarded as "1" or "yes" with IPTG induction, and "0" or "no" without IPTG induction. In addition, the signal transduction of the induction and repression effects have a time scale of several seconds from on-state to off-state or vise versa. Therefore, Q_1 can be set to "1" or "0" for the cases of IPTG addition or not described by Eq. (28), which is much simpler than the development of Eq. (13).

$$Q_1 = \begin{cases} 0 & \text{no IPTG} \\ 1 & \text{IPTG} \end{cases} \tag{28}$$

The carbon catabolite repression control mechanism is related with the concentration of cAMP, which is an activator of CAP protein and is reversely correlated with the energy charge of the cell. The relationships between substrate concentration and intracellular cAMP concentration can be described by Eq. (23). Similar with Q_1, Q_2 has the activated or non-activated states under high or low cAMP conditions. But, unlike IPTG which has an almost constant concentration during the cultivation process, the intracellular cAMP concentration is always changing with the changes of the substrate concentration resulted from the cell consumption or the feeding of the substrate. Therefore, different from Q_1 that has the discrete states of "0" or "1", Q_2 is described using unstructured Hill equation for activator as a function of intracellular cAMP concentration:

$$Q_2 = \frac{\beta \cdot X_{cAMP}{}^{\gamma}}{k_{cAMP}{}^{\gamma} + X_{cAMP}{}^{\gamma}} \tag{29}$$

Where, k_{cAMP}, β and γ are the constants. Combining Eq. (23) and (29), Q_2 becomes the function of substrate concentration (S) of the cultivation medium. The sharpness of Q_2 function can be adjusted by the parameters. With the consumption of substrate as shown in Fig. 4A, Q_2 increases from about 0.3 to 1. The intracellular plasmid replication rate is described by Eq. (24). Combing with Eq. (24), the total plasmid copy number can be described by Eq. (30).

$$\frac{d[N_P]_T}{dt} = r_P \cdot [X]_T \tag{30}$$

Where, X, the cell concentration; the footnote "T" indicates the total concentration in the fermentation broth. As discussed earlier, the transcription rate is not increased linearly with the increase of plasmid copy number, as the promoters of the plasmid and the chromosome compete for the mRNA polymerase. The effect of plasmid copy number on the transcription rate is described by Q_3 of Eq. (25). Then, combining with Eq. (26), the total mRNA can be described by Eq. (31) using the unstructured model.

$$\frac{d\left[X_{mRNA}\right]_T}{dt} = r_{mRNA} \cdot \left[X\right]_T \tag{31}$$

Similarly, total MT production can be modelled by Eq. (32):

$$\frac{d\left[X_{MT}\right]_T}{dt} = r_{MT} \cdot \left[X\right]_T \tag{32}$$

The equations for the specific growth rate, cell growth, and substrate consumption are:

$$\mu = \frac{\mu_{\max} \cdot \left[S\right]_T}{k_m + \left[S\right]_T} \cdot \left(1 - \frac{\left[X\right]_T}{\left[X_{\max}\right]_T}\right) \tag{33}$$

$$\frac{d\left[X\right]_T}{dt} = \mu \cdot \left[X\right]_T \tag{34}$$

$$\frac{d\left[S\right]_T}{dt} = -\frac{1}{Y_{X/S}} \cdot \frac{d\left[X\right]_T}{dt} - \frac{1}{Y_{MT/S}} \cdot \frac{d\left[X_{MT}\right]_T}{dt} \tag{35}$$

Where, $X_{\max}$, the maximum cell concentration; k_m, the substrate affinity constant; S, the substrate concentration; $Y_{X/S}$, the cell yield from the substrate; $Y_{MT/S}$, the product yield from the substrate. The RFP fluorescence intensity curve is almost proportional to the MT production curve except that a time delay for the maturation of RFP, which can be modelled by Eq. (36):

$$\frac{d\left[F\right]_T}{dt} = k_F \cdot \frac{d\left[X_{MT}\right]_T}{d\left(t - t_L\right)} \tag{36}$$

Where, k_F, the constant; t_L, the time delay for the fluorescence. By using the unstructured model constructed in this section and the experimental data of section 2, some of the model parameters are calculated and the other unknown model parameters are optimized using genetic algorithm (GA) by minimizing the aimed function calculated from errors between model predictions and the measured data. The details of model parameter optimization using GA is introduced in section 5. By using the unstructured model constructed in this section and the model parameters, the production process of MT fusion protein is simulated, and the results are shewn in Fig. 4.

From Fig. 4, it shows that the model fits the experimental data very well, and is suitable for modelling the recombinant protein production. With the increase of cell concentration, the substrate concentration decreases (Fig. 4A). During the simulation, the initial and the maximum plasmid copy numbers are set to 10 and 30, respectively. The initial value for aimed mRNA is set to 0 with the aimed gene under non-induced state. As shown in Fig. 4B, the plasmid copy number decreases with the increase of cell growth before 5th h of

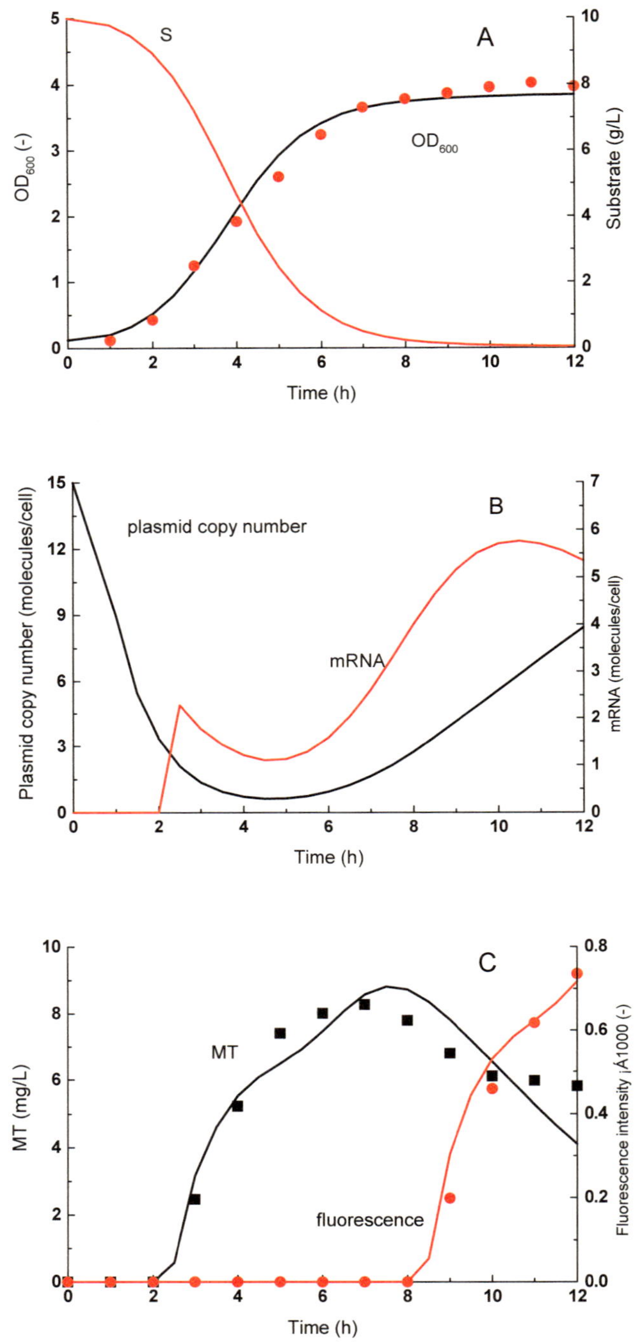

Fig. 4. Simulation of the production process of MT fusion protein. Lines, model predictions; dots, measured data.

cultivation (Fig. 4.A), which is modelled by Eq. (24). The number of intracellular aimed mRNA molecules increases immediately after the addition of the inducer of IPTG at 3rd h of the cultivation (Fig. 4B), modelled by Eq. (26). From Fig. 4, it shows that the aimed mRNA time profile is not proportional to the time profile of plasmid copy number, resulted from the effects of aimed gene regulation, mRNA polymerase competition, mRNA degradation *et al.*. The MT fusion protein production and the RFP fluorescence time courses are shown in Fig. 4C. MT production increases after addition of IPTG at 3rd h of cultivation and reaches the maximum value at 7th h, then decreases because of degradation. The RFP fluorescence is 6 h delay than MT production (Fig. 4C). The reason for the time delay of RFP fluorescence should be the time consumed for maturation of red chromophore which undergoes a time period of oxidation (Verkhusha, 2004).

5. Model parameters and the optimization using genetic algorithm (GA)

Some of the model parameters have clear physiological meanings and can be obtained by theoretical calculation or by experimental measurements. $X_{\max}$ and t_L can be obtained directly from Fig. 2; $\mu_{\max}$ can be calculated from the growth curve of Fig. 2; $Y_{X/S}$ can be calculated from the measured data; $Y_{MT/S}$ can be estimated from the biochemical pathways of protein synthesis; $N_{P.\max}$ is obtained from general knowledge about the plasmid copy number of *E. coli*; $k_{P.\max}$ is chosen arbitaryly as 2.5 times of $\mu_{\max}$. The other model parameter values are optimized using GA. The differential equations are solved using 4th order Runge-Kutta method.

Genetic algorithm is a search heuristic that mimics the process of natural evolution, which is proved useful in solving sophisticated optimization problems as well as in optimization of biological model parameters (Lin et al., 2004). A standard GA is used in the optimization, which has the operations of coding, initialization, mutation, hybridization, decoding, fitness calculation, selection, and reproduction procedures exerted on individuals (or chromosomes) in a population. The potential solution (individual) is coded as a binary vector, called a chromosome, the elements of which were called genes and situated in predefined positions, indicated as alleles (Fig. 5). One gene codes for one model parameter. The gene number n of one chromosome equals to the number of model parameters, so that each chromosome codes for all parameters of the model and enable to calculate the model prediction error with the set of model parameters coded by the chromosome. In GA, one population contains m individuals (or chromosomes) so that m model prediction errors can be calculated for the m chromosomes, and the fitness of each chromosome can then be calculated and used for the selection procedure. In this study, one gene is coded by a binary string of 10 bits. Then, n parameters are represented by a binary string of $n \times 10$ bits (Fig. 5). The population of m chromosomes can be represented by a $m \times 10n$ array. The initialization procedure is performed to randomly assign initial values of "0" or "1" to the $m \times 10n$ array. The hybridization procedure is applied to two randomly selected chromosomes called parents, and two new chromosomes created by the exchange of one or more parts randomly selected from the parent chromosomes, which occurred based on a probability called the hybridization rate. The mutation procedure is applied by turning over one or more randomly selected bits in the $m \times 10n$ array from "0" to "1" or from "1" to "0", which occurred based on a probability called the mutation rate. Decoding was performed to transform the binary number of each gene in the chromosome to a decimal system using the following equation:

$$D_{mn} = D_{\min} + \frac{B_{mn}}{2^Z - 1} \cdot (D_{\max} - D_{\min}) \tag{37}$$

Where, m, the ordinal rank of the chromosome; n, the ordinal rank of the gene in the chromosome; Z, the digits of the binary vector for one gene; B, the binary value coded by the corresponding gene; D, the decimal value transformed from B; and D_{max} and D_{min}, the decimal values of the maximum and minimum limits of the corresponding parameter. Selection and reproduction are performed to select individuals (chromosomes) to create a mating pool for reproducing offspring. The selection procedure is stochastic with the fitted chromosomes, judged by fitness (or objective function J), indicating a better chance of being selected. A low value of J is defined as a high fitness, with J defined as follows:

$$J = \frac{1}{R \cdot K \cdot L} \cdot \sum_r^R \sum_k^K \sum_l^L \left(\frac{Y_{rkl}^* - Y_{rkl}}{Y_{rkl}} \right)^2 \tag{38}$$

Where, R, the number of experiments; K, the number of measured variables; L, the number of measured points of one variable; Y_{rkl}^*, the model output; and Y_{rkl}, the measured value in the experiments. In order to give each variable the same importance in the optimization, the relative error $\left(Y_{rkl}^* - Y_{rkl}\right) / Y_{rkl}$ is used so that J had no unit. Another advantage using the relative error instead of the absolute error $\left(Y_{rkl}^* - Y_{rkl}\right)$ in calculating J is to enable the data points of one variable at different sampling time have the same importance in the optimization. A flow diagram of the GA used for the model parameter optimization is

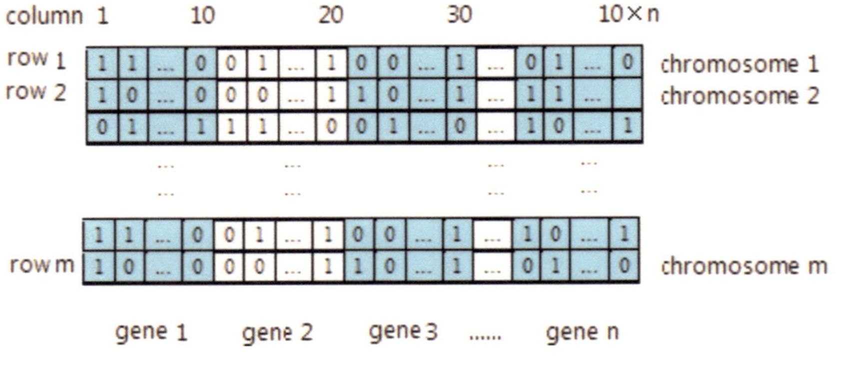

Fig. 5. The structure of the chromosome and the $m \times 10n$ array for m chromosomes of n genes.

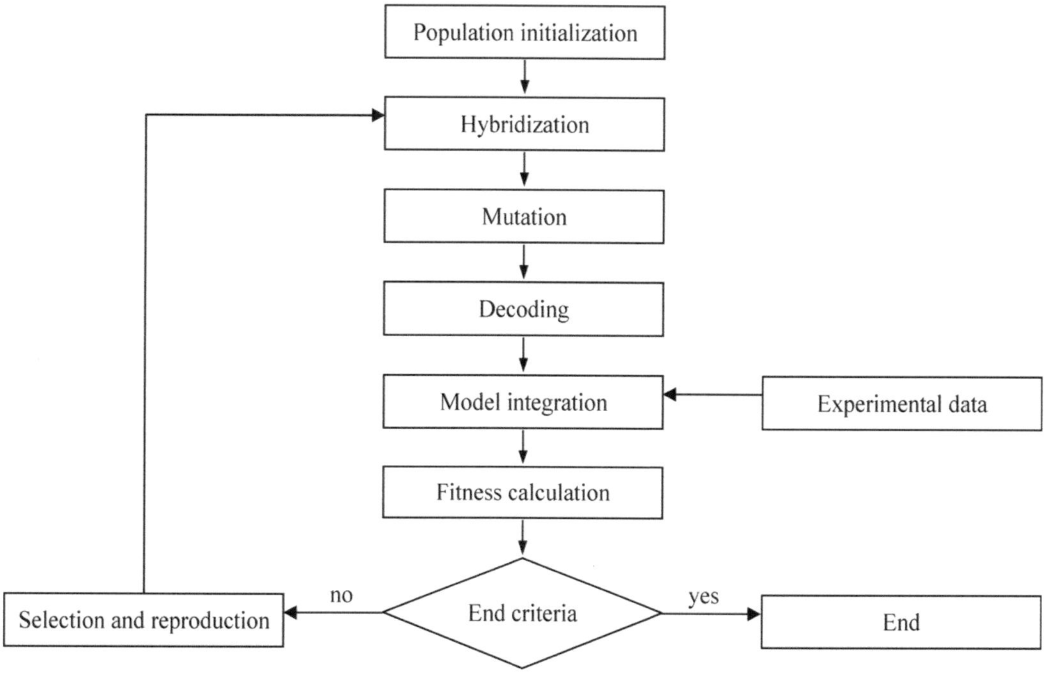

Fig. 6. The flow diagram of GA calculation in model parameter optimization.

shown in Fig. 6. In this research, the 4th order Runge-Kutta method is used to solve the differential equations and GA is used to minimize J in Eq. (38). A population size of 50, hybridization rate of 0.2, and mutation rate of 0.05 are used in GA optimization. GA programming using LabView for model parameter optimization was reported (Moore, 1995). In LabView, there are sub VIs of GA (located in: Control toolkit for LabView, ICTL) and also the 4th order Runge-Kutta method (located in: Functions/Mathematics/ Differential equations) (Fig. 7). In addition, the softwares written in MatLab, VisualBasic et al. can also be linked with LabView and used for the same purpose.

In optimization of the unknown model parameter values using GA, the known value model parameters are also refined in the mean time to eliminate the possible errores made in the measurements. Each of the measured value is set as the middle value of a small range and the value is searched within the small range by GA in the refining process to minimize the aimed function.

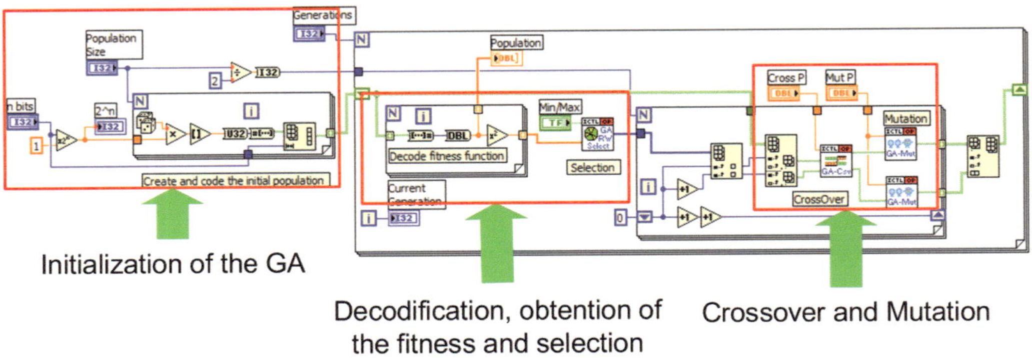

(A)

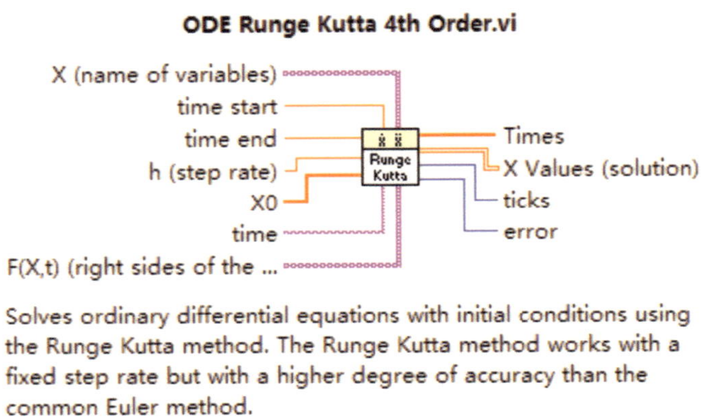

(B)

Fig. 7. (A) The VI of GA and (B) the VI image of 4th order Runge-Kutta method from the manuals of LabView.

6. Conclusion

The production of MT fusion protein is modelled using structured and unstructured models. The unstructured model developed in this research is suitable for bioprocess prediction and optimization. The data driven and graphical programming software of LabView has the advantages of high efficiency in programming, having many handy sub VIs for various applications, and especially easy in constructing data acquitation and on-line monitoring and control system. The mathematical models developed in LabView is easily incorporated into the future developed on-line model based predictive control system.

7. References

Abeles, R.H.; Frey, P.A. & Jencks, W.P. (*1992*). Biochemistry. *Jones & Bartlett Publishers, Boston, Mass*, p.383

Cherian, M. G. & Apostolova, M. D. (2000). Nuclear localization of metallothionein during cell proliferation and differentiation. *Cell Mol. Biol.*, 46, 347-356.

DE Boer, H.A.; Comstock, L. J. & Vasser, M. (1983). *Proc Natl Acad Sci USA*, 80:21-25.

Elinder, C. G.; Jönsson, L.; Piscator, M. & Rahnster B. (1981). Histopathological changes in relation to cadmium concentration in horse kidneys. *Environ. Res.*, 26, 1-21.

Feldman, S. L.& Cousins, R. J. (1976). Degradation of hepatic zinc-thionein after parenteral zinc administration. *Biochem. J.*, 160, 583-588.

Hong, S. H.; Toyama, M.; Maret, W. & Murooka, Y. (2001). High yield expression and single step purification of human thionein/metallothionein. *Protein Expr. Purif.*, 21, 243-250.

Lee, S. B. & Bailey, J. E. (1984). Genetically structured models for lac promotor-operotor function in the *Escherichia coli* chromosome and in multicopy plasmids: lac promotor function, *Biotechnol. Bioeng.*, 26,1381-1389.

Lin, J.; Lee, S. M. & Koo Y. M. (2004). Model development for lactic acid fermentation and parameter optimization using genetic algorithm, *J. Microbiol. Biotechnol.*, 14(6), 1163–1169.

Masters, B. A.; Kelly, E. J.; Quaife, C. J. ; Brinster, R. L. & Palmiter, R. D. (1994). Targeted disruption of metallothionein I and II genes increases sensitivity to cadmium. *PANS*, 91, 584-588.

Moore, J. H. (1995). Artificial intelligence programming with LabVIEW: genetic algorithms for instrumentation control and optimization, *Computer Methods and Programs in Biomedicine.*, 47, 73-79.

Moffatt, M. and D. Denizeau (1997) Metallothionein in physiological and physiopathological processes. *Drug Metabolism Reviews* 29: 261-307.

Nordberg, M. (1998). Metallothioneins: historical review and state of knowledge. *Talanta*, 46, 243-254.

Onosaka, S. & Cherian, M. G. (1982). Comparison of metallothionein determination by polarographic and cadmium-saturation methods. *Toxicol. Appl. Pharmacol.*, 63, 270-274.

Saito, S. & Hunziker P. E. (1996). Differential sensitivity of metallothionein-1 and-2 in liver of zinc-injected rat toward proteolysis. *Biochim. Biophys. Acta*, 1289, 65-70.

Sens, M. A.; Somji, S.; Garrett, S. H.; Beall, C. L. & Sens, D. A. (2001). Metallothionein isoform 3 overexpression is associated with breast cancers having a poor prognosis. *Am. J. Pathology.*, 159, 21-26.

Su, Y.; Lin, J.; Lin, J. & Hao, D. (2009). Bioaccumulation of arsenic in recombinant *Escherichia coli* expressing human metallothionein. *Biotechnol. Bioprocess Eng.*, 14, 565-570.

Velázquez, R. A.; Cai, Y.; Shi, Q. & Larson, A. A. (1999). The distribution of zinc selenite and expression of metallothionein-III mRNA in the spinal cord and dorsal root ganglia of the rat suggest a role for zinc insensory transmission. *J. Neurosci.*, 19, 2288-2300.

Verkhusha, V. V.; Chudakov, D. M.; Gurskaya, N. G.; Lukyanov, S. & Lukyanov, K. A. (2004). Common pathway for the red chromophore formation in fluorescent proteins and chromoproteins. *Chem. Biol.*, 11, 845-854.

Yang, F.; Zhou, M.; He, Z.; Liu, X.; Sun, L.; Sun, Y. & Chen Z. (2007). High-yield expression in *Escherichia coli* of soluble human MT2A with native functions. *Protein Expr. Purif.*, 53, 186-194.

6

Hysteresis Modeling of Soft Magnetic Materials using LabVIEW

Septimiu Motoasca
Transilvania University of Brasov
Romania

1. Introduction

This chapter deals with analytical modeling of hysteresis cycle using the powerful mathematical tools from LabVIEW. For magnetic materials one of the most important characteristics is the hysteresis cycle. In numerous technical applications it is necessary to have a mathematical representation of magnetic characteristics in form $M = f(H)$ or $B = f(H)$ in order to calculate magnetic field especially in various rotating machines or electromagnetic apparatus.

There are many physical models used for modeling the hysteresis cycle. Many of them are not so easy to implement, require too many data to be introduced or are time consuming. Two models are most used in practice: Preisach model and Jiles-Atherton model. In this chapter is presented the way to realize the program using LabVIEW VI's for these two models and comparison between the modeled data and measured ones.

A new simple analytical model using straight-line segments and arcs of circle to express the hysteresis cycle is also presented. This program for modeling the hysteresis cycle having the smallest amount of input data possible is suitable for soft magnetic materials. The easiness of using this model consists in the fact that it uses only nine parameters as input data, is very quick computed and give a good approximation of the measured hysteresis cycle. There are two variants of the program used for this model one using the LabVIEW VI and MatLab script block and other using only LabVIEW VI's.

2. Preisach model

2.1 Theoretical aspects of classical Preisach model

In this model, the ferromagnetic material is considered a basic set of fields called *elementary dipoles*, *Preisach dipoles* or *Preisach operators*. Each dipole is characterized by a rectangular hysteresis cycle and asymmetric [30] (Figure 1).

Each dipole can be in any time in a positive saturation state (1) or negative saturation (-1). Transition between states is determined by the magnetic field value H compared with values $h_{of} = of$, $h_b = b$ Field called critical or tipping.

If a state of saturation dipole is negative (-1) and the value of H increases above the $H = h_a = a$ it toggles the state (1). To return to its original state, the field will be decreased to below $H = h_b = b$ $(b < a)$.

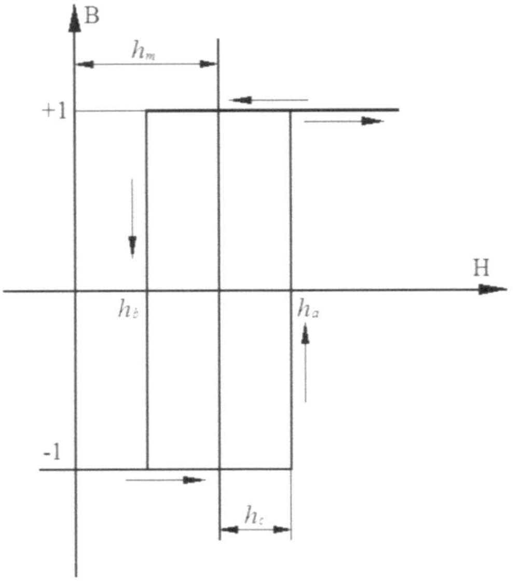

Fig. 1. Elementary Cycle (dipole) Preisach.

The problem to characterize the actual material is finding a statistical distribution of elements according to the values of variables *of* and *b*. This distribution is represented in the plane (*a*, *b*) and is called the Preisach distribution *p*(*a*, *b*) . With this distribution function is determined the global flux (magnetization), at a time of material.

Physical interpretation of the model can be given for weak fields, in agreement with the Neel theory of magnetism that consider that energy of moving Bloch wall has a stepped profile.

The idea can be extended to more intense fields, considering the lock-release mechanism walls cvasistationary regime.

Some properties of classical Preisach model are listed below:

- Property removal: each maximum (respectively minimum) local input size erase all maxims (respectively minima) above that are lower (respectively higher) value;
- Matching property of the minor cycles: minor cycles measured between the same extreme values of the magnetic field are equaled (congruent);
- Symmetry property that results from cyclical developments of *H* between values $-H_1$ and $+H_1$ produces symmetrical cycles. So symmetrical cycles obtained are one inside another, with no intersections.

Subsequent studies led to the conclusion that removal properties and the matching is necessary and sufficient conditions for a hysteretic system are properly represented by the classical Preisach model.

Must be mentioned the limitations imposed by this model, which means, eventually, an approximation of a real phenomenon:

- Model is static, not taking into account how variables change over time. The model need only the extremes of input size;
- Reversible magnetization phenomena are not taken into account;
- Phenomenon of habituation is ignored; *reptation* phenomenon of minor cycles is not modeled, closing cycles are minor points well established as the clear property.

For calculation of magnetic induction or magnetization is using the formula:

$$B(t) = \iint p(a,b) \cdot sign\left[m(a,b)\right] da\, db \tag{1}$$

where:

$p(a, b)$ represent the Preisach function which will be represented as a triangle in the space (a, b) $sign[m(a, b)]$ is the sign of Preisach elementary operator m(a, b). This operator changes sign in concordance with the magnetic field strength variation.

The identification operation for classical Preisach model involves determining the distribution function of the dipole unitary $p(a, b)$. For this goal it can be proceed in two ways:

- Search function is divided in small rectangles of points (a_i, b_j) like a mesh and in each rectangle a value $p(a_i, b_j)$ is inserted resulting from the experimental data;
- Is assumed to known an analytical form of function (eg. Gaussian distribution) and identified based on measurements only the needed function parameters.

For determining a mesh function $p(a_i,b_j)$ based on experimental data, two main methods are known:

- Biorci method [9] (requires 3N points for determining probabilities: the 1N from first magnetization curve and 2N on the descending major hysteresis cycle unless the cycle is considered symmetric, otherwise requires 5N points and additionally are needed another 2N points on the ascending branch of a major hysteresis cycle).
- Mayergoyz method (method requires more experimental data than the method Biorci ($2N^2$ instead of 3N), but accuracy is improved).

2.2 LabVIEW program using Preisach model

As previously mentioned, modeling hysteresis cycles were done using LabVIEW program, given the possibility of modular programming, using scripts in MatLab, obtaining handy charts and ported to other applications and the possibility to change inputs in real-time when program run continuously. The full program is presented in Annex 1.

The first step in modeling program using Preisach hysteresis cycle was to make a triangle in the Preisach space (a, b) which have a predefined number of points and create some Preisach function (also called weights) in each cell (a_i, b_j), respecting model properties listed above .

For this step, the block presented in Figure 2 was done, using the LabVIEW programming environment, in the block diagram. At the end of this block is obtainded a Preisach triangle with a simple analytical form of distribution so as to obtain symmetrical distribution of weighting point's a_i, b_j.

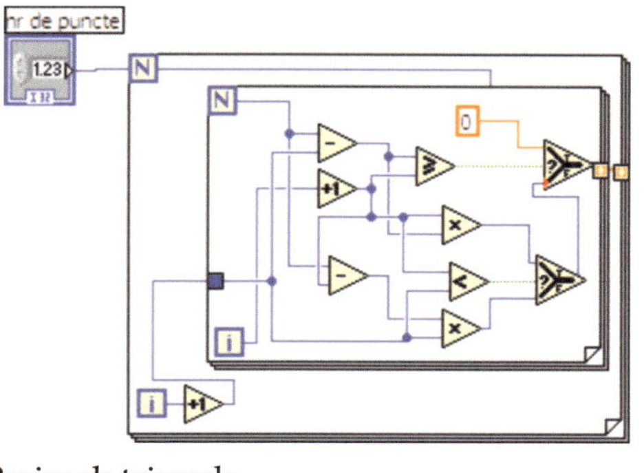

Fig. 2. Block performing Preisach triangle.

In this block , two cycles *for* was used to create space (a_i,b_j) , and in each element of the cell is introduced an analytical value of the Preisach function.
The result of this block may be highlighted on a chart is shown in Figure 3.
This analytical model was made only as a demonstration but the analytical form which must be inserted in each cell need much more calculations for real case tacking account of great number of data needed as input which must be inserted manual in each cell.
In figure 3, it can be seen Preisach distribution weights for N=100 points and arrangement according to two variables *a* andr *b*. It can be observed that is respected the principle of symmetry that is set for the Preisach model.
Next step that should be done is tilted fields according to an incremental or decremented change as a input function corresponding change in magnetic field strength *H* of a certain shape.

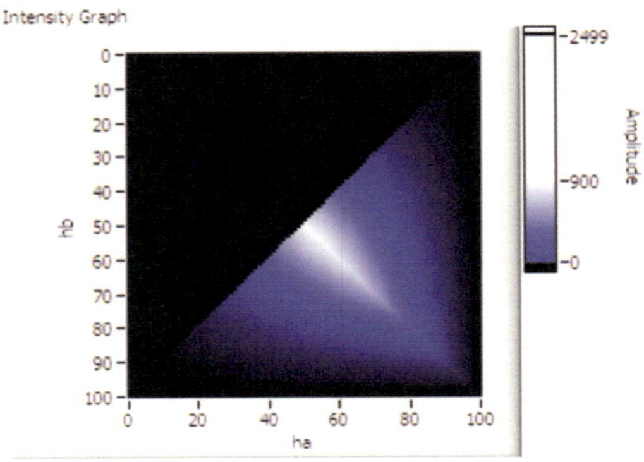

Fig. 3. Preisach triangle obtained at the exit of the first block.

For example, I used a saw-tooth function in which the amplitude is reduced to simulate the phenomenon of demagnetization. Function used as entry can be of another form (eg. sinusoid). It also may be introduced from an external file, like the change of the shape of a magnetic field strength as experimentally measured.

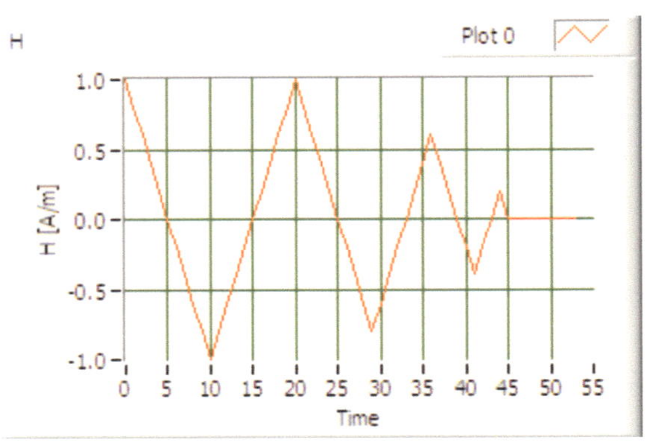

Fig. 4. Shape variation of the magnetic field intensity *H*.

For this case, the function used is shown in Figure 4, it was highlighted on a chart obtained from the LabVIEW environment. This function was created using LabVIEW environment by introducing the function values in a column matrix.

This waveform obtained is used as input in a block, shown in Figure 5, which carries out basic fields tilted to plus to minus and vice versa depending on the passage above a certain value of H. Also on that block entry is placed the previously obtained Preisach triangle.

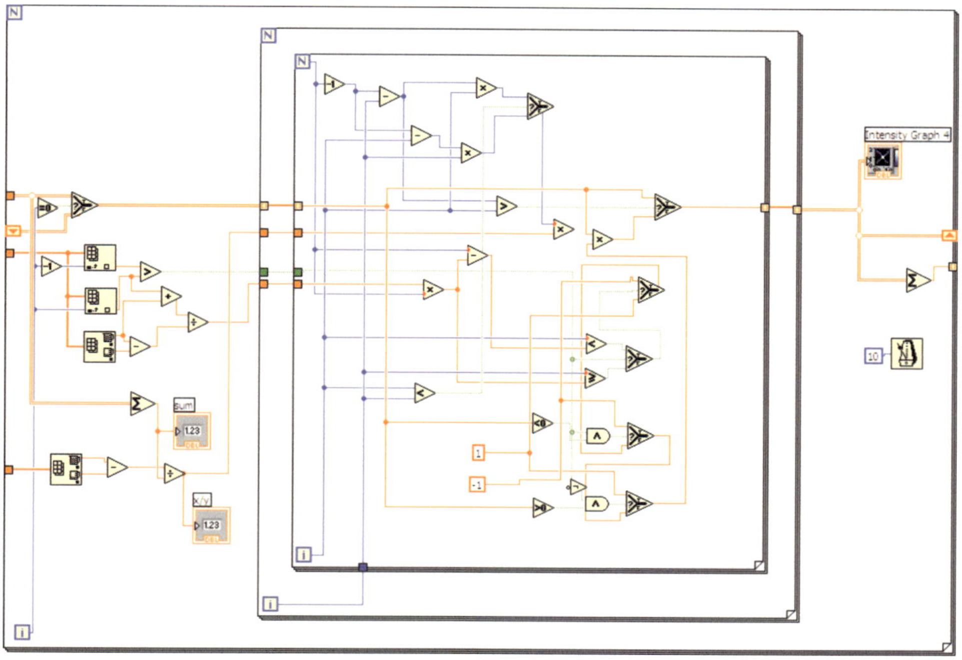

Fig. 5. Block tilting elementary Preisach domain.

This block has three loops *for* in which the Preisach triangle is decomposed in each elementary area. The first loop's is for H input waveform decomposition in the values for each step of time and is designed to save the final after making Preisach triangle areas in other two loops for.

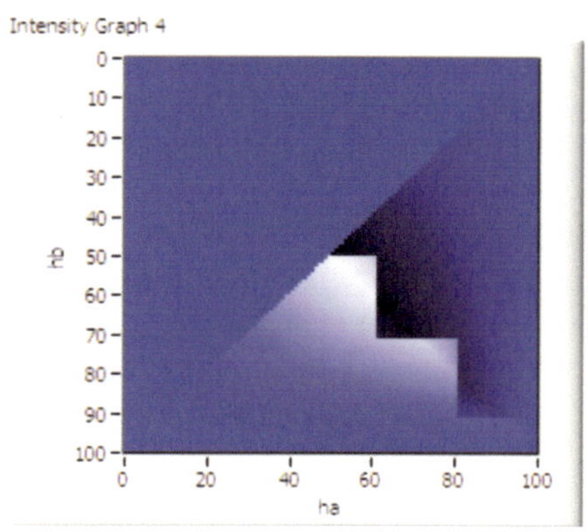

Fig. 6. Demagnetization triangle after having gone through the entire cycle.

In the first loop *for* was introduced a timer which makes the program to run in a given time to be able to see in the graphs in front panel the application of tilted fields on Preisach

Triangle. Preisach triangle undergoes changes during each step and the final position can be seen on a graph shown in Figure 6.
The other two loops *for* are used for the Preisach triangle decomposition in elements and the value of each element is tilted from plus to minus or vice versa taking into account the variation of input waveform.
Using the results obtained from this block and summing Preisach elements is obtained a waveform for magnetic induction or magnetization. Introducing the waveform of Magnetic field and obtained waveform for magnetic induction as input to a XYgraph is obtained the hysteresis cycle shown in Figure 7.

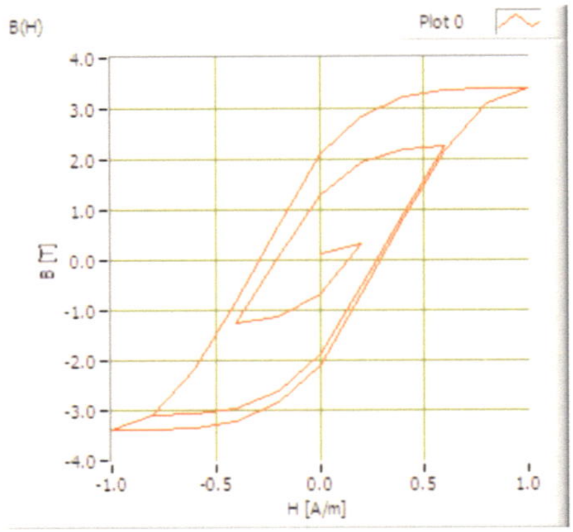

Fig. 7. Hysteresis cycle obtained using the program developed in LabVIEW .

The most difficult part of the Preisach model is the calculation of Preisach elementary functions (weights). In our theoretical model we not used the experimental data because is very difficult to calculate and populate the triangle considering 300 points on first magnetization curve and descending branch of hysterezis cycle. We tried several options for calculating the weighting coefficients using analytical methods but the appearing equations are very difficult to solve for experimental data.
Therefore, we made another Preisach modeling program that has as input the experimental measured values and weights were calculated using only the descending branch of the major hysteresis cycle considering that is a symmetrical cycle. This program is presented in the next subchapter, the method of calculating the weights being a personal contribution to this model.
It can be concluded that this model is quite easy to implement but requires finding a large weighting calculation and correlation with experimental data. The Preisach analytical functions that calculate weights can not give a sufficiently good approximation for the model. The full program is presented in Annex 2.

2.3 Modified Preisach method

To calculate the weights have been proposed several methods [4], [7], [15], [35], [38], [65]-[72]. In this chapter, is presented a method for calculating weights using only the descending branch of the major hysteresis cycle.
For this case, first builds a Preisach triangle that initially will have only half the amount of space populated with + 1 value and 0 otherwise.

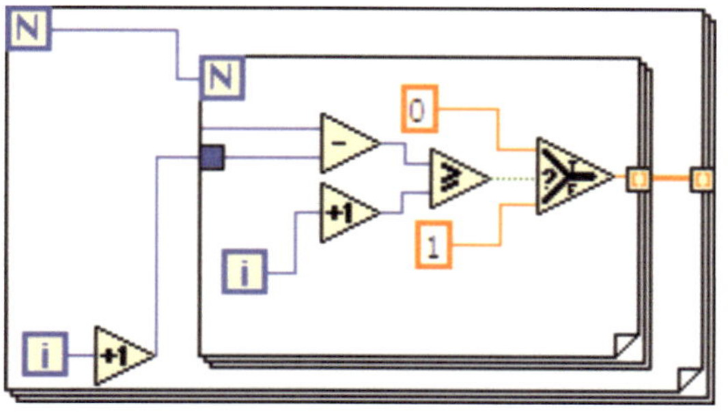

Fig. 8. Making Preisach triangle.

This first triangle will be changed in a block shown in Figure 9. As input for this block is used the triangle made in the block shown in Figure 8 and measured data values for the descending branch of major hysteresis cycle.

Before making the calculation of the weights of Preisach triangle, was an interpolation of experimental data for descending branch of hysteresis cycle so that the number of experimental data to correspond to the value of the n points chosen to achieve Preisach triangle.

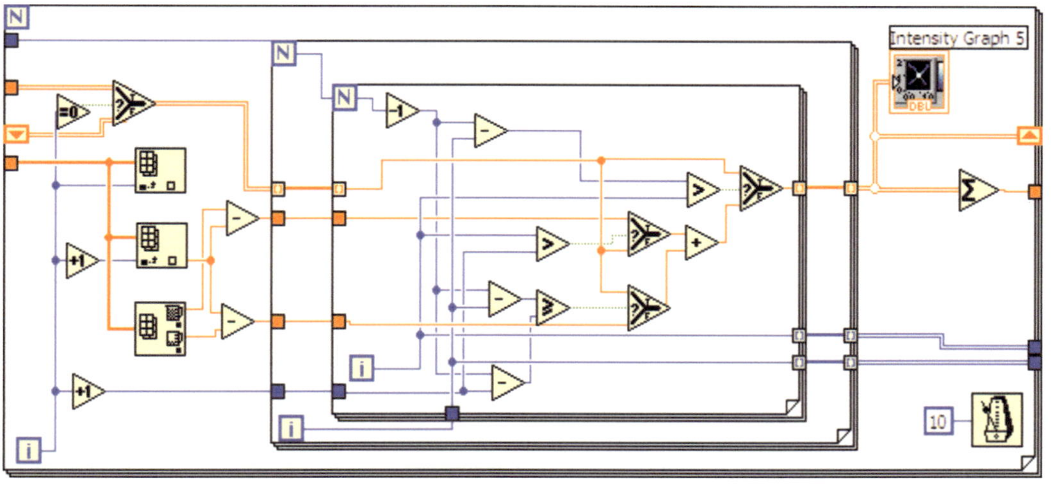

Fig. 9. Calculating the weights of block cells Preisach triangle .

Operation is performed for calculating the weights in n steps. Using data for the magnetic flux density was measured dividing the weights so that each step is calculated weights for a whole range of values of h_b and all possible values of h_a. Considering that the hysteresis cycle is symmetric around the origin can be considered the same values and ascending branch of a major hysteresis cycle. To first step considered in the first cell is obtained by subtracting the value derived from the saturation value (B_s = B0) the following item (B1) on the downward curve. The rest of the remaining cells, the total amount will be B1. In the next step, the first cell remain as previously calculated. Cells of the next line (h_b = ct.) for the next step will be the total value B1-B2 and the remaining cells are considered the overall value B2. This reasoning is repeated until reaching a negative saturation value.

By reversing these values are inserted upward branch of the same values and thus succeeded in dividing each line (h_b = ct.) component weights in their cells, taking into account the ascending branch.
The block in Figure 10 is tilted out of the cells for varying Preisach triangle field obtained in this case the measured values.

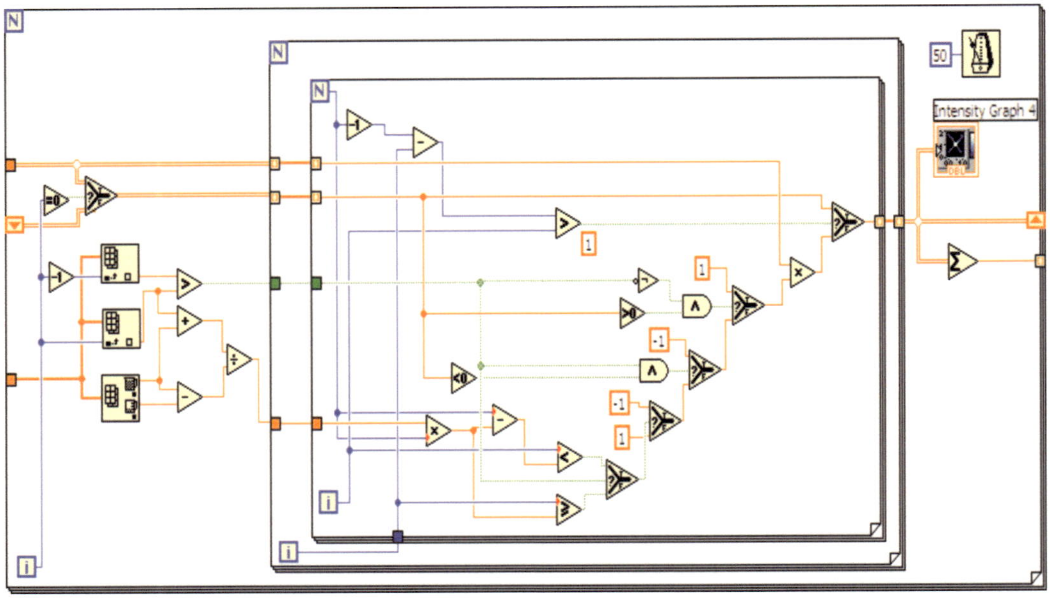

Fig. 10. Preisach triangle block tilting for varying magnetic field strength .

For example, were used as input values measured using the DC to determine first order return curves . Figure 11a is shown as the variation of the magnetic field and in Figure 11b , is shown as the variation of magnetic induction measured .

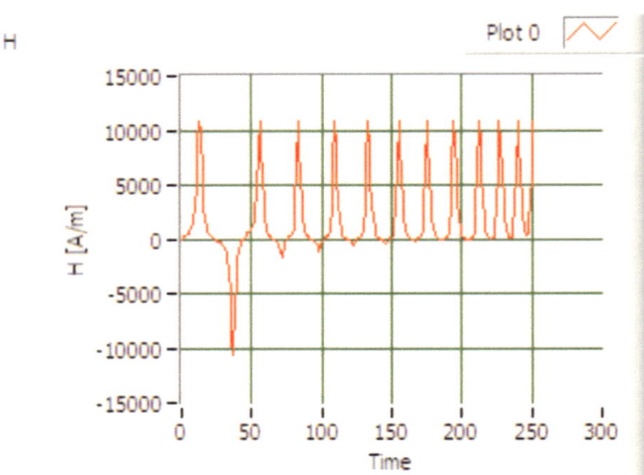

Fig. 11a. Shape variation of the magnetic field intensity.

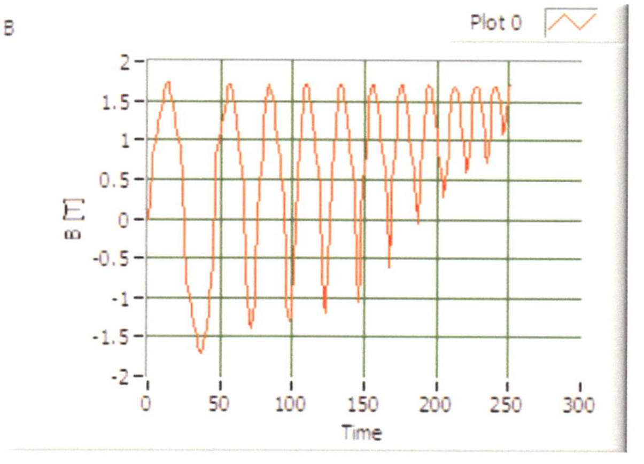

Fig. 11b. Shape variation of magnetic induction measured.

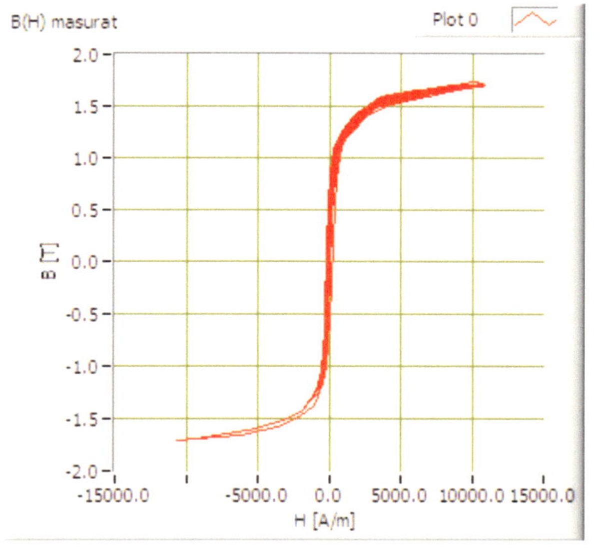

Fig. 11c. Hysteresis cycle obtained from measured data.

In Figure 11c is shown the hysteresis cycle as obtained from measured data.
In Figure 12 is presented the modeling results using this method for calculating the weighting Preisach.

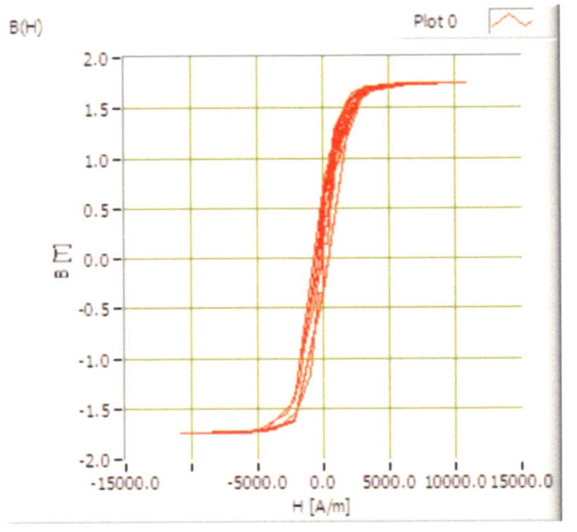

Fig. 12. Cycle Preisach modeling method using the computer program presented

For better illustration, in Figure 13, 3D representation was achieved resulting Preisach triangle.

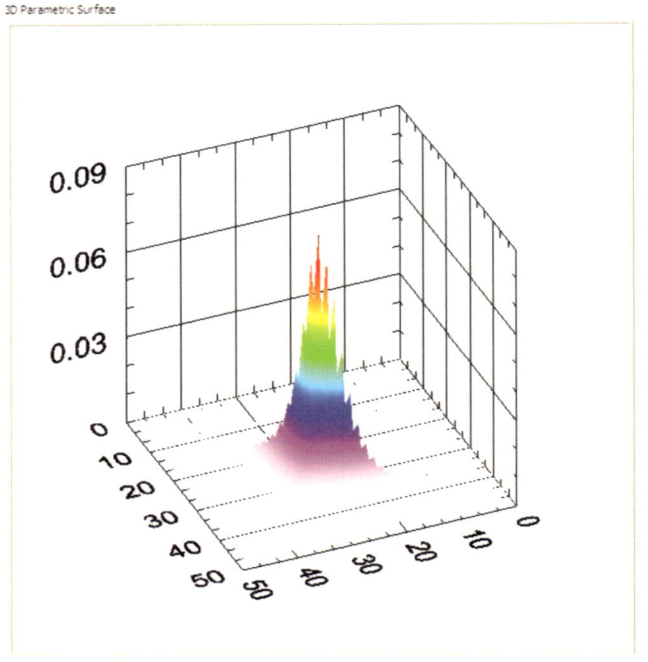

Fig. 13. 3D representation of the Preisach triangle

It appear that the modeling approach may not exactly follow the measured curve but if is choose more points for Preisach triangle the modeling cycle will be closer to the experimentally obtained one. It should be noted that the Preisach method is evident shortcomings in this case, some places having predetermined cycle end which cannot follow the experimental measurements.

This way of modeling is good for a fairly large number of entry points. This shortcoming can be overcome using software interpolation between the points and we obtain the descending branch.
Interpolation method also introduces its errors in the program. Very small variations around a value, as is apparent in our case around positive saturation will stop all at the same point. Full program in block diagram and the front panel results are presented in Annex 3.

3. Jiles - Atherton model

3.1 Langevin model his eyesis the paramagnetism

The first microscopic model of magnetic materials was presented by Langevin. He takes ***m*** total magnetic moment moment of an atom including spin and orbital moment of movement . If the magnetic field strength *H*, then the potential energy is calculated using the formula:

$$w_m = -\mu_0 \mathbf{m}\mathbf{H} = -\mu_0 m H \cos\Theta \tag{2}$$

where: Θ is the angle made between vectors: magnetization and applied magnetic field strength.
Langevin assumed that the atomic magnetic moments ***m*** in paramagnetic materials do not interact. Using the classical Maxwell-Boltzmann statistical probability that an atom to have energy w_m has the expression:

$$p(w_m) = e^{-\frac{w_m}{kT}} \tag{3}$$

where : - k = 1.381 10^{-23} J / K is Boltzmann's constant and
- T is absolute temperature.

When the electric field intensity vector will have the same direction as magnetization vector can talk about inner model describing the relationship between these two sizes. If the directions of the two components differ then be considered a model vector.
Eddy current losses are dependent by the frequency excitation field and are not negligible. If these addition losses and other types of losses may be neglected then the proposed model can be a model independent of frequency.

3.2 Theoretical aspects on Jiles - Atherton model

Model proposed by Jiles and Atherton in 1983 presents a series of equations to determine the magnetization of ferromagnetic materials taking into account the principles of physics. After this the model has been continually improved by other authors. This model is widely used to achieve hysteresis cycles and required to calculate or identify only five parameters.
It seems that this way of identifying the parameters is the great shortcoming of this method. Tried to identify parameters based on measured data is not so easy at it seems. Ideal is to find a mathematical system to calculate the parameters in order to obtain a minimum error between measured and simulated curves.
The Jiles - Atherton model are the two mechanisms underlying the magnetization:

- domain wall displacement;
- growth areas in the direction of the magnetic field is applied against those who are pointing in other directions .

In the Jiles - Atherton model the magnetization is composed of two terms: reversible magnetization and irreversible magnetization.

$$\mathbf{M} = \mathbf{M}_{irr} + \mathbf{M}_{rev} \tag{4}$$

The irreversible component is given by the irreversible movement of domain walls. Magnetizația reverse is reversible once the growth areas.
Hysteresis cycle can be drawn based on the equilibrium energy density within the material.

$$w = w_{mag} + w_{hys} \tag{5}$$

Energy density which is generated by the irreversible movement of domain walls can be calculated using the formula:

$$dw = \mu_0 k dM_{irr} \tag{6}$$

where: k - is a *pinning* factor.
Ferromagnetic materials interact in neighboring areas, so it is introduced the concept of effective magnetic fields acting on unit volume.
Consequently, the magnetization will be regarded as a function of magnetic field strength actually considering moving energy loss generated by irreversible domain wall:

$$dw_{bloh} = \mu_0 k\delta \frac{dM_{irr}}{dH_e} dH_e \tag{7}$$

where: $\delta = sign(dH_e / dt)$.
Modification of irreversible magnetization can be obtained from the calculation of energy. Energy consumed by the material is divided into two parts: the exchange energy and energy loss through hysteresis.

$$\mu_0 \int M_{an}(H)dH = \mu_0 \int M(H)dH + \mu_0 \int k\delta \frac{dM}{dH} dH \tag{8}$$

hence:

$$M_{an}(H) = M(H) + k\delta \frac{dM}{dH} \tag{9}$$

If during the process of magnetization, the anhisteretic magnetization has values lower than this leads to a solution for irreversible magnetization physically impossible, as if the domain walls can not move.
Solution of differential equation is:

$$dM_{irr} = \begin{cases} \frac{1}{k\delta}(M_{an} - M_{irr})dH_e & if\ M_{an} > M_{irr} \\ 0 & if\ M_{an} < M_{irr} \end{cases} \tag{10}$$

Reverse magnetization may be taken into account by introducing the coefficient *c*. which defines the equation as:

$$M_{rev} = c(M_{an} - M_{irr}) \tag{11}$$

Hence the total magnetization became:

$$M = cM_{an} + (1-c)M_{irr} \tag{12}$$

If its value is inserted M the differential equation is obtained

$$dM = \begin{cases} \dfrac{1-c}{k\delta}(M_{an} - M_{irr})dH_e + cdM_{an} & if\ M_{an} > M_{irr} \\ cdM_{an} & if\ M_{an} < M_{irr} \end{cases} \tag{13}$$

Each step can be determined from the previous value of the magnetization using formula:

$$dM_{j+1} = \begin{cases} \dfrac{1}{k\delta}(M_{an} - M_j)dH_e + cdM_{an} & if\ M_{an} > M_{irr} \\ cdM_{an} & if\ M_{an} < M_{irr} \end{cases} \tag{14}$$

This formula is used for numerical implementation of the model proposed by Jiles and Atherton.

In the literature [56]-[59], [89], [93], are proposed several methods of identification of parameters but it seems that no procedure is too easy, requiring input rather difficult and experimental features. To determine the values of input parameters need to know more points on the hysteresis cycles obtained by experimentally means:

- coercive magnetic field strength (H_c) ;
- remnant magnetization (M_r) ;
- saturation coordinates (H_s, M_s) ;
- susceptibility in coercitivity point
- susceptibility at point of remanance
- susceptibility at the saturation point
- anhisteretic susceptibility
- initial susceptibility
- maximum susceptibility

Parameter identification procedure based on these initial data is described in [15]. There is an easy procedure and therefore no result is as expected, the cycle obtained with large deviations from the shape obtained experimentally. For this reason we opted for a process for identifying the parameters by calculating the error between the curves obtained experimentally and modeled by the method of Jiles - Atherton.

3.3 LabVIEW modelling program using the Jiles - Atherton model

Jiles-Atherton model was implemented using LabVIEW programming environment for the reasons listed before. In figure 14 is presented in the LabVIEW program. As can be observed in Figure 14 the model was implemented in a cycle *for* to make the calculation of magnetization in each step, and can implement equations (14) for recurrence.

Magnetic field intensity values can be obtained using a generator as a sine wave or taking data from a file containing the actual measured values, which are find using block for retrieving data from files from virtual instruments and accessing the *PATH* of the file. To calculate total magnetization the cycle must be brought to saturation point. It is obtained from measured data or can be inserted in a parameter input box B_s from front panel of the program.

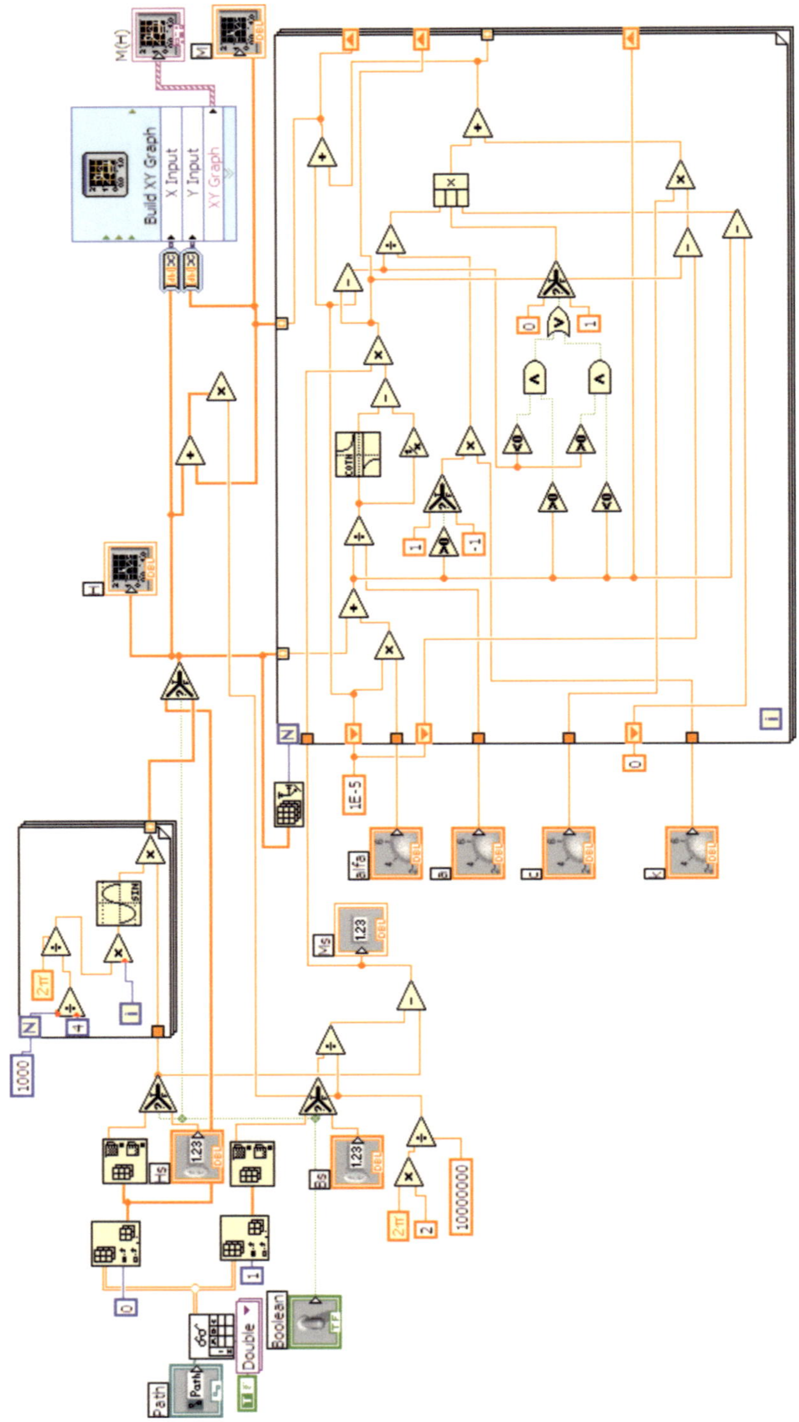

Fig. 14. Block diagram of LabVIEW program for modeling Jiles-Atherton.

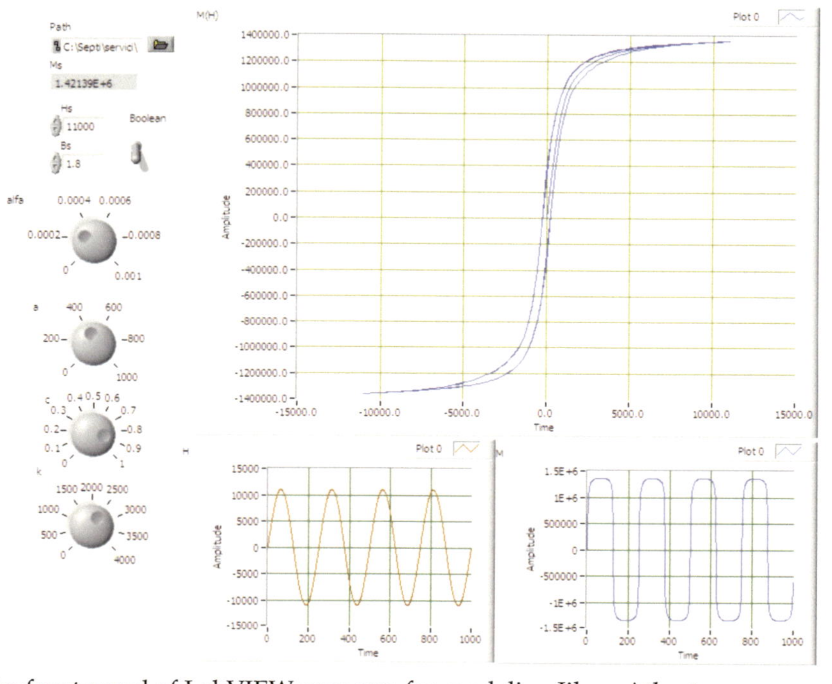

Fig. 15. The front panel of LabVIEW program for modeling Jiles - Atherton .

In figure 15 are presented the waveforms for H and M and hysteresis cycle as a graphic $M(H)$.

To give validity to the model this was compared with measured data and a program to minimize errors between modeled and measured cycle was proposed. This program is presented in Annex 4.

4. Analytical-geometric model

4.1 Theoretical aspects of analytical-geometric modeling

According to the Nicolaide model presented in [68]-[70], the major hysteresis cycle can be modeled using arcs of circle and straight-line segments in a satisfactory manner. To achieve the design it must be made several simplifying assumptions on the hysteresis cycle like the hysteresis cycle is considered symmetrical and centered at the origin.

In the present study taking into account the special characteristics of soft magnetic materials, we have adapted the method from [68]-[70] to studied case and obtain a much more simplified model requiring a small amount of input data.

Based on these simplifying assumptions one can construct a cycle branches, other details are obtained automatically by reversing field and magnetic induction or magnetization values, depending on the cycle shape.

As can be seen in Figure 16, for modeling downward branch is necessary to know some reference points as follows:

1. saturation point in quadrant I, characterized by the magnetic field saturation value H_S and magnetic induction B_S and slope tangent to the cycle at this point;
2. point 2 between two arcs , characterized by values H_2 and B_2;

3. remnant induction B_r (which implicitly means that $H_r = 0$);
4. coercive magnetic field strength H_c (which implicitly means that $B_c = 0$);
5. coordinates of point 5 where the loop starts tilting cycle (which will be calculated);
6. coordonates of point 6 at joint of two arcs characterized by coordinates H_6, B_6;
7. negative saturation point, characterized by $-H_S$-B_S.

In addition to work [84]-[86] where was used 11 parameters we considered that under appropriate conditions for soft magnetic materials, some of these parameters can be obtained from other conditions, and we restrict the number of parameters to only nine.
These parameters are: H_S, B_S, n_S (slope of the tangent at the point of saturation) H_2, B_2, B_r, H_c, H_6, B_6. Accurate representation is given on how to choose the coordinates of points 2 (H_2, B_2) and 6 (H_6, B_6). We try to develop a program to change the position of point 2 and 6 in order to have the smallest error between the cycle of measured and modeled in this way.

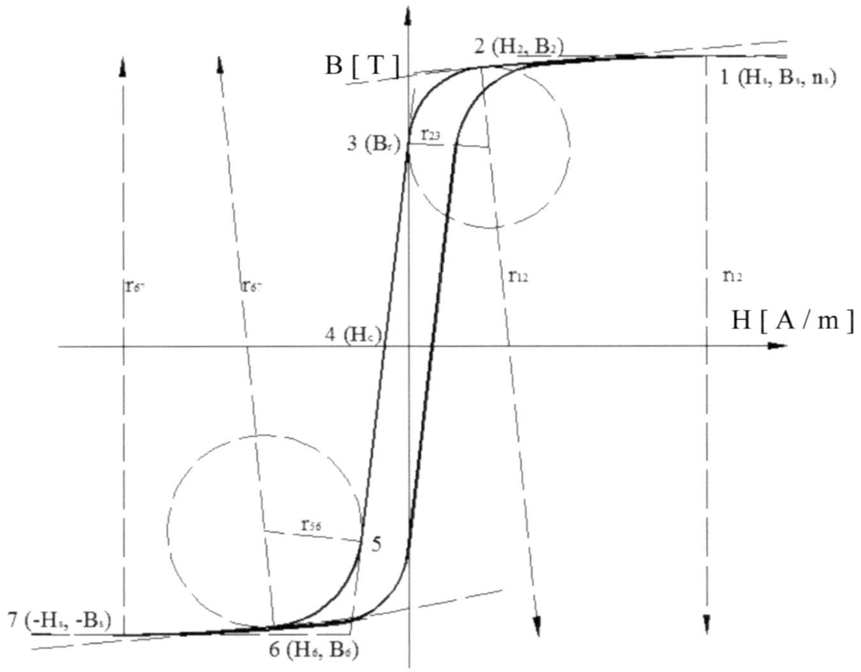

Fig. 16. Considered reference points for modeling hysteresis cycle

In Figure 16 is shown that between point 1 and point 2 is traced an arc of circle which is tangent to the point (H_S, B_S), tangent slope is known n_s and passing through point 2, whose coordinates are known (H_2, B_2).
Finally knowing the arc of a circle can be calculated from the slope of the tangent to the arc of a circle in section 2. Between point 2 and point 3 is plotted a different arc. The slope of the tangent point 3 is calculated using the coordinates of two points 3(0, B_r) and 4(H_c, 0). 2-3 arc is tangent to the slopes calculated previously in arc 1-2 and to straight-line segment 3-4. Between 3 and 5 point is a straight-line segment passing through 4 and has previously calculated slope with points 3 and 4. Coordinates resulting from the calculations forc arc 5-6 as the date of the intersection points between straight line which passes from points 3 and 4 and intersect the arc 5-6 in point 5. For this reason the point 5 is obtained intersecting a circle

obtained from point 6 which must be tangent to the slope in point 6 and to the straight line determined by point 3 and 4. In the arc 6-7 is calculate the slope in point 6 as in case in which is calculated in point 2. Coordinates of point 7 is obtained taking into account the symmetry condition. Linking the arcs and straight-line segment we obtain the descending branch and using an inversion technic taking into account the symmetry principle is btained the ascending branch of hysteresis cycle.

4.2 LabVIEW program for modeling hysteresis cycle

Figure 17 is shown modeling program using LabVIEW software. For solving analytical equations of circular arcs and straight segments, we used a MatLab script window. LabVIEW program was used because of its flexibility to integrate scripts in MatLab and the ease with which experimental data can be stored in text files.

It is noted that block entry into MatLab scripts are 10 input parameters of the nine parameters are input parameters above and the tenth is a step that gives the number of points needed for representation.

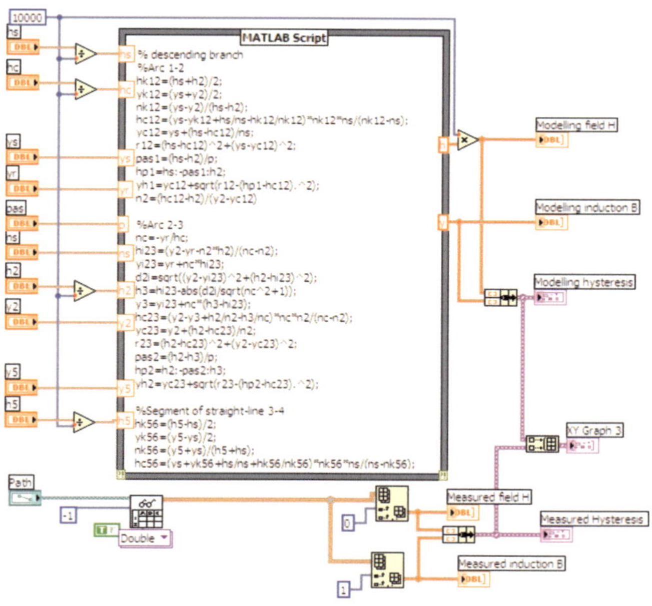

Fig. 17. LabVIEW program wish to use analytical modeling by arcs and line segments .

To see how well the program approximates the experimental data was achieved overlap values obtained by modeling with experimental values stored in text file in the location given by the block "path". The result of this representation can be seen in Figure 18.

As can be seen in the window each spring MatLab script was treated separately and has developed a sampling interval between two field values considered for early and late spring using variable step introduced by the operator as input parameter.

Using this step each spring is obtained by a column matrix for magnetic field strength and magnetic induction value. These matrices are concatenated, achieving one matrix with different values of magnetic field strength magnetic flux density values. Using these two matrix representation can be achieved descending branch of the hysteresis cycle.

To obtain the upward branch of the hysteresis cycle is made denying the two columns values obtained previously, given the condition of symmetry and centering the zero major hysteresis cycle. Resulting cycle is shown in Figure 18. For comparison, measured using a cycle using the Epstein and installation of measurement in Brockhauss Messtechnik. This measurement cycle was extracted from an excel file obtained by exporting data from MPG program.

The program, using the call block file path and measured data are collected and induction magnetic field strength values and shown on the same graph shown in Figure 51.

It should be noted that the two cycles overlap quite well in the saturation, with sharp differences in the curves around May remanence. These errors can be minimized if they choose the optimized values of point 2 and 6 but the difference would be too small to be seen.

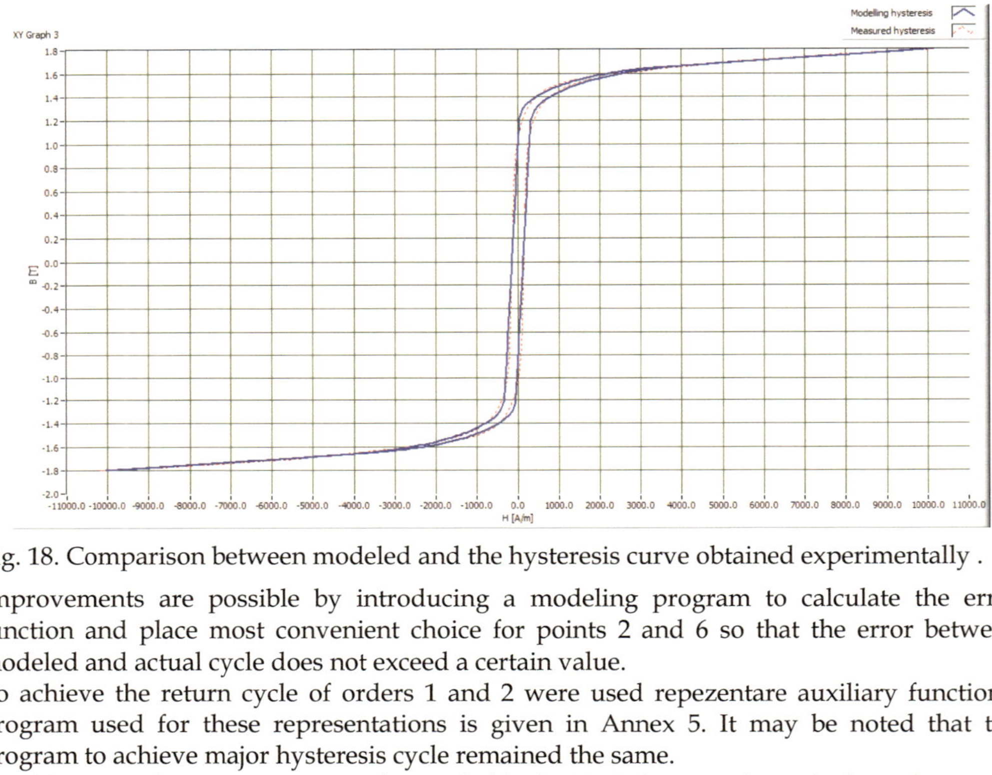

Fig. 18. Comparison between modeled and the hysteresis curve obtained experimentally .

Improvements are possible by introducing a modeling program to calculate the error function and place most convenient choice for points 2 and 6 so that the error between modeled and actual cycle does not exceed a certain value.

To achieve the return cycle of orders 1 and 2 were used repezentare auxiliary functions. Program used for these representations is given in Annex 5. It may be noted that the program to achieve major hysteresis cycle remained the same.

In addition to this program were also made blocks MatLab script that calculates the return of the first order curves upward and downward.

For easy use, I used buttons for choosing points that reversing the upward branch downward. In this way can choose any point on these branches. In the event that they want certain points, well defined, these buttons can be replaced by dialog boxes for entering a numerical exact values. Full program and graphics on the front panel are presented in Annex 5.

5. Acknowledgement

This paper is supported by The National University Research Council of Romania (CNCSIS) under the contract number 848/2009

Annex 1 Preisach classical method

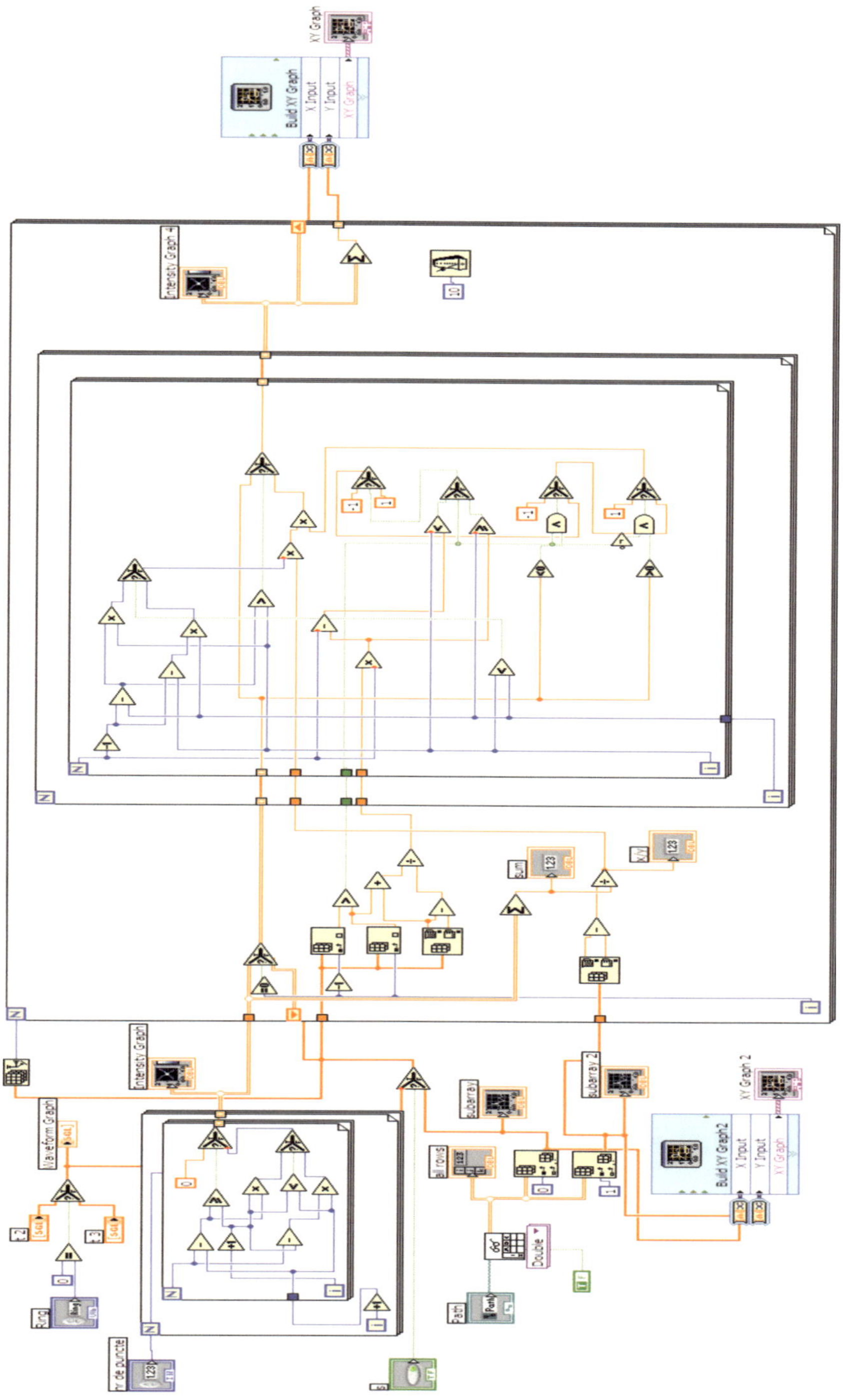

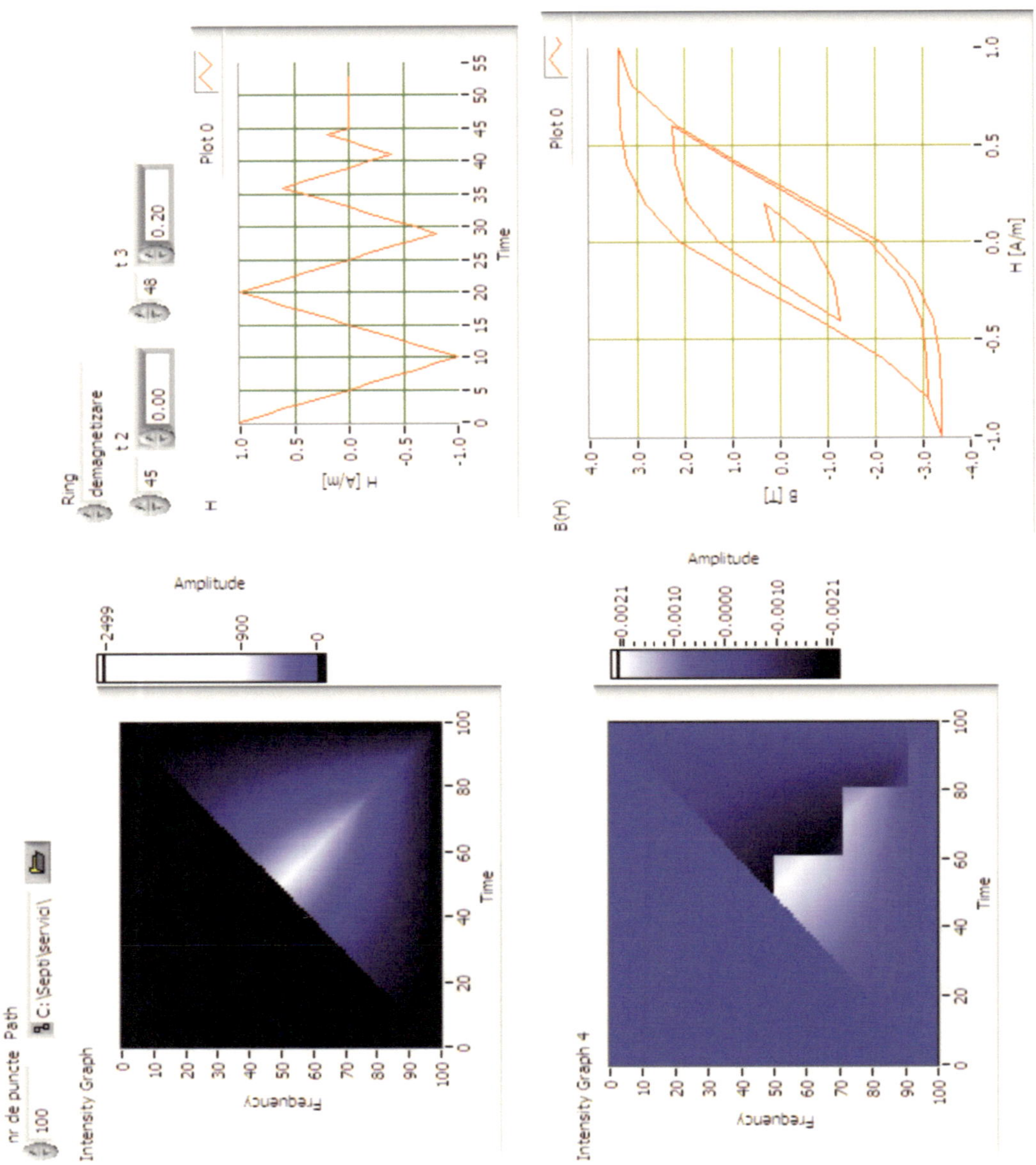
nr de puncte
Path
C:\Sept\servici\
Intensity Graph
Frequency
Time
Amplitude
Intensity Graph 4
Ring
demagnetizare
t 2
t 3
H
Plot 0
H [A/m]
B(H)
B [T]

Annex 2 Method modified Preisach

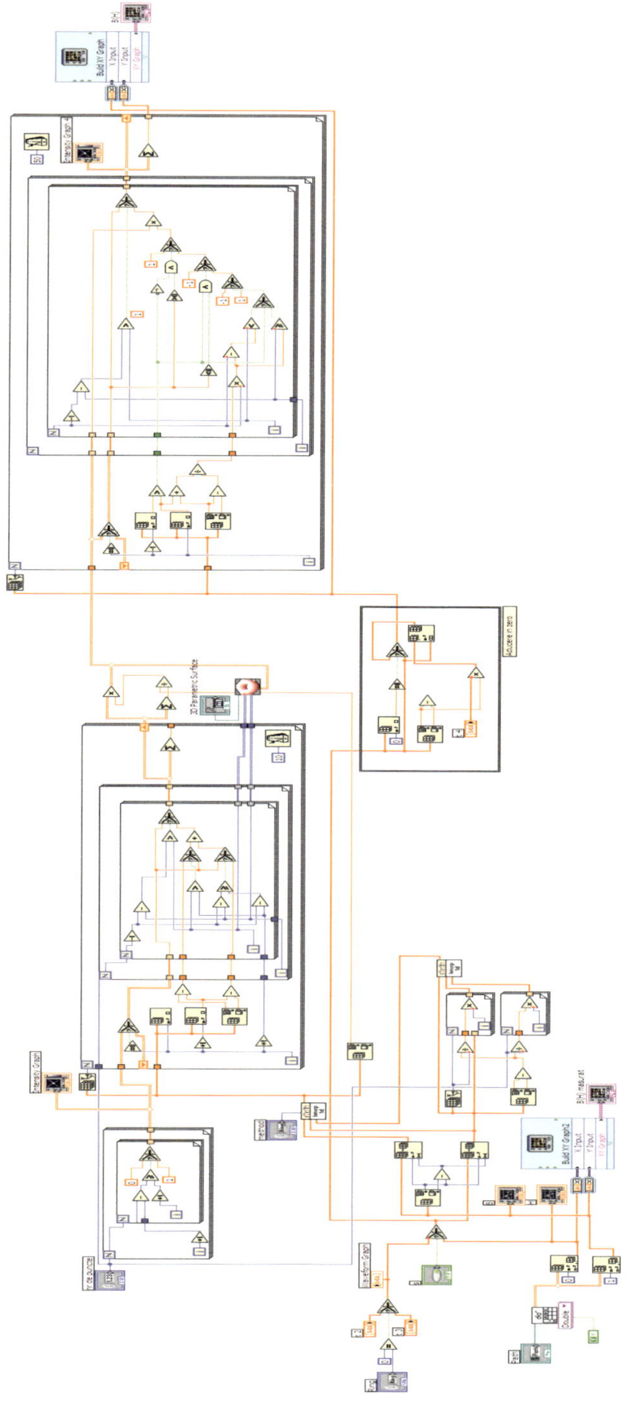

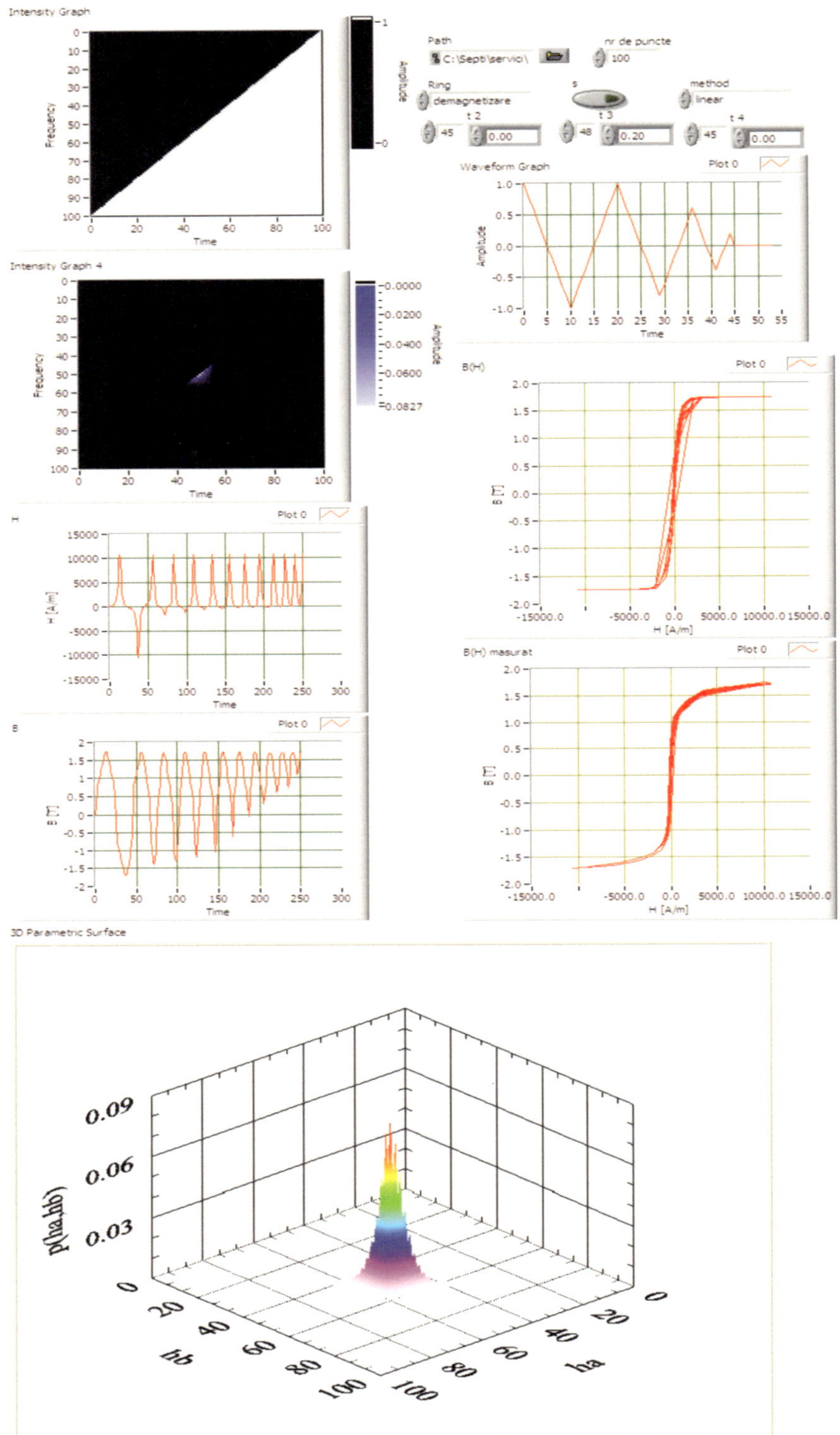
Intensity Graph
Frequency
Time
Amplitude
Intensity Graph 4
Path
C:\Septi\servici\
nr de puncte
100
Ring
demagnetizare
s
method
linear
t 2
t 3
t 4
Waveform Graph
Plot 0
B(H)
B [T]
H [A/m]
B(H) masurat
H
B
3D Parametric Surface
p(ha,hb)
hb
ha

Annex 3 Method Jiles - Atherton

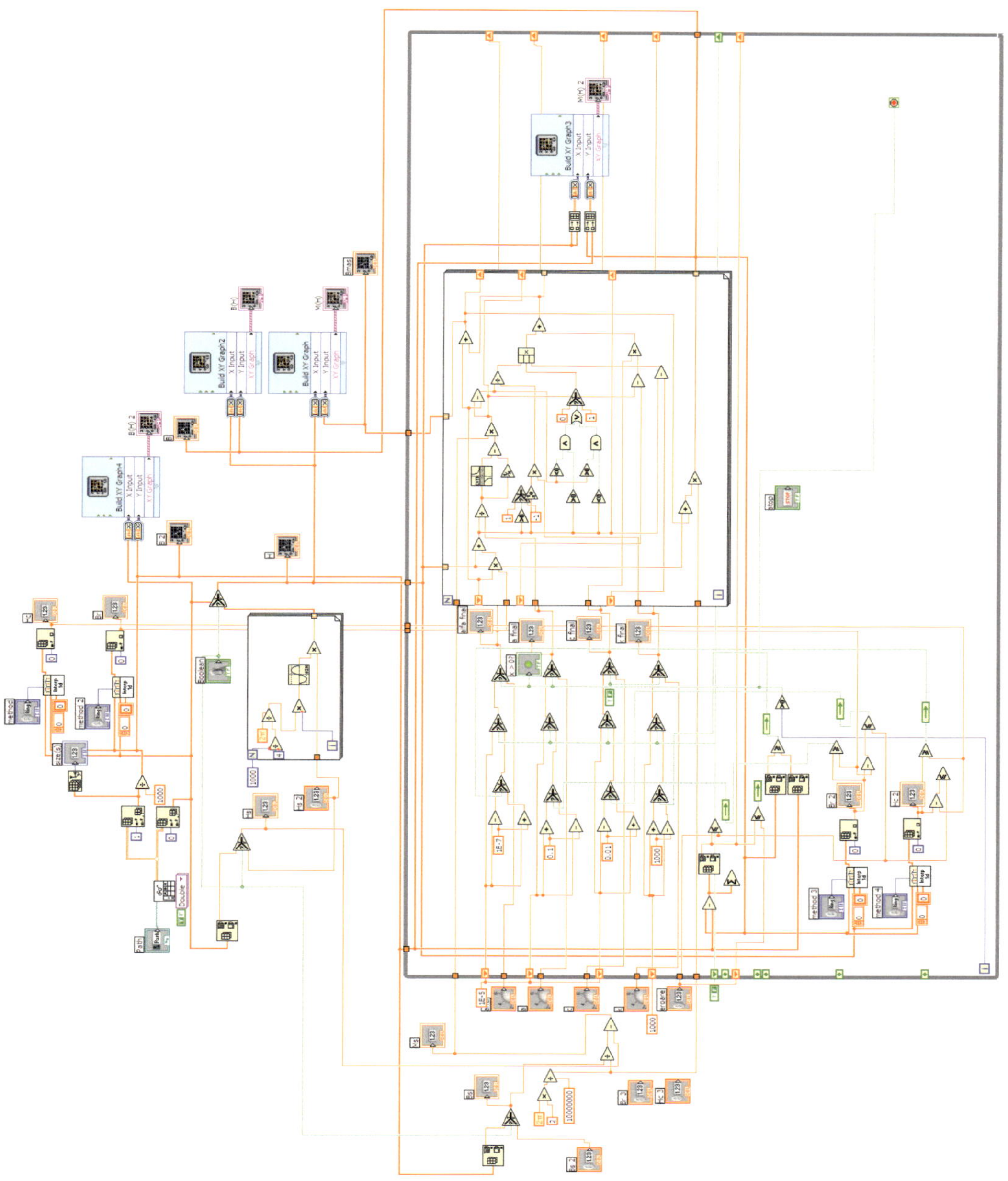

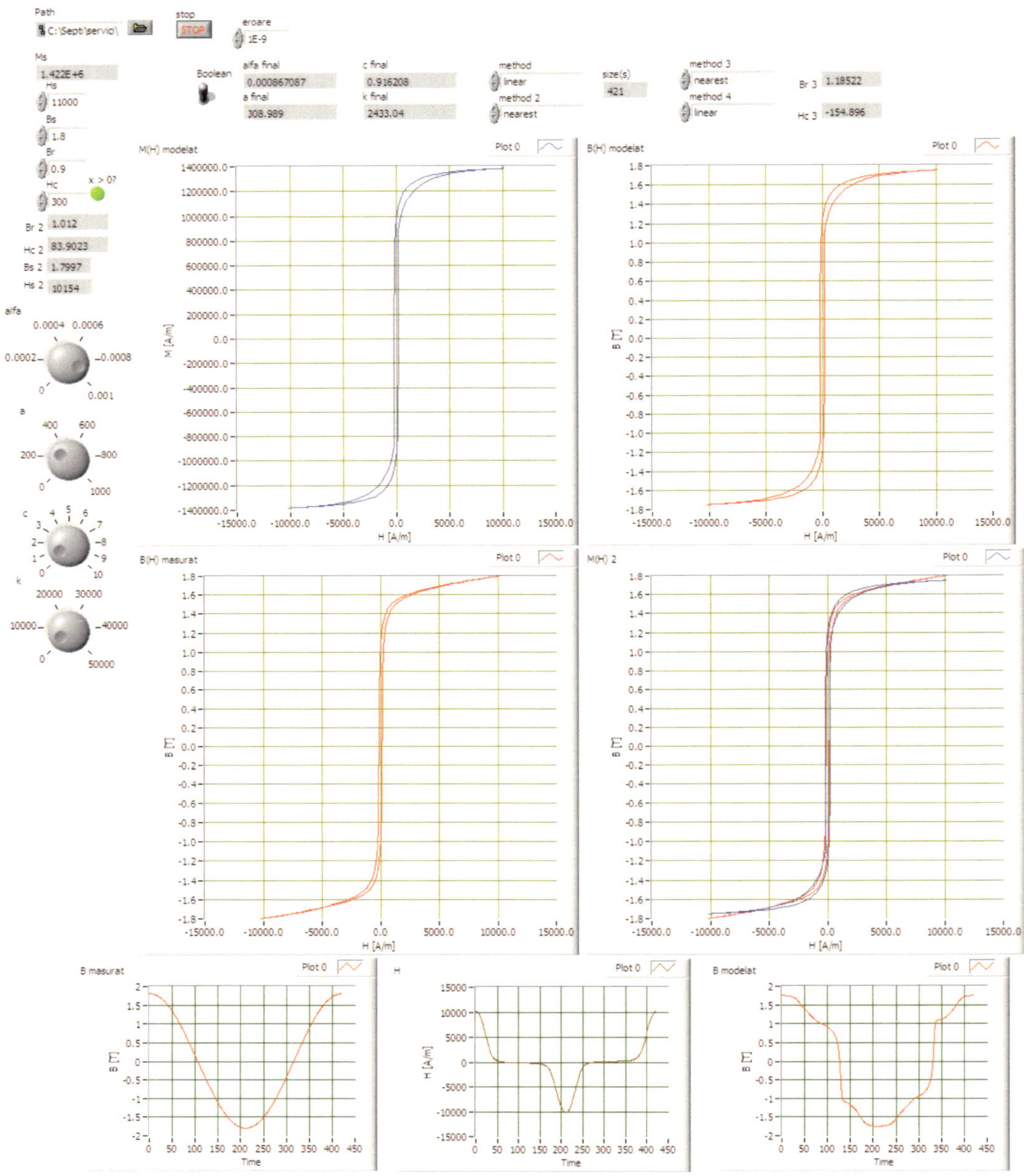
Path
C:\Sept\servio\
stop
STOP
eroare
1E-9
Ms
1.422E+6
Hs
11000
Bs
1.8
Br
0.9
Hc
300
x > 0?
Br 2 1.012
Hc 2 83.9023
Bs 2 1.7997
Hs 2 10154
alfa
a
c
k
Boolean
alfa final
0.000867087
a final
308.989
c final
0.916208
k final
2433.04
method
linear
method 2
nearest
size(s)
421
method 3
nearest
method 4
linear
Br 3 1.18522
Hc 3 -154.896
M(H) modelat
B(H) modelat
B(H) masurat
M(H) 2
Plot 0
M [A/m]
B [T]
H [A/m]
B masurat
H
B modelat
Time

Annex 4 Analytic-geometric method

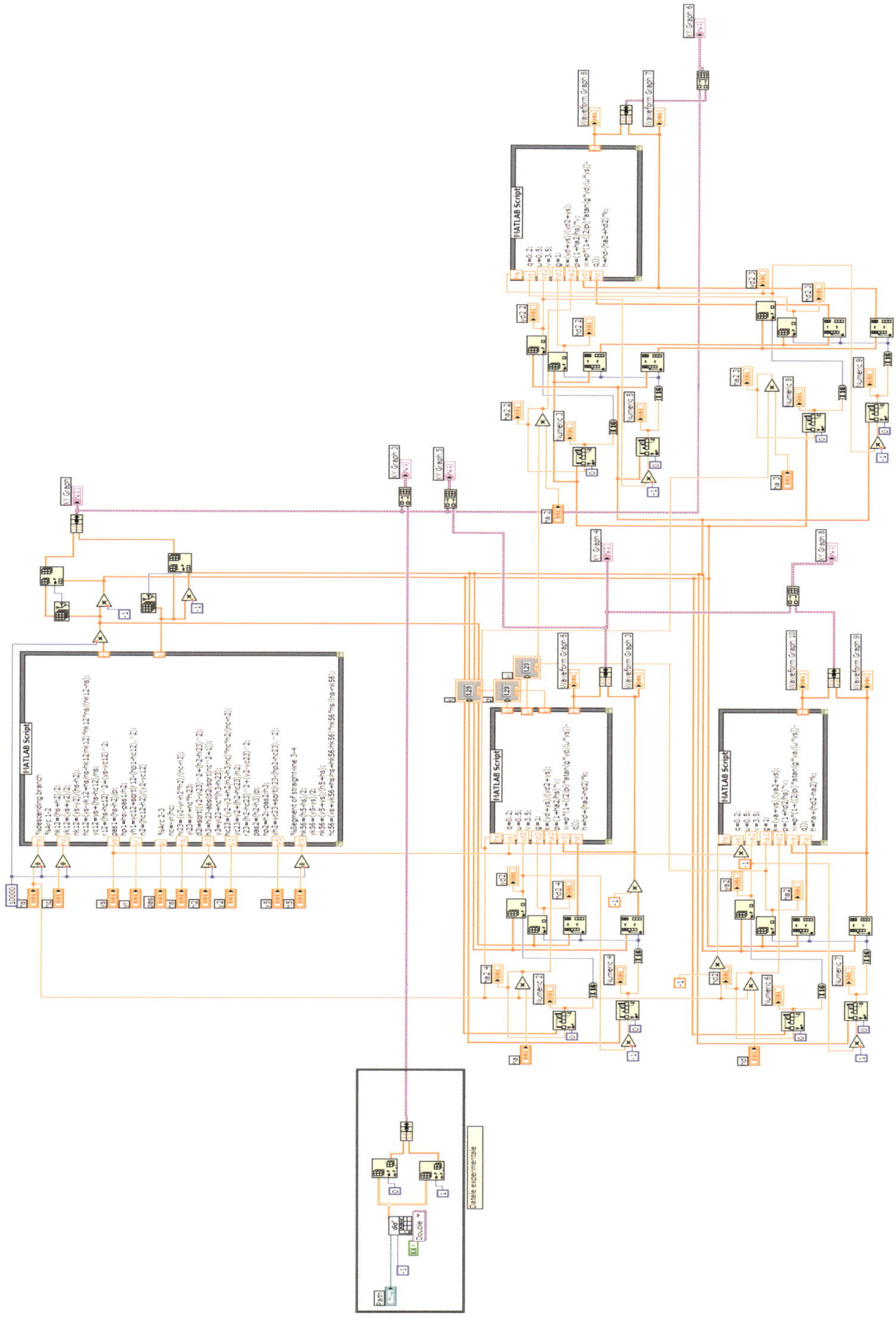

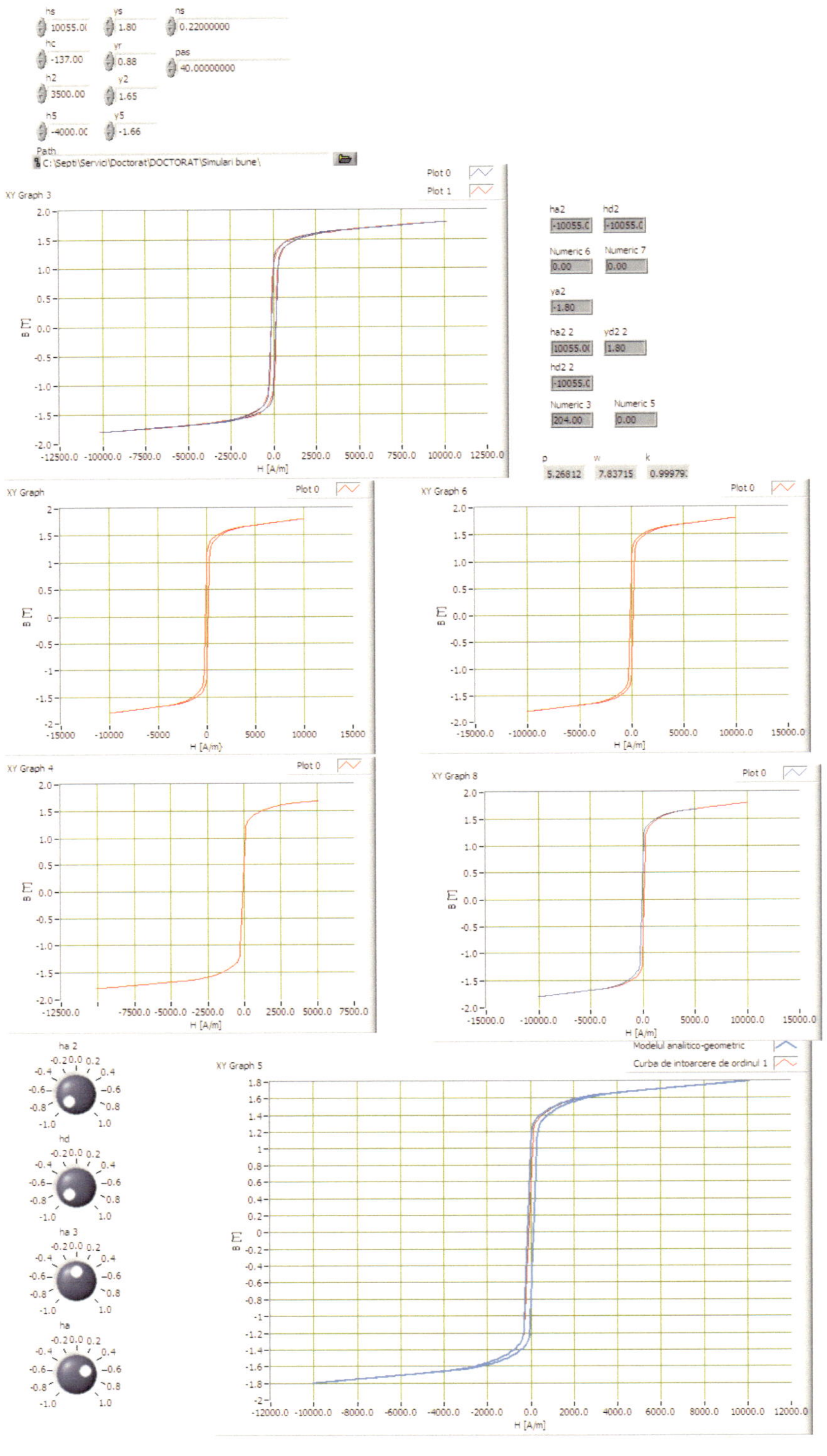
hs
10055.0(
ys
1.80
ns
0.22000000
hc
-137.00
yr
0.88
pas
40.00000000
h2
3500.00
y2
1.65
h5
-4000.0(
y5
-1.66
Path
C:\Sept\Servici\Doctorat\DOCTORAT\Simulari bune\
Plot 0
Plot 1
XY Graph 3
B [T]
H [A/m]
ha2
-10055.(
hd2
-10055.(
Numeric 6
0.00
Numeric 7
0.00
ya2
-1.80
ha2 2
10055.0(
yd2 2
1.80
hd2 2
-10055.(
Numeric 3
204.00
Numeric 5
0.00
p
5.26812
w
7.83715
k
0.99979:
XY Graph
XY Graph 6
XY Graph 4
XY Graph 8
XY Graph 5
Modelul analitico-geometric
Curba de intoarcere de ordinul 1
ha 2
hd
ha 3
ha

6. References

[1] FMEA, A., M., Mirmiran, A., *A New Model for Steel Members hysteresis*International Journal for Numerical Methods in Engineering , No. 45 , 1999 , pp 1007-1023 .

[2] Andrew, P., Stancu, A., Adedoyin, A., *Modeling of Viscosity Phenomena in Models of hysteresis With Local Memory,* Journal of Optoelectronics and Advanced Materials vol 8 , no. March , 2006 , pp 988-990 .

[3] Bennett , L. , H. , Vajda F , Atzmony , U. , Swartzendruber , L. J. *Accommodation Study of the Nanograin Iron Powder*IEEE Transactions on Magnetics , 32 (5) , 1996 , pp 4493-4495 .

[4] Bertotti , G. *Dynamic generalization of the scalar Preisach model of hysteresis,* IEEE Trans . Magna . , No. 28 , 1992 , pp 2599-2601 .

[5] Bertotti , G. *General Properties of Power Losses in Soft Ferromagnetic Materials,* IEEE Trans . Magna . , No. 24 , 1988 , pp 621-630 .

[6] Bertotti , G. *Hysteresis in Magnetism.* Academic Press , Inc. . , 1998 California, USA.

[7] Bertotti , G. , Basso , V. Pasquale , M. , *Application of the Preisach Model to the Calculation of Magnetization Curves and Power Losses in Ferromagnetic Materials,* IEEE Trans . Magna . , No. 30 , 1994 pp 1052-1057 .

[8] Bertotti , G. Fiorillo , F. , Pasquale , M. , *Measurement and Prediction of Dynamic Loop Shapes and Power Losses in Soft Magnetic Materials,* IEEE Trans . Magna . , No. 29 , March , 1993 , pp 3496-3498 .

[9] Biorci , G. Pescetti , D. *Some Remarks on hysteresis*J. Appl . Phys . , No. 37 , 1966 , pp 1313-1317 .

[10] Bossavit , A. *Computational Electromagnetism,* Academic Press , 1998 Boston.

[11] Bottauscio , O. , Chiampi , M. , Chiarabaglio , D. *Advanced Model of Laminated Cores for Two -Dimensional Magnetic Field Analysis,* IEEE Trans . Magna . , No. 36 , 2000 , pp 561-573 .

[12] Bottauscio , O. , Chiampi , M. , Chiarabaglio , D. , Raguso , C. , Repeto , M. *Ferromagnetic hysteresis and Magnetic Field Analysis,* ICS Newsletter , No. 6 , 1999 , pp 3-7 .

[13] Bottauscio , O. , Chiampi , M. , Chiarabaglio , D. , Repetto , M. , *Preisach -type hysteresis in Magnetic Field Computation Models,* Physica B : Condensed Matter , No. 275 , 2000 , pp 34-39 .

[14] Bottauscio , O. , Chiampi , M. *Laminated Core Modeling under Rotational Excitations Including Eddy currents and hysteresis*J. Appl . Phys . , No. 89 , 2001 , pp 6728-6730 .

[15] Bottauscio , O. , Chiarabaglio , D. Chiampi , M. , Repetto , M. , *A Periodic Magnetic Field Solution Using Hysteretic Preisach Model and Fixed -Point Technique,* IEEE Trans . Magna . , No. 31 , 1995 , pp 3548-3550 .

[16] Bozorth , R. , M. *Ferromagnetism.* D. Van Nostrand Co. . Inc. . Princeton, 1951 New Jersey.

[17] Burzo , E. *Physics of Magnetic Phenomena,* Romanian Academy Publishing House , Vol 1 , 1979 , Bucharestknow .

[18] Cardelli , E. Della Torre , E. , Faba , A. *Experimental Verification of the deletion and Congruency Property in Si- Fe Magnetic Steels,* Modeling hysteresis and Micromagnetics 2009 , some , Gaithersburg , Maryland, USA

[19] Cardelli , E. Della Torre , E. , Faba , A. *Properties of a Class of Vector Hysterons*Journal of Applied Physics , No. 103 , 2008 , 07D927 .

[20] Cardelli , E. , Faba , A. *Vector hysteresis Measurements via Single Disk Tester,* Physica B , No. 372 , 2006 , pp 143-146 .

[21] Cheng , K. , W. , E. Lu , Y. , Ho , S. , L. *Hysteresis Modeling of Magnetic Devices Using Dipole Distribution*IEEE Transactions on Magnetics , Vol 41 , No. 5 , 2005 .

[22] Chiampi , M. , Chiarabaglio , D. , Repetto , M. , *The Jiles - Atherton and Combined Fixed - Point Technique for Time Periodic Magnetic Field Problems With hysteresis,* IEEE Trans . Magna . , No. 31 , 1995 , pp 4306-4311 .

[23] Del Moral Hernandez , E. Muranaka , C. , S. , Cardoso , J. , R. , *Identification of the Jiles - Atherton Model Parameters Using Random and deterministic Searches,* Physica B 275 , 2000 , pp 212-215 .

[24] Del Vecchio , R. , *An Efficient Procedure without hysteresis Modeling Complex Processes in Ferromagnetic Materials,* IEEE Trans . Magna . , No. 16 , 1980 , pp 809-811 .

[25] Del Vecchio , R. , *Computation of Losses in Electrical Steels Nonoriented From the Classical Viewpoint*J. Appl . Phys . , No. 53 , 1982 , pp 8281-8286 .

[26] Del Vecchio , R. , *The Inclusion of hysteresis Processes in the Special Class of Electromagnetic Finite element calculations,* IEEE Trans . Magna . , No. 18 , (1982c) , pp 275-284 .

[27] Della Torre , E. *A Preisach Model for Accommodation,* IEEE Trans . Magna . , No. 30 , 1994 , pp 2701-2707 .

[28] Della Torre , E. *A Simplified Vector Preisach Model,* IEEE Trans . Magna., No. 34 , 1998 , pp 495-501 .

[29] Della Torre , E. *Hysteresis Modeling II : Accommodation,* IEEE Trans . Magna . , No. 23 , 1987 , pp 2823-2827 .

[30] Della Torre , E. *Magnetic hysteresis,* IEEE Press, New York , 1999

[31] Della Torre , E. , Pinzaglia , E. Cardelli , E. *Vector Modeling - Part I : Generalized hysteresis model,* Physica B , Vol 372 , 2006 , pp 111-114 .

[32] Della Torre , E. , Pinzaglia , E. Cardelli , E. *Vector Modeling - Part II: Ellipsoidal vector hysteresis model . Numerical Application to the 2 - D Houses,* Physica Male , Vol 372 , 2006 , pp 115-119 .

[33] Dlala , E. Arkkio , A. *Measurement and Analysis of hysteresis of High-Speed Torque on Induction Machine,* Electric Power Applications, EIT , Vol 1 , No. 5 , 2007 , pp 737-742 .

[34] Dlala , E. Belahcen , A. , Arkkio , A. *Vector Model of Ferromagnetic hysteresis Magnetodynamic Steel Laminations,* Physica B : Condensed Matter , Vol 403 , No. 2-3 , 2008 , pp 428-432 .

[35] Dlala , E. , Saitz , J. , Arkkio , A. *Inverted and Forward Preisach Models for Numerical Analysis of Electromagnetic Field Problems*IEEE Transactions on Magnetics , Vol 42 , No. 8 , 2006 , pp 1963-1973 .

[36] Dlala , E. , Saitz , J. , Arkkio , A. *Modeling Based on Symmetric hysteresis Minor Loops*IEEE Transactions on Magnetics , Vol 41 , No. 8 , 2005 , pp 2343-2348 .

[37] Doong , T. , Mayergoyz , I. , D. *Implementation of hysteresis on Numerical Models*IEEE Transactions on Magnetics , Vol 21 , No. 5 , 1985 , pp.1853 - 1855 .

[38] Fuzi , J. *Depends hysteresis model computationally Efficient Rate,* COMPEL , No. 18 , 1999 , pp 445-457 .

[39] Fuzi , J. , Helerea , E. Iványi , A. *Experimental Construction of Preisach Models for Ferromagnetic Cores,* PCIM / PQ , Nuremberg , 1998 .

[40] Fuzi , J. Ivanyi , A. *Two features of hysteresis Rate - Dependent Models, Physica B : Condensed Matter,* No. 306 , 2001 , pp 278-280 .

[41] Fuzi , J. , Kadar , G. *Frequency Dependence in the Product Preisach Model*J. Magna . Magna . Mater . , No. 254-255 , 2003 , p. 278-280 .

[42] Fuzi , J. *Type Vector Preisach hysteresis Two Models,* Physica B , No. 343 , 2004 , pp 159-163 .

[43] Hantila , F. *A Method of Solving Stationary Magnetic Field in Non - Linear Media,* rev. Roum . Sci . Techn. - Electrotechn . et Go. , No. 20 , 1975 , pp 397-407 .

[44] Hantila , F. *Mathematical Models of the Relation Between B and H for non-linear media,* rev. Roum . Sci . Techn. - Electrotechn . et Go. , No. 19 , 1974 , pp 429-448 .

[45] Hantila , F. , Preda , G. , Vasiliu , M. *Polarization Method for Static Fields,* IEEE Trans . Magna . , No. 36 , 2000 , pp 672-675 .

[46] Helerea , E. , electrical materialsÃ and electronics , Ed MatrixRom , Bucharest , 2003

[47] Henze , O. , Rucker , W. , M. *Identification procedures of Preisach model, IEEE* Transactions on Magnetics , Vol 38 , No. 2 , 2002 , pp 833-836 .

[48] Henze , O. , Rucker , W. , M. , Jesenik , M. , Gorican , V. , Trlep , M. , Hamler , A. , Stumberger , B. , *Hysteresis model and Examples of Ferromagnetic Material,* IEEE Trans . Magna . , Vol 39 , No. 3 , 2003 , pp 1151-1154 .

[49] Hutchinson , W. , B. , Swift , J. G. *Anisotropy in Some Soft Magnetic Materials*Gordon and Breach Science Publishers Ltd. , Texture , Vol 1 , 1972 , pp 117-123 , UK .

[50] Ionita , A. , D. Ionita , V. *Software Tools for interoperable between Materials with Electromagnetic Problems involving hysteresis,* Proc . of twond Int . Conf on Advances and Applications of GID , 2004 , pp.147 -150 .

[51] Ionita , V , Ionita , A. , D. *Use of Magnetic Material Models in Electromagnetic CAD*Journal of Optoelectronics and Advanced Materials Vol 6 , No. 3 , 2004 , pp 1013-1016 .

[52] Ionita , V. , Crânganu - Cretu , B. , John D. *Quasi - Stationary Magnetic Field Computation in Hysteretic Media,* IEEE Trans . On Magnetics , Vol 32 , No. 3 , 1996 , pp 1128-1131 .

[53] Ionita , V. , Crânganu - Cretu , B. , Ionita , A. , D. *Object- Oriented Software for Advanced Characterization of Magnetic Materials,* IEEE Trans . on Magnetics , Vol 38 , No. 2 , 2002 , pp 1101-1104 .

[54] Iványi , A. *Hysteresis Models in Electromagnetic Computation,* Akademia Kiadó , Budapest , 1997 .

[55] Jiles , D. C. *A Generalized Self Consistent Model For The Calculation of Minor Loop in The Theory of Hysterezis Excursion*IEEE Transaction on Magnetics , Vol 28 , 1992 , pp 2602-2604 .

[56] Jiles , D. , C. Atherton , D. L. *Ferromagnetic Hysterezis*IEEE Transaction on Magnetics , Vol 19 , 1983 , pp 2183-2189 .

[57] Jiles , D. , C. Atherton , D. L. *Theory of Ferromagnetic Hysterezis*Journal of Magnetism and Magnetic Materials , Vol 61 , 1986 pp 48-60 .

[58] Jiles , D. , C. Thoelke , J. , B. , Devine , M. , *Numerical Determination of hysteresis Parameters for the Modeling of Magnetic Properties Using the Theory of Ferromagnetic hysteresis,* IEEE Trans on Magnetics , Vol 28 , No. 1 , 1992 , pp 27-35 .

[59] Jiles , D. , C. Thoelke , J. B. , *Theory of Ferromagnetic Hysterezis : Determination of Model Parameters from Experimental hysteresis Loops,* IEEE Trans on Magneticws , vol 25 , no. May , 1989 , pp 3928-3930 .

[60] Kis , P. , Iványi , A. *Parameter Identification of Jiles - Atherton Model With Non - Linear Least -Square Method,* Physica B , Vol 343 , 2004 , pp 59-64 .

[61] Kis , P. , Kuczmann , M. , Füzi , J. Iványi , A. *Hysteresis Measurements in LabVIEW,* Physica B , Vol 343 , 2004 , pp 357-363 .

[62] Krejc , P. , *Vector hysteresis Models,* Eur . Jnl . Appl . Math . , Vol 2 , 1991 , pp 281-292 .

[63] Kuczmann , M. *Scalar hysteresis Measurement Using FFT*Journal of Optoelectronics and Advanced Materials , Vol 10 , No. 7 , 2008 , pp 1828-1833 .

[64] Lavers , J. , D. , Biringer , P. , P. , Hollitscher , H. *A Simple Method for Estimating the Minor Loop hysteresis Loss in Thin Laminations,* IEEE Trans . Magna ., vol 14 , 1978 , pp 386-388 .

[65] Lavers , J. , D. , Biringer , P. , P. , Hollitscher , H. *Estimation of Core Loss When the flow waveform Contains the Essential Plus single Odd Harmonic Component,* IEEE Trans . Magna ., vol 13 .

[66] Lin , D. Zhou , P. , Badics , Z. , Fu , W. , N. , Chen , Q. , M. , Cendes , Z. , J. A New Model for nonlinear anisotropic Soft Magnetic Materials, Proceedings of COMPUMAG , 2005 , CSY0084 .

[67] Makaveev, D., Dupre, L., De Wulf, M., Melkebeek, J., *Combined Preisach–Mayergoyz-Neural-Network Vector Hysteresis Model for Electrical Steel Sheets,* Journal of Applied Physics, Vol. 93, No. 10, 2003, pp. 6738-6740.

[68] Nicolaide, A., *Magnetism and Magnetic Materials,* Transilvania University Press, Brasov, Romania, 2001.

[69] Nicolaide, A., *A New Approach of Mathematical Modelling of Hysteresis Curves of Magnetic Materials,* Rev. Roum. Sci. Techn. - Electrotechn. Et Energ., Vol. 48, No. 2-3, 2003, pp. 221-233.

[70] Nicolaide, A., *An Approach to the Mathematical Modelling of the Hysteresis Curves of Magnetic Materials: The Mirror Curves,* Rev. Roum. Sci. Techn. - Electrotechn. Et Energ., Vol. 52, No. 3, 2007, pp. 301-310.

7

Modeling in Respiratory Movement Using LabVIEW and Simulink

Zhonghai He and Yuqian Zhao
Department of automation engineering, Northeastern University at Qinhuangdao Qinhuangdao,
China

1. Introduction

The rapid pace of change in modern medicine makes training on simulation platforms an absolute necessity. With the microprocessors the sophistication of simulators exploded. More recently medicine has developed simulators that are becoming increasingly sophisticated, especially in anesthesia training but also to train intensive care personnel. This is an area that will rapidly advance in the future and will have great impact on medical education medical. Unfortunately, the current state of development for simulated procedural environments remains rather limited and the availability of validated metrics of skills acquisition is just beginning. There are two impulse to push respiration simulation forward, as list following.

1.1 Optimize mechanical ventilation

Mechanical ventilation is on the one hand the lifesaving therapy in intensive care medicine by all means. On the other hand this therapy can even aggravate the pulmonary status of the critically ill patient. Mechanical damage of the lung tissue is the predominant reason for ventilator induced lung injury (VILI). To avoid VILI, the physicians make great efforts to develop lung protective ventilation strategies (Grinnan, 2005). Lung protective ventilation considerably improves the outcome of mechanically ventilated and critically ill patients as it avoids extensive mechanical stress of the lung tissue and hence its irreversible damage. A valid analysis of respiratory mechanics is a prerequisite for lung protective ventilation. This analysis is always based on mathematical models. The equation of motion is the commonly accepted mathematical model of the respiratory system which provides the basis for the most clinically applied methods of respiratory mechanics analysis.

1.2 Medical patient simulator

Learning through hands-on experience is the best teaching method, but when reality is dangerous, events are rare and errors are costly, for instance in medical training, simulators are the preferred tools for teaching. The medical patient simulator (MPS) is one such tool used to train medical students and anesthesia residents. Sophisticated physiological and pharmacological mathematical models control mechanical actuator embedded in and adult-sized mannequin to create life-like physical signs and symptoms that health care personnel use to make clinical diagnoses and to guide therapeutic interventions. As respiration is one of the most important physiology, the MPS has a self-regulating spontaneous breathing system that used pressurized gases in appropriate concentrations the enhance realism.

2. History of model construction

It has been long known that the mechanical properties of the airways and respiratory tissues exhibit different types of nonlinear behavior. In 1915 Rohrer suggested that the frictional pressure loss across the airways is a quadratic function of the volume flow rate. This Q dependence, originating from the nonlinear fluid mechanical aspects of gas flow in the airways, causes airway resistance to increase with increasing flow amplitude. Alternatively, in 1939, Bayliss and Robertson found that most of the viscous energy dissipated in the lung tissues during cyclic deformation did not depend on the flow rate but did depend on the amplitude of excursions, or tidal volume.

The first modern model as we know is described by Otis et al (1956) used to systematically examine the behavior of an inhomogeneous lung from a theoretical point of view. They assumed that the pressures to which the lungs are subjected are sine waves and inferred that time constant inequality could be responsible for the decrease in apparent compliance and resistance. Based on some reasonable approximations a single pulmonary pathway is regarded mechanically as consisting of a volume-elastic part having a compliance C, and a part having a resistance R, in series, which is the fundamental model of latter more complicated respiratory model. The success to this model is due to its simplicity, its immediate physiological interpretation, and its sensitivity to changes in lung mechanics.

The practical lung simulator is introduced by Clare E. Barkalow (1974, 1984). He invented a pneumatic lung analog for simulating spontaneous breathing and for testing of ventilatory devices used with spontaneously breathing patients and a kit for modifying training test lungs. The lung analog is comprised by mechanical parts and is the prototype of PneuView lung simulator of Michigan Instruments Inc.

The introduction of computers has made it possible to change quickly between different simulator settings. Meyer (1983) designed a microcomputer-controlled respiratory servo system, using a hydraulically operated cylinder-piston and solenoid valve assembly. The flexibility in selecting different breathing patterns allowed the implementation of complex sequences of breathing manoeuvers. Myojo (1989) described a breathing simulator with a split/cam valve without a piston/cylinder or bellows, the opening of the split/cam valve was controlled by a stepper motor under microcomputer control. This system allowed inspiratory flow patterns to be simulated as seen during spontaneous breathing, although it was not reported whether it was possible to change breathing patterns during simulation. Jansen (1989) described a computerized ventilator system for animal studies. Instead of the hydraulic system of Meyer, they used an electromechanical system, which was relatively small and easy to implement in the construction of a ventilator.

Verbraak adapted the idea of computer control and published series papers (1991, 1995, 2001, 2003) to drive a physical lung model for use in the pulmonary function laboratory to test lung function equipment. They use this computer-controlled mechanical lung model to perform pulmonary function tests on special breathing patterns in a body plethysmograph. The extended integration of hardware and software offers many new possibilities and advantages over the former simulators. The properties of components which simulate elastance and airway resistance of the lung are defined in software rather than by the mechanical properties of the components alone. The lung model consists of three components: the actual lung model, an electromechanical servo system and a computer system to control the model.

Meka (2004) present a new bellow-less lung simulator utilizing a fixed-volume pressure controller to simulate spontaneous breathing as an alternative to the traditional bellows-driven mechanical lung system in the human patient simulator. The lung simulator simulates carinal pressure, which allows for simulation of actively breathing or ventilated patients. The bellow-less lung simulator drives up the precision of model because more action must be calculated by software.

It is well known that the large airway resistance is a nonlinear function of flow, and that total respiratory resistance depends on tidal volume, and is different on inspiration and expiration, being a continuous function of time during the respiratory cycle. It is a nonlinear phenomenon coupled with the airway collapse mechanism, seen as effort independence of flow for driving pressure exceeding a threshold value. Bernhard Quatember (2003) creates a mathematical nonlinear pressure-flow model with the following characteristic: avoid oversimplification model, airway partition by dynamic relationship, some mechanic parameters variation caused by pathology, and tries to model very precisely the tracheobronchial tree. However, there are still some points should be added in his model: first, airway collapse sometimes plays an important role; second, turbulent characteristic in large bronchi can not be neglected; third, more comprehensive pathology should be taken into account in modelling.

In 1998 Adam G. Polak (1998) has been constructed a complex, nonlinear forward model, including exciting signal and static recoil pressure lung volume descriptions and 132 parameters. In this case, the structural complexity is achieved at the expense of model linearization. It has been shown that lung heterogeneity plays an important role in respiratory system pathology and influences results of lung examinations. Experimental and model studies on the respiratory system demonstrate that heterogeneous constriction of airways accompany asthma and can be a crucial determinant of hyper-responsiveness via an increase in lung impedance.

In 2003 Adam G. Polak presented a computational model to predict maximal expiration through a morphometry-based asymmetrical bronchial tree. A computational model with the Horsfield-like geometry of the airway structure, including wave-speed flow limitation and taking into consideration separate airflows from several independent alveolar compartments has been derived. The airflow values are calculated for quasistatic conditions by solving a system of nonlinear differential equations describing static pressure losses along the airway branches. Then in 2006 he (Polak, 2006) use the nonlinear model to analyze the characteristic of lung mechanical ventilation.

In 2008 Adam G. Polak again investigated a model-based method for flow limitation analysis in the heterogeneous human lung. Flow limitation in the airways is a fundamental process constituting the maximal expiratory flow-volume curve. Its location is referred to as the choke point. In this work, expressions enabling the calculation of critical flows in the case of wave-speed, turbulent or viscous limitation were derived. Then a computational model for the forced expiration from the heterogeneous lung was used to analyse the regime and degree of flow limitation as well as movement and arrangement of the choke points. The conclusion is that flow limitation begins at similar time in every branch of the bronchial tree developing a parallel arrangement of the choke points.

3. Fluid dynamics theory used for respiratory model

3.1 Flow and resistance

Flow (Q) is the movement of air. Flow is dependent on a pressure gradient (Δp) and is inversely related to the resistance to flow (R). This relationship is described in the following equation: $Q = \Delta p / R$. In the lungs, two types of flow are present - laminar flow and turbulent flow. In general, turbulent flow is present in large airways and major bifurcations, whereas laminar flow is present in the more distant airways.
The steady flow is parabolic flow with radius and obtain Poiseuille theorem. In airways governed by laminar flow, resistance is related to the radius (r), airway length (l), and gas viscosity (η) through Poiseuille's Law ($R=8\ \eta l / \pi r^4$). This equation highlights the strong relation of the radius on resistance. The turbulent flow shape is equal in center pipe and flow equation described by Rohrer's equation.
In a normal individual maximal inspiratory flow is limited only by muscle strength and total lung and chest wall compliance. Resistance to flow is minimal and does not limit inspiration. Maximal expiratory flow is initially limited only by expiratory muscle strength (when the airway radius is large and resistance is minimal). However, as the airway lumen decreases, resistance to flow will increase and flow is limited by resistance.
The wave speed theory of flow limitation is derived from fluid mechanics. When airflow approaches the speed of wave propagation within the airway wall, flow will be limited. According to this model, the cross-sectional area of the airway, the compliance of the airway and the resistance upstream from the flow limiting segment all contribute to flow limitation. This theory has been well validated during expiration, when vital capacity is between 0% and 75% of the total lung capacity. At a vital capacity greater than 75% of total lung capacity, it has been difficult to limit flow by increasing pleural pressure in normal individuals. Therefore, traditional teaching indicated that early expiration is primarily limited by effort dependent muscle strength. However, a recent model in normal individuals showed that peak expiratory flow was limited by mechanical properties of the lung (in accordance with the wave speed mechanism), and not by muscle strength (Tantucci, C., 2002). As peak flow normally occurs at around 80% of total lung capacity, the wave speed theory can be used to explain expiratory flow limitation from a vital capacity of 80% and less.

3.2 fluid theorems

A. Generalized Navier-Stokes equation
The basic equation of fluid dynamic is Navier-Stokes equation, as equation (1):

$$X - \frac{1}{\rho}\frac{\partial p}{\partial x} + \nu\nabla^2 u_x = \frac{du_x}{dt} \tag{1}$$

where p is pressure, u_x is velocity vector in x direction, x is body force, ρ is density, ν is kinetic viscosity.
B. Bernoulli energy equation
From classic fluid mechanics we obtain the following energy equation for a respiratory system in a closed loop pipe system with varying diameters

$$z + \frac{p}{\rho g} + \frac{u^2}{2g} = C \tag{2}$$

where z is spatial position, C is a constant value.

C. Conservation of mass

In steady flow, flow is continuous, mass conversation requires that

$$Q_{m1} = Q_{m2},\ Q_{m1} = \rho_1 Q_1 dt \tag{3}$$

Compliance with mass conservation law requires that flow rate in parent vessel must equal the total flow rate in children vessels on each branching level. Assuming that flow rate is constant for individual airway the continuity equation is expressed by

$$Q_0 = Q_1 + Q_2 \tag{4}$$

At a lung bifurcation the flow in the parent vessel Q_0 equals the sum of flow in two children segments Q_1 and Q_2 respectively.

D. Poiseuille theorem

Laminar flow is smooth, with molecules moving in parallel, concentric streams without eddies, and the molecules at the edge of the tube move more slowly than those in the middle. Laminar flow in Newtonian fluids (fluids with constant viscosities) is governed by Poiseuille's law. Poiseuille's law relates the air flow Q [ml/s] through airway with the difference in airway segment pressure at the two ends of vessel segment Δp created by the respiratory muscle, radius r, length L, and viscosity μ of the air:

$$R = \frac{8\mu L}{\pi r^4} \tag{5}$$

The resistance of air through vessels is most strongly dependent on radius, with the fourth power relationship. Because of fluid friction air flow velocity within vessel varies from none in wall proximity to maximum value in the center of the vessel creating parabolic velocity profile. Average velocity (with respect to cross-section) inside air vessel segment is determined as:

$$U_m = \frac{\Delta p * r^2}{8\mu * L} \tag{6}$$

E. Rohrer's equation

When flow rate through a tube reaches a critical velocity, turbulent flow occurs. In turbulent flow, the molecules swirl in eddies and vortices rather than in an orderly way, so that the molecules have a rotational as well as a linear velocity. Irregularities and corners in the tube facilitate turbulence. Conversion from laminar flow to turbulent flow approximately halves the flow for a given pressure drop.

If the flow is in high speed, the composition is altered, or if the internal part of the conduit is modified, the flow will become turbulent, and the equation to describe this phenomenon will be the following second-grad equation, as described by Rohrer (1915):

$$\Delta p = K_1 \times Q + K_2 \times Q^2 \tag{7}$$

where K_1 is the linear coefficient and K_2 is the angular coefficient of the straight line.

F. General pressure loss

The airflow values are calculated for quasistatic conditions by solving a system of nonlinear differential equations describing static result in the semi dynamic maximal expiratory flow-volume (MEFV) curve. This phenomenon has been described by Lambert et al. (1982) using the conservation of momentum (static, incompressible flow case):

$$\frac{dP}{dx} = \frac{-f(x)}{1-S_{ws}^2(x)} = \frac{-f(x)}{1-\frac{\rho q^2}{A^3(x)}\left(\frac{\partial A}{\partial P_{tm}}\right)} \tag{8}$$

Where dp/dx is the gradient of lateral pressure along the bronchus, $S_{ws} = u/c$ is the local speed index equal to the ratio between flow (u) and wave (c) speed, q is the volume flow in the bronchus, ρ denotes gas density, A is the cross sectional area, and $\partial A/\partial P_{tm}$ is the elementary compliance of the airway wall dependent on transmural pressure P_{tm}. The elementary dissipative pressure loss f (pressure drop per unit distance) is described by the following empirical formula (Renolds, D.B., 1982):

$$f(x) = (a + bR_N(x))\frac{8\pi\mu q}{A^2(x)} \tag{9}$$

Where a and b are scaling coefficients, R_N the local Reynolds number and μ is gas viscosity.

4. Anatomical and physiology knowledge of airway and lung

4.1 Physiological characteristic

One of the most important problems in all the respiratory passageways is to keep them open to allow easy passage of the air to and from the alveoli. To keep the trachea from collapsing, multiple cartilage rings extend about five sixths of the way around the trachea. In the walls of the bronchi, less extensive cartilage plates also maintain a reasonable amount of rigidity yet allow sufficient motion for the lungs to expand and contract. These plates become progressively less extensive in the later generations of bronchi and are gone in the bronchioles, which usually have diameters less than 1.5mm (Guyton, 2002). The bronchioles are not prevented from collapsing by the rigidity of their walls. Instead, they are kept expanded by the same transpulmonary pressures that expand the alveoli. That is, as the alveoli enlarge, so do the bronchioles.

Under normal respiratory conditions, air flows through the respiratory passageways so easily that less than 1 cm of water pressure gradient from the alveoli to the atmosphere is sufficient to cause enough airflow for quiet breathing. The normal airway resistance of an adult is 0.1-0.3 kPa.s/L. The greatest amount of resistance to airflow occurs not in the minute air passages (diameter<1.5mm) of the terminal bronchioles but in some of the larger bronchi (diameter>1.5mm) near to the trachea, typically 80% in larger bronchi to 20% in minute passages in health physiology. The reason for this high resistance is that there are relatively few of these larger bronchi in comparison with about 65,000 parallel terminal bronchioles, through each of which only a minute amount of air must pass. Yet in disease conditions, the smaller bronchioles often do play a far greater role in determining airflow resistance, for two reasons: (1) because of their small size, they are easily occluded; and (2) because they have a greater percentage of smooth muscle in the walls, they constrict easily.

4.2 Morphometric model of the lung and the corresponding fluid dynamic

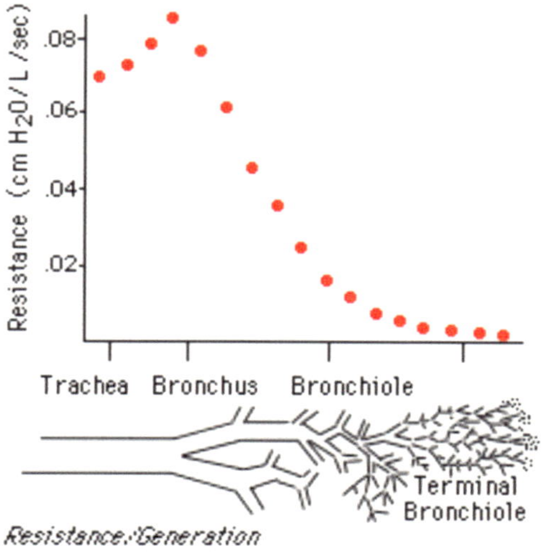

Fig. 1. Typical airway resistance value for every generation

1	2	3	4	5	6	7	8
0.0701	0.0732	0.0788	0.0856	0.0769	0.0620	0.0459	0.0360
9	10	11	12	13	14	15	16
0.0248	0.0161	0.0118	0.0074	0.0056	0.0037	0.0031	0.0025
17							
0.0019							

Table 1. Resistance for passage airway, same value with Fig. 1

The morphometric model used to describe the behavior of the respiratory system is based on the symmetrical model proposed by Weibel (1963). In this model the tracheobronchial tree is divided into 24 generations, where generation 0 is the trachea, generation 1 is extrapulmonary bronchus, generations 2 to 6 are larger intrapulmonary bronchi with cartilage, generations 7 to 16 are bronchioles with smooth muscle, generations 17 to 22 are all respiratory bronchioles, and generation 23 corresponds to alveolar sacs. The airways multiply by regular dichotomy. Starting from the trachea, each branch of a given generation divides into two identical daughters, therefore generation n has 2^n branches. In a spontaneous breathing, normal person, the medium-sized bronchi are the site of greatest resistance (Ball, Wilmot C., 1996), see the data (table 1) and graph (figure 1) of airway resistance.

4.3 Collapsible tube model and flow limitation

Limitation of flow is caused by airway wall collapsing, which follows the drop of transmural pressure (i.e. the difference between internal lateral and external pressure) along a bronchus. There are a few mechanisms influencing the decrease of transmural pressure in quasi-static conditions. The first of them is the loss of pressure due to frictional and turbulent dissipation of gas energy. It entails the drop of internal pressure and then narrowing of an elastic airway. This change in the cross-sectional area of the bronchus forces increase of gas velocity, thus enlargement of the kinetic component of gas energy. This

convective acceleration absorbs a part of potential energy (thus also of lateral pressure), producing additional decrease of transmural pressure. It was theoretically discussed and shown that these two processes can produce flow limitation themselves. Additionally, when flow velocity approaches wave-speed of pressure disturbance propagation along the airway wall, the loss of lateral pressure is strongly amplified, and the airway narrows much quicker than in case of frictional or turbulent dissipation alone. In effect, increasing driving pressure tries to develop faster airflow, but any growth of flow would have produced faster airway collapsing, overcoming the expansion of pressure, and finally, flow remains constant. The wave-speed theory predicts flow over most of vital capacity (V_C, the maximal volume of air that can be expired after deep inspiration), but the other mechanisms may limit flow at low lung volumes.
The wave velocity in fluid-filled collapsible tube is the following equation:

$$c = \left(\frac{A}{\rho} \frac{dp}{dA} \right)^{1/2} \tag{10}$$

where A is the mean cross-sectional area of the tube, p is the transmural pressure in the tube (the inner minus the outer pressure), and ρ the fluid density. The equation crops up in the study of wave propagation in pulmonary passages.
The principal characteristic of pliable, collapsible tubes is that, as the pressure therein changes, so does the cross sectional area. Similarity of Eq. (10) to that for propagation of waves in a compressible gas is evident once it is realized that such waves involve variations in density rather than the cross-sectional area; so, if A is replaced by r, this results in

$$c = (dp/d\rho)^{1/2}$$

An interesting phenomenon arising in collapsible tubes with internal flow is that of flow limitation. As the upstream pressure p_1 is increased relative to the downstream one p_2, thus as $p_{1-2} = p_1 - p_2$ is increased, there exists a limit in the flow-rate Q; if p_{1-2} is increased further, no further increase in Q is possible. This, obviously, is very counter-intuitive from the point of view of rigid-pipe hydraulics.

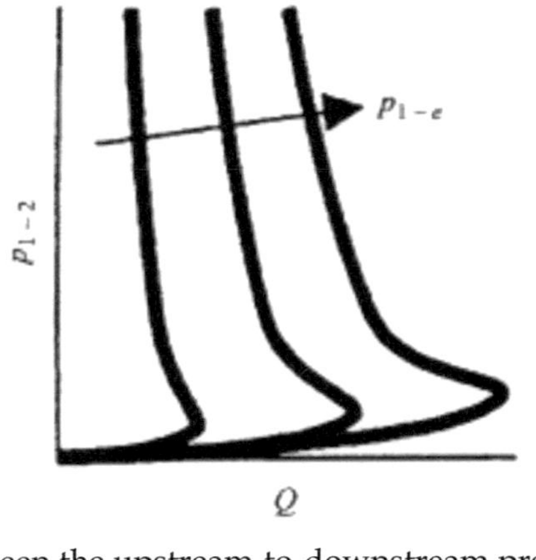

Fig. 2. The relationship between the upstream-to-downstream pressure difference p_{1-2} in a collapsible tube conveying fluid

As seen in Fig. 2, obtained from experimental measurements by Bertram (1995), for a constant transmural pressure at the upstream end of the tube, denoted by p_{1-e} (e standing for external), and varying p_{2-e}, as p_{1-2} increases there is a limit for Q, a maximum value; three such cases are shown in the figure for three different values of p_{1-e}. In fact, the flow rate decreases somewhat with increasing p_{1-2} beyond that yielding the maximum Q. This corresponds to the so-called "negative effort dependency" in maximal flow expiration. In an appealing analogy, flow limitation is likened to flow over a waterfall, where the flow-rate is independent of the level of the downstream reservoir. One of the mechanisms associated with flow limitation in collapsible tubes is the so-called wave-speed mechanism, with strong analogy to gas dynamics. One may calculate

$$\frac{dQ}{dp} = \frac{A}{\rho U}\left(1 - \frac{U^2}{c^2}\right) \tag{11}$$

where Q is the volumetric flow-rate in the collapsible tube, p the transmural pressure, A the cross-sectional area, U the flow velocity corresponding to any particular A (both A and U vary along the tube), and c the wave speed as in Eq. (10).
It is obvious that as

$$\frac{U}{c} \to 1$$

There is a discontinuity associated with a maximum flow rate in the collapsible tube. This is also associated with so-called elastic jumps. Thus, in all this, the analogy to choked flow and shock waves in gas dynamics is quite strong.

4.4 Airway segment based on different fluid dynamic performance

Based on anatomical structure the entire respiratory system (including airway and lung) can be divided into two zones: conductive zone (generation 0 to 16) and respiratory zone (generation 17 to 23). In conductive zone the airway resistance is the main effective factor. At the same time in respiratory zone the compliance is the dominant parameter. The last 7 generations (respiratory zone) are modeled as a single viscoelastic element with constant values; chest wall is combined in lung compliance value.

A. Thoracic cage and respiratory muscles

The lung and airways were assumed to be enclosed within a rigid-walled thoracic cage, with the airways open to the atmosphere. The intrapleural space was assumed to be subject to a time-varying, spatially averaged driving intrapleural pressure $[P_{pl}(t)]$, which was assumed to be equivalent to the average pressure in the pleural space acting on the lungs and produced by the muscles of respiration. Excursion in P_{pl} was dictated by the effort generated by the subject.

B. Alveolar region

Alveolar region (of volume V_A) was assumed to exhibit nonlinear, time-varying viscoelastic behavior. Static elastic behavior of the lung ($P_{el} vs. V_A$) was described by a hysteretic pressure-volume (P-V) relationship. The extent of hysteresis in P_{el} was presumed to be a function of breathing effort, which, in turn, was assumed to be proportional to P_{pl} (reflecting muscular effort). Hence, the dependence of P_{el} on P_{pl} served to define the well-known hysteretic path. Viscous dissipative characteristics exhibited by lung tissue were characterized by using a constant lung tissue resistance R_L.

C. Peripheral airways

Peripheral airways were characterized by a resistance (R_s) that was inversely proportional to V_A. Airway closure during forced expiration causes occlusion of these airways at low alveolar volumes. Because of the effect of large intrathoracic pressures generated during the effort-dependent portion of forced expiration, R_s was modified to be a function of both V_A and P_{pl}.

D. Collapsible airways region

Collapsible airway region (of volume V_c) was characterized in terms of a volume-dependent resistance and a volume-pressure relationship $(V_C - P_{tm})$. The functional importance of this collapsible segment has since been confirmed by analyze the input impedance spectrum vs. frequency and demonstrated that adequate reconstruction of pressure-flow data could not be achieved with a conventional single-compartment resistive-compliant model. Previous studies have demonstrated that in lumped models expiratory flow limitation during the FVC maneuver cannot be simulated without the presence of this collapsible segment. Verbraak et al. (1991) modeled the elastic properties of the compressible segment as a family of curves dependent on the lung elastic recoil. This more complex approach proved to be of little benefit in achieving good fits to subject data.

E. Upper airway region

Upper airway region (of volume V_D) was assumed to be rigid, with its resistance to airflow characterized by a nonlinear, flow-dependent Rohrer resistor.

Summarized from fluid dynamic analysis the conductive zone can be segmented into two parts, i.e., the larger airway and the small airway, which have different flow behaviors. For lung simulator aim we segment the airway by fluid dynamic performance of different generations. Existed analysis (Polak, 2006) reveals three sections of the bronchial tree with distinct resistive properties. Generations 0–6 are characterized mainly by turbulent dissipation of the head pressure, laminar flow and airways collapsing dominate in generations from 7 to 16 (Mauroy, 2004), and lastly, flow in generations from 17 to 23 is approximately laminar, where compliance, not resistance, is the main parameter.

4.5 Different pathology and segments they influenced

The respiratory ventilation functional obstruction can be divided into two main types: restrictive hypoventilation and obstructive hypoventilation. The restrictive hypoventilation is mainly cause by two factors: respiratory muscle activation decrease and compliance decrease of lung. The disease such as fibrosis, pneumothorax, pulmonary overventilation, lung edema, can cause compliance decrease. In simulation model, the muscle decrease can be simulated by muscle driven pressure, and the aforementioned lung diseases have influence on lung compliance. The obstructive hypoventilation is mainly caused by airway stricture or obstacle. The disease typically emphysematous, asthmatic lung and larger airway occluded are obstructive.

The obstructive hypoventilation can also be divided into two types: central airway obstacle and peripheral airway obstacle. The central airway obstacle can further divided into extrapleural and intrapleural obstacle. The extrapleural obstacle locate in trachea and main bronchi which extrapleural, correspond to generations 0 and 1. The extrapleural obstacle shows inspiration difficult. The intrapleural central airway obstacle locate in bronchi

intrapleural and is expiration difficult. To show this different localization obstacle, we must subdivide the upper airway into two segments: the extrapleural segment and intrapleural segment which have different symptom in respiratory disorders.
For the purpose of modeling, the pulmonary system has to be simplified to elements which represent specific physical features of the lung. The lung model was restricted to serial inhomogeneity with respect to both resistance and elastic properties of the airways. The currently prepared mathematical model is based on serial model consists of one alveolar compartment connected to ambient air by a tube representing the airways. All alveoli were lumped to one compartment V_A, which was connected to ambient air by a tube representing the lumped airways. This tube consisted of four parts in series: one for the small airways, a compressible segment in between, one for the large airways intrapleural, and the last one for large airways extrapleural. The alveolar compartment and the intrapulmonary airways were influenced by the intrathoracic pressure, which was equal to pleural pressure P_{pl}. In preliminary result, the serial model of lung can be schemed in figure 3.

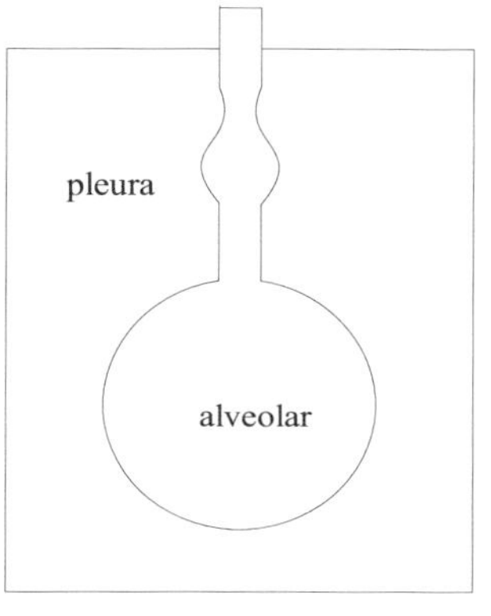

Fig. 3. Serial lung model with airway segment

5. Respiratory model with different complication

5.1 Simple linear model

There are many models describe breathing movement with different complication. It is possible to construct a model with a single volume-elastic unit and a single flow-resistance unit (e.g. a rubber bellows connected to a glass tube) which conforms mechanically to simple linear model.
The simplest and fundamental model consisting of a volume-elastic part having a compliance C and a resistance R in series. These equations are analogous to equations which define electrical capacitance and electrical resistance, respectively. If the total pressure across the system at any moment is Δp , then

$$\Delta p = \frac{1}{C} V + RQ \tag{12}$$

Since the compliance and resistance of a single pathway are constants, the total pressure will be determined at any instant by the volume of the unit and the rate and direction of flow at that instant.

Recent studies have shown that this first-order model is, however, an oversimplified representation of nonlinear, multicompartment respiratory mechanics. In fact, it is well known that the large airway resistance is a nonlinear function of flow, and that total respiratory resistance depends on tidal volume, and is different on inspiration and expiration, being a continuous function of time during the respiratory cycle. Parameter estimates based on the first-order model, therefore, do not depend solely on patient condition but also on experimental condition, because the model involves linearization around the working point.

5.2 Complicated compliance nonlinear model

The numerically simulated model features a two component resistance, representing the series association of a linear resistor with a flow-dependent resistor. The latter models nonlinear tracheal tube characteristics, and the former lumps the linear part of the tracheal tube resistance together with the equivalent linear resistor of the respiratory system. The model of elastance was proposed with a volume-independent and a volume-dependent component. The equation of motion that represents this model is:

$$P_{aw} = \left(K_1 + K_2\left|Q(t)\right|\right)Q(t) + \left(E_1 + E_2V(t)\right)V(t) + P_0 \tag{13}$$

where Paw(t) is the pressure measured at the airway opening at time t, Q(t) the flow, V(t) the volume and P0the constant.

The basic model values used in this work ($E_1 = 50cmH_2OL^{-1}$, $E_2 = -80cmH_2OL^{-2}$, $K_1 = 10cmH_2OL^{-1}s$, $K_2 = 5cmH_2OL^{-2}s^2$) lie within the range observed in data obtained from animal experiments described elsewhere (Jandre et al., 2004). The negative E_2 suggests alveolar recruitment throughout the respiratory cycle.

5.3 Nonlinear simulation model of breathing mechanics with airway segment

In this model, the viscoelastic properties of the tracheobronchial airways are characterized by nonlinear relationships, whereas the behavior of the alveolar space and chest wall are assumed to be linear. The airway behavior is described by a physiological representation, incorporating a mechanism causing expiratory flow limitation, which has proved useful for the clinical interpretation of lung function tests and for describing the dependence of total respiratory resistance on frequency and tidal volume, in line with experimental evidence. Airway resistance was divided into the following three components:

1. upper airway resistance, R_u, modeled by a nonlinear Rohrer resistor depending on flow:

   $$R_u = K_1 + K_2\left|Q\right| \tag{14}$$

   where the constant K_1 represents resistive properties for laminar flow, and the constant K_2characterizes an additional resistive term, significant at higher flow rates when turbulence may occur;
2. intermediate airway resistance R_i, depending on the airway compression due to transmural pressure. This segment was modeled as a cylinder of constant length, the radius and hence volume (v_c) of which vary with transmural pressure. On the basis of Poiseuille's law, the corresponding resistance is described by

   $$R_i = K_3\left(\frac{v_{c\max}}{v_c}\right)^2 \tag{15}$$

where the constant K_3 represents the value of R_i when airway volume reaches its maximum admissible value v_{cmax}; and

3. lower airway resistance R_i , depending on lung volume (v). Since R_i decreases with increasing lung volume, it was described by the following relationship:

$$R_l = \frac{K_4}{v} \tag{16}$$

Where K_4 is a positive constant.

On the basis of experimental data the elastic characteristic of the intermediate airway segment is approximated by the relationship:

$$\frac{v_c}{v_{c\max}} = \frac{1}{1+\exp\left[-a\left(p_{tm}-b\right)\right]} \tag{17}$$

where a and b are constants and P_{tm} is the transmural pressure. Differentiating v_c with respect to p_{tm}, we obtain the intermediate airway compliance C_{aw}.

Finally, since this chapter is aimed at establishing respiratory model have the nonlinear mechanical properties of the tracheobronchial airways, the alveolar space and chest wall were assumed to have a constant, purely elastic behavior and were represented by the constant elastance respectively.

6. Simulation method

6.1 General description

LabVIEW and Matlab are the two main programs used widely by engineer. LabVIEW is a well opened virtual instruments platform and widely used in automatic control and measuring technology. LabVIEW simplify development procedure of process control and testing software. Now, LabVIEW has become the main trend of measuring and testing technologies and instruments. With the strong hardware interface capability, LabVIEW can communicate with other hardware and acquire data easily. But LabVIEW has limited toolboxes which confine the using field to large application program, in the case of complex applications having large data processing and complicate control algorithm, LabVIEW is not competent. Conversely, Matlab has very strong computing functions and stable algorithm library. Matlab provides precision and high efficiency toolboxes in almost all engineering computing fields. But it is not proficiency for interface compile. And data input, net communication, hardware control are also shortcoming of matlab. Because the two languages have complimentary specialties, we can combine the advantage by mixture programming. The data collected by LabVIEW can be sending to matlab for computing, and then processed data transfer back to LabVIEW for output control and display. Calling matlab in LabVIEW can control hardware easily and realize complex algorithm concurrently.

The Simulation Interface Toolkit provides methods for creating a LabVIEW user interface for a Simulink model, converting a Simulink model into a dynamic link library (DLL), and running a simulation model on an RT target. By combining the capabilities of Simulink and Real-Time Workshop with LabVIEW, the Simulation Interface Toolkit helps you import simulation models into LabVIEW.

6.2 Simplest model simulation

There are two distinct approaches to generating the simulated respiratory movement. The first is a simulation script and another one is model-driven simulation. The state-of-the-art medical patient simulator is physiological model driven simulator, so generating suitable physiological signal is the key task of medical patient simulator.

In order to describe the spontaneous respiratory model fundamentality in a simple and direct way, the following principles are adopted: structure of respiratory system is described by the simplest model, i.e., only lung compliance (C) and airway resistance (R) are taken into consideration; respiratory muscle pressure is used as input of model. With the above hypothesis, the constructed model can reflect the basic characteristic in general.

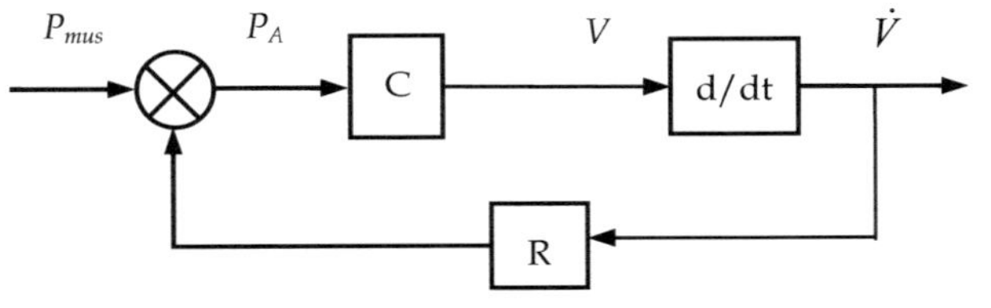

Fig. 4. Respiratory model based on muscle pressure driven

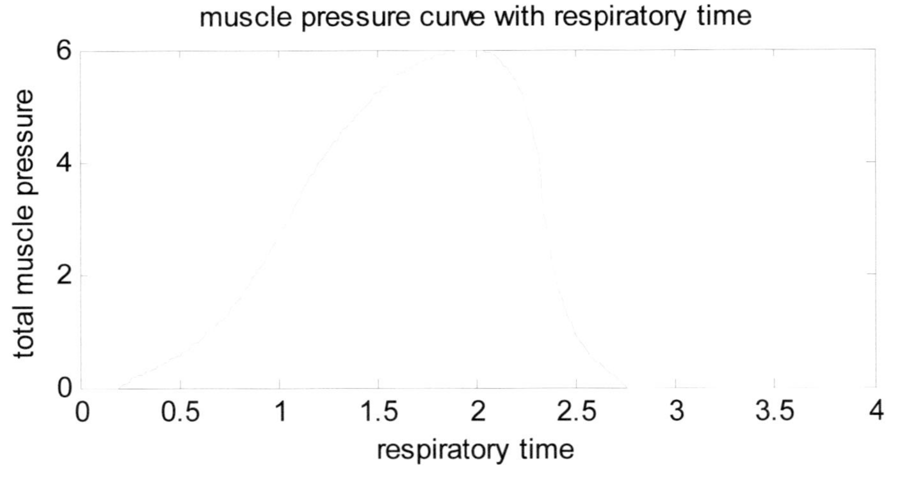

Fig. 5. Pressure waveform generated by respiratory muscle

The simplest mathematical model of respiratory system is linear model:

$$P_{mus} = \frac{1}{C}V(t) + R\dot{V}(t) \tag{12}$$

Which P_{mus} is respiratory pressure, generated by respiratory muscle, C is compliance, R is airway resistance, $V(t)$ is air volume breathed in lung, $\dot{V}(t)$ is air flow of respiratory, being the derivative of volume to time. In the model the compressibility of air is neglected as usual. There are two basic parameters in describing the respiratory system: compliance C and airway resistance R. Based on the linear model described above, the simplest respiratory model we established is shown in figure 4. The merits of the model are listed on the following: (1) simple model, most details are neglected; (2) from distinct principle, spontaneous respiratory can be concluded from the model; (3) extensive expansibility, every component can be complicated if needed, so that complexity of model's study can be selected as requirement.

The parameters of R and C in model can be selected as normal human; while the respiratory muscle pressure can be acquired precisely from the data of Jodat et al.(1966) image processing, as shown in figure 5. In Simulink the muscle pressure used as input, the breath mechanical parameters (*R* and *C*) is the linear response system, then the spontaneous respiratory waveform can be computed.

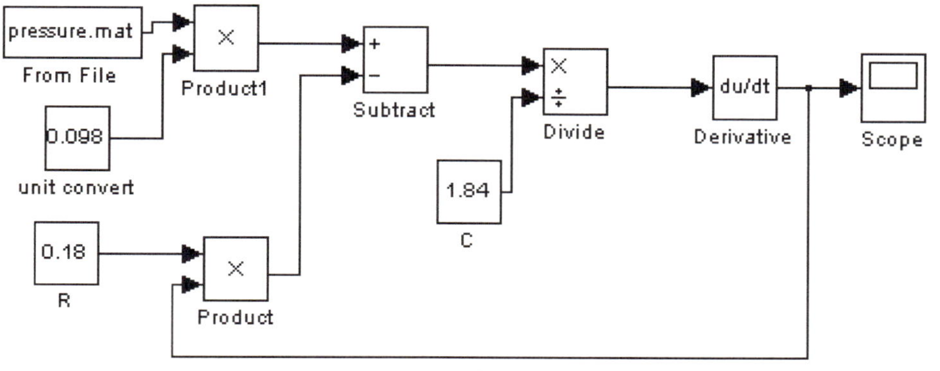

Fig. 6. Spontaneous respiratory model simulated by Simulink

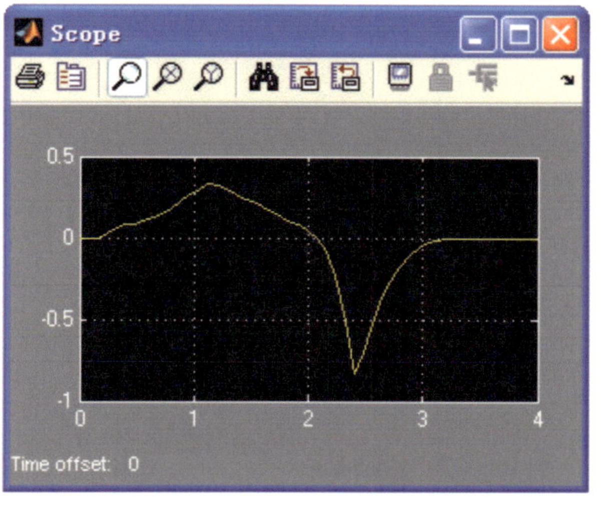

Fig. 7. Respiratory flow waveform by muscle pressure driven using Simulink

Typical parameters of human respiratory system is used in simulation, parameters being R=0.18kPa.s/L, C=1.84L/kPa (Tang, 1995). Particular Simulink model is shown in figure 6, and the simulation result shown in figure 7.

Compared with the respiratory flow given in reference (Bachy, 1986), it can be concluded that the two flow waves are very similar. They both have smooth inspiratory flow wave and rather sharp expiratory flow wave, but have the same volume in the two breath phase. The expiratory flow is originate from the relax of breath muscle, together with the delay of respiratory system to airflow. The two main facts make the expiratory flow being a sharp flow at the beginning and then a long time without airflow. Change the parameters of respiratory system, the shape of flow variate, and so is the frequency spectrum of flow waveform, which is in accordance with Benchetrit's (2000) conclusion. Because respiratory pressure waveform is not single frequency sine wave, change the pressure waveform will change the frequency spectrum of respiratory flow wave too, so pressure waveform generated by respiratory muscle is an influence factor to flow frequency spectrum. The frequency of the breath system can also be changed by variation of the mechanical parameters, which is similar to one-order RC circuit. The linear system can not create the non-existing frequency, however, the input (muscle pressure) of the linear system (breath system) the muscle pressure contain abundant frequency, as a result the output (airflow) also include harmonic frequency. Once the input and mechanical parameters do not change abruptly, the output will remain a suitable stable frequency content.

6.3 Adjustable respiratory mechanical parameters lung system

In our simulation, all mechanical parameters of the lungs (pressure, compliance, resistance, volume) can be reduced to airflow, which is the most important variable to be measured in clinical. We design a new approach to simulate the lung system, which has the following characteristics. First, the basic hardware structure of the lung is similar to Meka's (2004). Second, breath flow is tracked in stead of carinal pressure, which is the most important parameter in respiration and calculated by respiratory model. Third, the resistance and compliance are adjustable in the simulation model. The influence of the two facts, i.e., compliance (C) and resistance (R), to the breath can be observed distinctly in our model. Four, the entire system is small size as the advantage of bellows-less lung simulator.

Current simulator models the flow in and out the lung to simulate physically character of respiratory system. We design the lung simulator based on the breath principle. This paper construct normal human respiratory system model, combined the widely used respiratory model and muscle pressure driven power. Then the breath flow wave is tracked by proportional valve controlled by calculated output voltage.

There are two main methods for simulation that are widely used, one is Simulink in matlab, and another is control design and simulation module in LabVIEW. Compared with matlab, LabVIEW not only easy to realize parameter collection and control parameter output, but also convenient to realize in hardware. As to Simulink in matlab, after the realization on algorithm, it is usually needed to transform to C language in order to combine with hardware, compile language is necessary sometimes. We have done the simulation in Simulink (He, 2009(a)), and we met the foregoing difficulty, i.e., how to realize the algorithm on hardware. In this chapter, we give the simulation method based on LabVIEW. Because of different simulation way between the two programs, different models are used base on same principle.

Not similar to the Simulink model, the convenient way to construct the respiratory model in Control Design and Simulation module in LabVIEW is to use linear system theory. An electro-acoustic analogy (Ma, 1983) is used to develop an electric model of the respiratory system in despite of its exact anatomical structure. In order to describe the spontaneous respiratory model fundamentality in a simple and direct way, the following principles are

adopted: structure of respiratory system is described by the simplest model, i.e., only lung compliance (C) and airway resistance (R) are taken into consideration; respiratory muscle pressure data is used as input of model into the linear system; transfer function is generated by first-order RC circuits. With the above hypothesis, the constructed model can reflect the basic characteristic in general. Then the output is calculated by linear system theory and realized in LabVIEW by CD linear simulation.vi located in Control Design and Simulation module. The final output represents the volume variation of every breath. After differentiate the volume, respiratory flow is gained that can be traced by hardware.
The simplest mathematical model of respiratory system is linear model (Otis, 1956):

$$P_{mus} = \frac{1}{C}V(t) + R\dot{V}(t) \tag{12}$$

Then the transfer function of volume of compliance can be calculated as

$$F(S) = \frac{1}{RCS+1} \tag{18}$$

Which P_{mus} is respiratory pressure, generated by respiratory muscle, C is compliance, R is airway resistance, V(t) is air volume breathed in lung, $\dot{V}(t)$ is air flow of respiratory, being the derivative of volume to time. In the model the compressibility of air is neglected as usual.
Typical parameters of human respiratory system is used in simulation, parameters being R=0.18kPa.s/L, C=1.84L/kPa (Tang, 1995). The related LabVIEW program is shown in figure 8, and the simulation result shown in figure 9.
Compared with the respiratory flow given in (Bachy, 1986), it can be concluded that the two flow waves are very similar. Change the parameters of respiratory system, the shape of flow change, and so is the frequency spectrum of flow waveform, which is in accordance with Benchetrit's (2000) conclusion. Because respiratory pressure waveform is not simple sine wave, changing the pressure waveform will change the frequency spectrum of respiratory flow wave too, so pressure waveform generated by respiratory muscle is an influence factor to flow frequency spectrum.

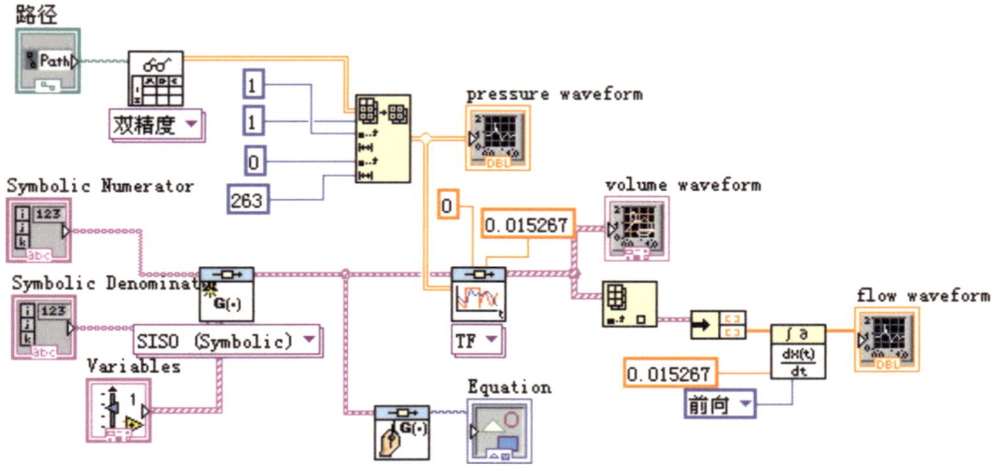

Fig. 8. Block diagram of respiratory simulation using transfer

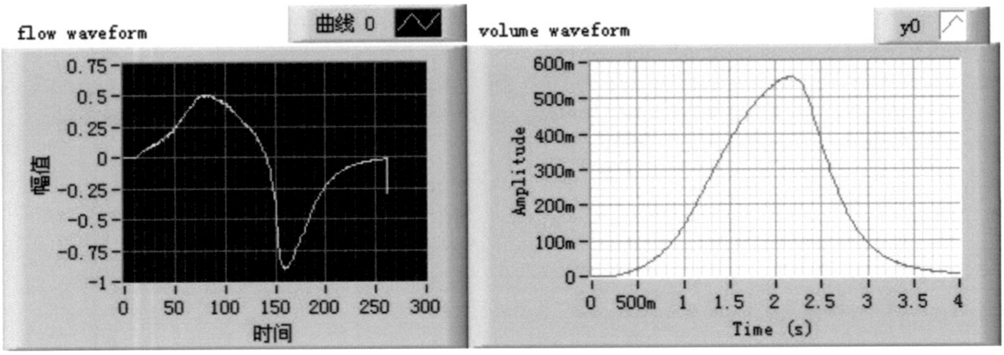

(a) (b)

Fig. 9. The simulation results calculated by transfer function of the respiratory
(a) flow waveform of one breath cycle (b) volume curve of one breath cycle

We used a fixed volume flow controller to generate the required airway flow. The flow controller is based on the ideal gas law. Air compression is neglected in this model, which is common practice. Flow is generated inside a fixed volume at a constant temperature by adjustment of the orifice of proportional valves. In flow is generated when gas is pumped into the fixed volume, and likewise out flow is generated when gas is removed from the volume. The airway resistor was constructed in the direction of Mecklenburgh (1988). The flow system consists of a fixed-volume vessel (FVV), a positive pressure source, a negative pressure source, two proportional flow valves (PFV), a flow sensor, a computer with data acquisition card. The entire setup is illustrated in Fig.10. The two pressure sources are implemented by air pump and vacuum respectively.

The fixed-volume vessel is a cylindrical-shaped polyvinyl chloride (PVC) structure. The cylindrical shape reduces turbulent gas flow inside the container, and the PVC material allows for inexpensive, quick and easy assembly of the structure. The vessel has three openings to allow the flow of gas in and out of the FVV to simulate ventilation. The outlet also facilitates the fitting of standard clinical airway resistors. The vessel is sealed airtight using PVC cement to prevent any air leaks from the container.

The volume of the FVV was determined experimentally by measuring the flow rate for various vessel volumes. The size of the volume was chosen to balance time delay and controllability. Time delay increases for larger vessels, because the vessel needs to fill completely before the flow starts to rise. Controllability is affected mainly by the volume of the vessel. It is easier to control the flow in a larger vessel, because compressibility of gas increases the total vessel compliance. It is difficult to control the flow in a very stiff vessel, because a small addition of volume increases the flow rapidly. With the available materials, a volume of 0.64 l was realized.

Two proportional flow control valves (IQ valves co., P/N: 209090) were used for control flow in and out of FVV. Pulse width modulated (PWM) solenoid valve drivers (Burr-Brown Company, DRV101) were used to run the proportional flow valves. An added advantage of the PWM waveform was that it reduced valve magnetic hysteresis and minimized power loss and component overheating at high current levels. The duty cycle of the pulse width determined the amount of power delivered to the valve. A 16-bit DAQ card (NI, PCI-6221M, with 16 analog inputs and 2 analog outputs, all in 16-bits resolution) supplied the signal to adjust the duty cycle of the pulse width.

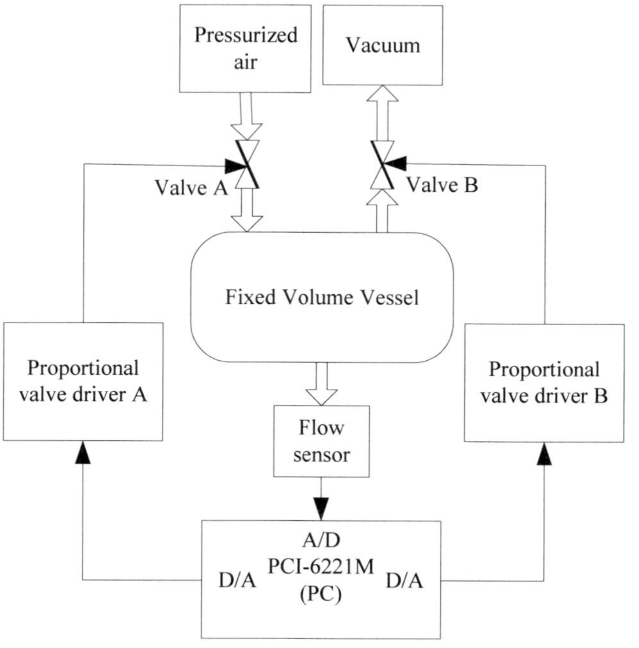

Fig. 10. Block diagram implementation of flow track design. Solid arrow lines illustrate electrical signal, hollow arrow lines illustrate airflow

A flow sensor (Honeywell, AWM5104) that outputs an analogue signal proportionally scaled to the applied flow was used to sample the flow of mouth. The analogue flow signal is conditioned and low-pass filtered using a 2nd-order digital Butterworth filter with a 50 Hz cutoff frequency to remove high-frequency noise due to turbulent flow inside the FVV. The analogue flow pressure signal was sampled with a 16-bit ADC, i.e., analog input in PCI-6221M.

There are many methods for the PID adjusting. The PID parameters were selected based on the extended step response curve methods. The steps for the PID parameters adjustment were as following:

1. digital controller does not worked in system, the process variable of controlling object was adjusted to the values near setpoint. The variable values were stabilized, and then unit step response curve was measured.
2. a tangent at inflexion in response curve is located. Delayed time τ and time constant T_m and ratio of the two parameters T_m/τ were calculated.
3. controlling degree was selected.
4. parameters T, K_p, T_i and T_d were calculated based on table (Gao, 2007).

The final parameters we selected were listed: P=3, I=0.8, D=0. The controller can be more efficient if adaptive-tuning scheme based on adaptive signal processing techniques was implemented to tune automatically.

Tracking result was shown in figure 11. It can be concluded that in the normal breath pattern the practical flow was very much alike to the theoretical flow curve. More details are to be exploited in future. And more pathology breath options should be studied to get a more complicated understanding to the flow tracking method.

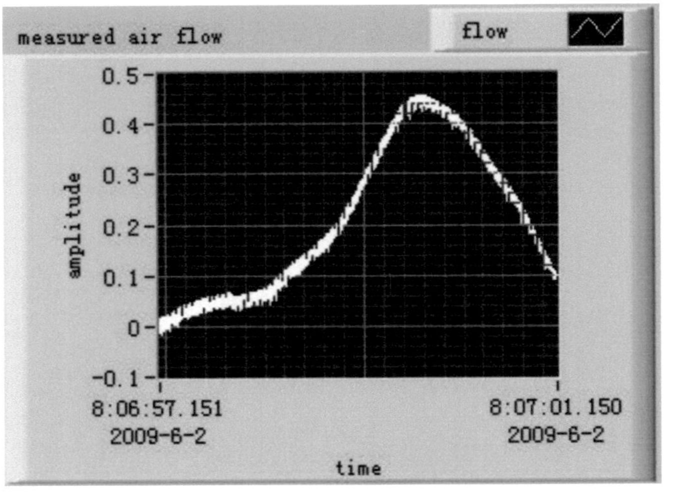

Fig. 11. Measured flow waveform by flow tracking algorithm using PID, which is very similar to the calculated wave.

6.4 Simulation of spontaneous respiration nonlinear model

There are two methods that we can use to simulate the respiratory system. First, simulink toolkits in matlab are the commonly used tool for simulation. But the simulink can not interface control system real-time, although it is powerful in model simulation. Second, the control design and simulation module in LabVIEW can also be used. On advantage of LabVIEW's interface convenience, the model design by control design and simulation module can be used in real actuator control very easy. But the disadvantage of the module is it can not design model by block. If the model is somewhat complicate, the control design and simulation module will become powerless. Fortunately, the National Instruments Company realize the problem, they provide a tool, i.e., simulation interface toolkits, used to transform Simulink model to LabVIEW program. Combine the advantage of powerful model construction of simulink and interface convenience with peripheral actuator of LabVIEW and the bridge tool simulation interface toolkits (SIT), we design a program based on LabVIEW with SIT interface with simulation model generated by simulink. The program can control actuator and designs the simulation model complicate, which take advantage while eliminate disadvantage of the two languages.

The equation of motion that represents the nonlinear model is (Jandre, 2005):

$$P = \left(K_1 + K_2\left|\dot{V}(t)\right|\right)\dot{V}(t) + E \cdot V(t) \tag{19}$$

The respiratory muscle pressure data from Jodat (1966) is used as input of model. We construct the nonlinear model of breath system using simulink, the following block in Fig. 12 being the model, parameters were selected from Tang (1995). The LabVIEW 8.6 and SIT 5.0 is used in the main program, DAQ is configured to output signal with PCI-6221M card equipped. The calculated flow wave is to be tracked by proportional flow valve. Fig.13 is part of front panel when SIT is used interface with simulink. Fig.14 is the simulated flow using the aforementioned simulation condition: respiratory muscle used as input, nonlinear parameter of resistance that flow-dependent is used, and compliance is fix number.

Compared with the flow wave generated with fixed resistance (He, 2009(b)), the inspiratory flow part has little change, but the expiratory flow parts are smoother. In general, the flow is more similar to the real curve. We have tried the two foregoing methods both respectively (He, 2009(a, b)). But we can not realize the simulation construction and output simulated result by one program. If the model is simple, the control design and simulation module in LabVIEW can competent for the task, as we have done in previous work. With the complicate of respiratory model, by practice, we conclude that the combination of simulink and LabVIEW bridged by simulation interface toolkits is the optimum option.

There are three main key points in the chapter: (1) the respiratory muscle pressure is used as system input, which is accorded with spontaneous breath principle; (2) respiratory model is more complicated and precise with resistance flow-dependent parameterized, and the computed flow is even similar to real breath; (3) LabVIEW is used as the main program to interface with peripheral equipment, simulink is used as model construction program to cope with model complication, SIT is used to bridge the two program efficiently. The mentioned program method should be the optimum solution by our practice.

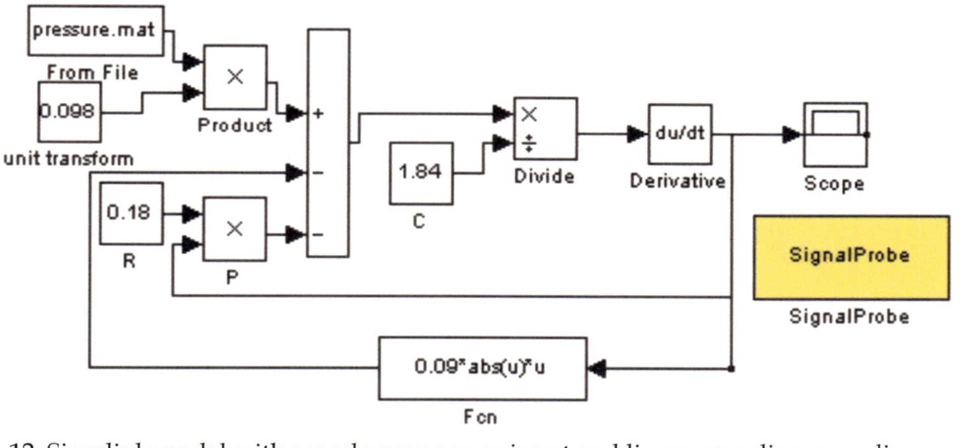

Fig. 12. Simulink model with muscle pressure as input and linear compliance nonlinear resistance varied with flow

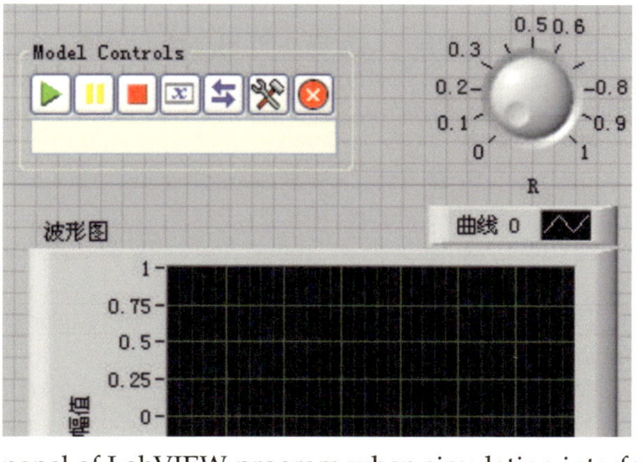

Fig. 13. Part of front panel of LabVIEW program when simulation interface toolkits are used to embed simulink mode

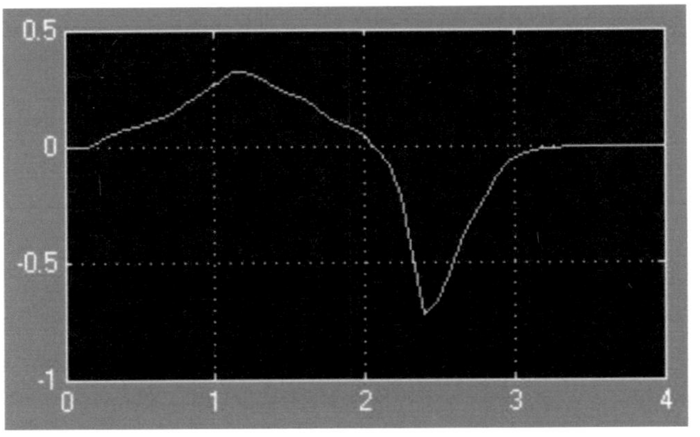

Fig.14. Simulation result of flow using muscle pressure as input and nonlinear airway resistance

7. Conclusion

In this chapter, respiratory model is studies including simple model and complicated nonlinear model. The realize method is introduced that have can control output flow. Two main simulate way, i.e., simulink and LabVIEW, are used to model the respiratory movement. The combined method that can integrate the advantage of the two method is illustrated for control aim. In general, this chapter provide a through introduction for respiratory modelling and control design.

8. References

Bachy, Jean-pierre, Eberhard, A., Baconnier, P. and Benchetrit, G. (1986). A program for cycle-by-cycle shape analysis of biological rhythms. Application to respiratory rhythm. Computer methods and programs in biomedicine, Vol. 23, 297-307.

Ball, W. C. (1996). Interactive respiratory physiology, John Hopkins School of Medicine, http://oac.med.jhmi.edu/res_phys/Encyclopedia/AirwayResistance/AirwayResistance.HTML

Barkalow, C. E., Morsley, K. C., (1974). Pneumatic lung analog. US Patent, 3808706.

Barkalow (1984). Pneumatic lung analog for simulation of spontaneous breathing and for testing of ventilatory devices used with spontaneously breathing patients. US Patent, 4430893.

Bayliss, L. and Robertson, G. (1939). The visco-elastic properties of the lungs. Quarterly journal of experimental physiology. Vol. 29, 27-47.

Benchetrit, G. (2000). Breathing pattern in humans: diversity and individuality. Respiration physiology, Vol. 122, 124-129.

Bertram, C.D. (1995). The dynamics of collapsible tubes. In: Ellington, C.P., Pedley, T.J. (Eds.), Biological fluid dynamics, 253-264.

Gao, Jinyuan, Xia, Jie (2007). Computer control systems. Tsinghua university press, Beijing.

Grinnan, D. C. and Truwit, J. D. (2005). Clinical review: Respiratory mechanics in spontaneous and assisted ventilation. Critical Care, Vol. 9, No.5, 472-484.

Guyton, Authur C., Hall, John E. (2002). Textbook of medical physiology (tenth edition). Beijing medical university press, Beijing.

He, Zhonghai (2009, a). Simulation study on human respiratory system based on muscle pressure driven. International conference on engineering computation. Hong Kong: IEEE computer society, 33-35.

He, Zhonghai, Shan, Fang, Sun, Meirong (2009, b). Adjustable parameters respiratory flow generation simulation method realized by LabVIEW. Third international symposium on intelligent information technology application, Nanchang, IEEE computer society, 299-301.

Jandre, F. C., Carvalho, A. R. S., Pino, A. V., Antonio G. (2005). Effects of filtering and delays on the estimates of a nonlinear respiratory mechanics model. Respiratory Physiology & Neurobiology, Vol. 148, 309–314.

Jandre, F., Pino, A., Lacorte, I., Soares, J., Giannella-Neto, A. (2004). A closed-loop mechanical ventilation controller with explicit objective functions. IEEE transactions on biomedical engineering, Vol. 51, 823-831.

Jansen, J. R. C., Hoorn, E., Goudoever, J., and Versprille, A. (1989). A computerized respiratory system including test functions of lung and circulation. Journal of applied physiology, Vol. 67, No. 4, 1687-1691.

Jodat, R. W., Horgen, J. D., and Lange, R. L. (1966). Simulation of respiratory mechanics. Biophysical journal, Vol. 6, 773-785.

Lambert, R. K., Wilson, T. A., Hyatt, R. E., and Rodarte, J. R. (1982). A computational model for expiratory flow. Journal of applied physiology, Vol. 52, No. 1, 44-56.

Ma, Dayou, Shen, Hao (1983). Acoustics handbook. Beijing, China: Science press.

Mauroy, B., Filoche, M., Weibel, E. R., Sapoval, B. (2004). An optimal bronchial tree may be dangerous. Nature, Vol. 427, 633-636.

Mecklenburgh, J. S. (1988). Construction of linear resistance units for a model lung. Medical & Biological Engineering & Computing, Vol. 26, 552-554.

Meka, V. V., van Oostrom, J. H. (2004). Bellow-less lung system for the human patient simulator. Medical & Biological engineering & computing, Vol. 42, 413-418.

Meyer, M. (1983). A versatile hydraulically operated respiratory servo system for ventilation and lung function testing. Journal of applied physiology, Vol.55, 1023-1030.

Myojo, T. (1989). Breathing pattern simulation using slit/cam valve. American industrial hygiene association journal, Vol.50, No.5, 240-244.

Otis, Arthur B., McKerrow, Colin B., Bartlett, Richard A., Mead, Jere et al. (1956). Mechanical factors in distribution of pulmonary ventilation. Journal of applied physiology, Vol.8, No. 4, 427-443.

Polak, Adam G. (1998). A forward model for maximum expiration [J]. Computers in biology and medicine, Vol.28, 613-625.

Polak, Adam G. (2003). Computational model for forced expiration from asymmetric normal lungs. Annals of biomedical engineering, Vol. 31, 891-907.

Polak, Adam G., Mroczka, J. (2006). Nonlinear model for mechanical ventilation of human lungs. Computers in biology and medicine, Vol. 36, 41-58.

Polak, Adam G.. (2008). A model-based method for limitation analysis in the heterogeneous human lung. Computer methods and programs in biomedicine, Vol. 89, 123-131.

Quatember, B. (2003). Human respiratory system: simulation of breathing mechanics and gas mixing processes based on a non-linear mathematical model. International

conference on health sciences simulation, University of Innsbruck, Innsbruck, Austria.
Renolds, D.B. (1982). Steady expiratory flow-pressure relationship of a model of the human bronchial tree, Journal of biomechanical engineering , Vol. 104, 153-158.
Rohrer F (1915). Flow resistance in human air passages and the effect of irregular branching of the bronchial system on the respiratory process in various regions of the lungs. Arch. Ges. Physiol, Vol. 162, 225-229.
Tang Yuansheng, Zhang Xiuzhen, Han diancun (1995). Parameters and concept of human medical. Jinan publishing house, Jinan.
Tantucci, C., Duguet, A., Giampiccolo, P., Similowski, T., Zelter, M., Derenne, J.P. (2002). The best peak expiratory flow is flow-limited and effort-independent in normal subjects. American journal of respiratory critical care medicine, Vol. 165, 1304-1308.
Verbraak, A. F. M., Bogaard, J. M., Beneken, J. E. W., Hoorn, E., Versprille, A. (1991). Serial lung model for simulation and parameter estimation in body plethysmography. Medical & biological engineering & computing, Vol. 29, 309-317.
Verbraak, A. F. M., Rijnbeek, P. R., Beneken, J. E. W., Bogaard, J. M., Versprille, A. (1995). Computer-controlled mechanical lung model for application in pulmonary function studies. Medical & biological engineering & computing, Vol. 33, 776-783.
Verbraak, A. F. M., Rijnbeek, P. R., Beneken, J. E. W., Bogaard, J. M., Versprille, A. (2001). A new approach to mechanical simulation of lung behaviour: pressure-controlled and time-related piston movement. Medical & biological engineering & computing, Vol. 39, 82-89.
Verbraak, A F. M., Mesic, S., Babuska, R., Hoogsteden, H. C. (2003). Computer-controlled mechanical simulation of the artificially ventilated human respiratory system. IEEE transactions on biomedical engineering, Vol. 50, No. 6, 731-743.
Weibel, E. R. (1963). Morphometry of the human lung. Springer-Verlag, Berlin.

Part 3

LabVIEW for Specific Processes and Applications

8

Automated MOS Transistor gamma Degradation Measurements Based on LabVIEW Environment

Slimane Oussalah and Boualem Djezzar
Centre de Développement des Technologies Avancées (CDTA)
Algeria

1. Introduction

In recent years, the study of the effects of ionizing radiation in thin gate oxides has received increasing attention. This is due not only to the appearance of new lithography tools for ultra low scale integration (ULSI) technologies, that use X- rays or e-beams, but also for the interest of space, medical, military or high-energy applications, where the complementary metal-oxide-semiconductor (CMOS) read-out circuitry will be subjected to a very hostile radiation environment.
A major concern in the reliability of metal-oxide-semiconductor field effect transistor (MOSFET) devices is the formation of interface traps and near-interface oxide traps; called also border traps; under hot carrier injection, irradiation and processing. Traps at or near the semiconductor/gate dielectric interface can cause degraded transconductance (Doyle et al., 1990), the shifting of threshold voltage (Tsuchiya et al., 1987) and may lead to dielectric breakdown (Chen et al., 1985). In order to improve the resistance of MOSFET devices to these effects, it is necessary to have a reliable method of determining the densities of both interface traps and oxide traps (Djezzar et al., 2004).
The reliable test procedure to predict radiation response of integrated circuits (IC's) from standard test laboratory, for example in space, is very important and requires a development of simple and rapid electrical characterization techniques easily mountable in production line. Therefore, intensive works have been carried out on the electrical characterization techniques for MOS gate oxide and Si/SiO_2 interface degradation caused by radiation (Schwank et al., 1993). The charge pumping (CP) technique (Groeseneken et al., 1984) is a valuable tool for all kind of traps characterization.
In this article, we present an automatic measurement bench programmable by the IEEE-488 bus that permits to characterize MOSFET device degradation induced by gamma radiation at low doses. This characterization permits to extract threshold voltage and flatband voltage for virgin and irradiated samples. Moreover, the determination of the breakpoint frequency that represents the limit between interface and border trap contributions to the charge trap is automatically extracted. The measurement bench is managed by a program, written by a graphical language LabVIEW. LabVIEW is a powerful, platform-independent, graphical programming development system which is ideally suited for data acquisition, storage, analysis, and presentation.

2. The LabVIEW environment

LabVIEW (short for Laboratory Virtual Instrumentation Engineering Workbench) is a program development application from National Instruments, much like various C or BASIC software development tools. It is, however, different from those applications in one important respect. LabVIEW uses a graphical language (G), to create programs in block diagram form while other programming tools use text-based languages. LabVIEW includes libraries of functions and development tools designed specifically for instrument control. It has application specific libraries for data acquisition, serial instrument control, data analysis, data presentation and data storage.

Nowadays, not only is LabVIEW everywhere (Fig. 1), but it offers something for every scientist and engineer. All levels of users, ranging from experienced to non-programmers, will benefit from the interactive, configurable tools, enabling LabVIEW to be used as a one integrated tool for measurement and automation throughout the design process.

The LabVIEW system provides an intuitive, graphical interface for the automated control of laboratory equipment. For each specific type of measurement, a virtual instrument (VI) is created. A VI can be regarded as the software equivalent of a single piece of laboratory test equipment, even though the measurement it represents may involve any number of different laboratory units.

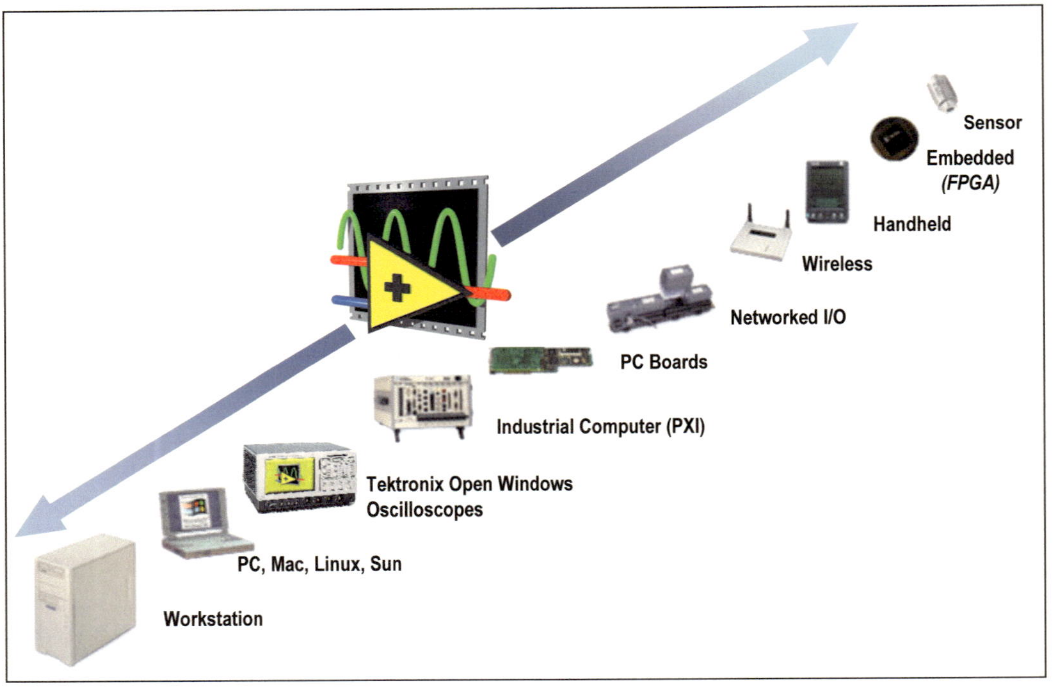

Fig. 1. LabVIEW is everywhere.

Each VI contains three main parts:

- Front Panel: how the user interacts with the VI.
- Block Diagram: the code that controls the program.
- Icon/Connector: Means of connecting a VI to other VIs.

All of the measurement parameters can be varied by manipulating a front panel (Fig. 2) which is the graphical equivalent of the push buttons and knobs on a test set, allowing a user who is not familiar with the programming to operate the setup easily

The Front Panel is used to interact with the user when the program is running. Users can control the program, change inputs, and see data updated in real time. Stress that controls are used for inputs- adjusting a slide control to set an alarm value, turning a switch on or off, or stopping a program. Indicators are used as outputs. Thermometers, lights, and other indicators indicate values from the program. These may include data, program states, and other information.

On the front panel of a VI, we place the controls and data displays for our system by selecting objects from the Controls palette, such as numeric displays, buttons, knobs, switches, meters, gauges, thermometers, tanks, LEDs, tables, arrays, charts, and graphs. When we complete and run the VI, we use the front panel to control our system whether we move a slide, zoom in on a graph, or enter a value with the keyboard. The front panel also serves to document the experiment; a hard copy yields results as well as all of the input parameters on one sheet.

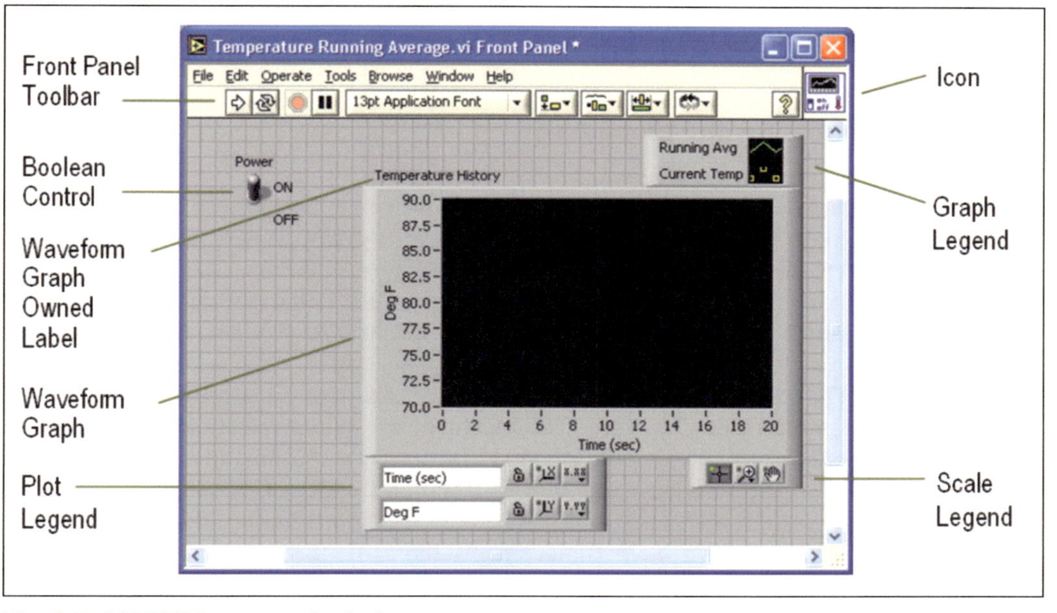

Fig. 2. LabVIEW front panel window.

The programming which coordinates the operation is accomplished graphically in the diagram panel Window using a dataflow language described by an example in Fig. 3.

To program the VI, we construct the block diagram without worrying about the syntactical details of text-based programming languages. We do this by selecting objects (icons) from the Functions palette and connecting them together with wires to transfer data among block diagram objects. These objects include simple arithmetic functions, Programming Structures, Signal Processing, advanced acquisition and analysis routines, network and file I/O operations, and more.

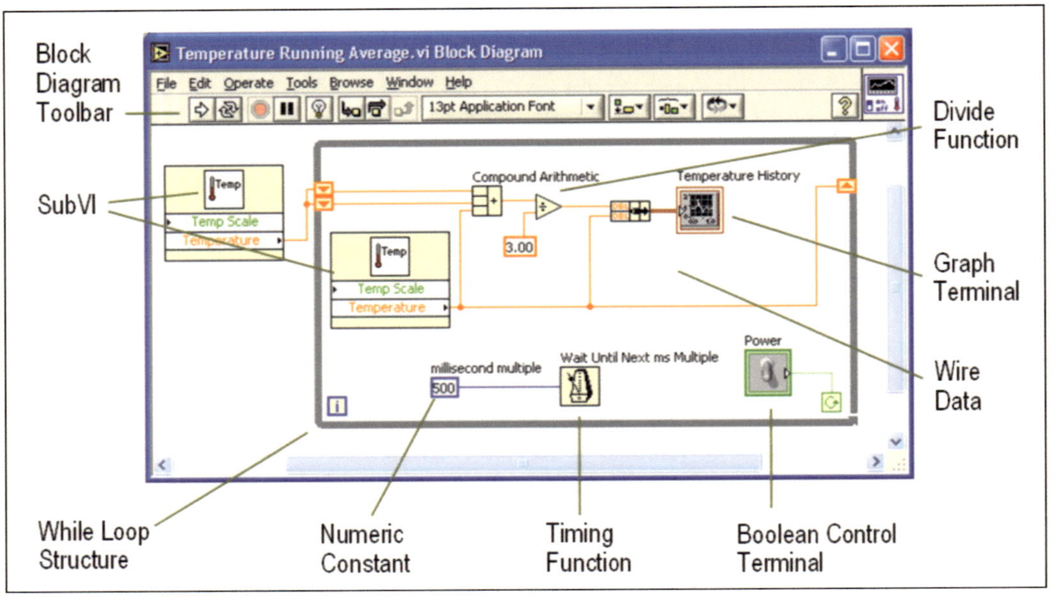

Fig. 3. LabVIEW block diagram window.

3. Set-up and experimental procedure

3.1 Device and irradiation details

Samples investigated in this work are test structures, which were designed in Microelectronics and Nanotechnology Division of CDTA (Centre de Développement de Technologies Avancées) and fabricated in ES2 (European Silicon Structure) foundry. The different NMOS transistors within test structures were fabricated using a conventional (soft process) dual layer metal CMOS 2 µm N-well technology on p-type silicon <100> substrate with normal concentration of 7.6x1015 boron/cm^3, N+-poly-silicon gate, and 40 nm thick gate oxide layer grown in dry O_2. The gate capacitance per area unit, C_{OX} is about of 8.6 10-8 F.cm^{-2}.
The radiation was performed at the CRS (Centre de Radioprotection et de Sureté) Laboratories, Algeria. Irradiation is performed at low doses up to 250 krad on non-packaged samples with gate lengths varying from 2µm to 20µm and width of 80 µm and 300 µm by using 1.25 MeV γ-rays at room temperature. The γ -ray was produced by 60Co cell with low-dose-rate of 200 rad/min. We have characterized the radiation effects at low doses on NMOS transistors. Thereafter, the electrical characterization is achieved by using standard charge pumping technique (CP) at high frequencies.

3.2 Experimental set-up

The experimental set-up details of the standard CP technique are shown in Fig. 4. The MOSFET source/drain terminals have been grounded, the gate terminal has been pulsed by applying a triangular pulse train with amplitude ΔV_G of various frequencies, and the substrate terminal has been grounded via a pico-ammeter. The measurements have been performed at room temperature and by using a sensitive Keithley 617 electrometer, Keithley 3940 multifunction synthesizer, and Karl Suss PA300 micro-manipulator semi-automatic probe station.

For all measurements, a reverse bias is applied to the source and the drain diodes. When the gate is pulsed between inversion and accumulation conditions (from above the threshold

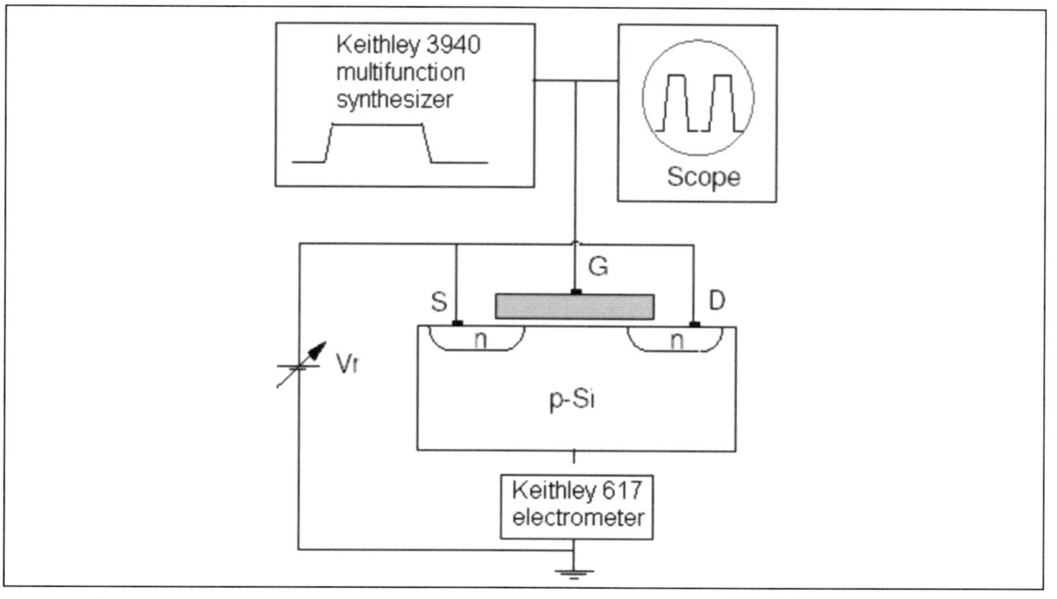

Fig. 4. Experimental setup for charge pumping measurement.

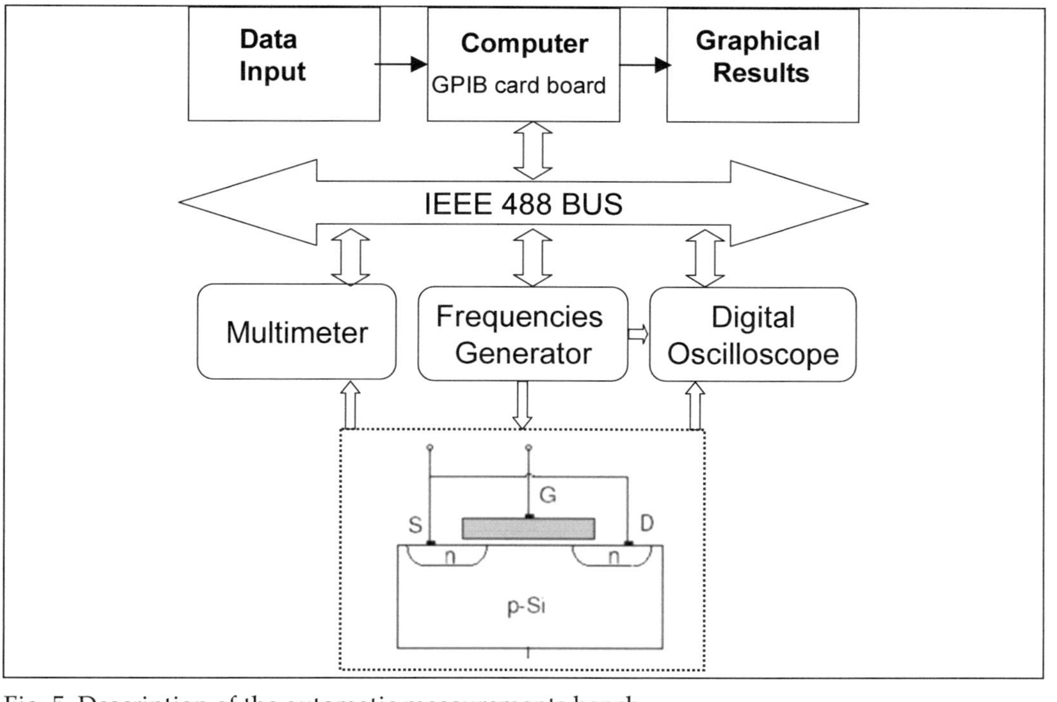

Fig. 5. Description of the automatic measurements bench.

voltage to below the flatband voltage), trapping and recombination of carriers under these non equilibrium conditions gives rise to a net DC current that can be measured at the substrate. For relatively high frequency pulses (1 MHz), the CP current is proportional to the average density of interface traps which are physically located within 1 nm of the semiconductor -dielectric interface (Paulsen et al., 1992).
The test circuit chip within the probe station were isolated from vibration and enclosed in a grounded faraday box to avoid both RF and light effects. A computer has been programmed to control the measurement system, record the data, and extract the parameters. The control of instruments has been realized by a program developed with the LabVIEW software via the GPIB IEEE-488 bus.
Since the whole system is in this case based on computer (Fig. 5), the data is easily ported in ASCII form to other programs or even shared via networking with other machines.

4. Theoretical background

A commonly used definition of threshold voltage is that gate voltage for which the surface potential (ϕ_S) in the semiconductor below the gate oxide is given by:

$$\phi_S = 2\phi_F \tag{1}$$

where ϕ_F (V) is the Fermi level potential.
Thus, the threshold voltage (Schroder, 1998) is given as follows:

$$V_{th} = \phi_{MS} + 2\phi_F + \frac{\sqrt{2q\varepsilon_{si}N_A(2\phi_F)}}{C_{ox}} - \frac{Q_{total}}{C_{ox}} \tag{2}$$

where,
q (C) is the electron charge,
ε_{si} (F/cm) is the permittivity of silicon,
N_A (cm^{-3}) is the substrate doping,
C_{OX} (F/cm^2) is the gate oxide capacitance per area unit,
ϕ_{MS} (V) is the metal-semiconductor work function difference,
Q_T (C/cm^2) is the total charge density in SiO_2/Si system.
According to the Deal nomenclature (Deal, 1980), there are four general types of charges associated with the SiO_2/Si system. Fleetwood (Fleetwood, 1992) has completed this picture of charges by introducing a new charge type termed border trapped charge (Q_{BT}) as illustrated in Fig. 6. Thus Q_T is given by (Djezzar et al., 2004):

$$Q_T = Q_F + Q_M + Q_{OT} + Q_{IT} + Q_{BT} \tag{3}$$

where,
Q_F (C/cm^2) is the fixed charge density,
Q_M (C/cm^2) is the mobile oxide charge density,
Q_{OT} (C/cm^2) is the oxide-trapped charge density,
Q_{IT} (C/cm^2) is the interface-trapped charge density,
Unlike fixed oxide charge, oxide trapped charge, and mobile oxide charge, interface trapped charge is in electrical communication with the underlying silicon. by substituting eq. (3) in eq. (2), V_{TH} can be written as:

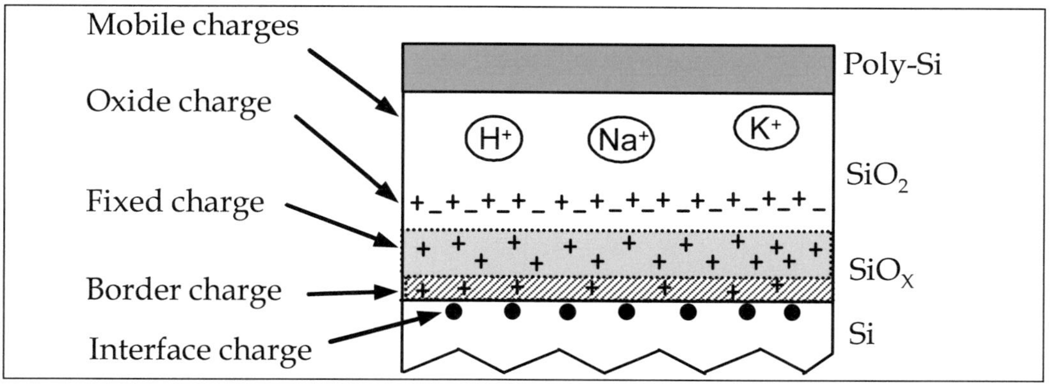

Fig. 6. Schematic illustration of different charges in MOS devices.

$$V_{TH} = \phi_{MS} + 2\phi_F + \frac{\sqrt{2q\varepsilon_{Si}N_A(2\phi_F)}}{C_{OX}} - \frac{1}{C_{OX}}(Q_F + Q_M + Q_{OT} + Q_{IT} + Q_{BT}) \quad (4)$$

When MOS transistors are exposed to various types of stress such as ionizing radiation, FN injection, or hot carrier injection, the gate oxide and SiO_2/Si interface are damaged. This degradation is induced by the creation of oxide-trapped charge (ΔQ_{OT}) and interface trapped charge (ΔQ_{IT}). The different charge increments are shown in fig. 2. Contrary to Q_{OT}, Q_{IT}, and and Q_{BT}, Q_F and Q_M are not affected by these ionizing stresses. Consequently, the threshold voltage shift caused by uniform stresses (FN stress or radiation effect) is given by:

$$\Delta V_{TH} = -\frac{\Delta Q_{IT}}{C_{OX}} - \frac{\Delta Q_{OT}}{C_{OX}} - \frac{\Delta Q_{BT}}{C_{OX}} \quad (5)$$

where,
ΔQ_{IT} ($C.cm^{-2}$) is the radiation-induced interface trapped charges,
ΔQ_{BT} ($C.cm^{-2}$) is the radiation-induced border trapped charges,
ΔQ_{OT} ($C.cm^{-2}$) is the radiation-induced oxide trapped charges.
Generally, the net radiation-induced oxide and border charges, ΔQ_{OT} and ΔQ_{BT} respectively, are positive and induce a negative shift in V_{TH}. However, ΔQ_{IT} can contribute either a net-negative or net-positive charge, depending on the position of the Fermi level at the silicon surface in inversion mode. Usually, the interface-trap is considered like an acceptor state for NMOS transistor and like a donor state for PMOS transistor. Therefore, ΔQ_{IT} is negative for n-channel ($\Delta Q_{IT} = -q\ \Delta N_{IT}$) and positive for p-channel ($\Delta Q_{IT} = q\ \Delta N_{IT}$) devices (Oldham, 1999). On the other hand, $\Delta Q_{OT} = q\ \Delta N_{OT}$ and $\Delta Q_{BT} = q\ \Delta N_{BT}$. Where ΔN_{IT}, ΔN_{OT}, and ΔN_{BT} are positive numbers per area unit.
So, ΔV_{TH} reads:

$$\Delta V_{TH} = \Delta V_{IT} + \Delta V_{OT} + \Delta V_{BT} \quad (8)$$

where,

$\Delta V_{IT} = -\Delta Q_{IT} / C_{OX} = q\, \Delta N_{IT} / C_{OX}$ (V) is the voltage shift caused by interface- trap increase,
$\Delta V_{OT} = -\Delta Q_{OT} / C_{OX} = -q\, N_{OT} / C_{OX}$ (V) is the voltage shift caused by oxide-trap increase,
$\Delta V_{BT} = -\Delta Q_{BT} / C_{OX} = -q\, \Delta N_{BT} / C_{OX}$ (V) is the voltage shift caused by border- trap increase.
The Equation 6 is only true when applying a DC signal or a low frequencies (less than a few kHz) AC signal train. Therefore, only ΔN_{OT} and ΔN_{IT} take part in standard charge pumping current at high frequencies. Thus, Equation 6 can be written as:

$$\Delta V_{TH} = \Delta V_{IT} + \Delta V_{OT} \tag{7}$$

Where, ΔV_{OT} is now the voltage shift caused by the oxide-trap increase at high frequency measurements.
After irradiation, I_{CP} (V_B) (where V_B is the base voltage of the gate signal) curves are laterally and vertically shifted. Figure 7 qualitatively illustrates the effect induced by ionizing radiation on CP curves. The lateral shift indicates the introduction of radiation-induced oxide- and interface-trap. However, the vertical one (increase of I_{CPM}) is indicative of the augmentation of interface-trap density, ΔN_{IT} (numbre/cm^2).

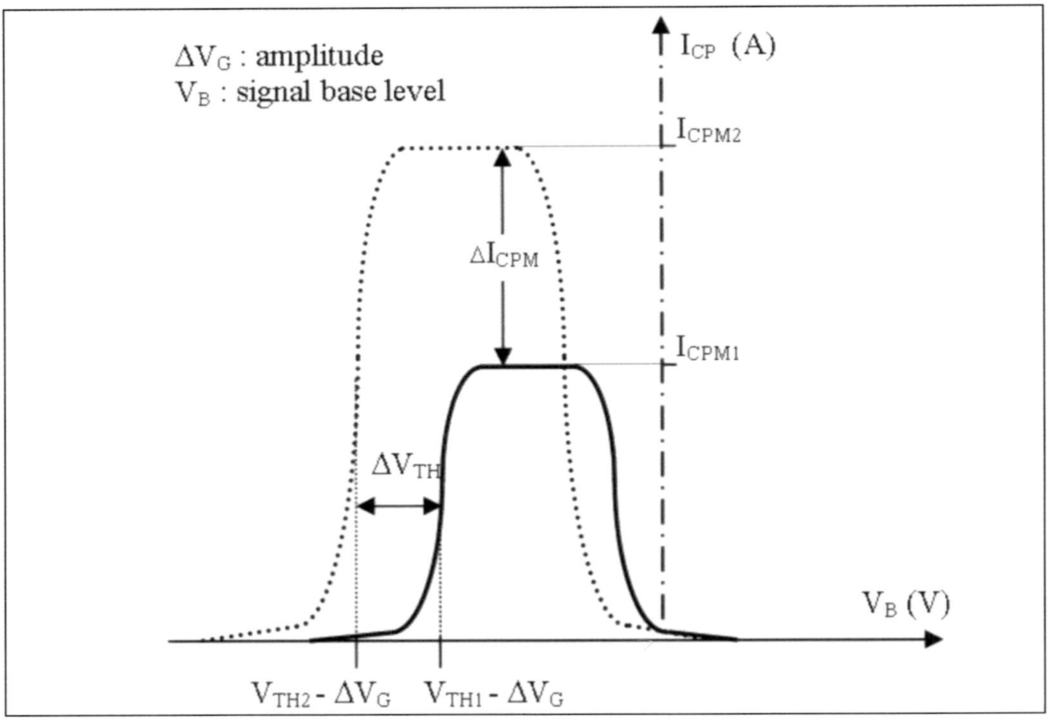

Fig. 7. Schematic illustration of standard charge pumping current curves. Solid line shows CP current before irradiation and Dashed line shows CP current after irradiation.

The I_{CPM} current is given by:

$$I_{CPM} = q.f.A_G.N_{IT} \tag{8}$$

Where,

q (C) is the elementary charge,
N_{IT} (cm^{-2}) is the interface and border-trap densities per area unit,
A_G (cm^2) is the gate area,
f (Hz) is the frequency.
Before irradiation, I_{CPM1} and N_{IT1} represent charge pumping current and interface-trap density respectively. After irradiation, I_{CPM2} and N_{IT2} represent charge pumping current and interface-trap density respectively. Then, the radiation-induced interface-trap density increase (ΔN_{IT}) is given by:

$$\Delta N_{IT} = N_{IT2} - N_{IT1} = \frac{I_{CPM2} - I_{CPM1}}{q.f.A_G} = \frac{\Delta I_{CPM}}{q.f.A_G} \tag{9}$$

Thus, ΔV_{IT} is given by:

$$\Delta V_{IT} = q\frac{\Delta N_{IT}}{C_{OX}} = \frac{\Delta I_{CPM}}{C_{OX}.f.A_G} \tag{10}$$

Using Equations 8 and 12, and ΔV_{OT} = -q $\Delta N_{OT}/C_{OX}$, we have expressed ΔN_{OT}, at high frequencies, as:

$$\Delta N_{OT} = \frac{\Delta I_{CPM}}{q.f.A_G} - \frac{C_{OX}}{q}\Delta V_{TH} \tag{11}$$

where, ΔI_{CPM} (A) is the radiation-induced maximum CP current increase.

5. Experiment

The I_{CP} (V_B) charge pumping measurements were made before and after each irradiation at 25°C. The irradiated NMOS devices were characterized after the latent interface-trap build-up (10^6 s) (Schwank , 1992). In other words, we made a long delay between irradiation and measurements. The I_{CP} (V_B) standard curves (Elliot curves) were extracted using a triangular signal with an amplitude of 3V and a frequency of 100 kHz. The technique consists in varying V_B (signal base voltage) from -6V to 2V. The high frequency value (100 kHz) is chosen basing on Q_{CP} (f) (charge recombined per cycle vs. frequency) measurements performed on our devices. The Q_{CP} (f) characteristics have explicitly shown that the border-traps contribution starts at 10 kHz as frequency as lowered. Consequently, 100 kHz are largely sufficient to avoid their interference with interface-trap.
We expose the experimental results in Fig. 8. All degraded NMOS transistors exhibit the same general features and behaviours as a function of total dose in charge pumping current I_{CP}(V_B) measured by CP technique. When MOSFET transistors are exposed to uniform degradation such as ionizing radiation, the threshold voltage is shifted. This shift is induced by the creation of oxide-trapped charge (ΔQ_{OT}) in the dielectric and interface-trapped charge (ΔQ_{IT}) in the Si/SiO_2 system. After irradiation, the curves obtained from CP technique (current measured (I_{CP}) vs. the base voltage of the gate signal (V_B)) are vertically and laterally shifted. The vertical shift represented by the increase of the maximum CP current, I_{CPM}, indicates the augmentation of the interface trap density, ΔN_{IT} (numbre/cm^2) (Fig. 8a).

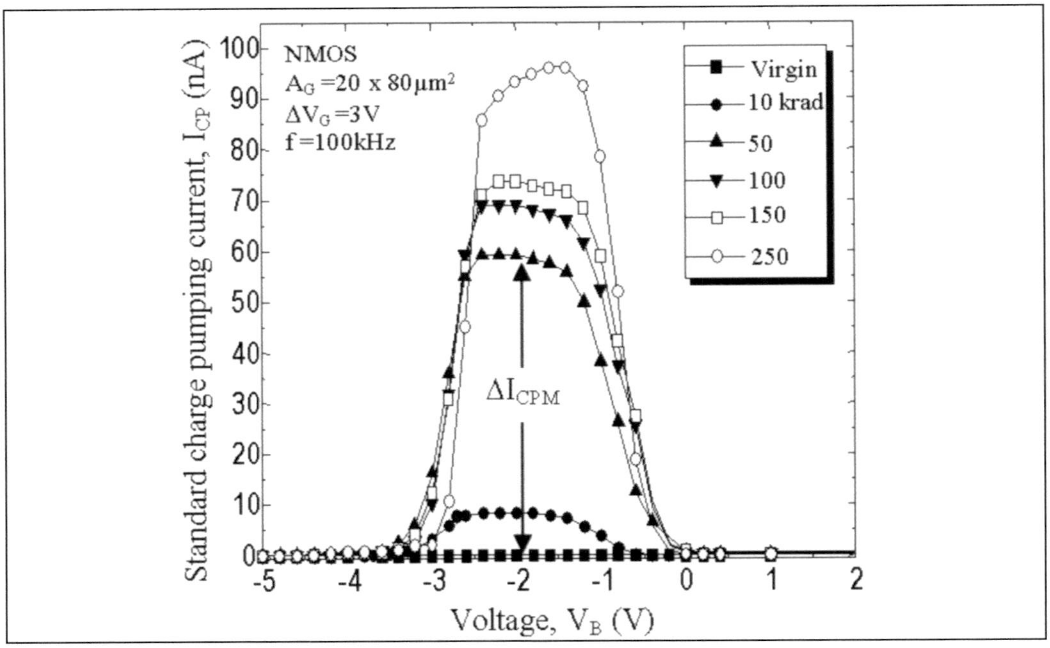

(a)

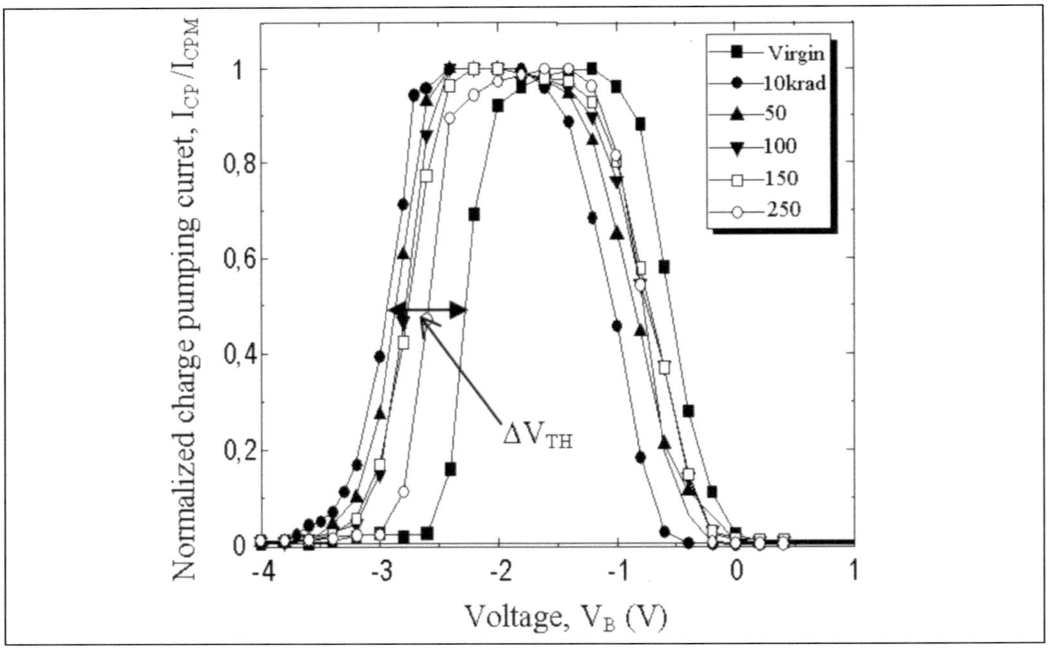

(b)

Fig. 8. Radiation effects on CP curves at high frequencies for different total gamma ray doses. (a) Standard CP current vs. V_B. (b) Normalized CP current vs. V_B.

However, the lateral one indicates the introduction of the radiation-induced oxide- and interface-trap (Fig. 8b). Fig. 8b gives the I_{CP} (V_B) normalized curves to their respective I_{CPM}, in order to illustrate well the lateral shifts induced by irradiation. These quantities are estimated, as shown in figure 8, from I_{CP} (V_B) curves at high frequencies.

Knowing ΔI_{CPM} and ΔV_{TH}, we are able to calculate ΔN_{IT} from equation 9 and also ΔN_{OT} from equation 11. This is very useful when we want to rapidly get information on the quality of irradiated oxide and SiO_2/Si interface and also if we intend to study the annealing of both radiation-induced oxide- and interface-trap.

Equations 9 and 11 shows clearly that ΔN_{IT} and ΔN_{OT} are is just dependent on experimental parameters ΔI_{CPM} and ΔV_{TH} (Djezzar et al., 2004). These quantities are estimated from I_{CP} (V_B) curves at high frequencies.

In Fig. 9, the front panel of the developed software loads two files, of virgin and irradiated MOS devices, respectively and calculates the lateral shift of threshold and flatband voltage, respectively caused by radiation-induced ΔN_{IT} and ΔN_{OT} (normalized charge pumping curves).

The software developed permits to extract the radiation-induced threshold voltage shift (ΔV_{TH}), the radiation-induced flatband voltage shift (ΔV_{FB}), the radiation-induced oxide-trap (ΔN_{OT}), and radiation-induced interface-trap (ΔN_{IT}) are extracted [Oussalah & Djezzar, 2007).

All of the relevant parameters are visible from this screen, as are the experimental results. The program loads a file of a virgin MOS device and extracts the threshold voltage, the flatband and other parameters.

In Fig. 9, we show the window front panel for the charge pumping base level sweep measurement.

The input parameters are:

- file path,
- the signal level,
- the working frequency
- the percentage at the V_{TH} is calculated
- the percentage at V_{FB} is calculated
- process parameters, like, substrate doping (cm^{-3}), oxide capacitor (F/cm^2) and gate oxide area (cm^2).

The extracted parameters by the software are:

- threshold voltage, V_{TH} (V),
- flatband voltage, V_{FB} (V),
- maximum charge pumping current, I_{CPM} (A),
- interface-trapped charge density, Q_{IT} (C/cm^2),
- interface trap density, N_{IT} ($1/cm^2$),
- V_{IT} (V),
- interface trap density, D_{IT} ($1/eV.cm^2$).

In Fig. 10, we show the window front panel for the charge pumping base level sweep measurement for virgin and irradiated MOS transistor. The program loads two files for virgin and irradiated MOS devices, and calculates the lateral shift of V_{TH} and V_{FB}, respectively caused by radiation-induced ΔN_{IT} and ΔN_{OT} (normalized CP curves).

The input parameters in the program software are:

- file path of the virgin MOS transistor,
- file path of the irradiated MOS transistor,
- the signal level,
- the working frequency,

- the percentage at the V_{TH} is calculated,
- the percentage at the V_{FB} is calculated,
- process parameters, like, substrate doping (cm^{-3}), oxide capacitor (F/cm^2) and gate oxide area (cm^2).

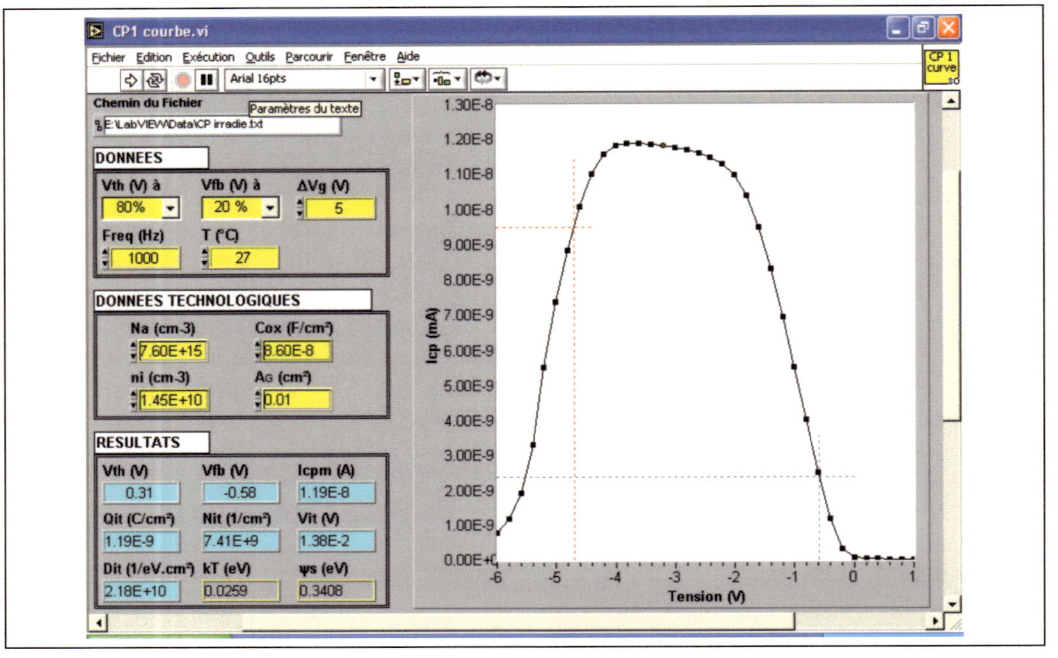

Fig. 9. LabVIEW front panel for the charge pumping base level sweep measurement.

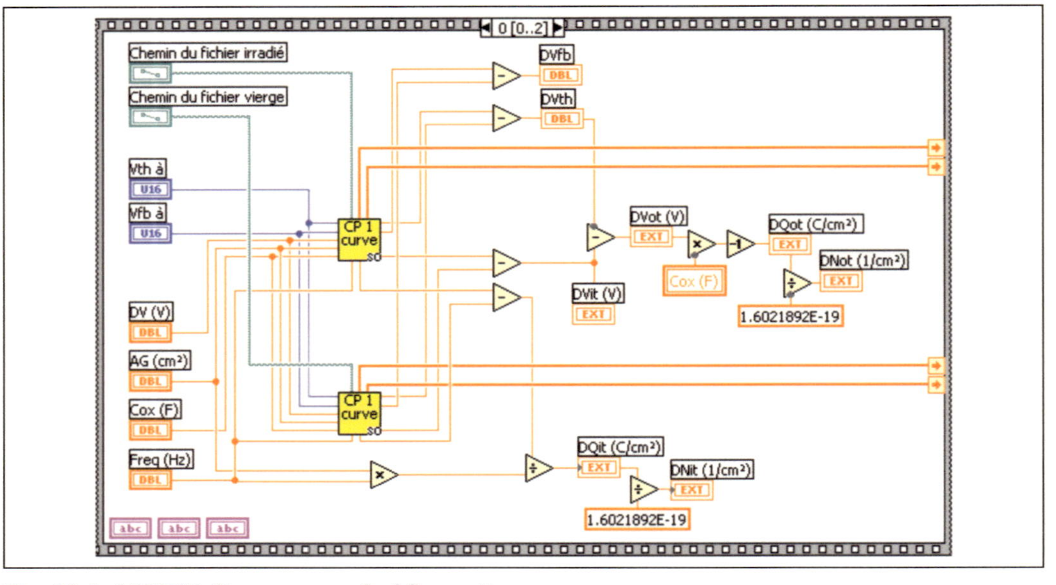

Fig. 10. LabVIEW diagram panel of figure 9.

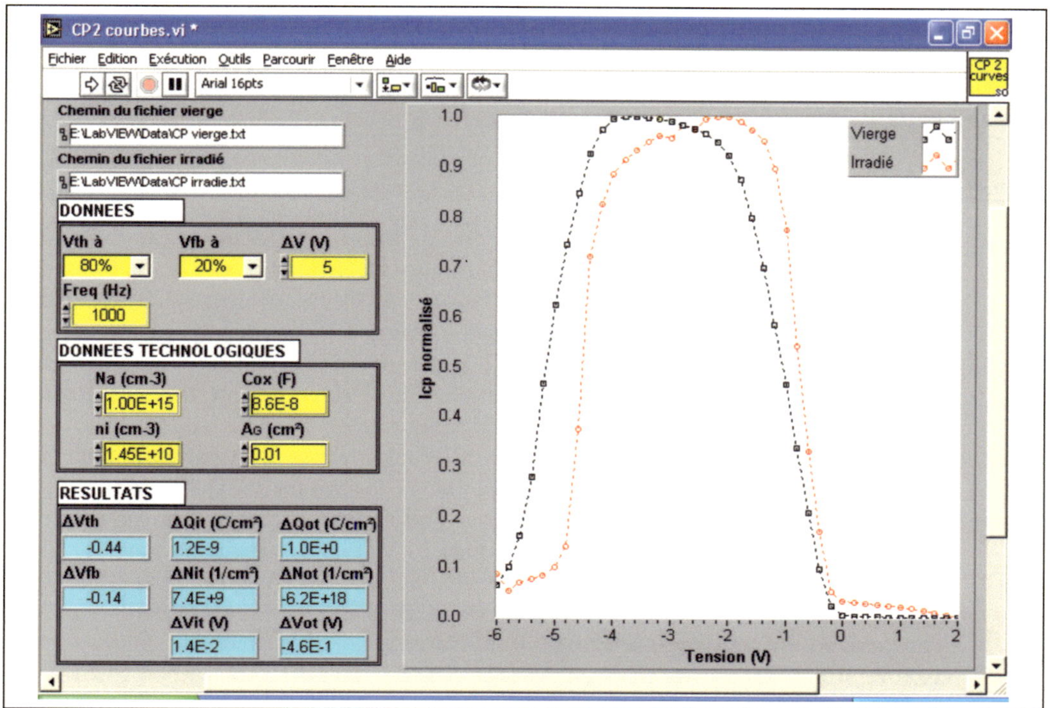

Fig. 11. LabVIEW front panel for the radiation induced parameters of the virgin and irradiated MOS transitor.

The extracted parameters by the program software are:

- threshold voltage shift, ΔV_{TH} (V),
- flatband voltage shift, ΔV_{FB} (V),
- oxide trapped charges density, ΔQot (C/cm^2),
- Interface trapped charge density, ΔQit (C/cm^2).
- Oxide trapped density, ΔNot (1/cm^2).
- Interface trapped density, ΔNit (1/cm^2).
- Voltage shift caused by interface- trap increase, ΔVit (V).
- Voltage shift caused by oxide-trap increase, ΔV_{OT} (V).

6. Conclusion

Experiments with LabVIEW software have been carried out to determine the effects of gamma radiation at low doses on trap densities in MOSFET devices. The threshold and the flatband voltages degradation due to the charge injection from gamma radiation effect at low doses are characterized with the developed software. Since ΔI_{CPM} and ΔV_{TH} are measured, the program is able to extract ΔN_{IT} and ΔN_{OT}. This is very useful when we want to rapidly get information on the quality of irradiated oxide and SiO_2/Si interface and also if we intend to study the annealing of both radiation-induced oxide- and interface-trap. This makes it a powerful tool for rapid and routinely electrical characterization in hardness assurance test of MOSFET's device qualification for space and strategic applications.

LabVIEW is a powerful environment for software development. It is widely used for instrument control, data acquisition and data analysis. LabVIEW's graphical way of programming allows fast and efficient developing of robust, user controlled applications for measurement, analysis anad visualization of data.

7. References

Doyle, B. S.; Bourcerie, M.; Bergonzoni, C.; Benecchi, R.; Bravis, A.; Mistry, K.R.; & Boudou, A. (1990). The generation and characterization of electron and hole traps created by hole injection during low gate voltage hot-carrier stressing of n-MOS transistors. *IEEE Transactions on Electron Devices*, Vol. 37, (August 1990) 1869-1876.

Tsuchiya, T.; Kobayashi, T.; & Nakajima, S. (1987). Hot carrier-injected oxide region and hot-electron trapping as the main cause in Si nMOSFET degradation. *IEEE Transactions on Electron Devices*, Vol. 34, (February 1987) 386-391.

Chen, I.C.; Holland, S.E. & Hu, C. (1985). Electrical breakdown of thin gate and tunneling oxides. *IEEE Journal of Solid-State Circuits*, Vol. 20, (February 1985) 333-342.

Djezzar, B.; Oussalah, S. & Smatti, A. (2004). A new Oxide-Trap based on Charge Pumping (OTCP) extraction method for irradiated MOSFET devices: part I (high frequencies). *IEEE Transactions on Nuclear Science.* Vol. 51, (August 2004) 1724-1731.

Schwank, J. R.; Fleetwood, D. M.; Shaneyfelt, M. R. & Winokur, P. S. (1993). A critical comparison of charge-pumping, dual-transistor, and midgap measurement techniques. *IEEE Transactions on Nuclear Science.* Vol. 40, (December 1993) 1666-1677.

Groeseneken, G.; Maes, H. E.; Beltran, N. & De Keermaecker, R. F. (1984). A reliable approach to charge pumping measurement in MOS transistors. *IEEE Transactions on Electron Devices*. Vol. 31, (January 1984) 42-53.

Paulsen, R.E.; Siergiej, R.R.; French, M.L. & White, M.H. (1992). Observation of Near-Interface Oxide Traps with the Charge-Pumping Technique. *IEEE Electron Device Letters.*, Vol. 13, N°12, (December 1992) 627-629.

Schroder, D.K. (1998). Semiconductor Material and Device Characterization. John Wiley and Sons, 2nd Edition, New York.

Deal, B.E. (1980). Standardized Terminology for Oxide Charges Associated with Thermally Oxidized Silicon. *Journal of the Electrochemical Society*, Vol. 127, Issue 4, (April 1980) 979-981.

Fleetwood, D. M. (1992). Border Traps in MOS Devices. *IEEE Transactions on Nuclear Science*, Vol. 39, (1992) 269-271.

Oldham, T.R. (1999). *Ionizing Radiation Effects in MOS Oxides*, World Scientific Publishing.

Schwank, J.R.; Fleetwood, D.M.; Shaneyfelt, M.R.; Winokur, P.S.; Axness, C.L. & Riewe, L.C. (1992). Latent Interface-Trap Buildup and its Implications for Hardness Assurance, *IEEE Transactions on Nuclear Science*, Vol. 39, (1992) 1953-1963.

Oussalah, S. & Djezzar, B. (2007). Automated MOS Transistor Degradation Measurements Based on LabVIEW. *Proceedings of the International Conference on design & Technology of Integrated Systems in Nanoscale Era*, Rabat (Morocco), pp. 217-220.

9

Time-Resolved Fluorescence Spectroscopy with LabView

Edgard Moreno, Porfirio Reyes and José M. de la Rosa
Instituto Politécnico Nacional
México

1. Introduction

1.1 Fluorescence phenomenon

The absorption and subsequent emission of light by organic and inorganic specimens is typically the result of physical phenomena known as luminescence, which occurs at electronically excited states. Luminescence is formally divided into two categories: fluorescence and phosphorescence, depending on the nature of the excited state. Fluorescence occurs when a photon excites an electron from the ground-state to a higher energy state, and the electron in the excited orbital is paired (of opposite spin) to the second electron in the ground-state orbital. Return to the ground state is spin allowed and occurs rapidly by emission of a photon producing fluorescence. The emission rate of fluorescence (fluorescence lifetime) is of the order of nanoseconds to microseconds. The lifetime τ of a fluorophore (fluorescence substance) is the average time between its excitation and its return to the ground state. Phosphorescence is the light emission from excited states, in which the electron in the excited orbital has the same spin orientation as the ground-state electron. Transitions to the ground state are forbidden and the emission rates are slow, in the order of millisecond to seconds (Lakowicz, 1991), (Lakowicz, 1999), (Gore, 2000), (Valeur, 2002).

The processes which occur between the absorption and emission of light are usually illustrated by a Jablonski diagram (figure 1). S0, S1 and S2 denote ground, first, and second electronic states. At each of these electronic energy levels the electrons can exist in a number of vibration energy levels denoted by 0, 1, 2, etc. The transitions between states are depicted as vertical lines to illustrate the instantaneous nature of light absorption (10^{-15}s). An electron is usually excited to some higher vibration level of either S1 or S2 and rapidly relaxes (10^{-12} s–10^{-15} s) to the lowest vibration level of S1. Return from level S1 to the ground state S0 produces fluorescence emission. Examination of the Jablonski diagram revels that the energy of emission is less than that of absorption. Hence, fluorescence occurs at lower energies or longer wavelength (Stokes shift). The amount of Stokes shift is a measure of the relaxation process occurring in the excited state, populated by absorption. Another property of fluorescence is that the same fluorescence emission spectrum is generally observed irrespective of the excitation wavelength. This is known as Kasha´s rule. Although fluorescence measurements are more sophisticated than an absorption (transmission) experiment, they provide a wealth of the information about the molecular structure, interaction and dynamics of species.

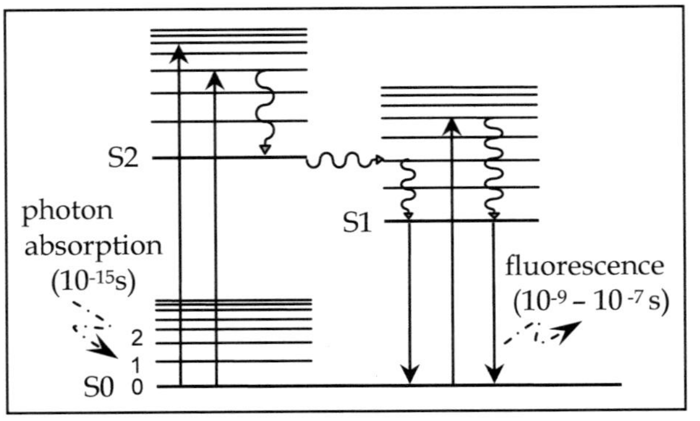

Fig. 1. A simple Jablonski diagram

Two important characteristics of a fluorophore are its quantum yield and its fluorescence lifetime. The quantum yield is the number of emitted photons relative to the number of absorbed photons, and it is given by equation (1). Γ is the decay rate by spontaneous emission and knr is the decay rate which do not produce radiation, and it is associated to energy losses by vibrational relaxations and internal conversions. The fluorescence lifetime τ is defined as the average time from the fluorophore excitation to the return to ground state, when the optical excitation is a δ impulse function and it can be expressed as (2).

$$Q = \frac{\Gamma}{\Gamma + knr} \tag{1}$$

$$\tau = \frac{1}{\Gamma + knr} \tag{2}$$

The population in excited state decays at rate Γ+ knr according to equation (3), where n(t) is the number of excited molecule. In fluorescence spectroscopy, instead of excited molecule n(t), an equivalent quantity as irradiance I(t) is measured. The result is an exponential decay of the irradiance as equation (4). The lifetime τ is the decay time from maximum value Io to its fraction 1/e.

$$\frac{dn(t)}{dt} = \frac{1}{\tau} n(t) \tag{3}$$

$$I(t) = Io \exp(-t/\tau) \tag{4}$$

1.2 Fluorescence measurements

Fluorescence measurements can be broadly classified into two types: steady-state and time-resolved. Steady-state measurements are those performed with constant illumination and observation, this is the most common type of measurement. The sample is illuminated with a continuous beam of light and the intensity of the emission is usually recorded as a wavelength function (fluorescence spectrum), as it is shown in figure 2. When the sample is exposed to light, steady state is reached almost immediately. Time-resolved measurements are used for measuring intensity decays. For those measurements, the sample is exposed to a pulse of light, where the pulse width is typically shorter than the decay time of the sample.

The intensity decay is recorded with a high speed detection system that allows the intensity to be measured on a nanoseconds timescale. Figure 3 shows an example of time-domain measurement of an excitation laser pulse and the fluorescent response pulse. Time-dependent measurements resolve fluorescence intensity decays in terms of lifetimes, and thus provide additional information about the intra and intermolecular dynamics of the fluorophore (the fluorescent compound of the sample) under study (Lakowicz, 1991), (Lakowics, 1999), (Gore, 2000).

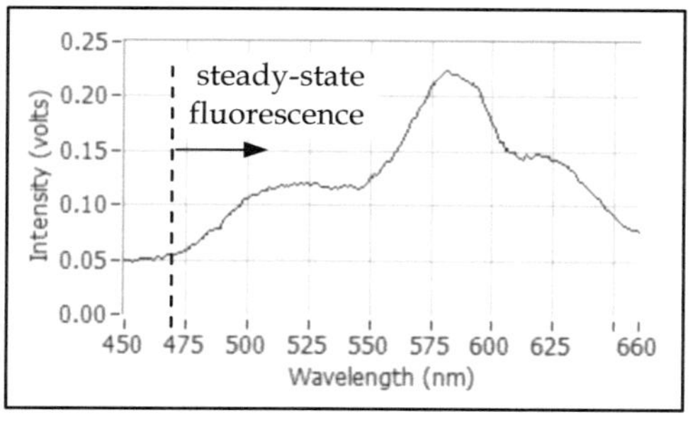

Fig. 2. Steady-state measurements

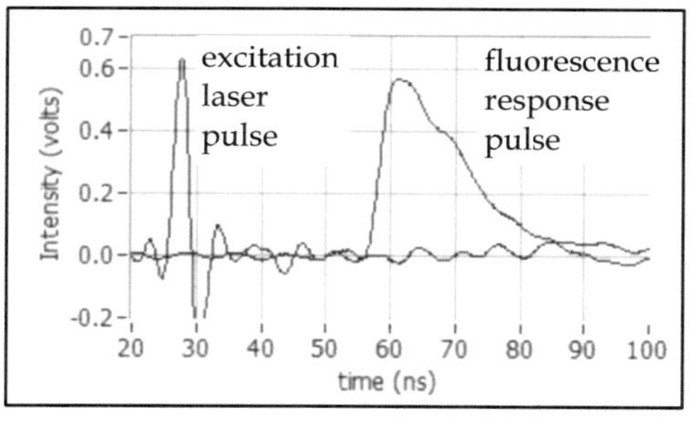

Fig. 3. Time-resolved measurements

There exists a rather simple relationship between steady-state and time-resolved measurements. The steady-state intensity Iss is an average of the time resolved phenomena over the intensity decay of the sample, as equation (5). The value of the intensity Io depends on the fluorophore concentration.

$$Iss = \int_0^{\infty} Ioe^{-t/\tau}dt = Io\tau \quad (5)$$

Figure 4 shows the general structure of a spectrofluorometer to measure steady-state and time-resolved fluorescence. Usually, the sample under study is excited with ultraviolet light, the sample emits florescence in all directions, and part of this emission is captured at the monochromator input. The monochromator output is a light with a single wavelength (λ) component of the input light, coming from the sample. The light from the monochromator output is captured by a photodetector (FD), which produces a current signal proportional to response fluorescence signal. This electrical signal is processed and acquired to be read by the computer.

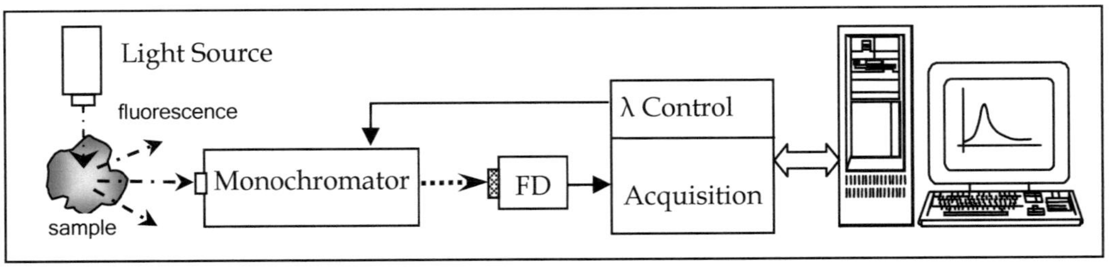

Fig. 4. General structure of a spectrofluorometer

The main differences between steady-state and time-resolved fluorometers are two: the light source (continuous or pulsed) and data acquisition process requirements. For steady-state measurements the values to acquire are constant, and thus there are not high speed requirements. The acquisition process uses real-time sampling technique. A low cost DAQ board or microcontroller is enough to acquire steady-state data. A time-domain fluorometer requires a high speed digitizer to resolve ns fluorescence decays. Normally this digitizer uses an equivalent-time sampling method to acquire temporal data on nanoseconds timescales. It is a common practice to use a digital oscilloscope as digitizer system.

1.3 Fluorescence applications

The spectrofluorometry is related to the measurement of the emission spectra produced by fluorescent samples, it is the most extensively used optical spectroscopic method in analytical measurements and scientific investigation to measure the concentration species in gases, liquids and solids. In the scientific research laboratory, fluorescence spectroscopy is being used or applied to study the fundamental physical processes of molecules, structure-function relationships and interactions of biomolecules (Gore, 2000), (Valeur, 2002). In-situ fluorescence measurements are too very important in others areas as the study of water and soil contamination (Anderson et al., 2003), the chlorophyll fluorescence in green plants to know their physiological and health status (Nesterenko et al., 2007), the study of chemical and physical changes in dairy products caused by processing and storage (Moller & Mortensen, 2008), or for adulteration assessment (Poulli et al., 2007).

The fluorescence spectroscopy is now widely used for biomedical purposes and clinical analysis. The fluorescence emission from the skin can be used to monitor changes induced by the UV radiation. *In vivo* spectrofluorometry has emerged as a powerful technique for biomedical research covering abroad spectrum, from study of cellular and tissue structures, to biological function and early detection of cancer (Paras, 2003), (Tuan, 2003). Optical biopsy refers to detection of cancerous state of a tissue using optical methods. This is a new area, offering the potential to use noninvasive or minimally invasive *in vivo* optical spectroscopic methods, to identify a cancer at its various early stages and monitor its progression. The basic principle utilized for the method of optical biopsy is that the emission fluorescence is strongly influenced by the composition and the cellular structures of tissues. The changes in tissue from normal state to cancerous state have been show to alter the fluorescence. Biomedical fluorescence spectroscopy is an extremely large and growing field of research (Paras, 2003), (Tuan, 2003).

2. Time-resolved fluorescence spectrometer

Figure 5 shows the experimental arrangement of a home made instrument to measure time-resolved fluorescence signals emitted by samples under study. The nitrogen laser (N_2) generates short light pulses to a beam divider, where part of the incident light is reflected toward a reference photodiode (PD). This detector produces an electric pulse, similar to laser pulse, which triggers the oscilloscope to start an acquisition process of the signals present on both oscilloscope input channels. Most of the laser pulse passes trough the divider to an optical chamber formed by a biconvex lens, an ultraviolet filter (337.1 nm) and a sample holder.

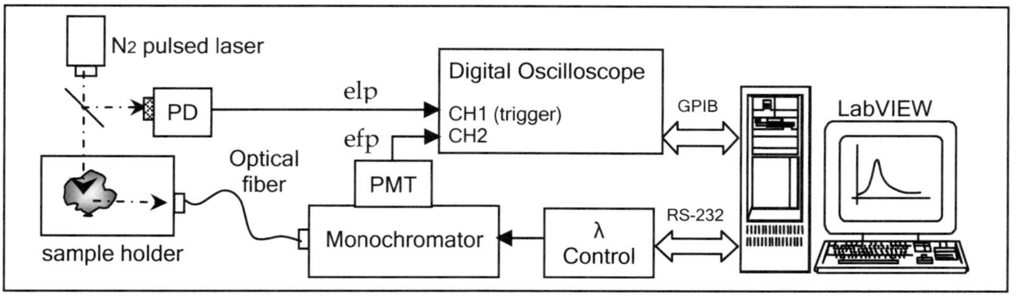

Fig. 5. Time-resolved fluorescence spectrometer

The response fluorescence pulse emitted by the sample is collected by an optical fiber and delivered to monochromator input. The luminous pulse at monochromator output is detected by a photo multiplier tube (PMT) and converted to an electrical current pulse. The laser (elp) and fluorescence (efp) electrical pulses are measured with oscilloscope channels 1 and 2, and the information registered of both signals is sent to a computer via a GPIB interface. These time-resolved signals correspond to a single monochromator output wavelength. The wavelength control communicates with the computer via a serial port RS-232. A control program was developed in the graphical language G of LabVIEW™ 7.1 to control the process, and to register and plot the time-resolved pulses.

2.1 Pulsed light source

When a fluorophore is excited with light, the emitted fluorescence propagates in all directions, and only a small fraction of fluorescence intensity reaches the monochromator input. Therefore a light source with relative high power emission is required. It has been common practice to use a nitrogen laser, as monochromatic pulsed light source in fluorescence spectroscopy. Now days the nitrogen laser can be replaced by a laser diode but at a higher cost. During the past years the light emitter semiconductor materials have been improved, lowering wavelengths up to deep UV region, and increasing emission powers, at lower costs than laser diodes (Geddes & Lakowicz, 2004). Figure 6 shows a home made nitrogen laser system. The nitrogen is injected to a discharge chamber at around 20 mbar. When the spark-gap (SP) is open the capacitors C_1 and C_2 are charging from the high dc voltage supply and a 10 MΩ resistors bank (inductance L behaves as short-circuit). The voltage trough capacitors increases exponentially up to the spark-gap threshold voltage, then C_1 discharges immediately trough the spark-gap, and C_2 discharges trough the nitrogen inside the chamber (now L behaves as open-circuit). The excited nitrogen by the discharge produces an ultraviolet light pulse (337. 1 nm) at chamber output. After discharge the spark-gap is open, L behaves as a short-circuit, and capacitors voltage start to increase again. The repetition rate of laser pulses is given by time constant RC (around 30 ms) and the applied high voltage. With 10KV a frequency rate near 30 Hz is obtained.

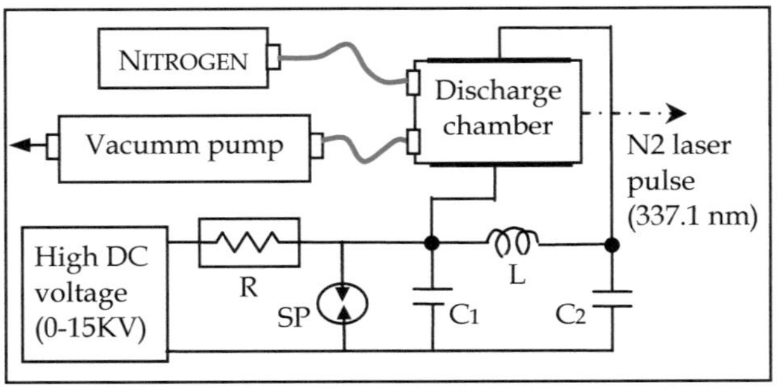

Fig. 6. Nitrogen pulsed laser

2.2 Monochromator

A monochromator is an optical system which decomposes an input light in its different wavelength components, and selects a single wavelength component at its output. Most of monochromators used in fluorescence spectroscopy contains a diffraction grating as dispersion element, since the inverse of the dispersion factor (D^{-1}) is constant at all wavelength. This parameter has nm/mm units and relates the effective wavelength bandwidth which goes trough the monochromator input slit, it is a quality factor of the monochromator (typical values: 2–8 nm/mm). The wavelength resolution is not important since the fluorescent emission spectra are wider than 5 nm. Normally, monochromators have input and output adjustable slits. The luminous intensity at any slit input is approximately proportional to the square of the slit width. For wider slits more light goes through the slit and then, the signal to noise ratio increases. A narrow slit improves the resolution at intensity expenses (Lakowicz, 1991), (Lakowics, 1999), (Gore, 2000).

For our spectrofluorometer we use a monochromator from Acton Research Corp., model SpectraPro 275, which is of the Czerny-Turner type with focal length of 275 mm. The instrument contains three selectable gratings for three different wavelength intervals. We use a grating with 2400 groves/mm for a 200 - 750 nm interval. The reciprocal linear dispersion factor D^{-1} is 3 nm/mm. The equipment includes a microprocessor control with menu driven software for scan control, grating selection, and change of scanning speed. All scanning functions and control parameters are selected locally from a keypad and a LCD display. Computer control is provided trough a standard RS-232 port.

2.3 Photodetectors

Perhaps the most used photodetector for time-resolved fluorescence spectroscopy is the photomultiplier tube (PMT), because two relevant characteristics: its high gain with low noise, which allows detecting weak fluorescence signals, and its fast response. A PMT consists of a photocathode covered with an emitter surface and a chain of electrodes (dynodes) which acts as amplification stages. The photocatode is supplied with a high negative potential (-1 KV to -2 KV) and dynodes also are supplied with negative potentials,

but less in magnitude for each dynode in the chain. The radiation reaching the photocatode produces emission of some primary electrons which are accelerated to the first dynode. When each one of these electrons hits the dynode several additionally electrons are emitted by collisions, and accelerated to the next dynode. The amplification process is repeated successively and the produced current is collected at the end of the chain (Lakowicz, 1999).
Other photodetector of growing use in steady-state fluorescence spectroscopy is the charge coupled device (CCD). This device consists of a thin silicon substrate with thousands or millions of small photodetectors elements, in one or two dimensional array. The substrate is coupled to metallic electrodes by means of silicon dioxide, and each element of the array functions as a MOS photodiode and capacitor (storage element). The charge related to the light intensity detected by each image element (pixel), is acquired sequentially and then converted into a digital format inside de same CCD (Spring, 2010).
An instrument with a single channel photodetecor like a PMT, produces a spectrum by means of the diffraction grating. For each grating position, a single point of information is registered. In contrast, a multichannel detector like CCD collects many points simultaneously; this permits to acquire a complete spectrum data in a single exposition. The acquisition speed of steady-state spectrum is much higher with a CCD (almost real time), compared with the acquisition speed with PMT (point by point). The major disadvantage of a CDD is its slow response time, or limited bandwidth, and then its application in time resolved spectroscopy is limited.
Now days there are complete PMT modules which include: a cd-cd converter to supply the high voltage required by the PMT, from a single +15 V supply, a cd voltage input to control PMT gain, and an output reference voltage. We use the PMT module H7732P-11 manufactured by Hamamatsu. This module contains a high sensitivity photomultiplier tube with 4x20 mm^2 of effective area of detection, a peak radiant sensitivity of 80 mA/W at 430 nm, 2 ns characteristic rise-time, and a capacitance of 4 pF. The output current pulse generated by the PMT is sent the oscilloscope through a coaxial cable. A voltage pulse is produced through the input impedance of the oscilloscope analog input. This impedance must be low enough to increase the bandwidth at the analog front end of the oscilloscope (see section 2.4)
In figure 5 a fraction of the laser pulse is reflected by a beam divider toward a reference photodiode. When the photodiode is negative biased, it produces an inverse current proportional to the light intensity, detected by its active area at the junction. The photodiode produces a current pulse similar to laser pulse which excites the sample. Also this reference current pulse is converted to a voltage pulse trough the input impedance of the oscilloscope analog input. This reference pulse is used as trigger signal to the oscilloscope to start the acquisition process on both input channels. We use the fast photodiode MRD500 with a response time of 1 ns on 50 Ω load, a sensitivity of 1 nA/mW/cm2 at 337.1 nm, and a capacitance of 4 pF.

2.4 Time-domain measurements

An automatic process for time-domain measurements involves the use of a digitizer (programmable digital system or digital oscilloscope), thus the continuous-time fluorescence pulse to measure has to be converted to a digital format in order to be recognized by the digital system. There are two basic sampling methods to perform the analog-to-digital conversion (ADC): real-time sampling and equivalent-time sampling. Equivalent-time sampling can by dived further into two sub-categories: random and sequential. Each method has distinct advantages depending on the kind of measurements being made (Lawton, 1986), (Nahman, 1978). Real-time methods require only a single occurrence of the signal to acquire an entire waveform, and the sampler operates at maximum speed to acquire as many points as possible in one sweep. Figure 7 shows the real-time sampling process with a sample rate = 1/Ts.

Equivalent-time methods, on other hand, require multiple occurrences of the signal to acquire the waveform. Samples are acquired over many repetitions of the signal, with one or more samples taken on each repetition. The sequential equivalent-time technique includes a trigger signal as figure 8 shows.

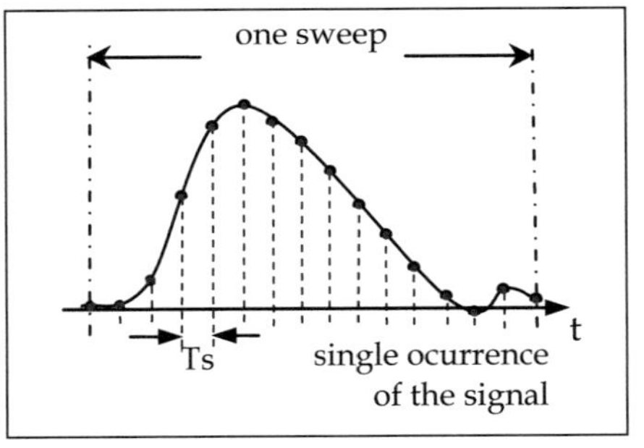

Fig. 7. Real-time sampling

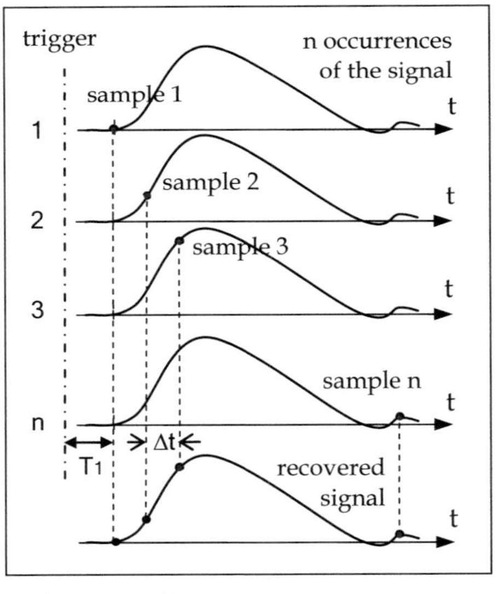

Fig. 8. Sequential equivalent-time sampling

When the first trigger is detected the first sample is taken after a fixed initial timeT_1. At the next period, a second sample is taken after a very short, but well defined, delay Δt from the time position of the first sample. When the next trigger occurs, the same time Δt is added to the previous delay and another sample is taken. This process is repeated many times, and after n periods of the signal, n samples have been taken to recover the waveform of the signal. If the sample point is shifted in sufficiently small steps Δt, this sampling method provides a very high bandwidths (65 GHz and higher) and timing resolution needed for time-resolved fluorescence signals. In random equivalent-time mode, portions of waveforms are acquired in real-time sampling during multiple trigger events. Over time, these portions are assembled into a complete waveform. Modern digital programmable oscilloscopes apply the three sampling techniques mentioned before, depending on the kind of measurements being made. In fluorescence spectroscopy, where nanoseconds times have to be resolved, the sequential equivalent-time is normally used.

To measure the reference and response signals in figure 5, we use the digital oscilloscope model 2440 from Tektronix®. This oscilloscope has 300 MHz analog input bandwidth, 500 MS/s maximum sampling rate, and 1 MΩ input impedance. This impedance can be programmed to be 50 Ω, as it is needed to measure the current signals coming from the photodetectors. Most of the oscilloscope features can be programmed from its rear panel, or from a computer via its GPIB port. We use the interface board GPIB-USB-HS from National Instruments, which is directly connected to the oscilloscope GPIB port. This board communicates with the computer via USB interface.

2.5 Bandwidth and rise-time specifications

Particularly we are interesting to time-resolve fluorescence lifetimes in nanoseconds order. For these very short times there are two important specifications of the acquisition system behavior to consider, these are its bandwidth analog front end BW(afe) and its equivalent rise time tr(afe). Bandwidth describes the analog front end's ability to capture an analog signal with minimal amplitude loss, and rise time slowing. Bandwidth is defined as the frequency at which the amplitude of the sampled signal decays 30% due to ADC performance. The rise time for a signal is defined as the time to transit from 10% to 90% of the maximum signal amplitude. Both concepts can be applied in general to signals, to systems, or to components, and they are inversely related by equation (6), which is based on the one pole model, R-C limited input response [Ardizzoni, 2007].

$$\mathrm{BW} = \frac{0.35}{\mathrm{tr}} \tag{6}$$

In our instrument the rise-time at analog front ends of the oscilloscope can be estimated from the time constant introduced by photodetectors output capacitance, and the impedance of the oscilloscope input channels. The rise-time for this RC circuit is given by tr = 2.2RC, where the input impedance R must be low enough to decrees rise-time (or to increase the bandwidth) at analog front end. The capacitance has a value of 4 pF for both photodetectors, and the input impedance is programmed to be 50 Ω, thus the rise-time at analog front end of both input channels is 0.44 ns or equivalently 800 MHz bandwidth according to equation (6). Not only the rise-time of the analog front end at acquisition system input, but also rise-times of oscilloscope and photodetectors contribute to slowing the input signal. The measured rise time tr(m) can be estimated by using a sum-of-squares technique as equation (7), where tr(exc) is the excitation pulse rise-time, and tr(eq) is the equipment characteristic rise-time (Weller, 2002). The equipment square rise-time can be expressed as equation (8), where each term in summation is the square rise-time of the k component in the measuring chain.

$$\mathrm{tr}^2(\mathrm{m}) = \mathrm{tr}^2(\mathrm{exc}) + \mathrm{tr}^2(\mathrm{eq}) \tag{7}$$

$$\mathrm{tr}^2(\mathrm{eq}) = \sum_{\mathrm{k}} \mathrm{tr}^2(\mathrm{k}) \tag{8}$$

Figure 9 shows a diagram with the main components in our electronic instrumental, where rise-times and bandwidths values are indicated for each component. Some of these values are given by manufacturers and others are calculated from equation (6).

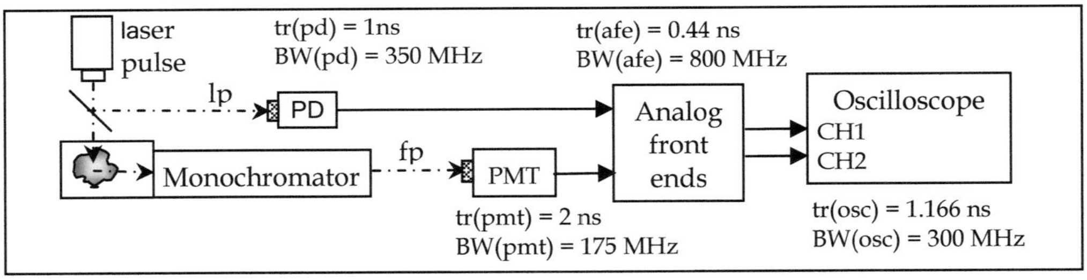

Fig. 9. Characteristic rise-times and bandwidths of each component of the measure chain

The laser pulse (lp) is detected by the photodiode (PD) and the fluorescence response pulse (fp) is detected by the PMT. From values in figure 9 and equation (8) we calculate for PD: $tr(eq)_{PD}$ = 1.59 ns, and for PMT: $tr(eq)_{PMT}$ = 2.35 ns. The laser pulse measured by the oscilloscope (figure 19, section 3.3) has a rise-time tr(lpm) = 1.78 ns, thus we can estimate the rise-time of the laser pulse as follows:

$$tr(lp) = \left(tr^2(lpm) - tr^2(eq)_{PD}\right)^{1/2} = 0.821\,\text{ns} \tag{9}$$

If the sample does not emit fluorescence (distillated water, per example) the laser pulse enters directly to monochromator, and then the measured signal corresponds to the system response and we can write the following expression:

$$tr^2(spm) = tr^2(lp) + tr^2(eq)_{MC\text{ - }PMT} \tag{10}$$

where tr(srm) is the rise-time of the system response pulse measured by the oscilloscope (figure 19) with a value of 5.64 ns, and $tr(eq)_{MC\text{-}PMT}$ is the equipment rise-time including monochromator rise-time. From values obtained we can assume $tr^2(srm) >> tr^2(lp)$, and then $tr(eq)_{MC\text{-}PMT}$ is approximately equal to tr(srm). This is the characteristic rise-time which slowing the fluorescence response signal, and it is mainly caused by the monochromator rise-time, for which we estimate tr(mc) = 5.13 ns. Other used form to quantified the slowing of the input signal is by means of the system temporal resolution, which is expressed in terms of pulse widths Δt as equation (11) (Lakowicz, 1991).

$$\Delta t^2(m) = \Delta t^2(exc) + \Delta t^2(eq) \tag{11}$$

3. Spectrofluorometer control program in LabView

A control program was developed in the graphical language G of LabVIEW 7.1 environment. This program controls the monochromator to generate a wavelength (λ) sweep, and reads the information of the time-resolved signals (excitation and response) measured by the oscilloscope in each λ value. The program was designed to execute one of three main functions, these are: a) *GoTo/Measure Noise*, b) *Sweep*, and c) *Open Files*. Following lines describe the algorithm for the main program.

S0) Serial Port Init.vi, goto λ.vi (250nm), actualλ = 250 nm ; initiation, sequenceS0
S1) while (STOP=false) ; sequence S1
case (Tab Control)
Go To / Measure Noise ; wait for a sub function Go to λ or Measure Noise = on
Sweep ; wait for a sub function Start = on
Open Files ; wait for a sub function Time Domain or Spectrum = on

In sequence S0, the serial port is initialized and the monochromator is positioned at 250 nm output wavelength, by means of the subvi "goto λ.vi". Then in sequence S1) a while sentence is executed for ever up to "STOP" control on the front panel (figure 16) is pressed. The function to execute is selected by means of a "Tab Control", for each function the panel shows the proper controls to start a sub function execution. Before reviewing the objects on the front panel we describe the program functions and developed subVI´s. Figure 10 shows a simplified diagram of the control logic during initial while sentence, when function *Go To/Measure Noise* is selected. For this function there are two sub function controls: if Measure Noise=on (as in figure 10) the respective algorithm is executed, if Measure Noise=off, means Go to λ=on, and then in the inner case structure, the "False" sentence executes the correspondence algorithm.

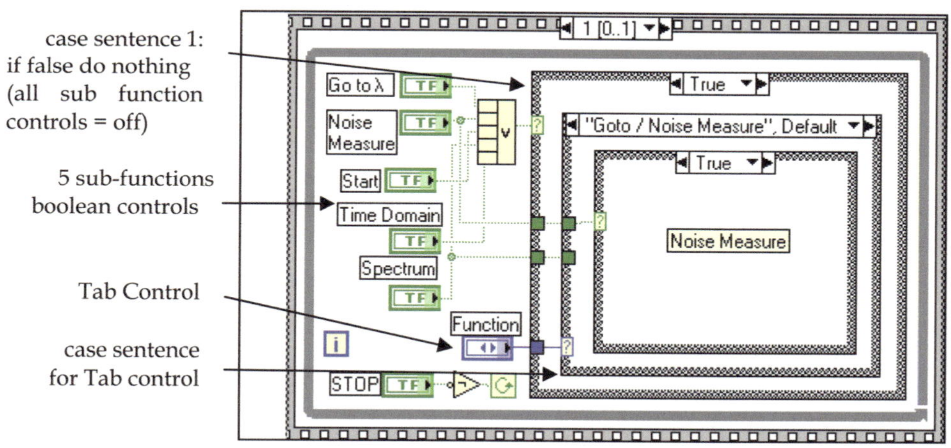

Fig. 10. Main while sentence S1

3.1 Functions and SubVi´s

Following lines describe the algorithms of program functions and developed subVI´s. Some LabVIEW diagrams are included.

a) Go To/Measure Noise

wait for (Go To λ or Measure Noise = on)
if Go To λ=on ; see diagram in figure 11
VER. Interval.vi ; verify valid values of λ, if not valid, do nothing and display an error message
goto λ.vi (λ to go) ; sends a command via serial port to move the monochromator from the actual value of λ (actualλ) to the destination value of λ (λ to go)
actualλ = λ to go

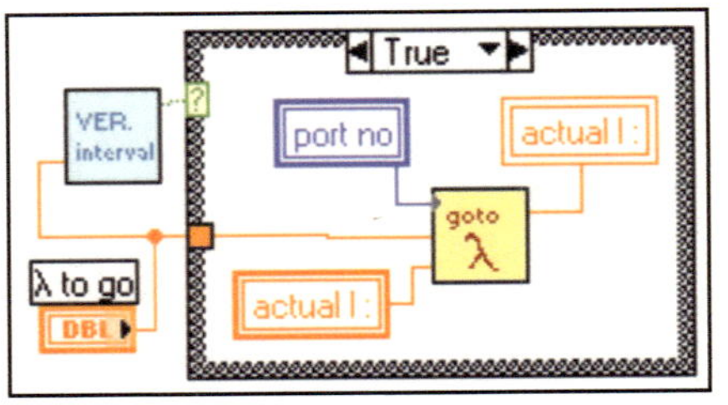

Fig. 11. Sub function Go To λ = on

if Measure Noise = on ; see diagram in figure 12

TM2440.vi (CH1, CH2, XInc) ; this sub.vi controls the oscilloscope via GPIB interface, to start a waveform acquisition of signals at channels 1 and 2. Acquisition ends when the oscilloscope had measured 16 waveforms of both input channels. The oscilloscope calculates average values of the waveforms measured, and send the averaged signals to subVi outputs CH1 and CH2, as k length arrays with k=1024 (fixed by oscilloscope). The output X inc corresponds to time interval used by oscilloscope during its temporal sweep. This subVi is a reduced and modified version from the original LabVIEW driver for the used oscilloscope.

noise1(k) = CH1

noise2(k) = CH2

time(k) = k*XInc

graph noise1(k) and noise2(k) vs time(k) in XY Graph "noise"

save data?

if yes "Write to Spreadsheet. vi"

The contents of arrays noise1(k) and noise2(k) are interpreted as noise information to be subtracted dynamically from the measured signals during the sweep function.

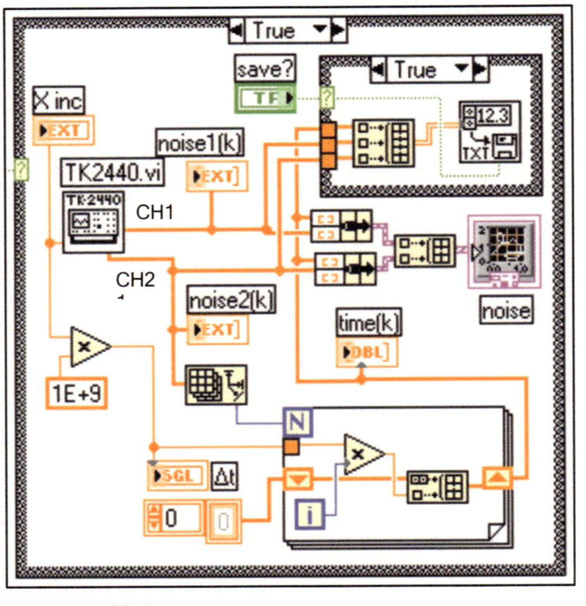

Fig. 12. Sub function Measure Noise = on

b) Sweep

wait for (Start =on)
VER. Interval.vi ; verify valid λ values
goto λ.vi (initialλ) ; move monochromator from actualλ to initialλ
actualλ = initialλ
while (finalλ > actualλ) ; sweep while
TM2440.vi (CH1, CH2, XInc)
lp(k) = CH1-noise1(k) ;laser pulse measurement with noise subtraction
fp(k) = CH2-noise2(k) ;fluorescence pulse measurement with noise subtraction
time(k) = k*XInc
graph lp(k) and fp(k) vs time(k) in XY Graph "temporal response"
nfp = max[fp(k)]/max[lp(k)]; because de laser pulse amplitude is not constant, it is necessary to normalize the fluorescence pulse amplitude at maximum peak
save in file: time(k), lp(k), fp(k)

Figure 13 shows a sequence where the file with the time-domain information is saved at locations given by the Path control and a string. This string is formed with the Base Name control and the value of actualλ, thus the file name contains the wavelength value at which the temporal data were measured. In the diagram there is a boolean constant to avoid saving time-domain data during the test procedures.

add element actualλ to array λ(j), and element nfp to array nfp(j) ; see figure 13
graph nfp(j) vs λ (j) in XY graph "spectrum" ; see figure 13
goto λ.vi (λactualλ + Δ λ)
actualλ = actualλ + Δ λ
save spectrum λ(j), nfp(j) ?; when sweep loop ends the complete spectrum can be saved

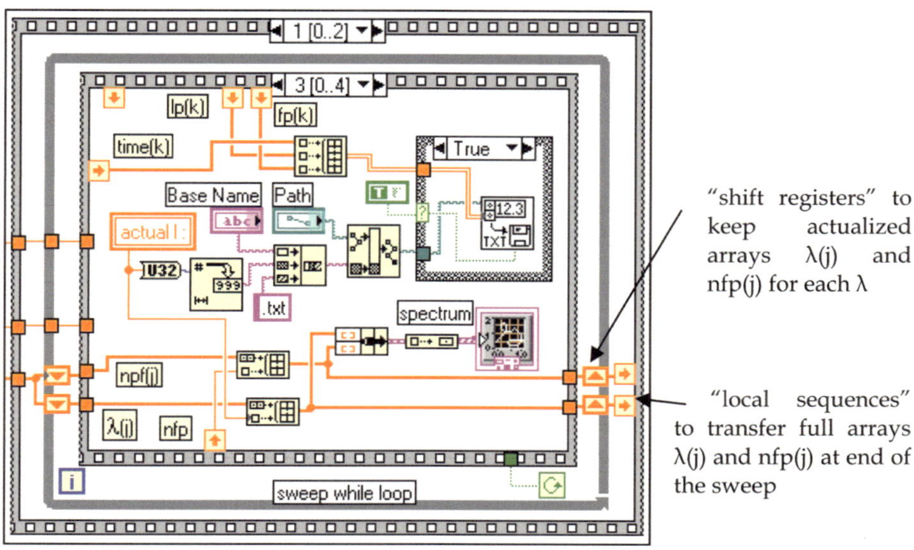

Fig. 13. A sequence of *Sweep* function to save time-domain data measured in a file with a name containing actual λ value

c) Open Files

wait for (Time Domain=on or Spectrum=on)

if Time Domain =on

open temps.vi ; this subVi can open several files with time-domain data and graph these in its own XY Graph. Each time that a new file is opened the graph is actualized. Because the subVi keeps in loop waiting for a new file to open, the information of this graph is transferred to the main panel XY Grap called "tempResponses", by means of "control references", as figure 14 shows.

if Spectrum=on

open spectra.vi ; this subVi performs similar to the previous one, but it opens spectra data. Also uses "control references"

SubVi: goto λ.vi (λ to go)

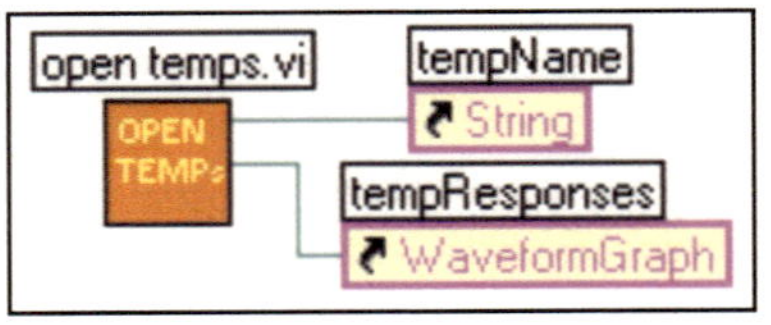

Fig. 14. "control references"

Figure 15 shows the two first sequences of subVi goto λ.vi. At left in first sequence, a string is ensemble to form the command "goto" recognized by the monochromator control. The command is sent to control via Serial Port Write.vi. Once the monochromator motor starts to move, it takes a time to reach the value of <u>λ to go</u> from <u>actual λ</u>. In second sequence this time is calculated according to maximum speed, and it is used as input to a delay element. It is important to reach <u>λ to go</u> before the oscilloscope starts an acquisition process.

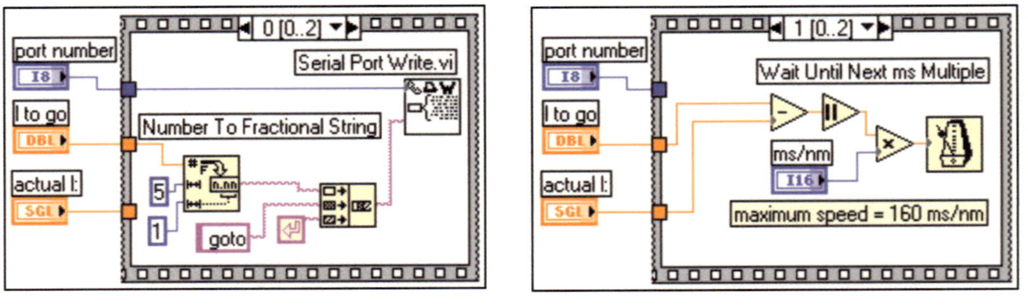

Fig. 15. First two sequences of SubVi goto λ.vi λ to go).

3.2 Front panel

The front panel of the developed program is shown in figure 16, where *Sweep* Function is selected by a Tap Control. At left there are 3 numeric controls to introduce λ values of the sweep to perform. At top there are two controls to introduce the Path and Base Name of the files to store time-domain information for a complete sweep. With selected values, the *Start* control is pressed to begin the sweep. First the monochromator output wavelength is controlled to move from actual λ (indicator at top-left corner on the panel) to initial λ, and then the oscilloscope is controlled to start waveform acquisition of laser pulse and fluorescence pulse. Each recorded laser and fluorescence pulses consisted on average

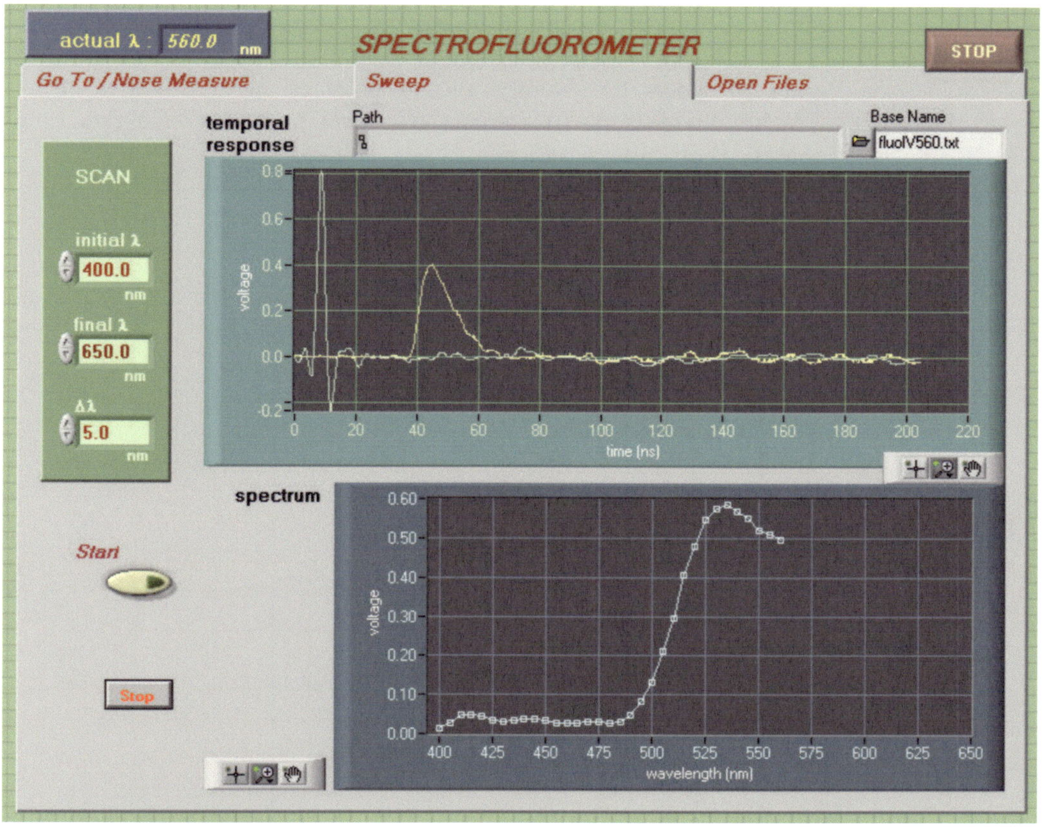

Fig. 16. Frontal Panel when *Sweep* function is selected and stopped at 560nm.

of 16 consecutive pulses computed by the oscilloscope before transfer to the computer. After receiving time-domain data from oscilloscope, the computer graphs the average time-resolved pulses on "temporal response" graph in figure 16, calculates the normalized peak fluorescence, and graphs this value on "spectrum" graph. The computer shifts the monochromator output wavelength by 5 nm and reset the oscilloscope for the next measurement. The sweep loop ends when final λ value is reached or Stop control is pressed (bottom-left corner). In figure 16 de sweep was stopped by "Stop" control, when monochromator was moving from 560nm to 565nm. The panels for other two functions show only their respective controls and indicators, similar to those in figure 16.

3.3 Measurements

Using the described spectrofluorometer and LabView program, we measured the fluorescence emitted by 3 substances with well known fluorescence life-times; these are fluoresceine, rhodamine 6G and rhodamine B. Their properties vary according to the used solvent. For distillated water as solvent, the life-time and wavelength at maximum emission of the fluorophores are: fluoresceine (4.03 ns, 517 nm), rhodamine 6G (4.08 ns, 555 nm) and rhodamine B (1.68 ns, 583 nm). Also we measured the fluorescence emitted by 3 mixtures of two fluorophores. For each fluorophore and mixture, were performed 6 wavelength sweeps from 400nm to 700nm with 5nm increments. The average spectra obtained for individual fluorophores are shown in figure 17, where λ value at maximum emission is indicated for each substance. Figure 18 shows the average spectra obtained for 3 mixtures of two components (50% each): fluoresceine-rhodamine 6G (f-r6G), fluoresceine-rhodamine B (f-rB) and rhodamine 6G-rhodamine B (r6G-rB).

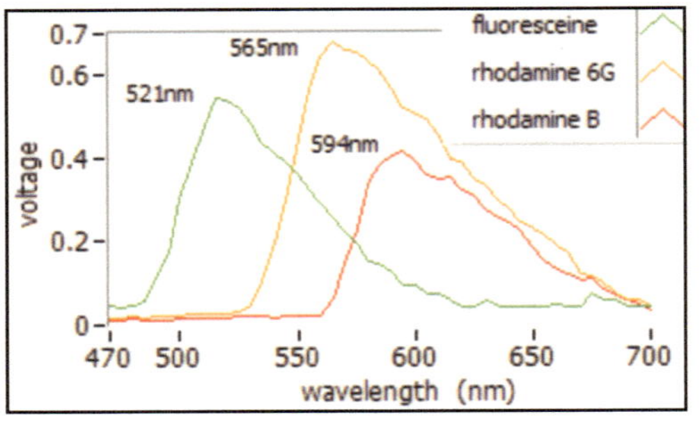

Fig. 17. Average spectra of fluorophores

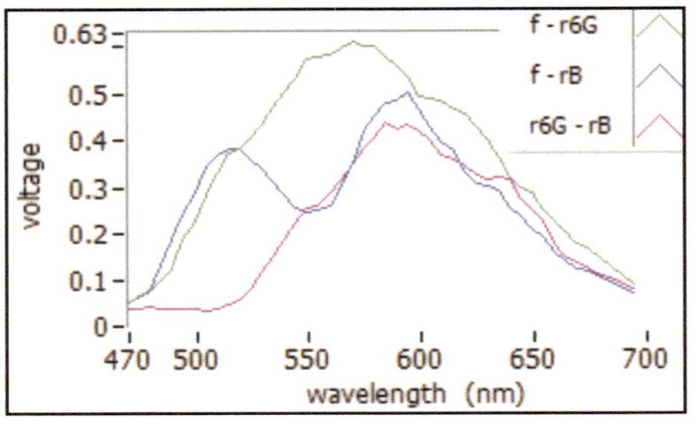

Fig. 18. Average spectra of mixtures

In figure 17 we observe that wavelengths at maximum emission peaks of the three fluorophores, are greater than the before mentioned reference values. These deviations may be produced because monochromator is out of calibration. In figure 18 the spectrum of mixture f-rB shows the emission peaks, one around 521 nm and other near 594 nm, both fluorophores. Because the spectra of the fluoresceine and the rhodamine 6G, and the spectra of the rhodamine 6G and the rhodamine B, overlap each other in a wider region. The wavelength at maximal emission in both mixtures are shifted in relation to their pure components.

Figure 19 shows the average time-resolved laser pulse and the system response pulse. This pulse was measured using distillated water as sample, which does not produce fluorescence. From recorded data we estimate for laser pulse tr(lpm) = 1.78 ns and FWHM(lpm) = 2.752 ns, and for system response pulse tr(srm) = 5.647 ns and FWHM(srm) = 13.28 ns. The average time-resolved fluorescence responses, measured for each fluorophore are shown in figure 20, where corresponding λ value is indicated. Figure 21 shows the average time-resolved fluorescence responses measured for each mixture at two different wavelengths. In section 4 we apply an analysis technique to estimate fluorescence life-times from the measured data.

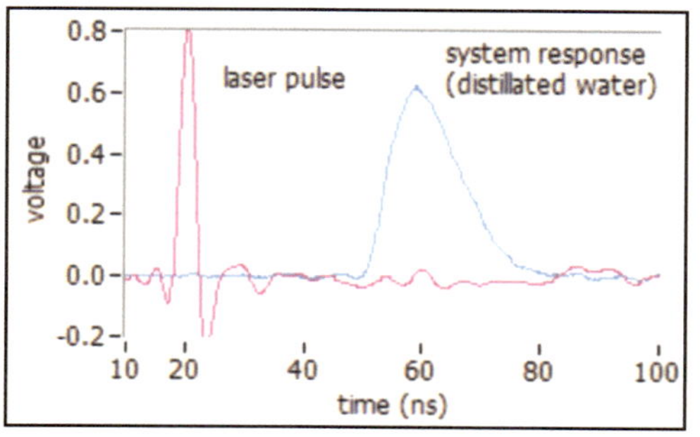

Fig. 19. Average time-resolved laser pulse and system response pulse

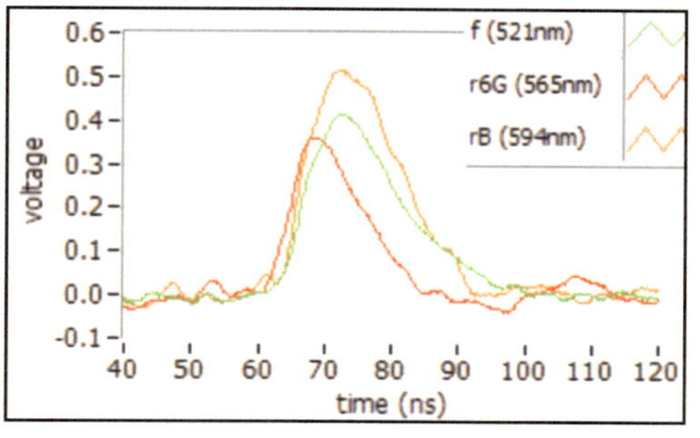

Fig. 20. Average time-resolved fluorescence responses each fluorophore

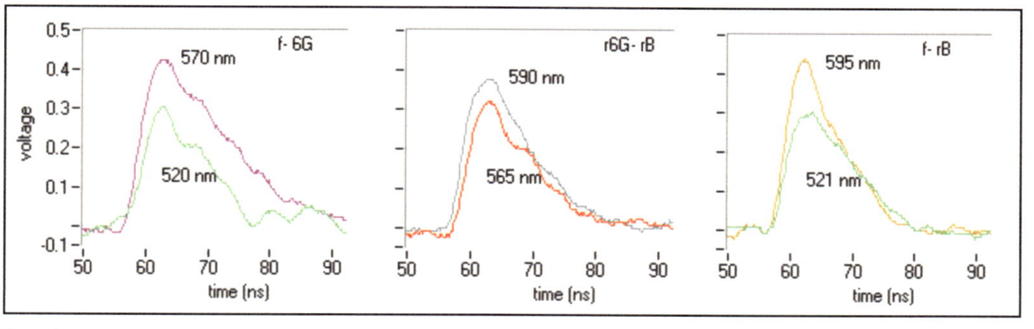

Fig. 21. Average time-resolved fluorescence responses of mixtures

4. Data analysis to estimate fluorescence lifetimes

In section 1.1 we stated that the fluorescence intensity due to a population of excited-state molecules decreases exponentially with time, following their instantaneous optical excitation, but equation (4) is only valid for δ impulse optical excitation. In practical time-domain spectroscopy, the excitation light pulse is of finite duration, and can be consider a δ function only if the florescence exponential decay is much greater than the excitation light pulse width. On other hand, there is not a direct relation between the exponential model of equation (4) with measured decays, meanly because the measurement instrumental introduces amplitude loss and rise time slowing of the signals to measure (section 2.5). Thus it is necessary to apply data analysis techniques to find the best estimation of fluorescence lifetimes.

4.1 Convolution integral and instrumental response

Mathematically, the fluorescence intensity decay data y(t) of a sample excited by a short pulse of light, is given by the convolution of the impulse response function h(t) (also called IRF) of the fluorescent sample, with the excitation light pulse f(t), i.e.

$$y(t) = h(t)*f(t) = \int_{-\infty}^{\infty} h(\tau)\, f(t-\tau)\, d\tau \tag{12}$$

The impulse response function h(t), represents the undistorted decay law of the sample which we want to estimate. If the excitation is an ideal δ function, the observed fluorescence y(t) is equal to the impulse response. In practice, the excitation light pulse is not a δ function, and then this pulse must be deconvolved from observed fluorescence intensity pulse to obtain h(t) (Lakowicz, 1999). As we mentioned, the inclusion of the instrumental to measure the florescence emitted by the sample, introduces distortions in the measured signal. To consider this, the data acquisition process can be represented as figure 22, where f(t) represents the excitation optical pulse, h(t) represents the fluorescence decay of the sample, y(t) is a signal with fluorescence information, s(t) represents the spectrometer response, and m(t) is the signal measured. The convolution of the complete system is given by equation (13).

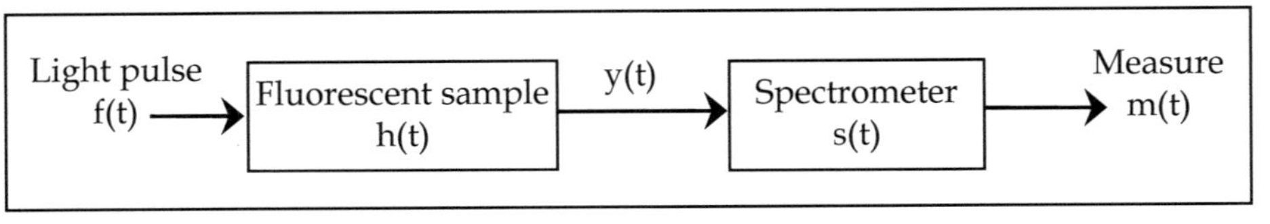

Fig. 22. Inclusion of the spectrometer response s(t) to measure the y(t)

$$m(t) = s(t) * y(t) = s(t) * [h(t) * f(t)] \tag{13}$$

To recover the fluorescence information from measured signals f(t) and m(t), the spectrometer response s(t) must be known. If the sample does not produce fluorescence (i.e. distillated water), thus h(t) = 1 and the measured signal represents the instrumental response: ir(t) = s(t)*f(t). Substituting this convolution in equation (13) yields:

$$m(t) = ir(t) * h(t) \tag{14}$$

Then, to estimate the intrinsic fluorescence h(t), the measured fluorescence m(t) must be deconvolved from the measured instrumental response ir(t).

4.2 Deconvolution techniques

Several deconvolution techniques have been developed to estimate the intrinsic fluorescence decay h(t) of a sample, from measured signals m(t) and ir(t). The measurement of these signals involves an analog to digital conversion process, where the signals are sampled in discrete times t_n. To be according with mathematical variables, we renamed our measured variables: $y(t_n)$ represents the fluorescence measured, and $f(t_n)$ represents the instrumental response. For discrete time the convolution of equation (14) becomes a summation as equation (15), where N is de number of samples, and T is the sampling interval.

$$y(t_n) = T \sum_{m=0}^{N-1} h(t_m)\, f(t_m - t_n) \tag{15}$$

As first approach we use the Fourier transform deconvolution method, which transforms the convolution in time-domain to a product in frequency-domain (O´Connor, 1979), i.e:

$$Y(\omega_n) = H(\omega_n)\ F(\omega_n) \tag{16}$$

In frequency-domain the intrinsic fluorescence $H(\omega_n)$ is calculated by division, and then $h(t_{n'})$ is found by the inverse Fourier transform of $H(\omega_n)$. It is suggested the use of the fast Fourier transform to greatly reduce the inherent oscillations produced during the inverse transformation process (0´Connor, 1979). Data analysis of time-resolved fluorescence spectroscopy includes identification of a set of fitting parameters that best describe the characteristics of the fluorescence decay. Typically the intrinsic fluorescence $h(t_{n'})$ found by deconvolution is assumed to be a multiple exponential decays function, from where lifetimes τ are obtained.

Among other methods, the most commonly used deconvolution technique is the nonlinear least-squares iterative reconvolution (LSIR) method. This technique applies a least-squares minimization algorithm to compute the coefficients of a multiexponential expansion of the fluorescence decay. A variant of classical LSIR method assumes the intrinsic fluorescence h(t) as an expansion on discrete time Laguerre functions, instead of a weighted sum of exponential functions (Maarek et all, 2000) (Jo et all, 2004). The Laguerre deconvolution technique uses an orthonormal set of discrete time Laguerre functions (LF) to expand the intrinsic fluorescence, i.e.:

$$h(t_n) = \sum_{j=0}^{L-1} c_j\, b_j^{\alpha}(t_n) \tag{17}$$

where c_j are the unknown Laguerre expansion coefficients, which are to be estimated from input data; $b_j^{\alpha}(t_n)$ denotes the j´th order discrete time LF; and L is the number of LFs used to model $h(t_n)$. The LF basis is defined as equation (18), where the Laguerre parameter ($0<a<1$) determines the rate of exponential decline of the LF (Maarek et all, 2000) (Jo et all, 2004). Inserting equation (17) into equation (15), the convolution becomes as equation (19).

$$b_j^{\alpha}(t_n) = \alpha^{(n-1)/2}(1-\alpha)^{1/2} \sum_{k=0}^{j} (-1)^k n^k \binom{n}{k}\binom{j}{k} \alpha^{(j-k)}(1-\alpha)^k \tag{18}$$

$$y(t_n) = \sum_{j=0}^{L-1} c_j\, \upsilon_j(t_n) \tag{19}$$

$$\upsilon_j(t_n) = T \sum_{m=0}^{k-1} b_j^{\alpha}(t_m)\, f(t_n - t_m) \tag{20}$$

In equation (20) $\upsilon_j(t_n)$ are the discrete time convolutions of the instrumental response with the LF. The unknown expansion coefficients can be estimated by generalized linear squares fitting of equation (19), using the measured discrete signals $y(t_n)$ and $f(t_n)$. This procedure involves the solution of a system of j equations. The optimal number of LFs and the value of the parameter α can be determined by minimizing the weighted sum of residuals:

$$\Phi = \sum_{n=0}^{N-1} w_n \left[y_0(t_n) - y_C(t_n) \right]^2 \quad (21)$$

where w_n is a weighting factor, $y_o(t_n)$ is the measured fluorescence, and $y_c(t_n)$ is the fluorescence computed by equation (15). Equation (15) is the convolution of the Laguerre expansion $h(t_n)$ of equation (17) with instrumental response $f(t_n)$. The iterative process ends when Φ reaches a minimum given value. The florescence decay lifetimes can by found by approximating the Laguerre expansion obtained to a multiexponential expansion.

4.3 Data analysis program

A data analysis program was developed in the graphical language G of LabVIEW 7.1 to estimate the intrinsic fluorescence decay $h(t_n)$, from deconvolution of the measured signals $y(t_n)$ and $f(t_n)$. This program applies the two deconvolution techniques described in section 4.2: Fast Fourier transform (FFT) and Laguerre expansion (LE). The intrinsic fluorescence $h(t_n)$ obtained with both methods is fitted to a simple exponential for a single fluorophore, or to double exponential for two compounds mixtures. From fitting results we can estimate the fluorescence lifetimes τ of the samples.

Before use the measured signals in any deconvolution method, they are first filtered to suppress undesired noises. The algorithm developed for noise filtering uses cursors resources of LabView. When this cursor facilities are used inside a while loop, it is possible to observe graphically the process results for different positions of the cursors. While the cursors in a graph are displaced, in other graph the process results are shown continuously. The filtering algorithm transforms the time-domain signals to frecuency-domain and a band-pass is selected by means of the cursors. The algorithm is described in following lines:

open a file with data t_n, $f(t_n)$ and $y_o(t_n)$, assign signals data to program variables f and yo ;
graph yo in a Waveform Graph "signals" (left graphs of figure 24) ;
obtain Fourier transforms of both signals: FFT{f} and FFT{yo}, using Real FFT.vi ;
graph FFT{yo} in XY Graph "FFT Real Mag" (right graphs of figure 24) ;
while (ok filter = off) ; while loop for dynamic processing, see figure 23
  read cursors positions in "FFT Real Mag" (blue traces in right graphs of figure 24) using property nodes, and find minimum and maximum x-indexes ;
  Cutoff.vi ; this subVI uses array functions to create a sub array with only the elements which are located between the cursor x-indexes, this means a cutoff of the signal outside the cursors positions. In graph "FFT Real Mag" x axes corresponds to frequency, thus the band-pass of the filter is the zone between cursors. The filtering process corresponds to a cut-off operation of the frequency spectrum.
  yo-filter = inverse Fourier transform of that part of the signal located between the cursors;
  graph yo and yo-filter in "signals" (left graphs in figure 24)

During while loop the cursors can be moved through the frequency-domain graph "FFT Real Mag". The effect of cursors displacement (select band-pass frequencies) can be observed continuously in time-domain graph "signals". This allows comparing the original and filtered signals dynamically. Figure 24 shows the result in time-domain (left graphs) for two different frequency band-pass (right graphs).

The instrumental response $f(t_n)$ is also filtered with the same band-pass selected with cursors. The filtering loop ends when the control "ok filter" on front panel is pressed.

After deconvolving by FFT, the useful information of the intrinsic fluorescence to be fitted is contained from its peak value to a minimum positive value. To cutoff signal in time-domain,

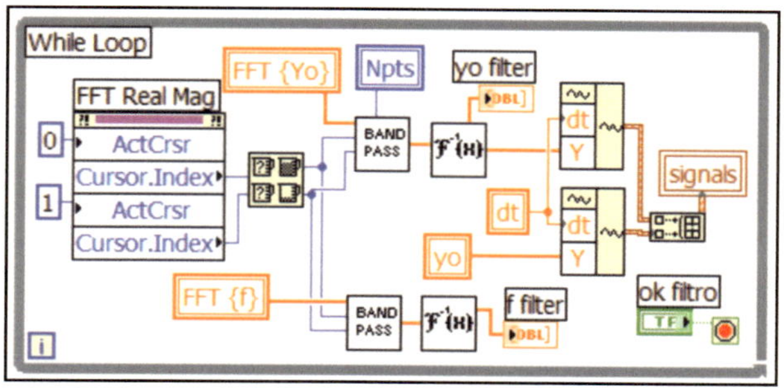

Fig. 23. Filtering process with cursors

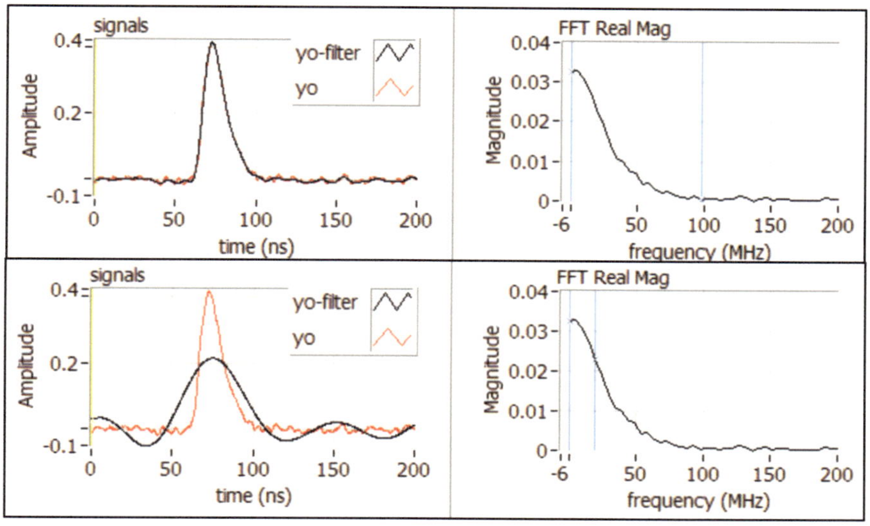

Fig. 24. Signals during filtering process

we use another while loop with dynamic cursors performance similar to that of figure 23. For fitting process we use the Levenberg-Marqurdt algorithm, which is already provided by LabVIEW as a SubVI. We assume a single exponential for a simple fluorophore, and double exponential for a two components mixture. The goodness of fit is tested by means of residuals of equation (20), where $y_c(t_n)$ is the fluorescence computed by convolving the best fit found for $h(t_n)$ and the instrumental response $f(t_n)$. Figure 25 shows the result for rhodamine6G at 565 nm.

The program for data analysis by Laguerre deconvolution technique uses the filtered signals and computes the Laguerre functions according to equation (18). The number of functions L and Laguerre coefficient α are given as known values. The algorithm sequence is as follows:

generate a set of Laguerre functions for given values of L and α, from equation (18)
computes $\upsilon_j(t_n)$ from equation (20)
ensemble the set of equations which minimize the sum of residuals Φ for coefficients c_j
adjust variables to the same time-length ; use of while sentence with dynamic cursors
c_j = Solve Linear Equations.vi ;LabVIEW function to find c_j coefficients
computes $h(t_n)$ from equation (17)
computes $y_c(t_n)$ from convolution of equation (15)
computes residuals $\Phi(t_n)$ from equation (21) ; $\Phi(t_n)$ = square error(t_n)

Levenberg Marqurdt.vi ;approximation to a simple exponential for a single fluorophore and to bi-exponential for two compounds mixtures to estimate fluorescence lifetimes

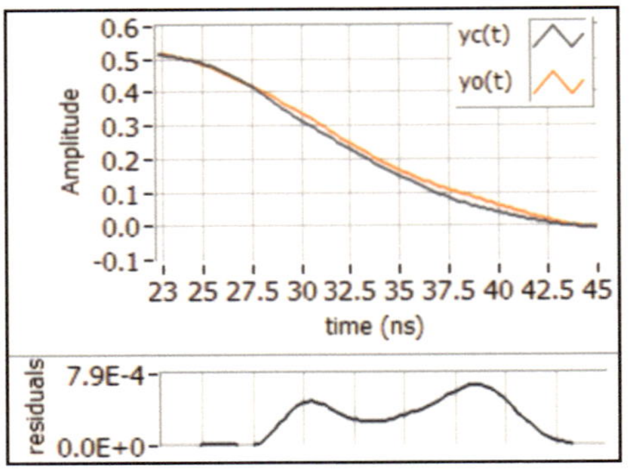

Fig. 25. Observed fluorescence and best fit

The analysis results are presented in terms of the fluorescence decay observed $y_o(t_n)$ and the fluoresce computed $y_c(t_n)$ with the best fit of the intrinsic fluorescence $h(t_n)$, as in figure 25. For a single fluorophore we use L=2 and for the mixtures L=3, α values were varied from 0.65 to 0.85.

4.4 Results

The performance of both deconvolution techniques FFT and LF is tested by means of the relative error (re), between reference value and the estimated lifetime, and the normalized mean square error (nmse). Table I summarizes the results obtained for each fluorophore at maximum emission peak wavelength, and table II summarizes the results for the mixtures, also at maximum emission peak wavelength. In tables refv is reference value from literauture, and estv is estimated value. From values in table I we observed that Laguerre expansion produces the best approximation for all fluorophores, with relative errors < -1%, and nmse values < 0.4%. Also, for mixtures in table 2 the best approximation is produced by

		FFT			Laguerre		
	refv (ns)	estv (ns)	re (%)	nmse (%)	estv (ns)	re (%)	nmse (%)
Fluoresceíne	4.01	4.12	2.23	1.15	3.99	-0.49	0.39
Rhodamine 6G	4.08	4.24	3.92	0.11	4.05	-0.73	0.09
Rhodamine B	1.68	1.59	-5.35	0.80	1.67	-0.12	0.24

Table 1. Results obtained for each fluorophore

	FFT					Laguerre				
	estv (ns)		re (%)		nmse	estv (ns)		re (%)		nmse
	τ1	τ2	τ1	τ2	(%)	τ1	τ2	τ1	τ2	(%)
f-r6G	3.92	4.17	-2.24	2.2	1.68	3.96	3.98	-1.25	-2.45	0.42
f-rB	4.03	1.49	0.49	-11.3	4.66	4.02	1.58	0.25	-5.95	0.86
r6G-rB	4.21	1.56	3.18	-7.14	2.56	4.08	1.71	0.12	1.78	0.82

Table 2. Results obtained for each mixture

Laguerre deconvolution technique, with relative errors < -1.25% for τ_1 and < -6% for τ_2. The nmse values are < 1%.

5. Conclusions

In this work we developed an automated spectrofluorometer prototype, which is able to perform time-resolved fluorescence measurements. The pulsed light source is a home made nitrogen laser, which generates UV pulses (337.1 nm) at 30 Hz rates, with FWHM = 2.75 ns. We use a monochromator from Acton Research Corp., model SpectraPro 275 which includes a microprocessor control to receive commands from a computer via a serial RS-232 port for scan control. To detect the fluorescence emitted by the sample, we use the PMT module H7732P-11 manufactured by Hamamatsu, which contains a high sensitivity photomultiplier tube with a peak radiant sensitivity of 80 mA/W at 430 nm, and 2 ns characteristic rise-time. To detect the laser pulse we use the fast photodiode MRD500 with a response time of 1 ns on 50 Ω load, and a sensitivity of 1 nA/mW/cm2 at 337.1 nm.

To measure the excitation pulse laser and the fluorescent response pulse, we use a digital oscilloscope model 2440 from Tektronix®. This oscilloscope has 300 MHz analog input bandwidth and 1 MΩ input impedance. This impedance can be programmed to be 50 Ω, as it is needed to measure the current signals coming from the photodetectors. The oscilloscope operation is programmed from a computer via its GPIB port. We use the interface board GPIB-USB-HS from National Instruments, which is directly connected to the oscilloscope and communicates with a computer via USB interface. For the complete spectrometer, we determine the characteristic rise-time of the instrumental (5.647 ns) and its temporal resolution (FWHM = 13.28 ns). This slowing of the input signal is mainly caused by the monochromator.

A control and acquisition program was developed in the graphical language G of LabVIEW 7.1 environment. This program controls the monochromator to generate a wavelength (λ) sweep, and reads the information of the time-resolved signals (excitation and response) measured by the oscilloscope in each λ value. The program was designed to execute one of three main functions: *GoTo/Measure Noise*, *Sweep*, and *Open Files*. With this program we measured the fluorescence emitted by 3 substances with well known fluorescence life-times: fluoresceine, rhodamine 6G and rhodamine B. Also we measured the fluorescence emitted by 3 mixtures of two fluorophores. For each fluorophore and mixture, were performed 6 wavelength sweeps from 400nm to 700nm with 5nm increments.

A data analysis program was developed in LabVIEW 7.1 to estimate the intrinsic fluorescence decay from deconvolution of measured signals. The program applies two deconvolution techniques: Fast Fourier transform and Laguerre expansion. The intrinsic fluorescence obtained with both methods is fitted to a simple exponential for a single fluorophore, or to double exponential for two compounds mixtures. From fitting results we can estimate the fluorescence lifetimes τ of the samples. LabVIEW provides an easy access to cursor resources. When these cursor facilities are used inside a while loop, it is possible to observe graphically the process results for different positions of the cursors. While the cursors in a graph are displaced, in other graph the process results are shown continuously. We used this while loop with dynamic cursors inside, to perform filtering, shifting, and cutting of signals.

From data analysis results, deconvolution by Laguerre expansion provides a good approximation with nmse values < 0.4% for single fluorophore and < 1% for mixtures. The Laguerre functions have been suggested as an appropriate orthonormal basis owing to their buil-in exponential term that makes them suitable for physical systems with asymptotically exponential relaxation dynamics (Jo et all, 2004). Because the Laguerre basis is a complete orthonomal set of functions, a unique characteristic of this approach is that it can reconstruct a fluorescenece response of arbitrary form. Laguerre deconvolution technique is a suitable approach for the analysis of time-domain fluorescence data of complex systems, since this technique has the ability to expand intrinsic fluorescence of any form, without any a priori assumption of its functional form.

6. References

Anderson, J.; Fischer, R.; Smith, C.; Webb, S. & Dennis, J. (2003). In situ detection of pathogen indicators using laser-induced fluorescence, *Proccedings of 2003 UCOWR Annual Conference "Water Security in the 21st Century"*, http://ucowr.siu.edu/proc/W1C.pdf.

Ardizzoni, J. (2007). High-Speed Time-Domain Measurements - Practical Tips for Improvement, Analog Dialogue, March 2007, 41-03.

Geddes, Ch. D. & Lakowicz, J. R. (2004). Lakowicz, *Reviews in Fluorescence 2004*, Kluwer Academic/Plenum Publishers, 0-306-48672-5 (eBook), New York, USA.

Gore, M.G. (2000). *Spectrophotometry and Spectrofluorimetry*, Oxford University Press, 2nd Edition, 0-19963812-8, New York, USA.

Jo, J.; Fang, Q.; Papaioannou, T. & Marcu, L. (2004). Fast model-free deconvolution of fluorescence decay for analysis of biological systems, *Journal of Biomedical Optics*, 9(4), 743 - 752.

Lakowicz, J. R. (1991). *Topics in Fluorescence Spectroscopy, Volume 1: Techniques*, Plenum Press, 0-3064-3874-7, New York, USA.

Lakowicz, J. R. (1999). *Principles of Fluorescence Spectroscopy*, Klumer Academic/Plenum Publishers, 2nd Edition, 0-306-46093-9, New York, USA.

Lawton, R.; Riad, S. & Andrews, J. (1986). Pulse and Time- Domain Measurements,. *Proc. IEEE, Vol.74, Jan. 1986*, 77-81.

Maarek, J-M.I.; Marcu, L.; Snyder, W.J. & Grundfest, W.S. (2000). Time-resolved Fluorescence Spectra of Arterial Fluorescent Compounds: Reconstruction with the Laguerre Expansion Techique, *Photochemistry and Photobiology*, 71, 178-187.

Moller, C. & Mortensen, G. (2008). Fluorescence spectroscopy; a rapid tool for analyzing dairy products, *J. Agric. Food Chem.*, 56, 720-729.

Nahman, N.S. (1978). Picosecond-Domain Waveform Measurements, *Proceedings of IEEE, Vol. 66, No.4*, April 1978, 441-454.

Nesterenko, T.V.; Tikhomirov, A.A. & Shikhov, V.N. (2007). Chlorophyll fluorescence induction and estimation on plant resistance to stress factors, *Zh. Obshch Biol.*, 68, 444-458.

O´Connor, D.V. & Ware, W.R. (1979). Deconvolution of fluorescente decay curves. A critical comparison of techniques, *The Journal of Physical Chemistry*, 83, 1333-1343.

Paras, N. P. (2003). *Introduction to Biophotonics*, Jhon Wiley&Sons, Inc., 0-471-28770-9, New Jersey.

Poulli, K.I.; Mousdis, G.A. & Georgiou, C.A. (2007). Rapid synchronous fluorescence method for virgin olive oil adulteration assessment, *Food Chemistr*, 105, 369-375.

Spring, K.R.; Fellers T.J. & and Davidson, M.W. (2010). Introduction to Charge-Coupled Devices (CCDs), Nikon Microscopy Fundamentals of Digital Imaging http://www.microscopyu.com/articles/digitalimaging/ccdintro.html

Valeur, B. (2002). *Molecular Fluorescence: Principles and Applications*, Wiley-BCH-Verlag, 3-527-29919-X, Federal Republic of Germany.

Vo-Dinh, T. (2003). *Biomedical Photonics Handbook*, CRC Press, 0-8493-1116-0, Florida, USA

Weller, D. (2002). Relating wideband DSO rise time to bandwidth: Lose the 0.35, *EDN*, Dec. 12, 2002, 89-94.

10

LabVIEW Applications for Optical Amplifier Automated Measurements, Fiber-Optic Remote Test and Fiber Sensor Systems

S. W. Harun, S. D. Emami, H. Arof, P. Hajireza and H. Ahmad
University of Malaya
Malaysia

1. Introduction

For the past 20 years, intensive researches in the fields of optoelectronics and fiber optic communications have resulted in the invention of new devices that revolutionized our life. The optoelectronics devices such as compact disc players, laser printers, bar code scanners, and laser pointers are some of the examples [1]. In fiber optic communications, revolution in the telecommunications system has been initiated by the introduction of higher bandwidth, more reliable telecommunication links with lower bandwidth cost [2]. Recently, fiber optic sensor technology has gained interest from the research community. Optical fiber sensors offer a number of advantages over conventional electrical sensing technologies, which make them attractive for a wide range of application areas. These advantages include intrinsic safety in chemically hostile or explosive environments, low susceptibility to electromagnetic interference, electrically passive operation and high sensitivity, compatible with composites, light weight and geometrical versatility [3]. Improvement in fiber optic technology creates a necessity for a virtual instrumentation system. A virtual instrumentation system is software used for developing a computerized test system, a measurement system, a calibration system, a control system for an external measurement hardware device and a display system for test or measurement data [4]. The best virtual instrumentation system that has been developed so far is LabVIEW. LabVIEW is an application development program that was developed by National Instruments in 1986 to integrate science and engineering tasks by interfacing computers with instruments for collecting, storing, analyzing, and transmitting data while, at the same time, providing an effective user interface. Different from other development software such as C/C++, FORTRAN, Basic, etc., LabVIEW utilizes its own integrated programming language known as the Graphical Programming Language, which uses graphics as code sequences in the application being developed, making the software development process significantly easier [5]. LabVIEW is powerful programming software that can interface with over 7,000 instruments to provide data acquisition, industrial measurement, automated testing, and instrument control. Integrated through LabVIEW, instruments such as sensors, optical time domain reflectometer (OTDR), oscilloscopes, optical spectrum analyzer (OSA) and RF generators can work alongside the GPIB hardware application software that makes fiber optic communication system research activities significantly easier [6].

In this chapter, applications of LabVIEW in automatic test measurement of fiber optic system are demonstrated. In the first section, the LabVIEW applications in fiber optic system and the basics of instrument connectivity are presented. Then, the aspects of hardware communication to external instruments through GPIB and serial interfaces are analyzed. Next, self-calibrating automated characterization system for depressed cladding applications is demonstrated utilizing the LabVIEW's GPIB interface. The automation system consists of a tunable laser source (TLS), optical spectrum analyzer (OSA), attenuator, laser diode controller, and a personal computer all networked using GPIB cables. Results of the manual and automatic measurements and the analysis of the measurement trace obtained from the optical time domain reflectometer (OTDR) are shown. Subsequently, the communication methods between the OTDR device and personal computer along with the details of the automation program developed using LabVIEW are presented. In the end, two applications of LabVIEW in fiber optic sensor system are discussed.

2. LabVIEW for fiber optic applications

Fiber optic systems have become in high demand for use in telecommunication and sensor systems. The optical systems, whether transmitting data across continents or providing real time measurement consist of dozens of components. These components are made from many different types of exotic materials and the manufacturing technologies are so new. Traditional labor intensive techniques cannot keep up with market demands, which require a cheaper solution. This section explains the automatic test measurement, fiber sensor and remote testing, which can be used to solve many problems in fiber optic system.

2.1 Self-calibration automated measurement

Automatic test measurement is a vital part of the telecommunication and fiber optic communication test scene today. Automatic test measurement enables self-calibrating test to be done very swiftly and accurately. The amount of time consumed in implementing a fiber optic sensor system forms the bulk of the development cost and thus it is necessary to reduce the troubleshooting time to the shortest possible. This can be achieved with the use of automatic test measurement techniques [6]. There are a variety of different approaches that can be used for automatic test measurement systems. Each type has its own advantages and disadvantages, and can be used to great effect in the right circumstances. Automatic test equipment and automatic test software are the two main types of test measurement systems. Equipments such as automatic optical inspection (AOI), automated X-Ray inspection (AXI) and In-Circuit Test (ICT) are common forms of automatic test equipment which are used today in optical and electrical science [4]. One the best solution in automatic test equipment is a board or unit that can be tested using a stack of remotely controlled test equipment. The most popular method of controlling the test equipment is the General Purpose Interface Bus (GPIB). There may also be an interface adapter necessary to control and interface with the item under test. While the GPIB is relatively slow and has been in existence for over 30 years it is still widely used as it provides a very flexible tool of test. This type of systems use test instruments on a board that can be slotted into a standard slot thus saving both space and cost when compared to the stand-alone. Laboratory test equipment can often be used as most items of lab test equipment have a GPIB port. The main drawback of GPIB is its speed and the cost of writing the programmes although packages like LabVIEW can be used to aid programme generation and execution in the test environment [5].

2.2 Fiber optic sensor

Fiber optic sensor is a device in which variations in the transmitted power or the rate of transmission of light in optical fiber are the means of measurement or control. The information could also be derived in terms of intensity, phase, frequency, polarization, spectral content, or other quantities. Physical parameters such as strain, temperature, pressure, velocity, and acceleration can be measured by fiber optic sensor. Immunity to electromagnetic interference (EMI) and radio frequency interference (RFI), elimination of conductive paths in high-voltage environments, inherent safety and suitability for extreme vibration and explosive environments, tolerant of high temperatures (>1450 C) and corrosive environments, light weight, and high sensitivity are the main advantages of fiber optic sensor over normal sensor [7]. Depending on the usage, fiber optic sensors can be divided into Extrinsic (or Hybrid) and Intrinsic (or All-Fiber) types.

Figure 1 shows an extrinsic sensor which consists of an optical fiber that transmits modulated light from a conventional sensor. A major feature of extrinsic sensors, which makes them so useful in such a large number of applications, is their ability to reach places which are otherwise inaccessible. In an extrinsic sensor, sensing takes place in a region outside of the fiber [8]. An intrinsic sensor relies on the properties of the optical fiber itself to convert signals from the environmental into a modulation of the light beam passing through it. Intrinsic sensors can modulate the intensity, phase, polarization, wavelength or transit time of light. Sensors which modulate light intensity tend to use mainly multimode fibers, but only single mode cables are used to modulate other light parameters. A particularly useful feature of intrinsic fiber optic sensors is that they can, if required, provide distributed sensing over distances of up to 1 meter [7].

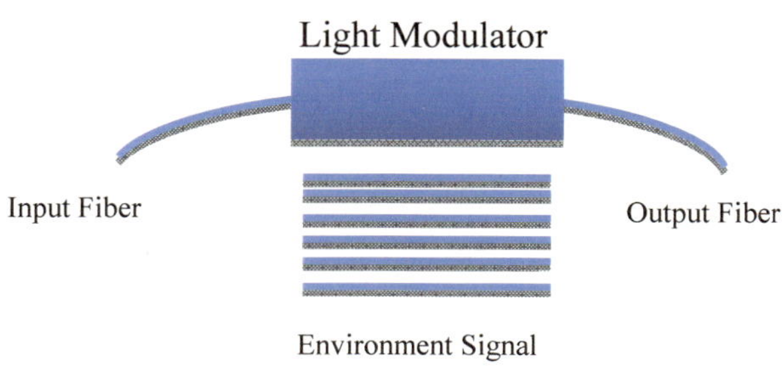

Fig. 1. Extrinsic sensor

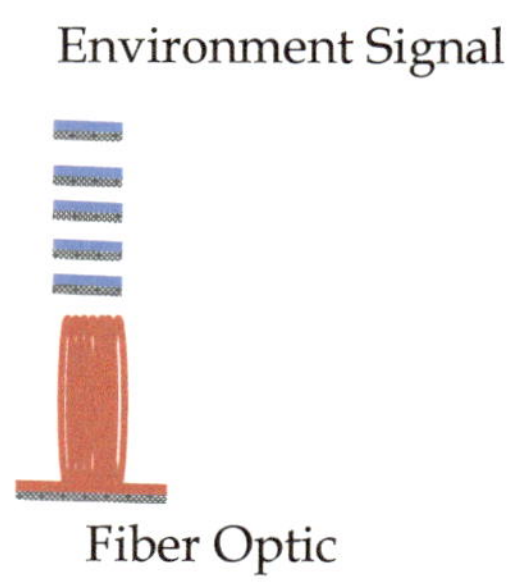

Fig. 2. Intrinsic sensor

Different types of fiber optic sensors are designed based on the characteristics of light modulated by the environmental effects. One of the most popular fiber optic sensors is the intensity based fiber sensor. Intensity-based fiber optic sensors depend on the principle that light can be modulated in intensity by an environmental effect. Multimode fiber reflective sensor and bending the fiber are two examples of fiber optic sensors. Figure 3 shows a displacement sensor using a multimode fiber. In this sensor, a light leaves the fiber end in a cone pattern, and strikes a movable reflector as shown in Figure 3. The intensity of reflected light is related to the distance of the fiber-reflector from the fiber's end [9].

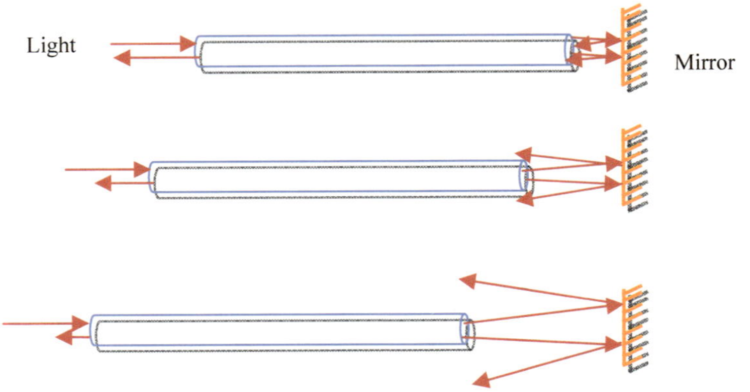

Fig. 3. An example of a fiber optic displacement sensor

Bending effect is another option which can be used to affect light intensity in an optical fiber. Figure 4 shows the fiber optic displacement sensor using the light intensity modulation based on the bending effect. As shown in the figure, the fiber loss increases as the deformer closer to the fiber. The displacement of the deformer is linearly dependent on the intensity of the transmitted light [10]. In interferometric fiber optic sensors, the optical phase of the light passing through the fiber is modulated by the field to be detected. This phase modulation is then detected interferometrically, by comparing the phase of the light in the signal fiber to that in a reference fiber [8].

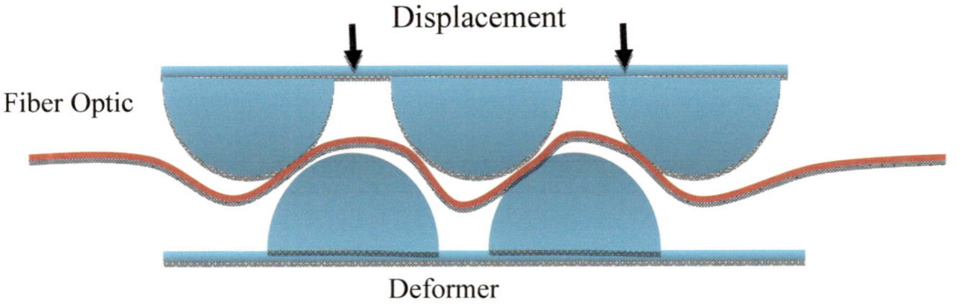

Fig. 4. Fiber optic displacement sensor based on bending effect

2.3 Remote fiber test system

A Remote Fiber Test System (RFTS) is used mainly for error detection in optical networks that may arise due to mechanical faults or quality losses in the optical fibers and connectors that form the optical communication network [11]. Optical Time Domain Reflectometer (OTDR) is the main device for measurement and software control of the measurement process in RFTS. Figure 5 shows a simple RFTS measurement system. The control unit is a personal computer which is used for pre and post-measurement management. The OTDR functions as a measurement unit and the optical power splitter divides an input power equally into output ports. The optical power splitter can be replaced by an optical switch [12].

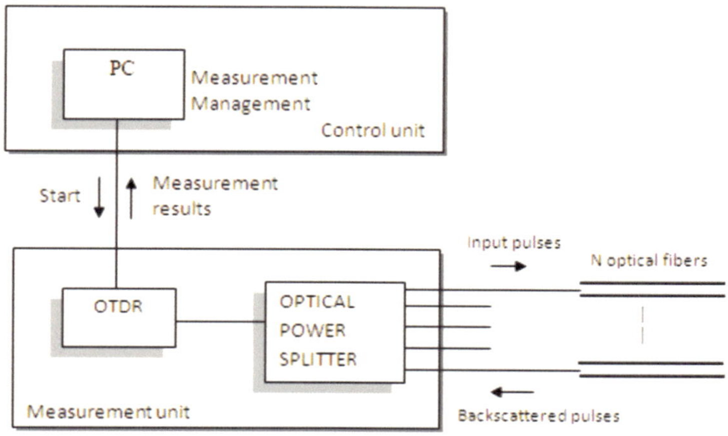

Fig. 5. RFTS measurement system.

The measurement process begins as the OTDR injects a short light pulse into the optical power splitter. In the splitter, the input power is divided into several output ports with power ratio specified by the splitter type. As the light pulse travels along the test fiber, a fraction of light is reflected back to the optical power splitter due to Rayleigh scattering and Fresnel reflection. All the scattered signals from the test fiber form a complex measurement trace as they reach the OTDR. Finally, the OTDR trace is saved in the computer memory and the analysis of the measurement result begins. In the standard RFTS, the error detection system is based on the measurement of the total loss in the optical link. Another approach that can be used is by comparing the reference and test measurement results. The reference measurement is collected just after the installation of the optical communication system [4]. As the test measurement is performed, the resulting test OTDR trace is compared with the reference trace. If the difference between the optical power level of the reference and the test measurement at certain measurement point exceeds the predefined threshold, the RFTS reports an error and stops the measurement. The time for the measurement to repeat is controlled by the user. The whole measurement process is software controlled and managed by LabVIEW [13].

3. Instrument communication methods

There are different types of communication methods available for controlling laboratory instruments as well as optical components. These methods are serial, parallel, GPIB, VXI,

PXI and others, which the choice is mainly based on the applications. Two most common instrument communication methods are GPIB and serial port communication. In 1965, Hewlett-Packard designed the Hewlett-Packard Interface Bus (HP-IB) to connect their line of programmable instruments to their computers. Because of its high transfer rates (nominally 1 MB/s), this interface bus quickly gained popularity. It was later accepted as IEEE Standard 488-1975. Today, the General Purpose Interface Bus (GPIB) is more widely used than the HP-IB. This is due to its ability to connect to different devices to the same GPIB bus. Any devices must have a unique GPIB address between 0 and 30, so that the data source and destinations can be specified by this number. Address 0 is assigned to the GPIB interface board. The GPIB has one Controller, usually a computer that controls the bus management functions. The LabVIEW GPIB VI automatically handles the addressing and most other bus management functions, saving user from the hassle of low-level programming. To use GPIB as part of in any virtual instrumentation systems, the GPIB driver software is required and can be installed in our computer according to the directions that accompany LabVIEW or the board. Installing a GPIB board is usually easy [14].

To configure the GPIB, serial interface or any communication method, NI Measurement & Automation Explorer (NI-MAX) simulation software can be used. The GPIB boards can be integrated with the NI-MAX so that it can be configured under the Devices and Interfaces tree easily. For the other GPIB devices, their installation procedures are described in the manual that comes with the GPIB board. Figure 6 illustrates the MAX windows which shows the GPIB interface number as 0. It is followed by an instrument with the primary address 2.

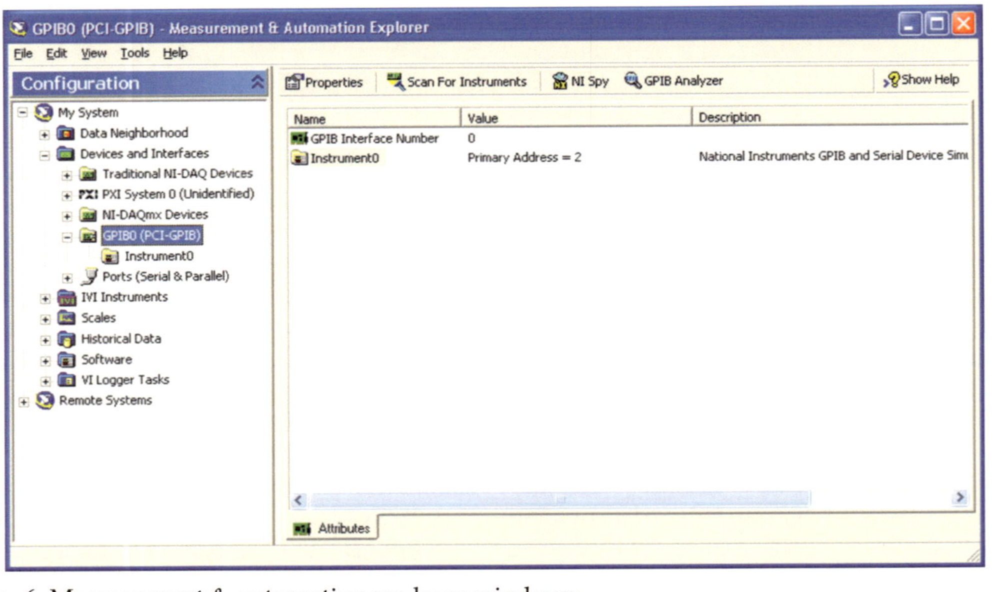

Fig. 6. Measurement & automation explorer windows

Serial communication is the other popular means of transmitting data between a computer and a peripheral device such as a programmable instrument or even another computer. Serial communication uses a transmitter to send data, one bit at a time, over a single communication line to a receiver. This method is normally used when data transfer rates are low or the data needs to be transferred over long distances. Serial communication is popular because most industrial computers have at least one serial port available. However, for laptops and smaller desktops that do not have a built-in serial port, an inexpensive USB-to-RS-232 adaptor can also be used. Serial communication requires that you specify four parameters: the baud rate of the transmission, the number of data bits encoding a character, the sense of the optional parity bit, and the number of stop bits. The requirements for port setting features are shown in the Ports (serial and parallel) menu in Figure 7. For the port binding, it is used for specifying the port to be used for the serial/parallel device. An alternative port can be selected to link to the ASRL resource, this setting does not change the logical port number (COMx) of the physical serial port, it only changes which COM port this VISA resource is binding to. After that, click the "Validate" button to test whether NI-VISA can access the resource with the specified configuration. The result shown on Figure 8 should pop up.

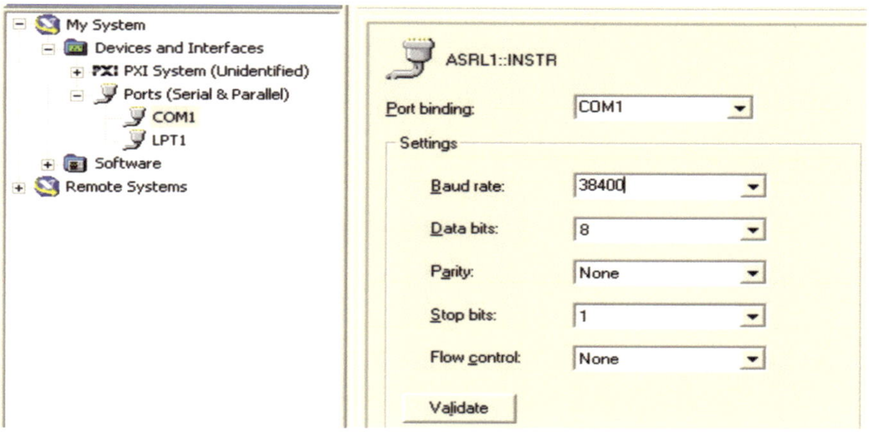

Fig. 7. Serial port setting

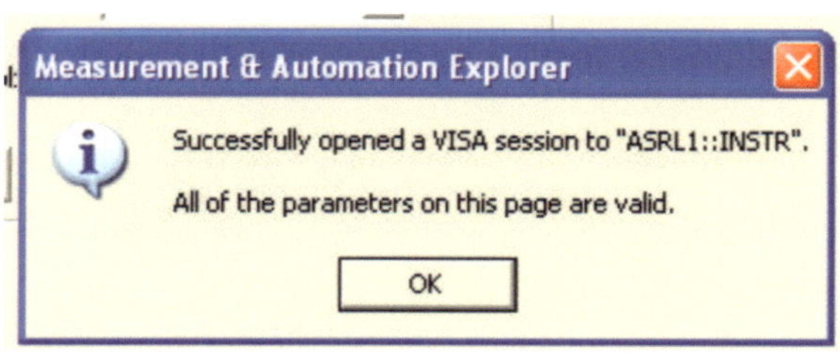

Fig. 8. Validation of NI-MAX

When a VISA session to "ASRL1::INSTR" is successfully opened, communication with the device can be started by going to the Property Node (Set) and modifying the value of the specified attribute as shown in Figure 9. The values for serial baud rate, serial data bits, serial stop bits, serial flow control and others are set to the same values as those chosen during Port Setting. Then click the execute button. Next, as shown in Figure 10, click the "Write" tab and fill up the blank box under the "Buffer" with a proper command ending with "\r\n" to initiate the communication with the serial device. The function of "\r\n" is just like the "ENTER" button on a personal computer keypad. Without "\r\n", the command is incomplete, and hence, NI-MAX cannot recognize it. This is the same as when the command at Hyper Terminal has been inserted, the "ENTER" key must be pressed to start the communication with the equipment such as OTDR.

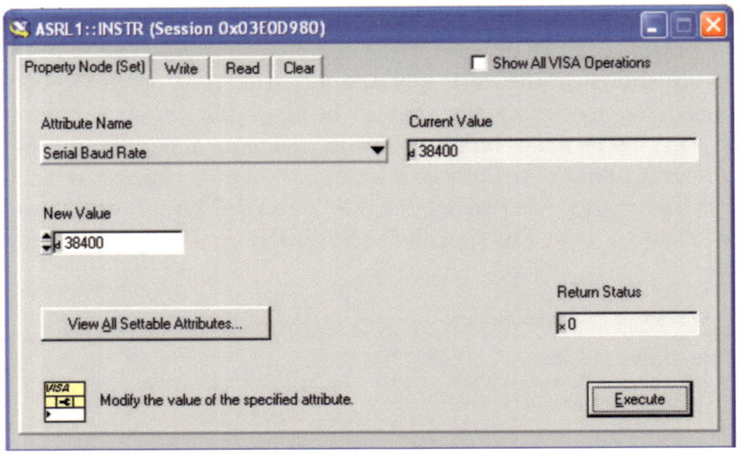

Fig. 9. Property node setting

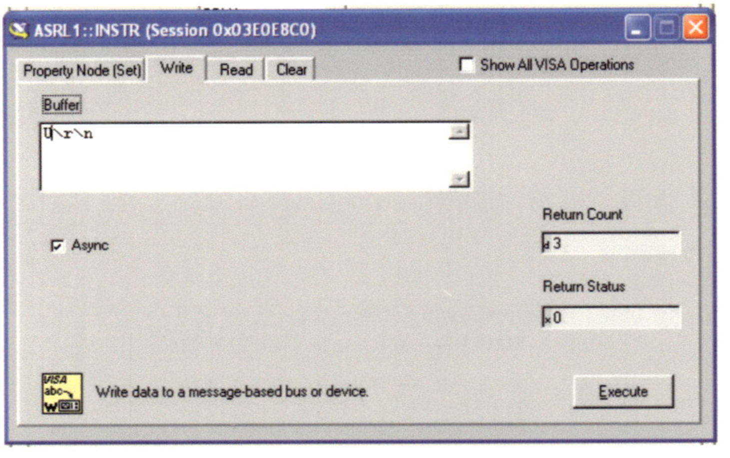

Fig. 10. Write buffer of NI-MAX

4. LabVIEW application examples

4.1 Self-calibrating automated characterization system for EDFA

Ultrahigh- capacity optical transmission systems are a vital component for 21st-century telecommunications networks that support various expanding information systems such as the Internet, mobile communications, and digital cable television [15].Wavelength-division-multiplexing (WDM)systems employing optical amplifiers such as the erbium-dopedfiber amplifier (EDFA) are considered the most effective solution to increase data transmission capacity [16–17]. The main characteristics of EDFAs are their gain and noise figure, and their values depend on the input signal wavelength, input signal power, and pump power [4]. The gain is determined by measuring the difference between the output signal power and the input signal power, whereas the noise figure is calculated from the gain, amplified spontaneous emission (ASE), and resolution of the optical spectrum analyzer (OSA). The accurate ASE level is measured using the interpolation technique, and thus, even a slight error in the initial measurement of the input power level will cause a cascading effect that will render the final ASE measurement invalid. In addition, the accuracy of the gain value is also dependent on the accuracy of the input measurement [5]. This makes the current manual measurement techniques not suitable for gain value measurement as even the slightest deviation in the initial input measurement will result in inaccurate gain values. As such, using manual measurement techniques for EDFA experiments could lead to inaccurate results and long experiment times. EDFAs are typically characterized using OSAs, tunable laser sources (TLSs), optical attenuators, laser diode controllers, and optical power meters. From experience, EDFA research with manual control of these instruments will lead to delays and inaccuracies in research due to the large number of values that have to be taken and recalibrated for each parameter. To cope with this problem, a self-calibrating automated measurement system for EDFAs has been developed based on the LabVIEW program and GPIB hardware.

The basic architecture of a standard EDFA is depicted in Figure 11. The setup consists of a piece of EDF, a wavelength division multiplexing (WDM) coupler, a pump laser and two isolators. In this work, a depressed cladding EDF (DC-EDF) with Erbium ion concentration of approximately 500 ppm is used as gain medium for amplification in S-band region. The EDF is pumped by a 980 nm laser diode to generate population inversion for amplification. A WDM coupler is used to combine the pump light with the input signal. Optical isolators are used to ensure unidirectional operation of the optical amplifier [15].

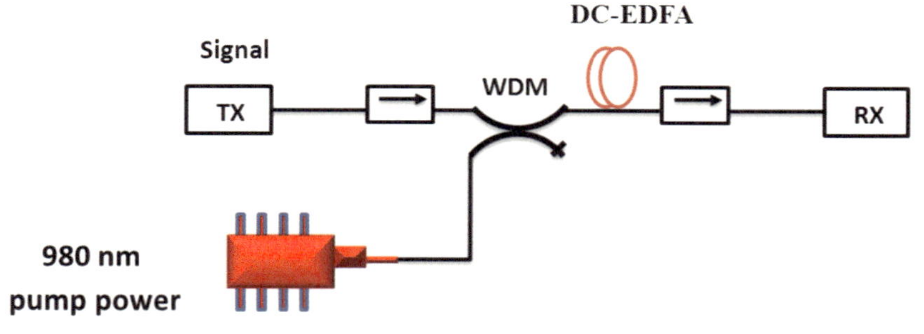

Fig. 11. Configuration of the EDFA

The automation system consists of a TLS, OSA, attenuator, laser diode controller, and a personal computer. All these instruments are networked using GPIB cables and are individually designated as Talkers, Listeners, and/or Controllers. By having these functions, all the involved instruments can automatically be controlled through a single computer for the input signal measurement; the experiment is setup as shown in Figure. 11, using only the TLS, attenuator, and OSA. Figure 12 shows the user interface of the automation system. The program has two main menus, i.e., the "input" menu and the "output" menu. Under the "input" menu, there are three submenus, i.e., "Multiwavelength/Power −30 dBm," "Multiwavelength/Power 0 dBm," and "Multipower." The "Multiwavelength/Power −30 dBm" submenu measures data by fixing the input power at −30 dBm and varying the input signal wavelengths. This submenu automatically changes the TLS wavelength values and determines the most accurate corresponding attenuation value to obtain a constant input power of −30 dBm. The OSA measures the output data and gives the necessary feedback to both the TLS and the attenuator, and the process repeats until the desired wavelength values and corresponding attenuation values are obtained.

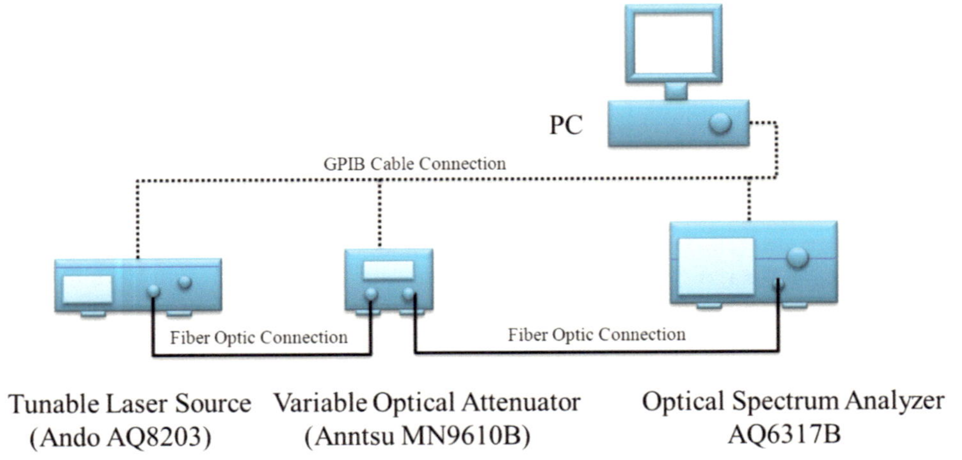

Fig. 11. The automation system for input signal measurement

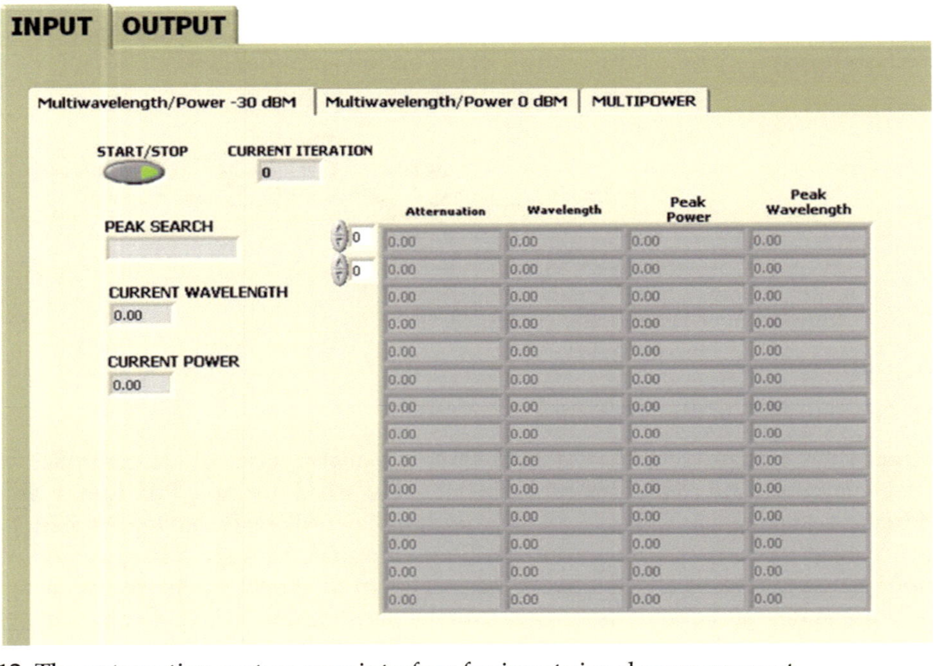

Fig. 12. The automation system user interface for input signal measurement

The automated measurement system is able to obtain a highly accurate input value by using a "while loop" subroutine that is contained within the application. The "while loop" will require the system to first obtain a rough attenuation value by adjusting the attenuation value so that the OSA is able to obtain a reading that is within ±0.9 dBm range of the required −30dBm value, as per the requirement of the multiwavelength menus or as per the required power as determined by the user in the multipower menu. Once the rough attenuation of the value has been determined, the system will then adjust the attenuation value based on the OSA readings to obtain the exact attenuation value required for the subsequent experiment. The "while" loop is illustrated in Figure 13. The submenu "Multiwavelength/Power 0 dBm" gathers data at a constant 0 dBm input power at different wavelengths. With regard to wavelength, the software is programmed for the S-band wavelength region from 1480 to 1530 nm. The "Multipower" submenu obtains the input power for a constant center wavelength, but at different input powers, which has been programmed from −40 to 5 dBm. All submenu functions are automatic, and the software records all required data on either diskette or hard disk.

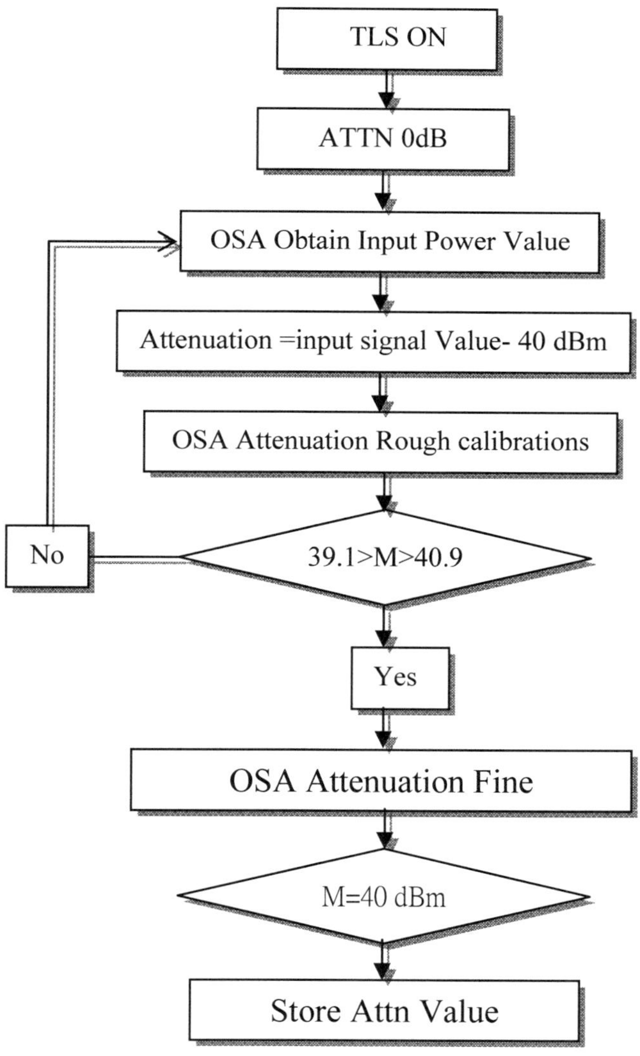

Fig. 13. "while loop" subroutine

For EDFA gain and noise figure measurements, the apparatus is set up as shown in Figure 14. The EDFA is placed between TLS and OSA, with the laser diode controller pumping the EDF (the pump power value must first be determined). The EDFA software "Output" menu is designed to automate this setup, as shown in Figure 15. Under the "Output" menu, there are two submenus, i.e., "Multiwavelength" and "Multipower." The "Multiwavelength" submenu obtains such output data as the gain, noise figure, ASE, peak power, and peak wavelength, and the obtained data are compared with the input data taken from the "Multiwavelength −30 dBm" or "Multiwavelength 0 dBm" submenu first. This comparison of input and output data is done to obtain the gain and noise figure values using interpolation techniques.

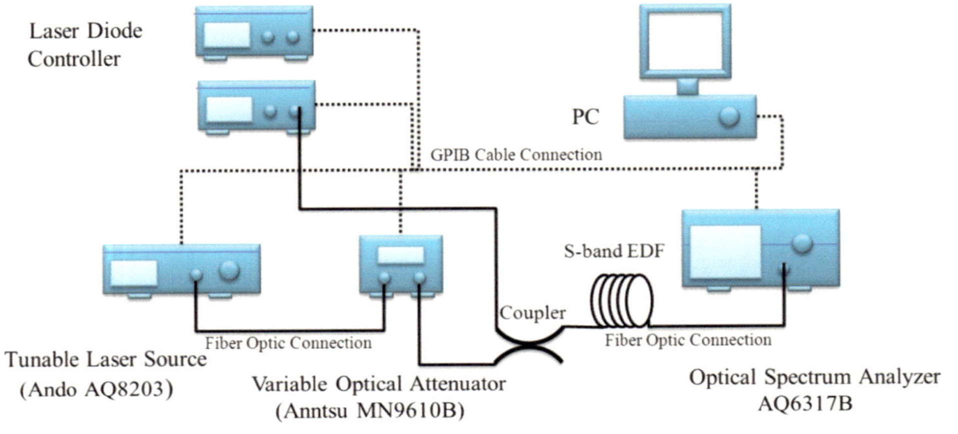

Fig. 14. The automation system for output gain and noise figure measurements

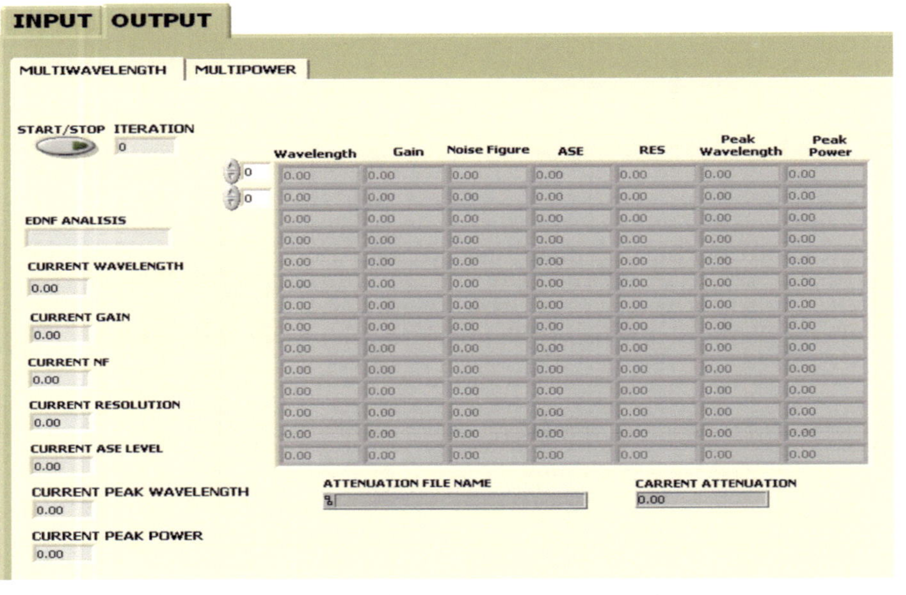

Fig. 15. The automation system user interface for gain and noise figure measurement

The "Multipower" submenu obtains output data at a center wavelength of 1500 nm but at different input powers. As with the "Multiwavelength" submenu, all data obtained from the "output" menu "Multipower" submenu are compared with data obtained from the "input" menu "Multipower" submenu to obtain values such as gain, noise figures, etc. All the "output" submenus plot graphs after one experiment cycle is complete, as shown in Figure 16, saving time for data analysis. In addition, the obtained data can also be stored in Word, Powerpoint, Excel, and other formats for further analysis. Figure 17 shows the flowchart for the automation system. The basic software design methodology possesses the required characteristics of being time efficient and the ability to accurately and consistently gather data while simultaneously reducing the uncertainty value, as these characteristics are very important in ensuring that the software can be utilized to gather data. The EDFA automation system is tested based on the aforementioned characteristics. The software is proven to reduce the EDFA testing time by more than 80%, as compared to manual EDFA testing methods.

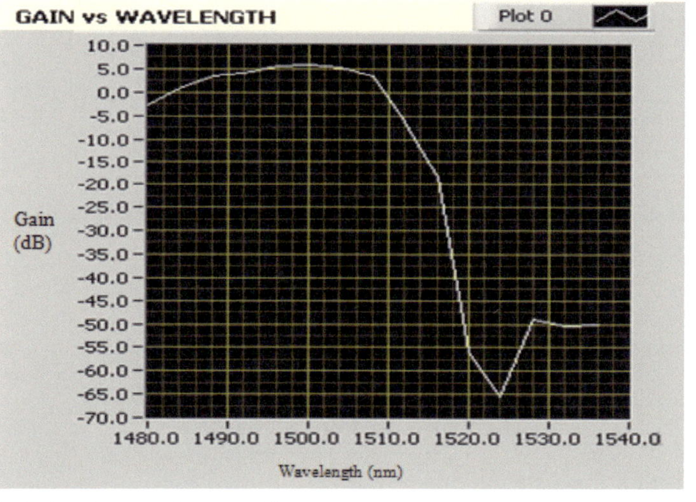

Fig. 16. S-band EDFA software "Output" menu

Accuracy is also increased, as at times, the experimentalist can make mistakes in acquiring and analyzing the data. By using the automation software, the human error factor can be eliminated, thus providing a higher degree of accuracy. The uncertainty value is also determined to be approximately ±0.012 dB, as compared to manual testing methods, as shown in Figures 18 and 19. However, each new experiment cycle will require the recalibration of equipment. This is due to changing environmental conditions such as temperature and experimental setup alignment, which have a significant effect on the measurements taken by the equipment. In addition, the optical connectors cannot be removed during the experiment cycle, and a recalibration must be performed by the automation software if the optical connectors are removed. For OSA calibration, standard lamps are frequently used to calibrate the OSA, whereas power measurements are made using a standard lamp and a power detector. In addition to increased accuracy and a reduction in the experiment time, the software also reduces the number of personnel needed for each experiment, thus allowing personnel to focus more on the interpretation of the acquired data. In addition, the software is designed to be user friendly and does not require specialist training to operate.

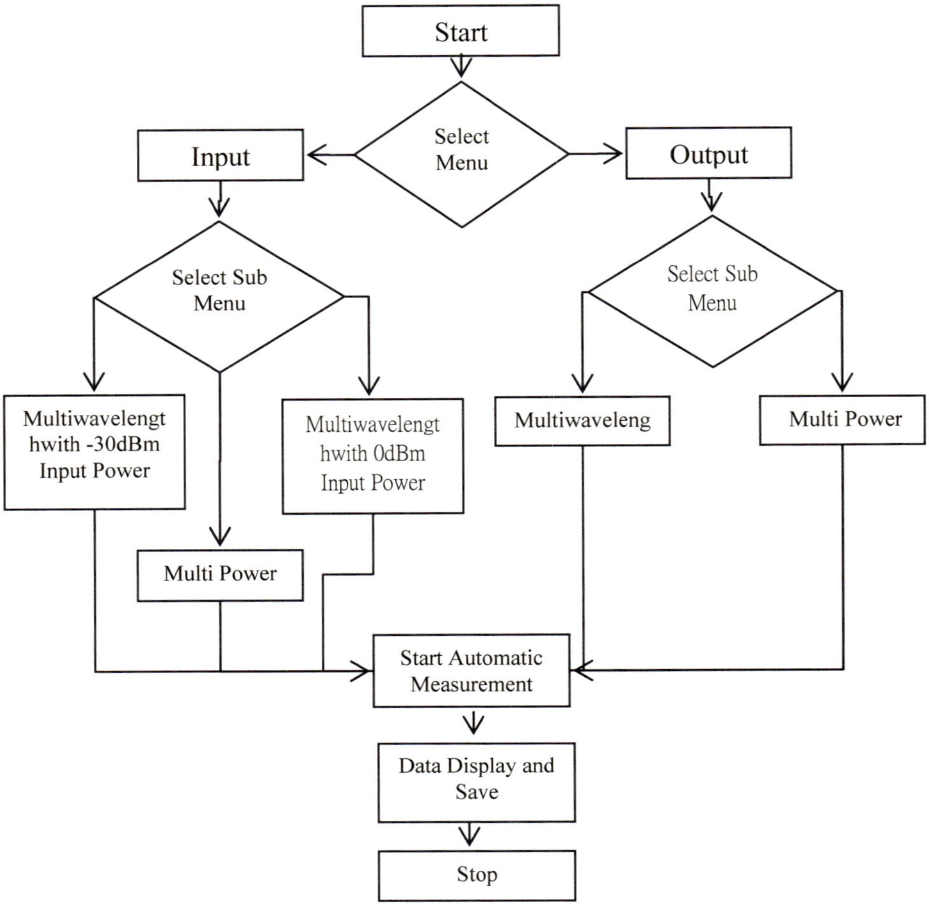

Fig. 17. Flowchart for the automation system.

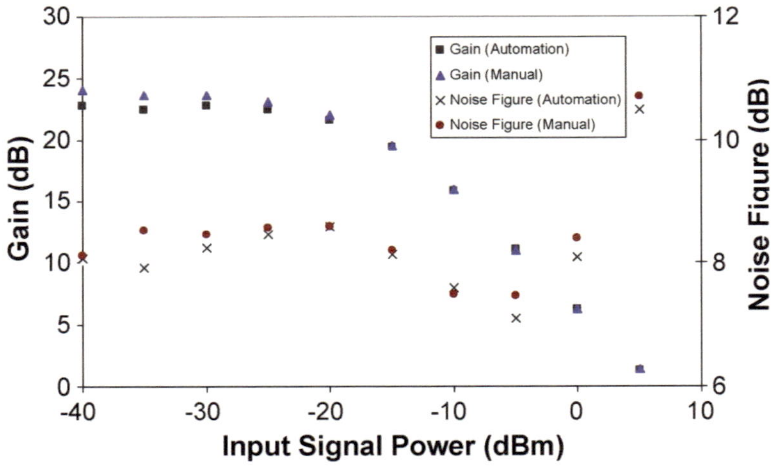

Fig. 18. Automate and manual EDFA's gain versus input signal power

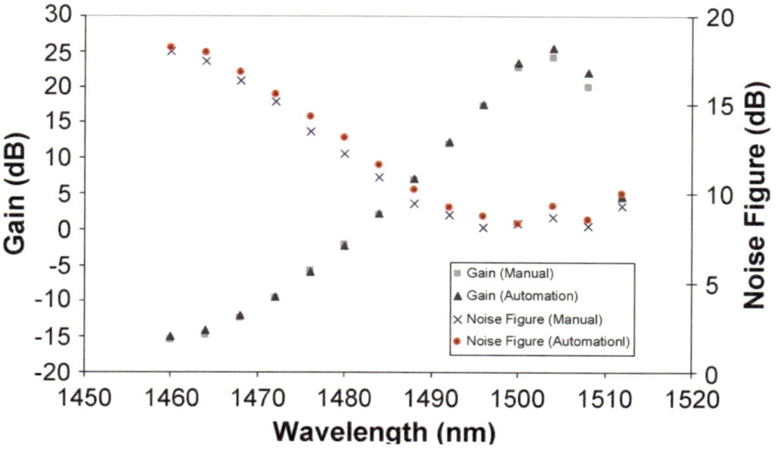

Fig. 19. Automate and manual EDFA's gain versus input signal wavelength

4.2 Remote fiber test system using Optical Time Domain Reflectometer (OTDR)

DWDM has increased fiber traffic capacity and thus it is important to proactively monitor and maintain the fiber networks. Due to huge penalties specified in Service Level Agreements (SLAs) and Quality of Service (QoS) commitments, carriers are keen to take measures in maintaining their fiber network. Optical Time Domain Reflectometer is a well-known optoelectronic instrument used for testing a fiber optic cable assembly in optical network [18]. An OTDR emits a pulsed ray into the fiber under test and acquired reflected ray. The strength of the return pulses is measured and integrated as a function of time, and is plotted as a function of fiber length. The plot can be used to analyse the optical fiber and detect the approximate location of the fault event that occurred. Different pulse widths in OTDR will affect the distance resolution and dynamic range. A longer laser pulse width will improve dynamic range and attenuation measurement resolution at the expense of distance resolution. This is useful for getting the overall characterization of a link, but is weak when trying to locate faults. A short pulse width will improve distance resolution of optical events, but will also reduce measuring range and attenuation measurement resolution [19]. Theoretically, OTDR has good distance measuring accuracy since it is software based and with its crystal clock possesses an inherent accuracy of better than 0.01%. Further calibration process is not needed since the practical cable length measuring accuracy is typically limited to about 1% [20].

Figure 20 shows the block diagram of an OTDR where a laser diode is driven by an electrical pulse generator that produces a train of short optical pulses. The backscattered optical power from the fiber through a directional coupler is detected by photodiode (PD). The detected waveform is amplified by an amplifier and converted to digital signal through the analog to digital converter (ADC) and then processed by the digital signal processing (DSP) unit. The timing of the DSP is synchronized with the source of the optical pulses so that delay in the propagation of each scattered pulse can be precisely calculated. Figure 21 is a typical commercial OTDR trace, showing among other things, the fiber attenuation. This figure shows that different losses will have different shapes in the trace. Hence, the analysis of the trace can be done to estimate the cause of a fault event [21].

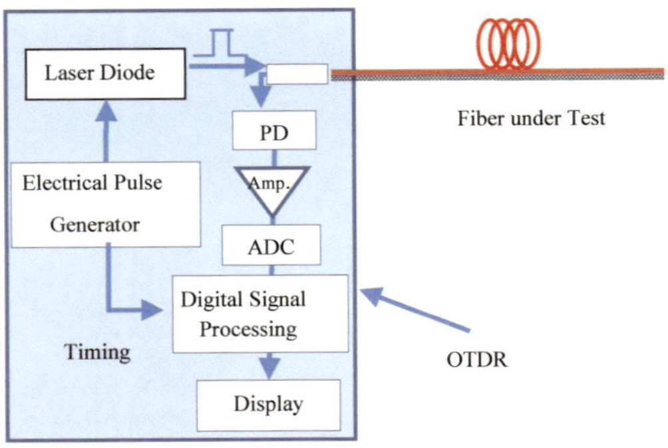

Fig. 20. Block diagram of an OTDR

One of the automation programs suggested for Remote fiber Test System is LabVIEW whose configurations will be explained in this section. The front panel or the graphic user interface of the automation program is shown in Figure 22. There are five sections in the program as indicated by arrow A, B, C, D and E. Section A is the communication settings required by LabVIEW to enable the communication link with the OTDR device. The settings in this section are VISA resource name, baud rate, data bits, parity, stop bits, flow control and timeout. The VISA resource name is the COM port which the RS-232C cable is connected to. Timeout sets the timeout value for the Write and Read operations. The baud rate, data bits, parity, stop bits and flow control must be set to the same value as the settings at the OTDR device and RS-232C cable in order for the communication link to be successful. Failure to do these will cause errors in the LabVIEW when running the automation program.

Section B is the setting for measurement conditions. Examples of measurement conditions are wavelength of the signal used, distance range, pulse width, attenuation, average time and index group. For the AQ7260 OTDR default setting, there are only two possible wavelengths which are 1310nm and 1550nm. The possible distance range is from 2km to

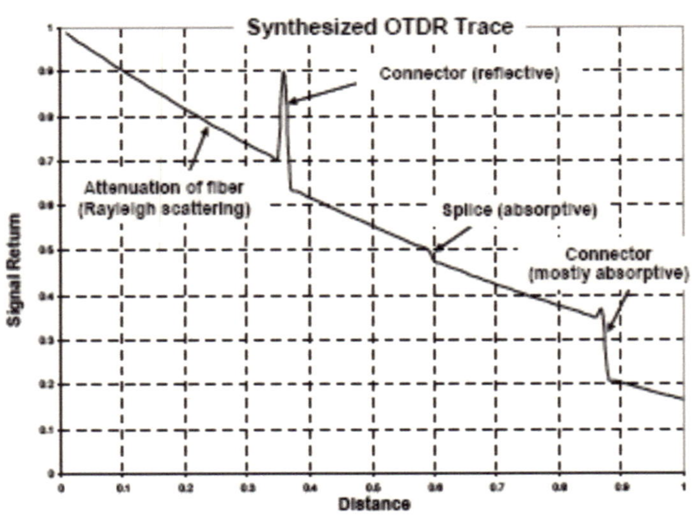

Fig. 21. Simulation of an OTDR trace.

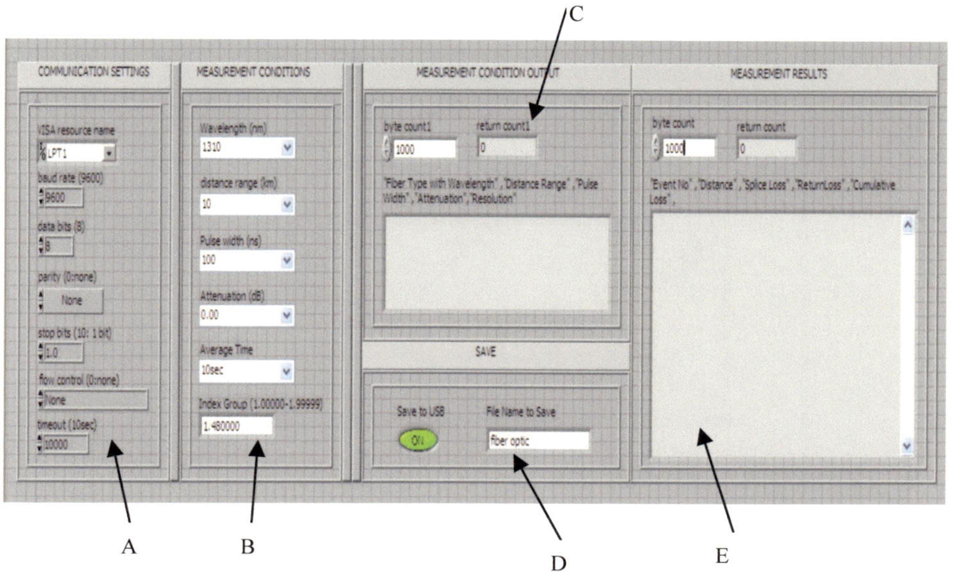

Fig. 22. Front panel of the automation program

640km. The pulse width is from 0ns to 20us as provided by the manufacturer. The possible attenuation settings are from 0dB to 26.25dB according to the AQ7260 OTDR user manual. Finally, the group index with is varying from 1.00000 to 1.99999. Next is the measurement conditions output given in Section C. The blank space will display the output of the "fiber type with wavelength, distance range, pulse width, attenuation and resolution of the measurement". The byte count1 value is set to more than the possible return count1 to prevent any loss of data. Users can enable or disable this function by clicking the "Save to USB" button. Finally, section E provides the measurement results. The measurement results in term of "event number, distance, splice loss, return loss, cumulative loss, dB/km, event type, and total span ORL" are shown in the blank area after the completed run of the program. For the event number, it will show "END" if the event is at end of the fiber, else it will show "1", "2" and so on according to the number of the detected event. Some of the measurement results will be neglected if they are not detected by the OTDR measurement, and the only display values are for those detected by the OTDR. The whole program consists of 6 main stacked sequences and 20 sub stacked sequences.

Figure 23 depicts the configuration for the distance range setting for the second main stacked sequence or the sub stacked sequence. VISA Write is used to write the data from write buffer to the device. The command for distance range is Rm\r\n, where "m" depends on the distance range chosen by the user. Figure 24 shows the configuration for pulse width programming. In the second sub stacked sequence, the command needed for the pulse width is PWm\r\n.

The configuration for the programming of group index is shown in Figure 25. The command needed is IORm\r\n, in this case, the "m" is the range from 1.00000 to 1.99999 depending on the value needed for the user. The "concatenate strings" function will combine the two constants (IOR and \r\n) and the control (value of group index) in the arrangement from top to bottom to form IORm\r\n. Thereafter, the concatenate output string will pass to

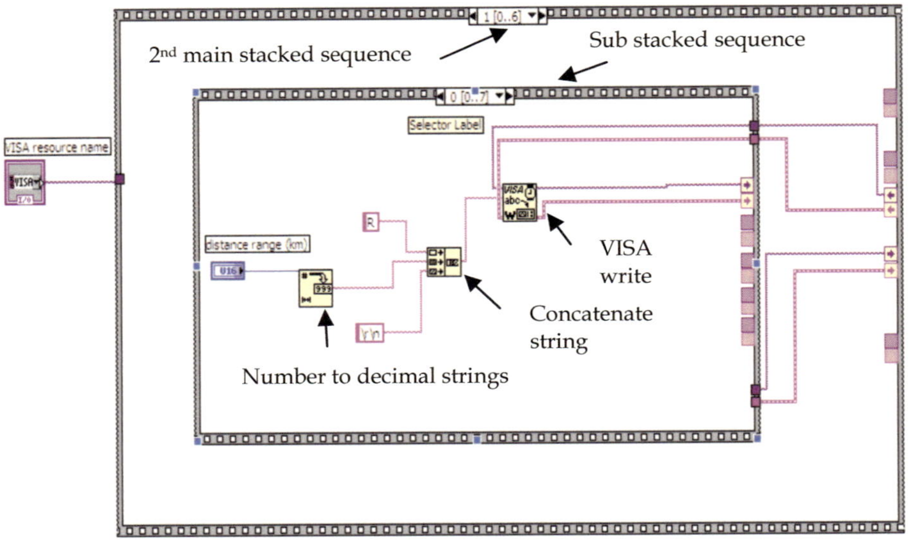

Fig. 23. Programming for distance range

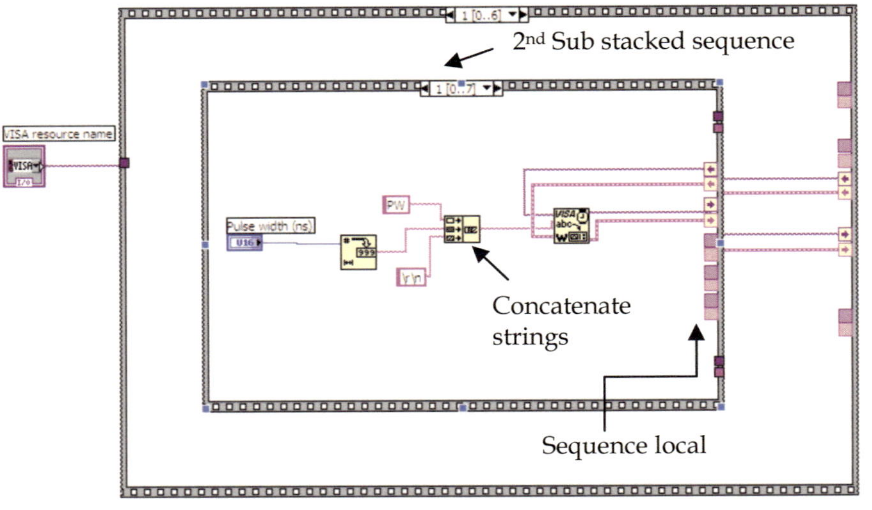

Fig. 24. Programming for pulse width

VISA Write to initialize the related operation. The next step is to initialize the OTDR device to start the measurement from the personal computer. The command needed to initialize the real time measurement is ST2\r\n. This command is sent to the VISA and the output is connected to the next sub stacked sequence. The duration needed for the OTDR measurement to be completed is approximately 15sec, so, a 20 second delay is applied to the next sub stacked sequence as shown in Figure 26 to ensure the measurement process is 100 percent complete. Then, to stop the measurement after 20 seconds, a stop measurement command is needed which is ST0\r\n, as shown in Figure 26. Without this stop command, the measurement will keep going without end.

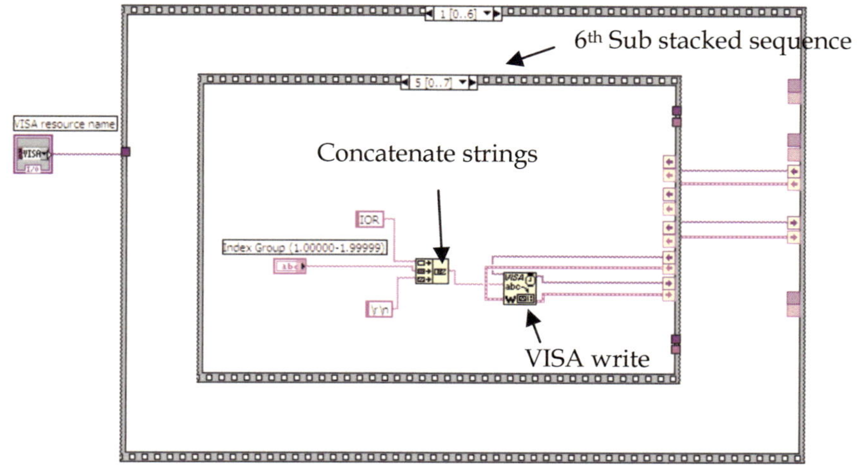

Fig. 25. Programming for group index

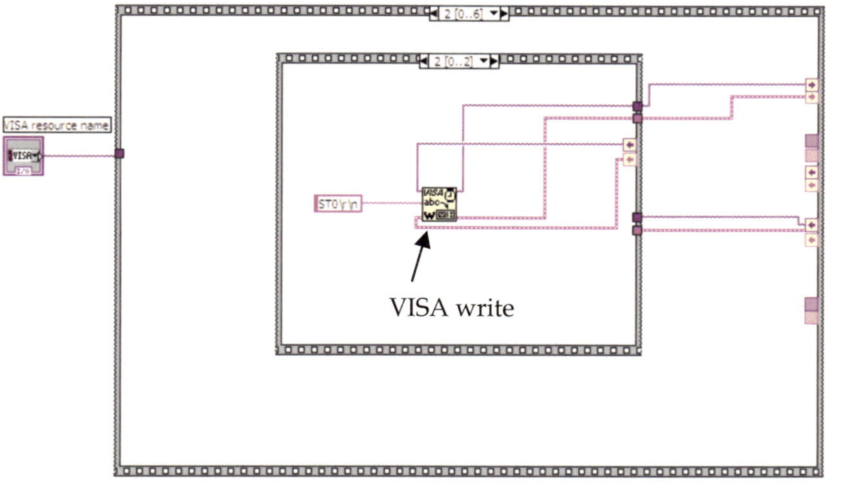

Fig. 26. Programming for stop measurement

For the automation program, the user has the option to choose whether they want to save a copy of the measurement trace and data or not. If the user does not wish to save the measurement trace, the program configuration at LabVIEW is as shown in Figure 27. The case structure is at the false condition (save function disable at the front panel). There is nothing to process or pass through during this sequence, hence, the program will continue to the next main sequence. If the user wishes to save a copy of the measurement results, the program configuration is shown in Figure 28. The case structure is at the true condition (save function enabled at the front panel). The configuration shown in Figure 28 is for the drive setting and file name to be saved for the measurement results. The command used is FDAmp\r\n (refer to Table 1), where "m" in this case is for drive setting and is equal to 5, which sets the drive used to save data to USB drive. While, "p" indicates any file name that the user wishes to save. The strings will be combined into a single output by the "concatenate strings" function and act as the input to the VISA Write. A delay is implemented to reduce the traffic to the OTDR to prevent the occurrence of a hang situation.

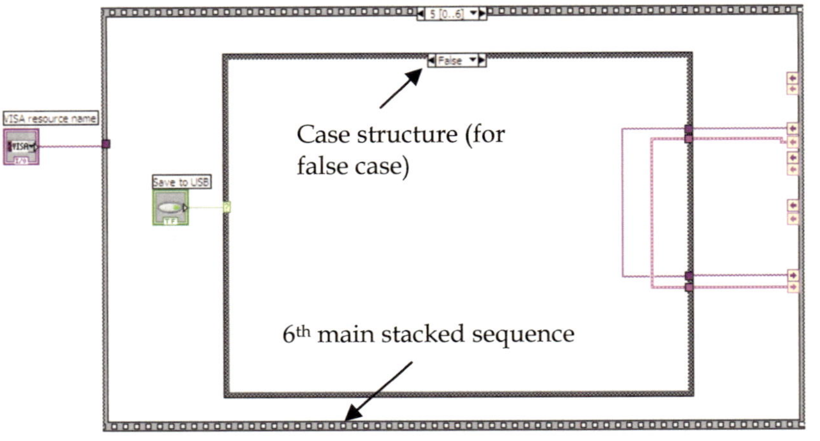

Fig. 27. Programming for false (save function disable)

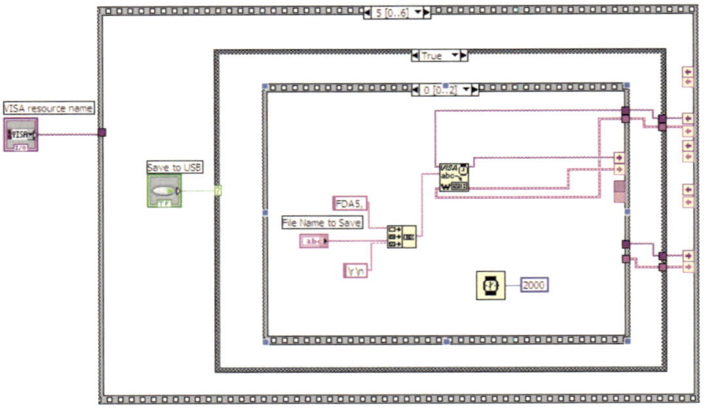

Fig. 28. Programming for true (save enable) case, drive setting and file name to save

Figure 29 shows the configuration to set the file type of the measurement trace. Examples of the possible file types are BMP, SOR (Telcordia) and so on. The command used here is FF7\r\n, which will set the file type to be saved in the SOR format. This file format will assist the user when analyzing or modifying the measurement trace by using Yokogawa OTDR Viewer software. Again, a delay is applied to reduce the traffic to the OTDR to prevent hang up. Finally the "data save" command is used to save the data. Figure 30 shows that the command FST\r\n is sent to the input of the VISA Write. Then, the measurement trace or data will be completely saved into the device (pen drive or thumb drive) plugged into the USB port of the OTDR device. A delay of few seconds is needed for the measurement trace or data to be successfully saved into the pendrive or thumbdrive.

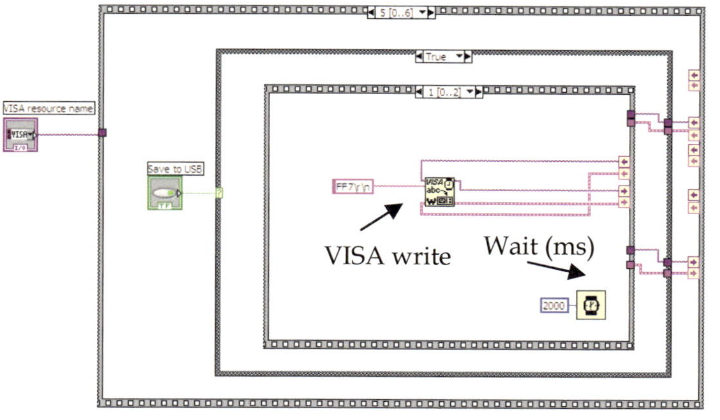

Fig. 29. Programming for "file type save"

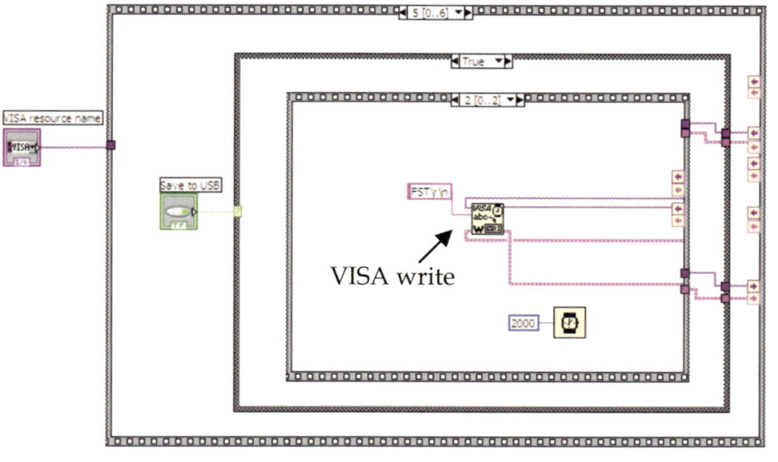

Fig. 30. Programming for data save.

The end of the program is as shown in Figure 31. This automation program ends with a VISA Close. The VISA Close closes a device session or event object specified by the VISA resource name. Finally, the simple error handling function indicates whether an error has occurred. If an error occurs during the program execution, it will return a description of the error and optionally displays it in a dialog box. In this section, the measurement data obtained from the automation program are presented. These data will be used to compare with the data obtained without using the automation program in the next section.

The results obtained from the automation program for 1310nm wavelength single mode fiber at 100ns, 200ns and 500ns pulse width are printed on the screen and shown in Figures 32, 33 and 34. The data shown are the event number, distance, splice loss, return loss, cumulative loss, dB/km, event type and the total return loss. The data are separated by comma and is ignored if there is no such data for the certain event. The event number is in accordance with the sequence of the events.

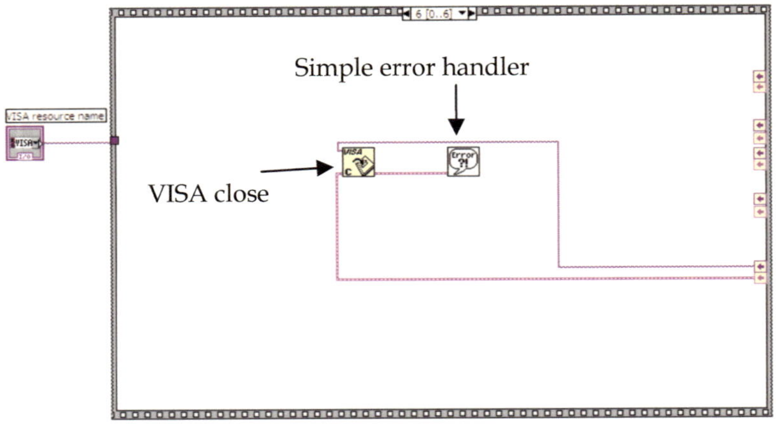

Fig. 31. Closes of the program

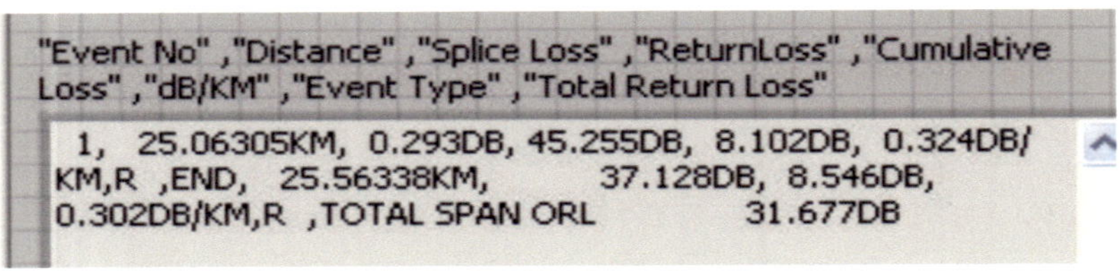

"Event No" ,"Distance" ,"Splice Loss" ,"ReturnLoss" ,"Cumulative Loss" ,"dB/KM" ,"Event Type" ,"Total Return Loss"

1, 25.06305KM, 0.293DB, 45.255DB, 8.102DB, 0.324DB/KM,R ,END, 25.56338KM, 37.128DB, 8.546DB, 0.302DB/KM,R ,TOTAL SPAN ORL 31.677DB

Fig. 32. 1310nm SMF at 100ns pulse width (automation program)

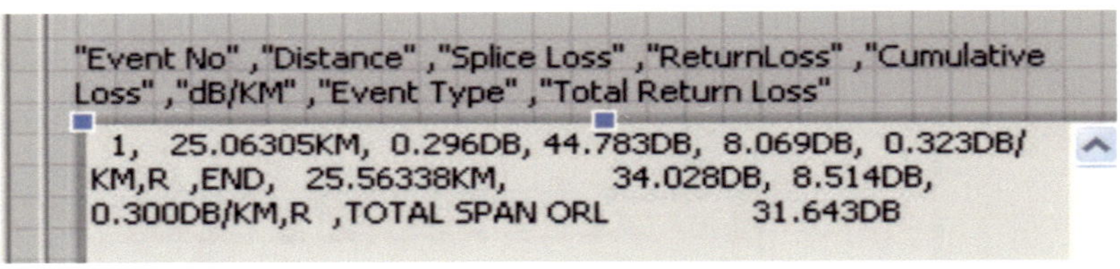

"Event No" ,"Distance" ,"Splice Loss" ,"ReturnLoss" ,"Cumulative Loss" ,"dB/KM" ,"Event Type" ,"Total Return Loss"

1, 25.06305KM, 0.296DB, 44.783DB, 8.069DB, 0.323DB/KM,R ,END, 25.56338KM, 34.028DB, 8.514DB, 0.300DB/KM,R ,TOTAL SPAN ORL 31.643DB

Fig. 33. 1310nm SMF at 200ns pulse width (automation program)

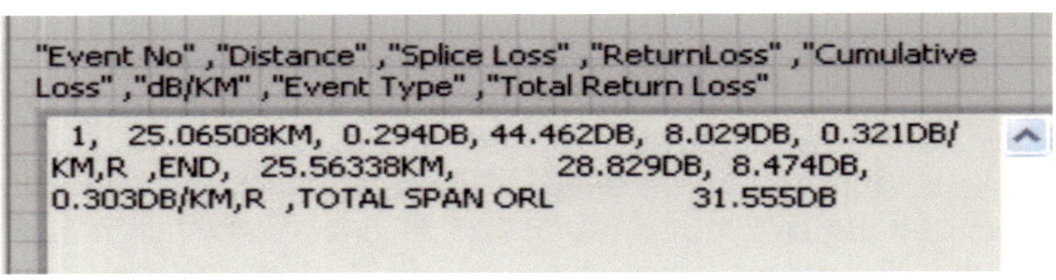

"Event No" ,"Distance" ,"Splice Loss" ,"ReturnLoss" ,"Cumulative Loss" ,"dB/KM" ,"Event Type" ,"Total Return Loss"

1, 25.06508KM, 0.294DB, 44.462DB, 8.029DB, 0.321DB/KM,R ,END, 25.56338KM, 28.829DB, 8.474DB, 0.303DB/KM,R ,TOTAL SPAN ORL 31.555DB

Fig. 34. 1310nm SMF at 500ns pulse width (automation program)

To verify the reliability of the automation program, a comparison between the results obtained from the automation program and the manually measured OTDR device is made. The data of Figures 35, 36 and 37 are obtained manually for 1310nm wavelength SMF at 100ns, 200ns and 500ns pulse width respectively. These results are compare with those obtained from the automation program. By comparing Figures 32, 33 and 34 with Figures 35, 36 and 37, it can be observed that the results are identical without any deviation. Hence, it is concluded that the automation program is very reliable and the results obtained from automation program are exactly the same as those obtained from the manually measured data from the OTDR device.

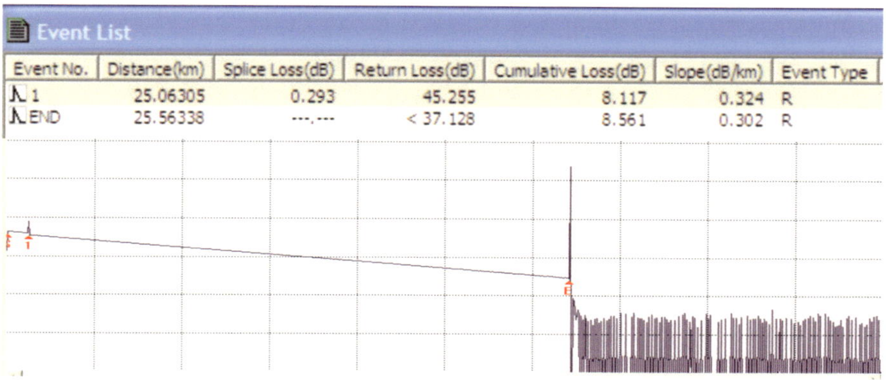

Fig. 35. 1310nm SMF at 100ns pulse width (manually measurement)

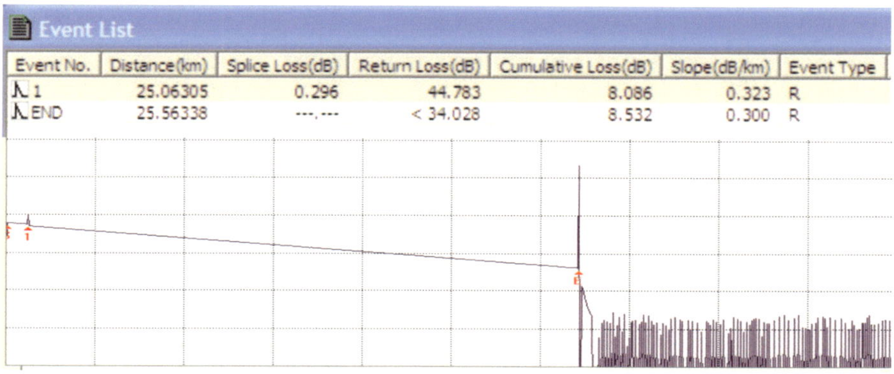

Fig. 36. 1310nm SMF at 200ns pulse width (manually measurement)

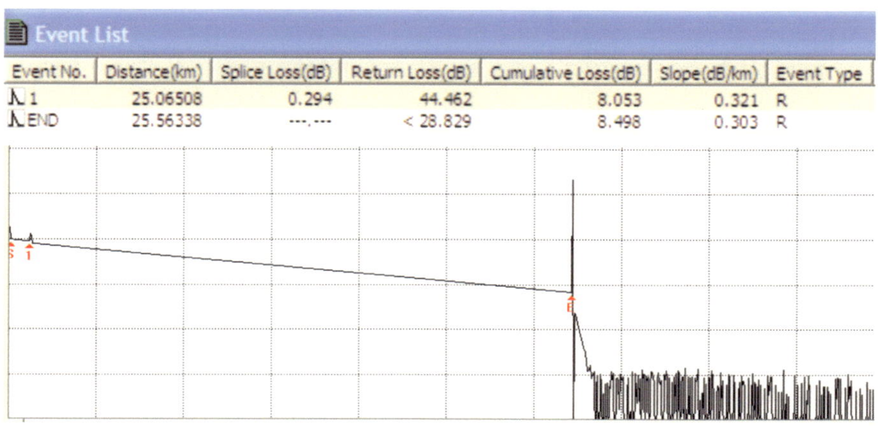

Fig. 37. 1310nm SMF at 500ns pulse width (manually measurement)

4.3 Automated fiber optic multiphase dynamic fluid differentiation measurement

Nowadays the main concern for many industries, especially those related to power production and more importantly the oil and gas industry is the discrimination of the immiscible phases of fluids in a flow system. The phase differentiation method is one of the effective, low-cost and highly accurate methods to discriminate phases in a flow system [22]. This ability to discern between the various phases of a flow system is important as this will ultimately affect the production outcome of the system. Oblique tips is one of the effective ways to achieve phase discrimination in fiber optic sensor. However, a proper automation and analysis software is necessary for the interpretation of the data from the optical probes [23], [24]. The LabVIEW software is a smart analysis program which is able to discriminate the individual phases of a multiphase system using Boolean logic and it presents the data in a real-time manner. Discrimination of the immiscible phases of fluids in a flow system using the phase differentiation measurement method is demonstrated by Kavintheran in 2007 [25]. The software was designed to monitor up to 8 individual sensor probes and it can also be configured to monitor two-phase or even three-phase flows.

The automated measurement of the phase differentiation measurement system is demonstrated in Figure 38. The system consists of four optic sensor heads, four laser diodes, four optical circulators, an optical coupler and an OSA. The laser diodes work as signal sources which send signal through the circulator to the optic sensors. The sensor head assembly is designed such that the sensor probes are arranged 90 degrees apart at 0, 90, 270 and 360 respectively. The reflected signal from the optic sensor head goes back to the circulator and is redirected to combine with reflections from the other laser sources through the OSA. The OSA is connected via GPIB hardware to a computer equipped with the LabVIEW software and a phase discrimination program that uses Boolean logic to accurately determine the various phase fractions of the multiphase system in real-time.

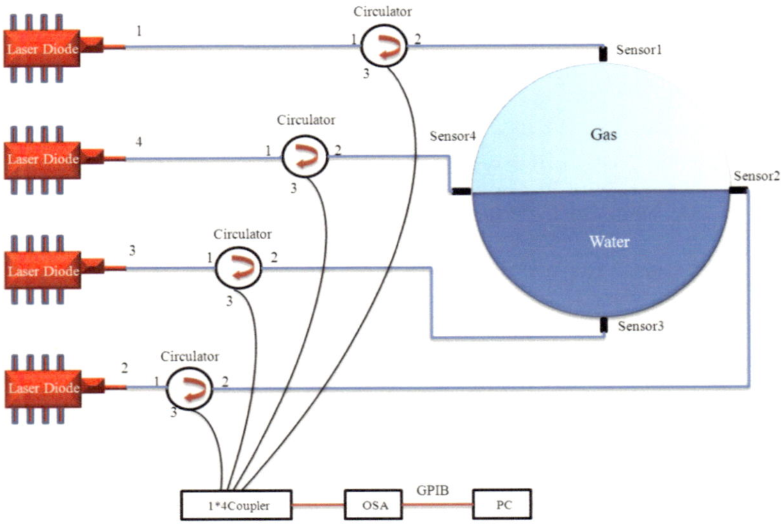

Fig. 38. Sensor probe location in sensor head assembly

The system is designed so that the output for each probe that computes a reflectivity between 0.015 and 0.040 generates a digital "1" which indicate water, and a digital "0" for each probe that computes a reflectivity of less than 0.015 to indicate air. The system incorporates a Boolean logic function that allows the phase level measurement to be determined accurately and also without any overlay in data. Figure 39 shows the flowchart for the operation of the program, while Figure 40 below shows the Boolean logic circuit. To detect three possible indications of the phase level, the Boolean logic function is designed to accommodate up to eight sensor probes. The three possible results are one-quarter water three-quarters air, three-quarters water one-quarter air and full water. Visual representation of the phase level is the result of the outputs of the logic circuit which is connected to the indicators. Each sensor probe is connected to an OR gate. In order to allow the logic functions to operate with only one input, OR gates are used. The OR gate allows the deployment of either four sensor probes or eight sensor probes. The program will refresh the phase fraction levels every 1 second, which is the scan time of the OSA [25].

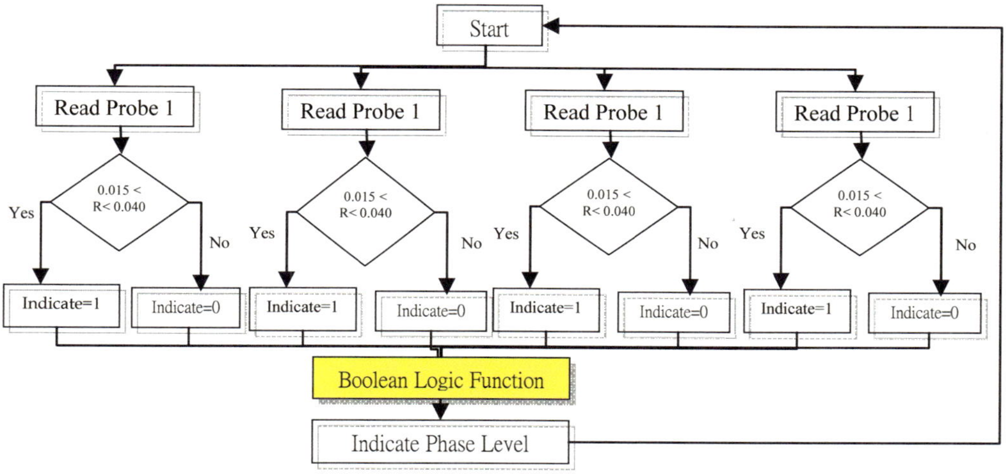

Fig. 39. Phase discrimination program flowchart

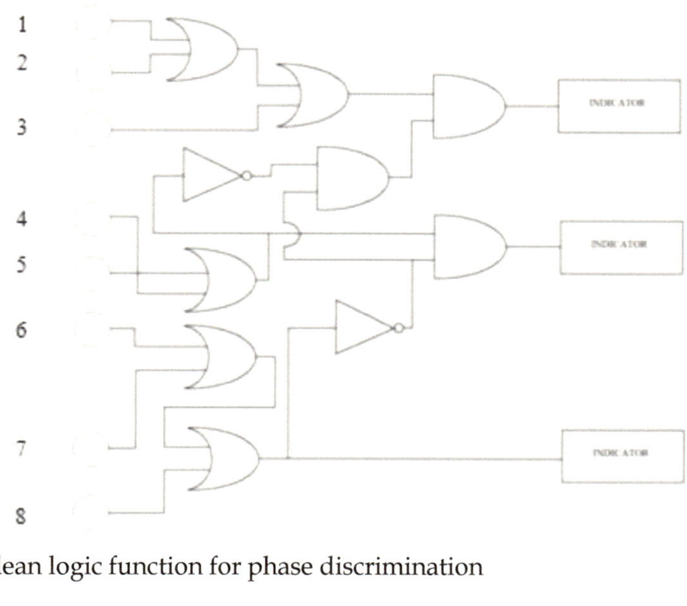

Fig. 40. Boolean logic function for phase discrimination

The reflectivity of the probes as a function of time when the water level in the flow system is at one-quarter is shown in Figure 41. As depicted, the reflectivity of probe 3 in water is shown to be 0.032 by the software, while the reflectivity's of probes 1, 2 and 4 is shown to be 0.002. To determine the phase level of the system, the Boolean logic function is done automatically and immediately. When digital "1" signal is generated by probe 3, it immediately passes through the respective logic gates to determine the phase level. Once this has been done, the system will represent the phase level using a diagram as shown in Figure 42. When the flow system is half-full, the reflectivity of probes 2, 3 and 4 is 0.0316, while the reflectivity of probe 1 remains at 0.002. Figure 43 shows the reflectivity of the four probes against time.

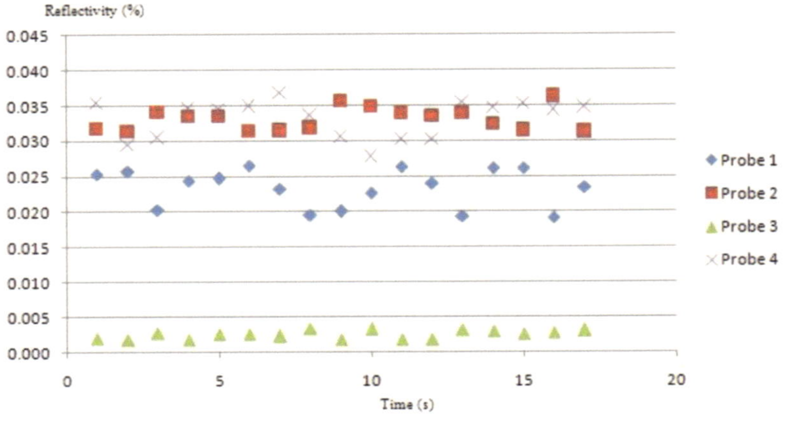

Fig. 41. Reflected power (dBm) of sensor probe vs. time for one-quarter full flow system

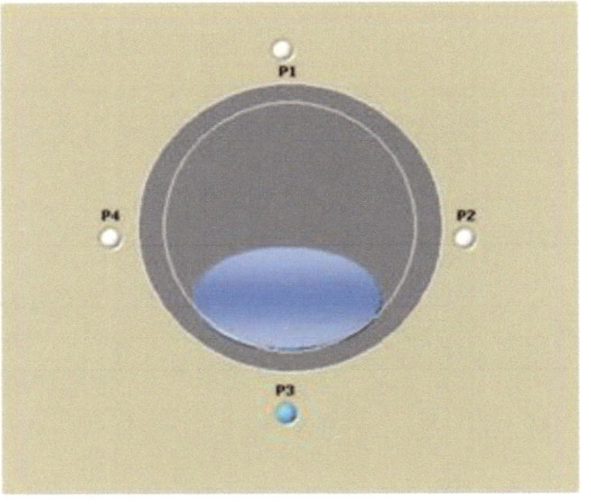

Fig. 42. LabVIEW phase level representation for one-quarter full flow system

Similarly, the Boolean logic gate function will determine the phase level of the system as shown in Figure 44. When all four probes detect water, the reflectivity of all four probes is 0.002, as shown in Figure 45. The Boolean logic system will then determine the phase level of the system to be fully water, and will indicate the condition of the system as shown in Figure 46.

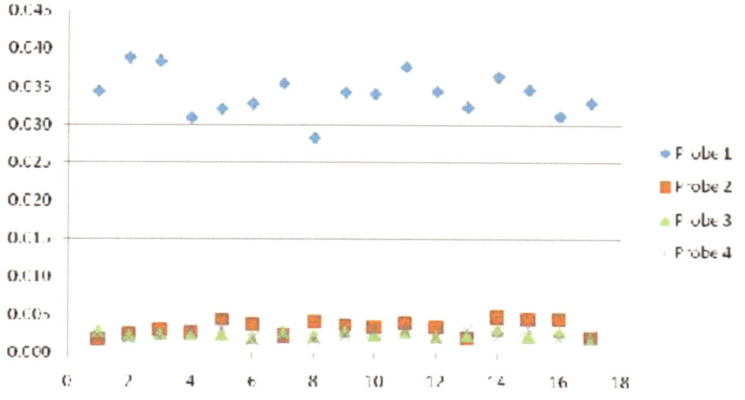

Fig. 43. Sensor probe reflectivity of vs. time for half-full flow system

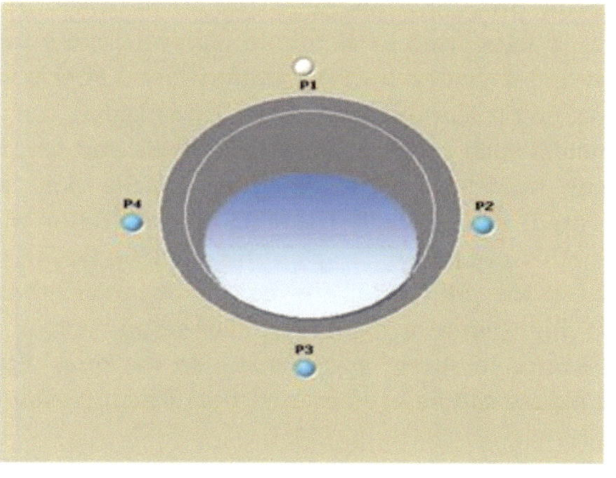

Fig. 44. LabVIEW phase level representation for half-quarter full flow system.

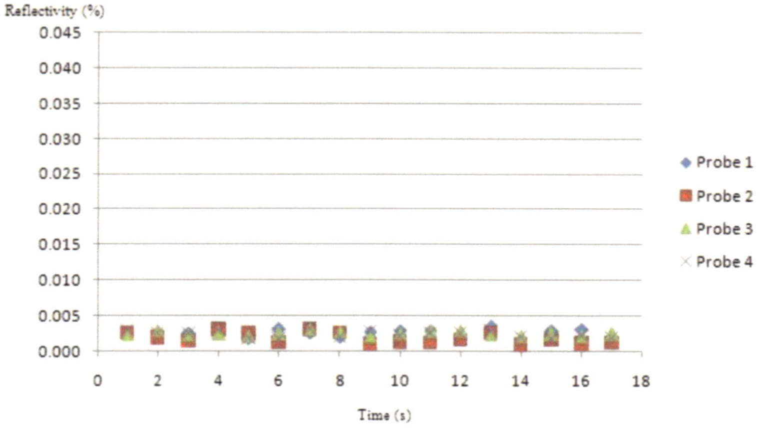

Fig. 45. Sensor probe reflectivity of vs. time for full flow system

Fig. 46. LabVIEW phase level representation for full flow system

4.4 Polarimetric fiber-optic pressure sensor

Due to the possibility of it being used to distribute high sensitivity sensors and of it being configurable in many different shapes, the polarization–based FOS is widely used. Recently different types of polarimetric sensors have been investigated for the measurement of various physical parameters such as: pressure, strain, stress and temperature. Polarimetric fiber optical sensors are sensitive to the variations in the polarization state of light transmitted by a single mode optical fiber. The state of polarization may vary according to physical factors such as stress, pressure, temperature, etc [26]. So far, the polarimetric fiber sensors demonstrated in the literature are based on interferometric schemes. In interferometric schemes high-birefringent (HB) polarization maintaining (PM) fibers are used. The proposed fibers have strong asymmetries so the quasi-degeneracy of the two orthogonally polarized modes can be avoided and thus forcing a single polarization mode under normal operations.

A low-cost distributed deformation sensor based on the change of polarization in a standard single-mode fiber of which data is obtained by the help of LabVIEW has been successfully developed by G. C. Contantin [27]. The schematics of the sensor is shown in Figure 47 which consists of a laser source, a mechanical polarization controller, a fiber polarizer and an optical receiver that is connected to a PC via a digital acquisition card (DAQ). The Power source consists of a laser diode and the biasing circuit. The laser source which is used is a telecommunications laser diode mounted inside a butterfly package. To acquire the diode temperature and monitor its temporal evolution, a laser diode is connected to a PC via a digital acquisition card. The light emitted by the laser source feeds the pressure transducer via the mechanical polarization controller that is used to align the incident polarization orthogonal to the transmission axis of the polarizer in the absence of the applied pressure stimulus. In this situation, the receiver reads a "0" voltage in the absence of any perturbations. It is also possible to align the light polarization in order to maximize the receiver reading in the idle state. As shown in Figure 47, the pressure sensor is made of a fiber sandwiched between two plexiglass plates [27]. Under pressure, the polarization state of the single-mode fiber changes and the value of the power transmitted from the fiber polarizer is affected. Therefore, if an optical power of zero is registered in the absence of perturbation, once pressure is applied to the transducer an optical power other than zero is obtained at the receiver [27].

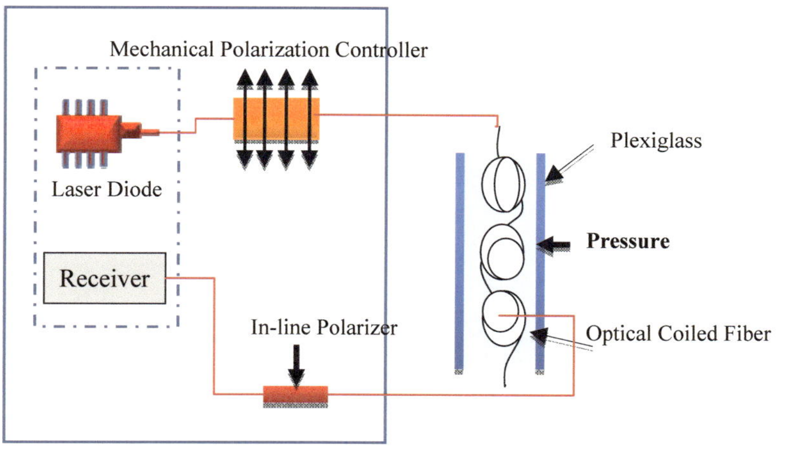

Fig. 47. Distributed deformation sensor schematic

Figure 48 shows the data acquisition program which has been developed with LabVIEW software. The main results obtained using the polarimetric fiber-optic pressure sensor is shown in Figure 49. In these figures, the dependency of the sensor output on time is shown. Figure 49(a) shows the output voltage (V) versus time in the absence of deformation. Figure 49 (c) presents the output normalized tension for different values of the pressure. The

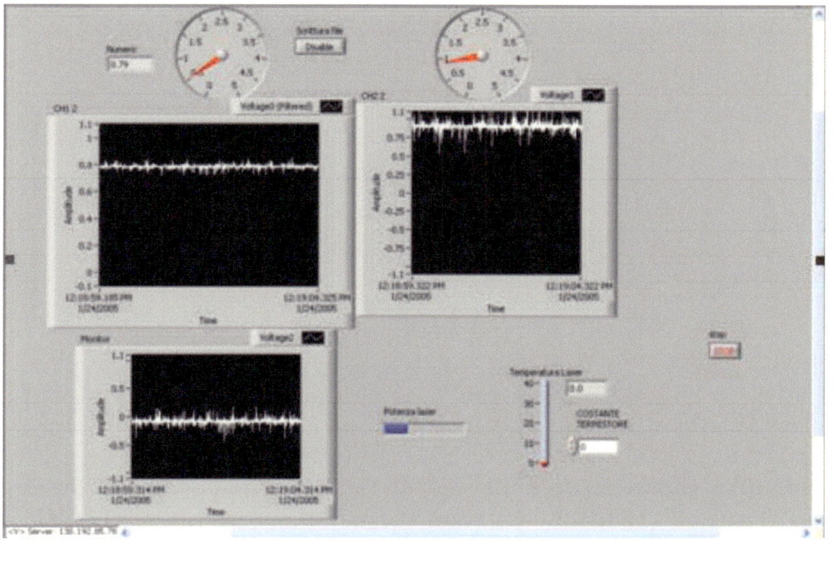

Fig. 48. Data acquisition program

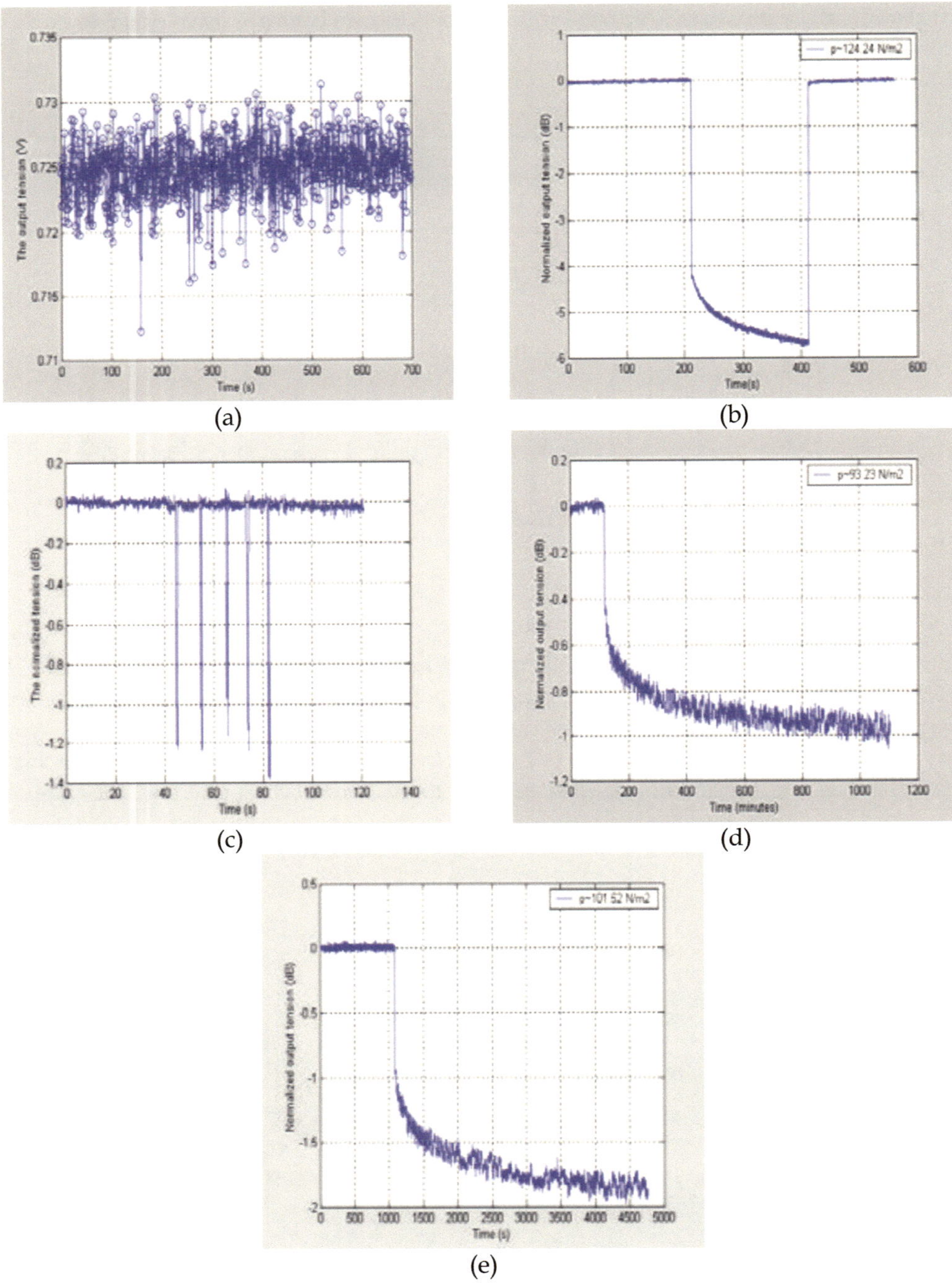

Fig. 49. Figure 49 (a) shows the dependence of the sensor output on time in the absence of deformation, Figures 49 (b), (d) and (e): show the output normalized voltage (dB) at constant pressure. Figure 49 (c): presents the output normalized tension for different values of the pressure. Figure 49(f): show the dependence of the sensor output on weight.

output normalized voltage (dB) at constant pressure is shown in Figures. 5 (b), (d) and (e). The normalized value is calculated by [27]

$$V_{norm} = \frac{V_{out} - V_{inf}}{V_{out(0)} - V_{inf}}$$

Where V_{norm} represents the output normalized voltage, V_{out} is the value of the acquired voltage, V_{inf}=− 0.5V is the lower limit of the output voltage and out (0) V is the output voltage in the absence of deformation.

4.5 Fiber Bragg Grating (FBG) sensor interrogation system

Recently in the field of architecture and civil, infrastructures such as long-span bridges, high-rise buildings, large dams, nuclear power stations, off shore platforms and others, there is a great demand for high performance sensors for structural health monitoring (SHM) systems to guarantee the efficiency/safety of the structures. Optical Fiber sensors such as the Fiber Bragg Grating (FBG) shows distinguishing advantages: immunity to electromagnetic interference and power fluctuation along the optical path and high precision. An FBG is a type of Bragg reflector constructed in a short part of optical fiber that reflects particular wavelengths of light and transmits all others. A key research area in FBG sensors is FBG fabrication, FBG demodulation and FBG encapsulation. In order to push forward the applications of the FBG sensors, reliability and accuracy of the FBG sensors must be ascertained. To achieve accuracy in the interrogation system, there is a great need in a monitoring program that could process the data and display the data collected for each sensor in graphical forms [28]. The optics, hardware and software architecture of such system was developed in year 2005 by Toh Yue Khing [29]. In this FBG fabrication system, digital filtering, peak detection and the ability to lock onto the reference wavelength are implemented by the LabVIEW program. In this research work, FBG is fabricated by using photosensitized optical fibers where the fiber reflective index is imprinted within the fiber core. The FBG sensor is fiber with different reflective indices which are connected in series to increase the number of sensors in a single fiber optic channel. Under tension or compression, changes in the reflective indices in the fiber will cause a shift in the reflected wavelength. By measuring the change in wavelength of the reflected light, the FBG interrogation system will be able to measure temperature, pressure or strain changes, depending on the types of material embedded in the FBG [29].

Figure 50 shows the interrogation System designed for the FBG fabrication system. As shown, a PCI-7831R FPGA Module, Fiber Fabry Perot Tunable Filter (FFP-TF), 8 photodiodes, 8 Pre-amps and an 8-Channel Fiber Optic Configuration are used in the system. Fiber Fabry Perot is a tunable filter which allows a narrow band of wavelength to pass through the fiber and filters the broad band laser. The Fabry Perot Tunable Filter is very sensitive to voltage change and serious noise disturbance produced by the electronic circuitry can also affect the accuracy of the result. Therefore, a high precision and low noise DAC voltage set is required. The PCI-7831R is a national instrument multifunction board featuring a user-programmable FPGA chip for onboard processing and flexible I/O operation. All analog and digital functionality is configured using the NI LabVIEW graphical block diagrams and the LabVIEW FPGA Module. When the PCI-7831R receives

instructions from LabVIEW to perform a scan, it will instruct the DAC to send out a whole range of voltage from 0 to 10V. At each change of DAC output, the FPGA will read from the 8 ADCs simultaneously and store the raw data onto the onboard memory. Once completed, data in the memory will be digitally filtered using the LabVIEW program.
The main software filters the noise from the data that is caused by both optical and electrical disturbance. Since the tunable filter is sensitive to temperature, the characteristic of the filter tends to drift over time. This drift will cause an error in the measurement. Thus, the software will automatically lock onto a reference FBG to obtain an accurate reading. The software front panel consists of two tabs. Figure 51 shows the sensor view tab. As shown in Figure 50, every peak in the FBG sensors is represented by the strain, pressure or temperature gauge. Any shift in wavelength of the FBG sensors will cause the measurement gauge to respond.

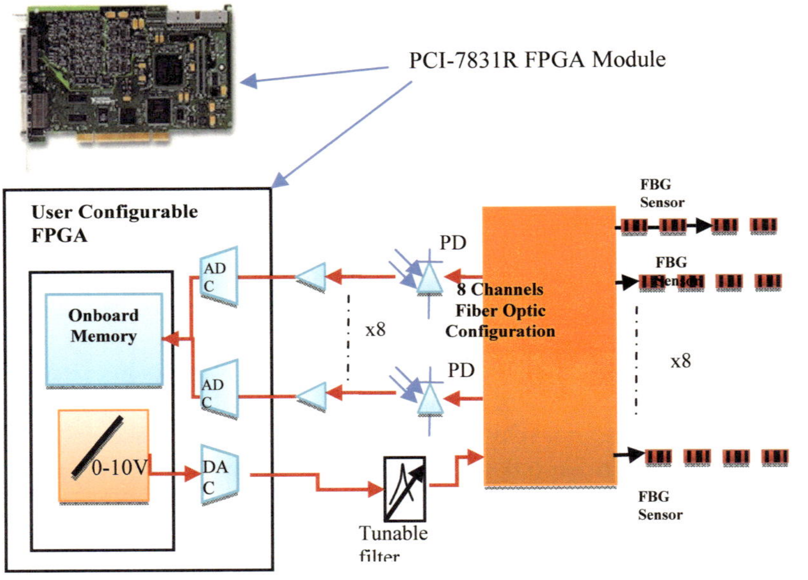

Fig. 50. Interrogation System design using FBGs

The scope view tab of the waveform acquired from the interrogation system developed for one of the channels is shown in Figure 52. These tabs consist of two scope displays. The top display shows the filtered data, while the bottom display shows the raw data from the Interrogation System. The first peak is the reference FBG and the rest of the 10 peaks are from 10 different types of FBG sensors. The shifting of peak 9 is caused by a change in pressure applied to the FBG sensor.

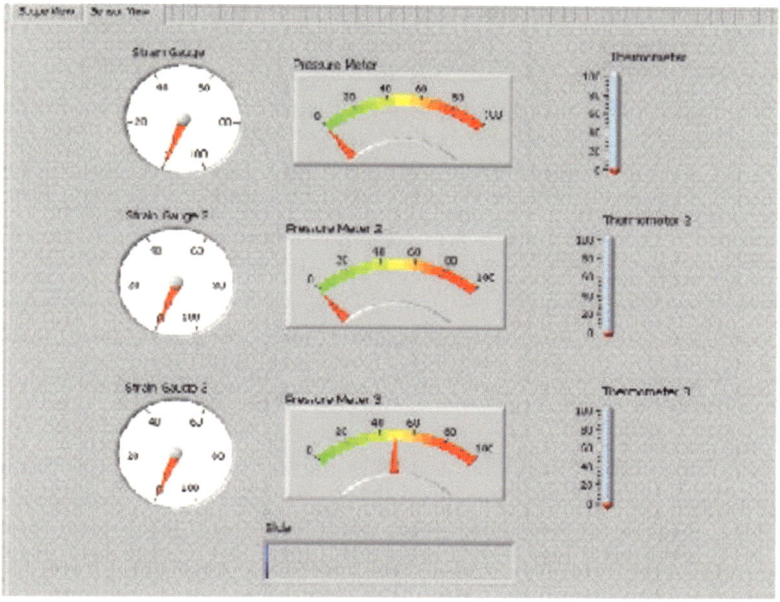

Fig. 51. Software front panel, sensor view tab

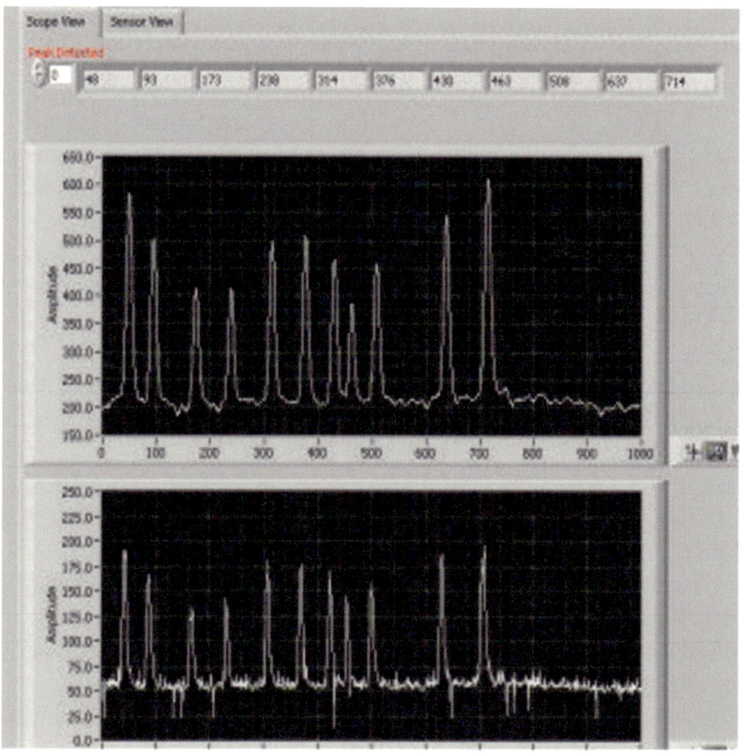

Fig. 52. Software front panel, scope view tab

5. Conclusion

The techniques and capabilities of LabVIEW development applied in fiber optic science are demonstrated. The application of LabVIEW in self-calibration and automatic measurement system, fiber remote test system and optical sensor are explained. The self-calibrating automated EDFA characterization system using the LabVIEW software and GPIB hardware is a more effective solution to testing. The overall experiment time is reduced by more than 80%, whereas data acquisition is more accurate and consistent with a low uncertainty value of ±0.012 dB. The automation program for remote fiber test systems using the optical time domain reflectometer (OTDR) is also presented. Polarimetric fiber-optic pressure sensor and multiphase dynamic fluid differentiation measurement are two examples of fiber optic sensors which are discussed. A low cost multi-channel interrogating system is developed with the NI PCI-7831R Module. This minimizes the electronic hardware configuration, simplifies and reduces the time required in the development process. The use of virtual instrumentation has not only provided a modern and interesting way for users to perform experiments but also reduced the amount of time necessary to make connections. The real-time display of quantities, such as gain, spectrum, temperature, strain power, and so on has made a great improvement in the users' ability to visualize these quantities and understand their relation to one another.

6. References

[1] B.E.A. Saleh and M.C. Teich, "Fundamentals of Photonics", Wiley, 1991

[2] Gred, Keiser "Optical Fiber Communications" Singapore: McGraw-HILL, 2000

[3] J. Chen, W. J. Bock, "A Novel Fiber-Optic Pressure Sensor Operated at 1300-nm Wavelength" IEEE Transactions on Instrumentation and Measurement 53(1), 10

[4] D. Derickson, "Fiber Optic Test and Measurement. Upper Saddle River," NJ: Prentice-Hall, 1998.

[5] R. A. Sherry and S. M. Lord, "LabVIEW as an Effective Enhancement to an Optoelectronic Laboratory Experiment", In Process Frontier Conference, pp. 897–900. 1997

[6] M.Z. Zulkifli, S.W. Harun, K. Thambiratnam and H. Ahmad, "Self-Calibrating Automated Characterization System for Depressed Cladding EDFA Applications using LabVIEW Software with GPIB", IEEE Transaction on Instrumentation and Measurement, vol. 57, no. 11, November 2008.

[7] A. W. Domanski, A. Gorecki and M. Swillo, "Dynamic Strain Measurements by Use of the Polarimetric Fiber Optic Sensors", IEEE Journal of Quantum Electronics, 31(8), 816 (1995).

[8] D. A. Krohn, "Fiber Optic Sensors: Fundamental and Applications", Instrument Society of America, Research Triangle Park, North Carolina, 1988.

[9] N. Lagokos, L. Litovitz, P. Macedo, and R. Mohr, "Multimode Optical Fiber Displacement Sensor", Applied Optic, Vol. 20, p. 167, 1981

[10] S. K. Yao and C. K. Asawa, "Fiber Optical Intensity Sensors", IEEE Journal of Selective Areas in Communication, SAC-1(3), 1983.

[11] Kreso Zmak, Zvonimir Sipus and Petar Basic, "A New Approach to Remote Fiber Testing in Optical Networks", 17th International Conference on Applied Electromagnettics and Communications, Croatia, 2003.

[12] U. Hilbk, M.Burmeister, B.Hoen, T.Hermes, and J.Saniter, " Selective OTDR Measurements at The Central Office of Individual Fiber Links in A PON", in Proc. Optical Fiber Communication Conference, Dallas, TX, Feb 1997, pp. 54-55, Paper TuK3.

[13] F.A Maier, H.Seeger, "Automation of Optical Time Domain Reflectometry Measurements", Hewlett Packard Journal, 46(1), pp 57-62, 1995.

[14] "GPIB Instrument Control Tutorial". National Instruments. August 2009.

[15] S. W. Harun, K. Dimyati, K. K. Jayapalan, and H. Ahmad, "An Overview on S-band Erbium-Doped Fiber Amplifiers," Laser Physics Letter, vol. 4, no. 1, pp. 10–15, 2007.

[16] S. W. Harun, F. Abd Rahman, K. Dimyati, and H. Ahmad, "An efficient gain-flattened C-band erbium-doped fiber amplifier," Laser Physics Letter, vol. 3, no. 11, pp. 536–538, 2006.

[17] N.M. Samsuri, S.W. Harun, and H. Ahmad, "Comparison of Performances between Partial double-Pass and Full Double-Pass Systems in Two-Stage L-Band EDFA," Laser Physics Letter, vol. 1, no. 12, pp. 610–612, 2004.

[18] Ozawa, K; Hishikawa,Y; Watanabe,K and Maki,H, "Remote Fiber Test System with Network Element Database and Geographic Information System", IEEE communication, vol. 2, page 1204-1207, 1999.

[19] R. Ramaswami, K.N.Sivarajan, "Optical Networks: A Practical Perspective" Morgan Kauffman Publishers, Los Altos, CA 1998.

[20] I. Yamashita, "The Latest FTTH Technologies for Full Service Access Networks", Proceedings of the IEEE, November 1996 Korea.

[21] D. N. Harres, B. Company, St.Louis, "Built-In Test for Fiber Optic Networks Enabled by OTDR", IEEE communication, 2006.

[22] C.P. Lenn, F.J. Kuchuk, J.Rounce and P. Hook, "Horizontal Well Performance Evaluation and Fluid Entry Mechanisms", Process of Social Petrol Engineering. Conferance and Exhibition, New Orleans, LA, SPE preprint 49089,. 1998.

[23] R.T. Tamos and E.J. Fordham, "Oblique-Tip Fiber-Optic Sensors for Multiphase Fluid Discrimination", Journal of Lightwave Technology, Vol. 17, No. 8, August 1999.

[24] R.T. Ramos, A. Holmes, X. Wu and E. Dussan, "A Local Optical Probe using Fluorescence and Reflectance for Measurement of Volume Fractions in Multi-Phase Flows", Meas. Sci. Technol., 12 (2001) 871-876.

[25] Kavintheran, Thambiratnam "Automated Fiber Optic Multiphase Dynamic Fluid Differentiation Measurement using LabVIEW Software with a Boolean Logic Function", ASEAN Virtual Instrumentation Applications Contest Submission, 2007.

[26] A. W. Domanski, A. Gorecki and M. Swillo. "Dynamic strain measurements by use of the polarimetric fiber optic sensors", IEEE Journal of Quantum Electronics QE-31(8), 816 (1995).

[27] G. C. Contantin, G. Perrone, S. Abrate, N. N. Puscaz "Fabrication and Characterization of Low-cost Polarimetric Fiber-Optic Pressure Sensor" Journal of Optoelectronics and Materials Vol. 8, No. 4, August 2006.

[28] Z. Zhou, T.W. Graver, L. Hsu, J. Ou, "Techniques of Advanced FBG Sensors: Fabrication, Demodulation, Encapsulation and Their Application in the Structural Health Monitoring of Bridges" Pacific Science Review, vol. 5, 2003

[29] Khing, T. Y.; Teck, P. K.; Voon L. K., Ee; L. T. & Wan, L. Y. (2005). Development of a Low Cost Fiber Bragg Grating (FBG) Sensor Interrogation System, ASEAN Virtual Instrumentation Applications Contest Submission.

11

Development of an Intelligent Bedsore Prevention System

Runjing Zhou
Inner Mongolia University
China

1. Introduction

Bedsore is a very common disease for long-term bedridden patients, and its main cause is that the human skins have been pressed too long in part areas, blood circulation obstruction lead to tissue necrosis. The conventional prevention measures include turning the body over at regular intervals by medical care personnel, using mattress and so on. Manpower nursing will increase the working strength of medical care personnel, and the common mattress only can be set to run periodically, it can not estimate the practical pressures of the different human body parts, as a result, if the time interval is set too long, maybe some parts can not be treated in time, and if the time interval is set too short, it will affect the rest of patient. A new method is put forward to improve the conventional bedsore prevention mattress, and the mattress is divided into areas to be controlled respectively. Several groups of stress sensor are used to measure the pressures signals in each area, and then the pressure signals are sampled to the computer. The LabVIEW virtual instrument is designed to analyze the measure pressure data, and estimate the state of every parts of the human body that have been continuously pressed. For the parts warned by the system, the LabVIEW instrument will send control signals to the corresponding pumps of the mattress.

2. System design and structure

The main cause of bedsore is that the part skin has been pressed too long, and the magnitude and duration of pressure are the crucial factors. According to the anatomical characteristics of human rachis, the pressures are bigger in four parts when the patient lies low, the four parts are head, scapular, sacrum and cruses. If these parts keep immobile for a long time, blood circulation of the corresponding parenchyma will be cumbered, and it will cause bedsore. According to amount of clinic experiments, in general, the pressure of sacrum is the biggest, that of the head and the scapular follows, and the pressure on cruses is the smallest among the four parts, therefore, the mattress can be divided into four areas, as shown in Fig. 1. Considering the position of the patient is not always in the center of the mattress, the numbers of stress sensor for practical system can be increased.

The whole system structure is shown in Fig. 2, pressure signals in each area of the mattress are conditioned and sampled to the computer, and then analyzed in the LabVIEW virtual instrument. Four pumps in different areas of the mattress are controlled by the signals from the virtual instrument.

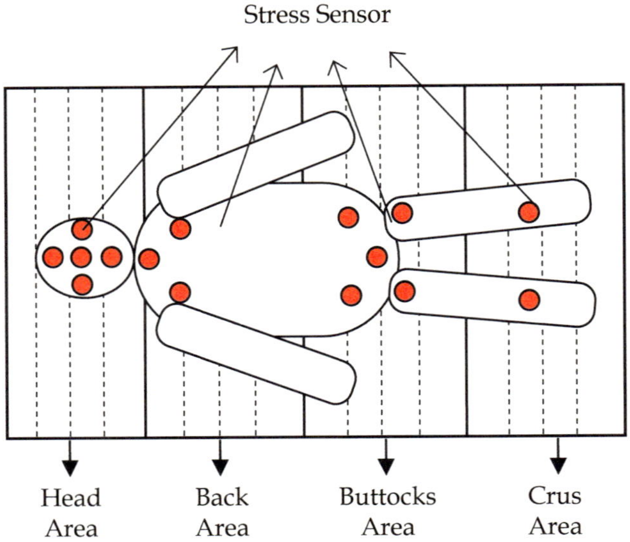

Fig. 1. Mattress partition and sensors distributing

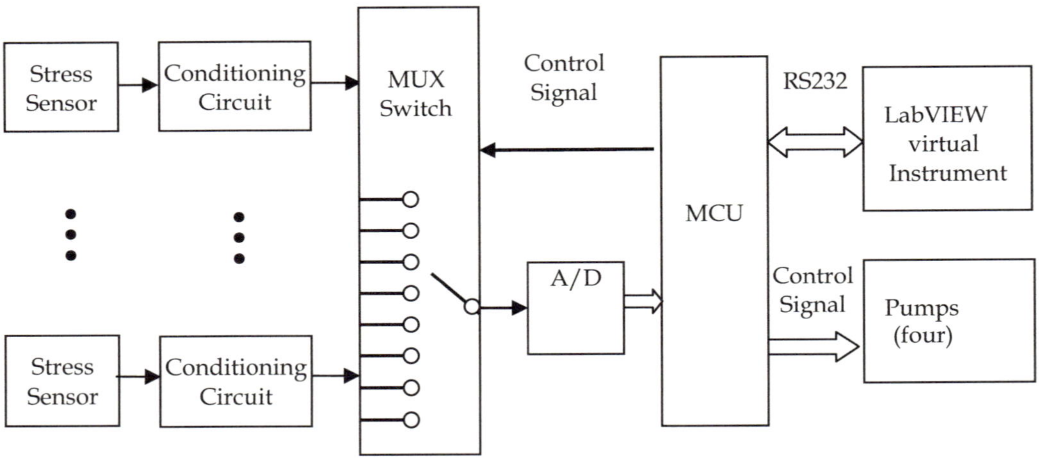

Fig. 2. System structure

3. Hard design

3.1 Pressure signal conditioning

3.1.1 Stress sensor selection

MPX2100 semiconductor pressure sensor manufactured by Motorola can convert pressure into a millivolt-level differential-mode voltage signal, the pressure sensor has good linearity, and the output voltage has a precise direct proportion with the pressure (Zhou, 2009). In addition, MPX2100 the compensation characteristics with temperature overcome the problem of the temperature drift of semiconductor pressure-sensitive semiconductor devices. So the system uses the MPX2100 pressure sensor, which can meet the system requirement. The physical map and pins map are shown in Fig.3 and Fig.4. MPX2100 has the following characteristics:

- As using a laser trimming technology to make the output of the bridge zero drift become small, generally less than ± 1mV;
- Having high sensitivity: 40mV± 1.5mV;
- Thermosensitive sensor compose of a temperature compensation network, in the range of -40 °C and +125 °C having a good temperature compensation effect, thereby enhancing the accuracy of the sensor;
- A better linearity (±0.25% F.S);
- A wide temperature range (-40 °C ~ +125 °C);
- Allowable large overload (400%).

Fig. 3. MPX2100 physical map

MPX2100 has 4 pins. Pin 1 connects to ground and pin 3 connects to the working voltage. Moreover, the output between pin 2 and pin 4 is differential-mode voltage signal which is proportional to the pressure.

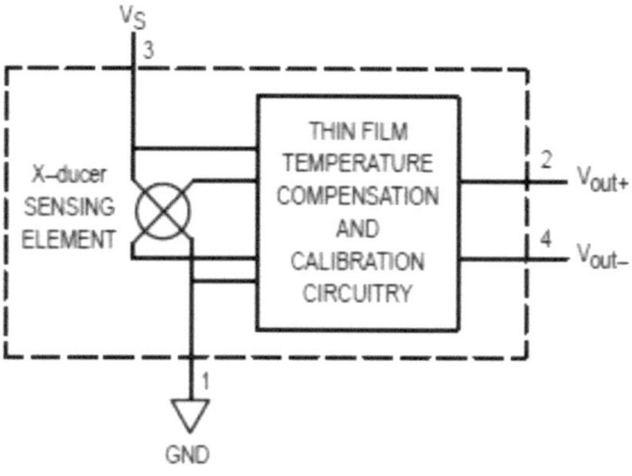

Fig. 4. MPX2100 pins map

MPX2100 is a piezoresistive pressure sensor, four equal resistors components are made by using diffusion technology on the silicon chip, which is constitute the Whiston bridge. Bridge have two power supply of voltage source power supply and constant current power supply. The principle of constant voltage source powered is shown in Fig.5.

When the pressure sensor under the pressure, a pair of arm resistance value increase ΔR, another pair of arm resistanc value decrease ΔR, resistance variation ΔR and stress is proportional, that is:

$$\Delta R = KP \tag{1}$$

The bridge output voltage is:

$$Uo = E\ (\Delta R\ /\ R) = (EK\ /\ R)\ P \tag{2}$$

The bridge output voltage is proportional to the pressure P.

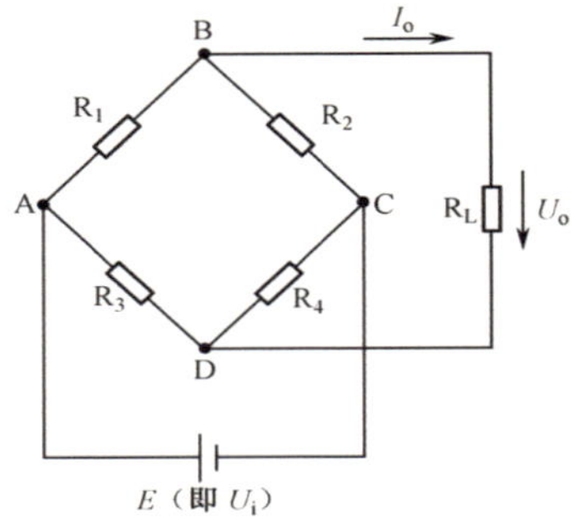

Fig. 5. Whiston bridge

3.1.2 Amplification circuit

The main amplification circuit is shown in Fig.6. The amplifier has a strong common-mode rejection ratio. It consists of two-stage amplifier, and the first-level is compose of integrated amplifier A1 and A2, as using the same type of operational amplifier, it can further reduce the drift. Resistors R1, R2 and R3 are composed of the same-phase input parallel differential amplifier with very high input impedance. The second-level comsist of inverse ratio amplifier by amplifier A3 and four resistances of R4, R5, R6 and R7, it will change a double-end input into a single-end output. The resistance is set as follows:

$$R1 = R3 \tag{3}$$

$$R4 = R5 \tag{4}$$

$$R6 = R7 \tag{5}$$

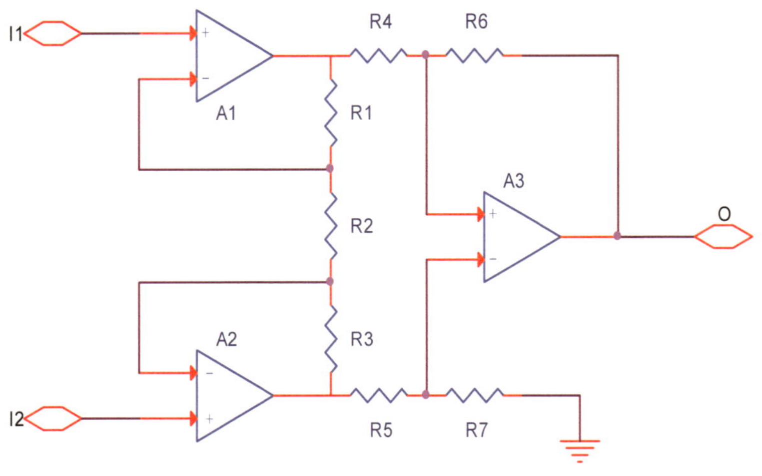

Fig. 6. Instrument amplifier circuit

According to the basic analysis method of operation circuit, the available output voltage is:

$$U_o = -\frac{R_6}{R_4}(1 + 2\frac{R_1}{R_2})(U_{I1} - U_{I2}) \quad (6)$$

To facilitate adjustment, the circuit increase a part of percentage of amplifier. At the same time, making the the output signal of the instrument amplifier circuit reverse, which is shown in Fig.7. RW is zero adjustment resistance.

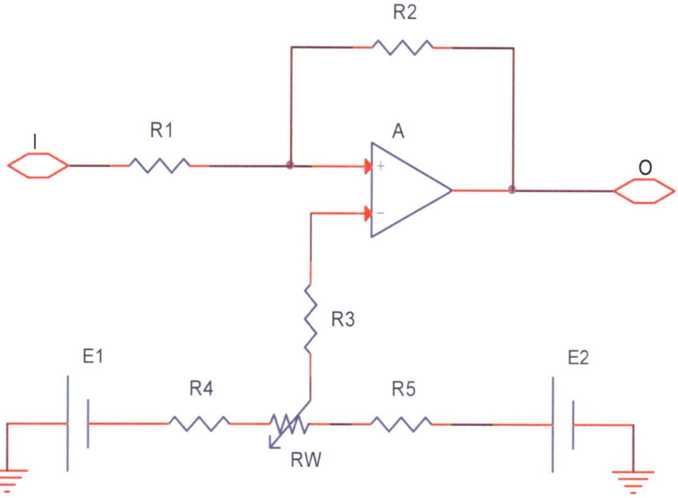

Fig. 7. Rate amplifier circuit

3.1.3 Integrated circuit design

Therefore, pressure measurement circuit is completed based on MPX2100. Integrated circuit is shown as follows. Pressure signal transmitted the signal to the multi-selector switch through IN1 port. Another 14-channel signal sampling circuit is the same with the Fig.8.

In the Fig.8, RW1 is the gain adjustment potentiometer; RW2 is zero adjustment potentiometer of the amplifier circuit. Amplifier circuit choose OP07CP as an amplifier, because it is an operation amplifier with low noise and a low offset voltage. In addition, the diode VD1, VD2 may play a protective effect on the circuit.

3.2 Control circuit

This system contain so much sensors, if sampling all sensor signals at the same time, the hardware design will be more complex. Multi-channel selection switch are timing of gating and cycle-sampled for the signal of every channel. For long-term bedridden patients, the pressure signal in different part of the human body changes relatively slow, so sampling period can be set slightly longer. Generally setting to one minute, it can meet the system requirement.

3.2.1 Microcontroller selection

So selecting AT89S52 microcontroller to design system not only meets the requirement of design but also can on-line program on the circuit board and taking convenient program debugging.

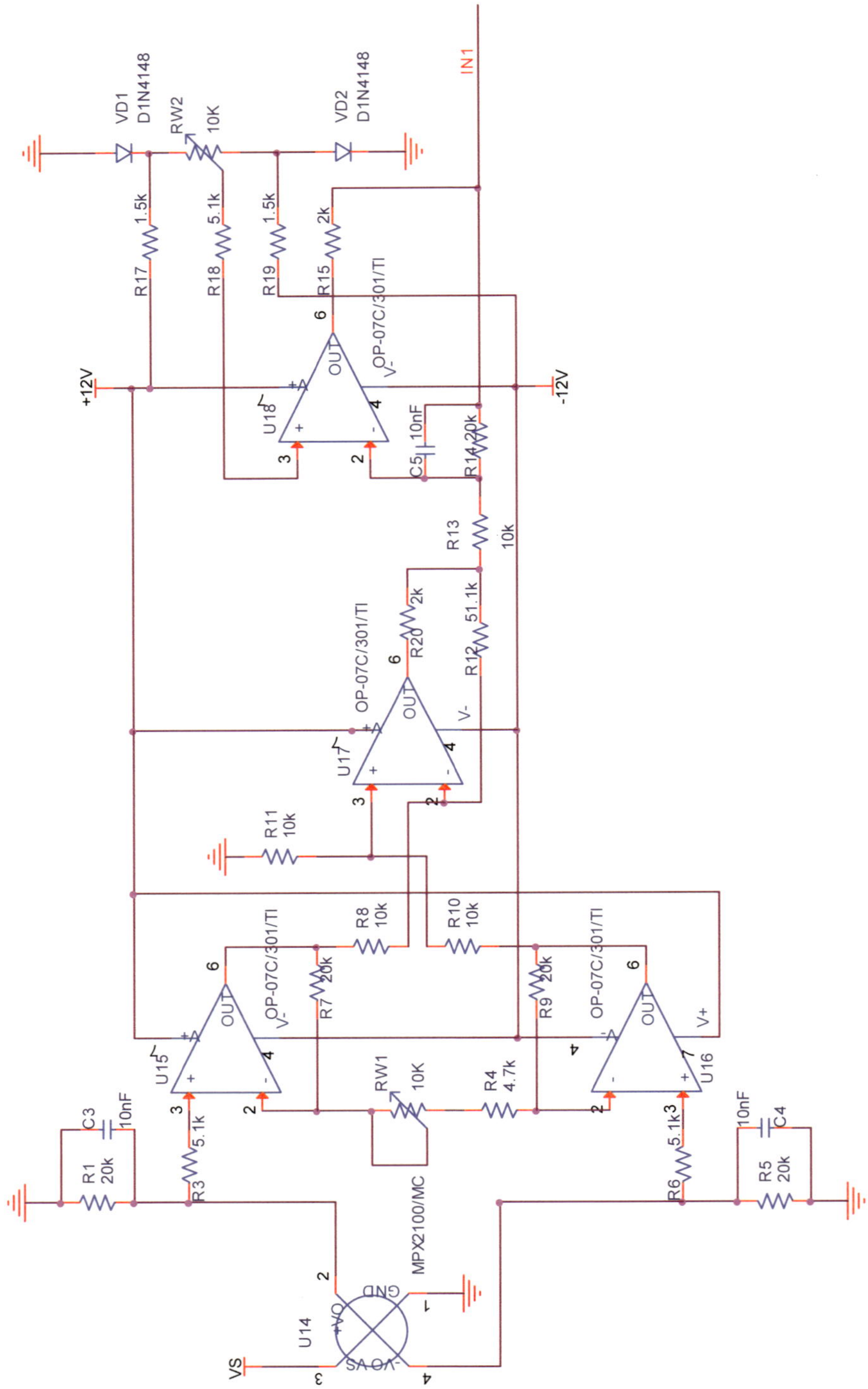

Fig. 8. Pressure measurement circuit

3.2.2 A/D converter selection

It is necessary to analyse sampled press signal in this design, taking the detail information of the signal, so sampled signal need to have higher resolution. Considering the performance-price ratio of hardware design, 12-bit A/D converter is selected to take a sample of data. The main function parameters of MAX1240 are as follows:

- A single supply(+2.7V ~+3.6V);
- 12-bit resolution;
- Low power consumption: 37Mw(73 KSPS),5μW (standby working mode);
- Internal provide track/hold circuit;
- Internal provide conversion clock.

The pin distribution of MAX1240 is shown in Fig.9, MAX1240 interface timing sequence is shown in Fig. 10.

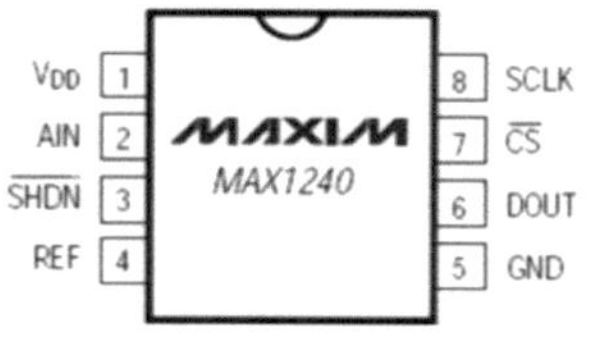

Fig. 9. MAX1240 pin distribution

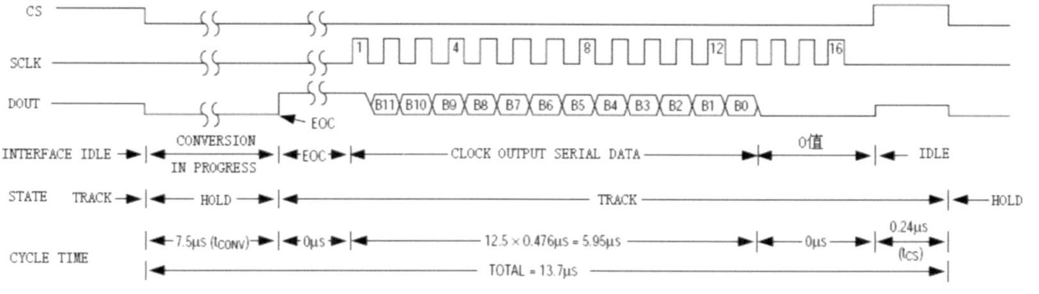

Fig. 10. MAX1240 working timing sequence

3.2.3 Serial communication circuit

Serial communication line is simple and reducing design cost, so it is used more widely to transfer data in the close distance with less demanding speed. Serial communication can be divided into two basic transmission forms of asynchronous communication and synchronization communication. Asynchronous transmission is characterized by the data discontinuous transmission on the transmission line, but the two communication parties must agree the character format and baud rate at first. Faster than asynchronous transmission, the hardware of synchronous transmission is more complex and also has a very strict requirement for the phase consistency of the synchronize clock pulse signal.

Serial communication has established a number of the consistent concepts and standards to make the computer, telephone and other communication devices communicate with each other. The concepts and standards conclude:

Transmission rate: transmission rate refers to the transmitting the bit number per second, so transmission rate is also called baud rate. Most CRT devices can work according to any baud rate of the range from 110 to 9600.

RS-232-C standard: RS-232-C standard make a regulation for two aspects, that is signal level standard and control signal standard. RS-232-C use the logic level of negative logic regulation, signal level is not compatible with the normal TTL level. RS-232-C standard use EIA level, in which the high level is +3V to +15V and the low level is -3V to -15V. But the high level of the standard TTL level is +2.4V to +5V and the low level is 0 to 0.4V. If transforming the two levels, the specialized level conversion chip is needed. At present, MAX3232 is usually used as level conversion chip. The main function parameter is as follows:

- 3.0~5.5V power supply;
- 300μA low supply current;
- Only connect 0.1μF capacitance

MCS_51 microcontroller has a full duplex serial port. Full duplex serial communication only need a output line TXD and a input line RXD. Serial communication mainly has two technical problems. The one is data transmission, the other is data conversion. Data transmission mainly solves some problems about standard, format and working mode in the transmission. Data conversion is the purpose to complete the conversion of string and parallel. MCS-51 serial port reception and sending both can work in the query or interrupt way with the use of very flexible. 51 microcontroller serial programming involved some major special function register, which is serial data buffer SBUF, serial port control register SCON, special function register PCON and interrupt allowable register IE.

3.2.4 The whole circuit of microcontroller

A/D converter power supply voltage is 3.3V, and taking supply voltage as the external reference voltage (Hu, 2003). SPI timing sequence can be programmed by the MCU software. MAX1240 sampling rate is much larger than the transmission rate, so the sampling rate of the whole hardware sampling system is decided by the transmission rate of serial port.

Baud rate of both communication sides is necessary ensure of making serial communication normal. Serial port select working mode 1, baud rate B is determined by the overflow rate S of timer T1 and it can use the following formula to express:

$$B = \frac{2^{SMOD} \cdot S}{32} \tag{7}$$

$$S = \frac{f_0}{12(2^n - X)} \tag{8}$$

Where X is the calculation initial value of timer T1, n is the number bits of the timer T1 (select working mode 2, n=8), the value of serial baud rate multiplier bit SMOD is 0. In this design, we should select the right size of the crystal oscillator to make the baud rate of system the same with the baud rate of setting in the PC. The baud rate generated by microcontroller is equal to 9600, so we select the 14.7456MHz crystal oscillator as the microcontroller crystal oscillator.

Where X is the calculation of initial value of timer T1, n the number of bits for the timer T1 (timer selection work 2, n = 8), the serial baud rate multiplier bit SMOD values to 0. We should choose the right size for the single chip crystal oscillator, the baud rate generated by the system and set the baud rate the same PC. This article hopes generated baud rate is equal to 9600 MCU, so select the 14.7456MHz crystal oscillator as a single chip.

3.2.5 Software design

The main tasks of the microcontroller which need to complete are data sending and data reception. The flow chart is shown in Fig.11, Data sending can send the data that the AD samples to the computer through the serial port. Data reception can receive the pressure signal processing results through the computer serial port, and make the corresponding control to the pump. The whole circuit of microcontroller is shown in Fig.12.

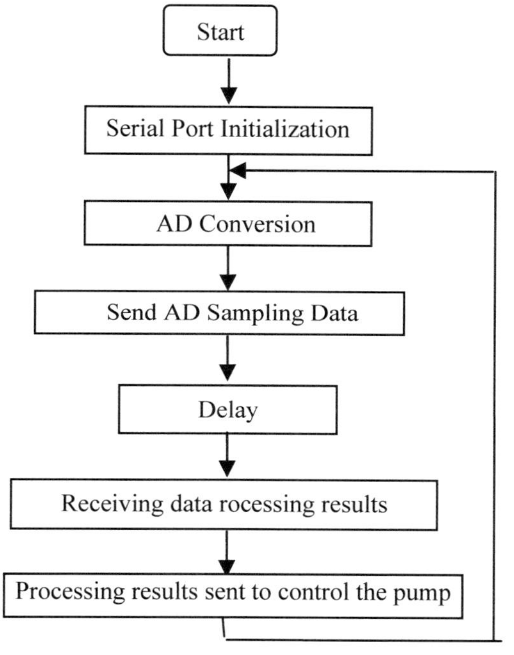

Fig. 11. Flow chart

Source Code:

```
#include <reg51.h>
#include<INTRINS.H>
#define uint unsigned int
#define uchar unsigned char
#define SomeNOP(); {}
uchar ch;
uchar cha;
unsigned char word1[16]={"Cha:  Val= "};   // Display Cache
bit read_flag= 0 ;
sbit dout=P1^0;
sbit sclk=P1^1;
sbit cs = P1^2;
sbit shdn=P1^3;
```

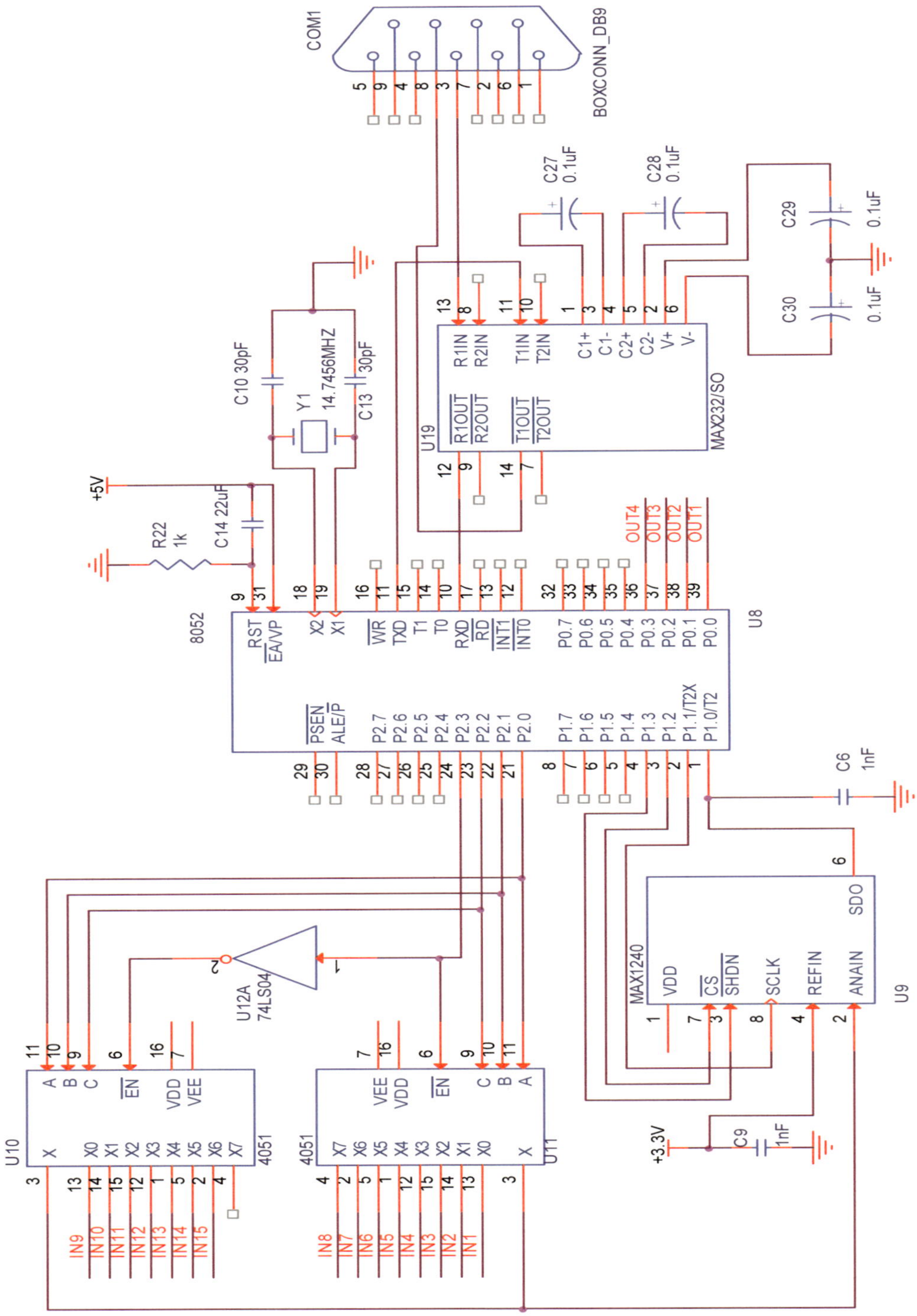

Fig. 12. MCU and its peripheral circuits

```
/************************1ms Delay Functions *********************/
delay1ms(uint t)
{
          uint i,j;
           for(i=0;i<t;i++)
            for(j=0;j<120;j++);
}
/********************* MAX1240 conversion process ********************/
void adconversion(void)
{ uint rice=0;
 uchar i;
float rice1=0;
 sclk=0;
 cs=0;
_nop_();
if(dout==0)
{_nop_();
_nop_();
_nop_();
_nop_();
_nop_();
_nop_();
_nop_();

if(dout==1)
         {
          for(i=0;i<12;i++)
          { sclk=1;
          _nop_();
          sclk=0;

     if(dout==1)
         {rice=(rice<<1) | 0x0001;}
         else
         rice=rice<<1;
          }
          cs=1;}
         }
word1[4]=(cha/10)+48;
word1[5]=(cha%10)+48;
rice1=(float)rice*1.220703125;//(2.5*rice*1000)/0xfff;
rice=(uint)rice1;
word1[11]=(rice%10000)/1000+48;
word1[12]='.';
word1[13]=(rice%1000)/100+48;
word1[14]=(rice%100)/10+48;
word1[15]=rice%10+48;
}
```

```
/**************** Serial port initialization process****************/
void UART_init()
        {
                TMOD=0x20;                      // timer 1 mode 2 : 8-Bit reload
                PCON=0x00;                      // Baud rate is not doubled
                SCON=0x50;                      // mode 1 bit UART, enable receiver
                TH1=0xFC;                       // reload value 9600 baud
                IE = 0x90;        //Enable Serial Interrupt
                TR1=1;                  //timer1 run
        }

/************* Serial communication function (send)**********************/
void putchar(unsigned char data1)  // Characters send function
        {
         SBUF = data1;
        while(TI == 0);
        TI = 0;
        }

void putstring(unsigned char *dat)   // string Send function
        {
         while(*dat != '\0')
         {
          putchar(*dat);
         dat++;
         delay1ms(5);
         }
        }

void Serialsent()                    // Send a string of specified bits
        {
        unsigned char c;
        for(c=11;c<16;c++)
                          {
                          SBUF=word1[c];
                          while(!TI);
                          TI=0;
                          delay1ms(10);
                          }
         }

/************* Serial communication function (receiver)*****************/
// Serial port receive interrupt function
void serial () interrupt 4 using 3
{
  if (RI)
        {
                RI=0;
                ch=SBUF;
```

```
                        read_flag= 1 ;
                        P0=ch;
                        delay1ms(1000);
                      }
}
/************************Main function **************************/
void main()
{
        UART_init();                                    // Serial port initialization
                do
                {
                P2=cha;
                adconversion();
                delay1ms(100);
                putstring("\r\n") ;
                Serialsent();
                delay1ms(50);
                cha++ ;
                }
        while(cha<15);

        putstring("\r\n");
        putstring("-----------\r\n");
        delay1ms(1000);
if (RI)   // If have received interrupt, get results and send it to P0
{                       RI=0;
                        ch=SBUF;
                        read_flag= 1 ;
                        P0=ch;
                        delay1ms(1000);
                      }
}
```

3.3 Pump control circuit

Pump control signal first use an inverter 74LS04 and a regional control circuit is shown in Fig.13. Then the other three regions control circuit is the same with the first pump control circuit.

3.4 Power supply module

3.4.1 Analysis of system power demand

In this design, the pressure signal conditioning circuit requires two groups of +5V and -5V analog power, the microcontroller requires 5V power supply, the operational amplifier of conditioning circuit requires +12V and -12V. A/D converter and MAX3232 need 3.3V digital power supply, while pump requires 12V power. To suppression the interference generated by digital circuit to the analog signal, the digital ground and the analog ground need to be isolated.

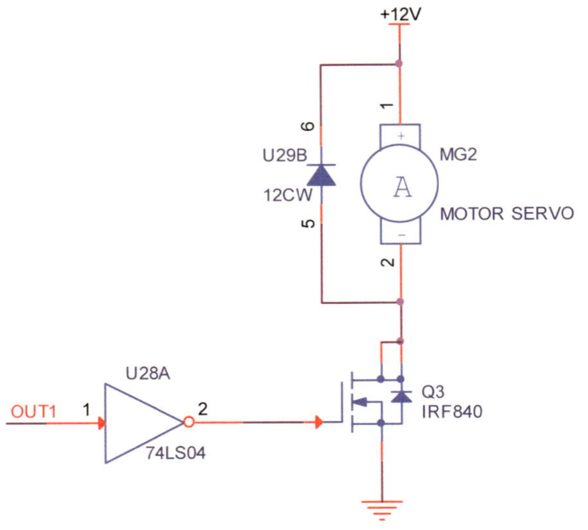

Fig. 13. Pump control circuit

According to the system design requirements and evaluating various factors, initially setting the basic parameters of the system power is as follows:

- Input Voltage: 12V AC voltage;
- Output voltage: +12 V,-12V, +5 V,-5V, +3.3 V;
- Output current: the major components required normal currents were several to tens of milliampere, so that the power supply current typically is less than 100mA.

3.4.2 Design of digital power

In order to reduce the power supply of system and improve power efficiency and reduce heat of the power system, low dropout regulator should be chosen. This design choice RT9163 series regulator to provide the required voltage, the main features of the chip are as follows:

- LDO: maximum voltage 1.4V;
- Fast transient response;
- ± 2% of total output regulation;
- 0.1% line regulation;
- 0.1% load regulation;
- Output Current: 0.5A;

+5V digital and analog power supply circuit is shown in Fig.14(a), output voltage of three-terminal regulator RT9163 is used as the +5V digital power supply, then the inductance L1 and capacitor Ct8 constitute of the LC low-pass filter, cutoff frequency is:

$$f_c = \frac{1}{2\pi\sqrt{L_1 \cdot C_2}} \approx 400Hz \tag{9}$$

Digital voltage filters high frequency noise by the LC filter, which can be used as analog power VCC. +5 V digital power supply followed by a three-terminal regulator RT9163 of 3.3V output is shown in Fig.14(b) and available +3.3 V digital power supply can be got.

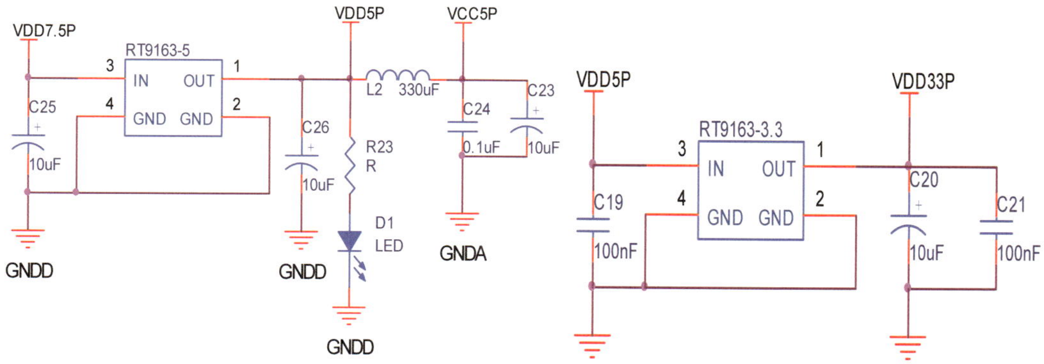

(a) +5 V digital power supply (b) +3.3 V digital power supply

Fig. 14. Digital power supply

3.4.3 Analog power supply

Analog power supply made the multi-level regulation of the three-terminal regulator block, and large-capacity electrolytic capacitors and high-frequency small capacitors make output to meet the voltage requirements. The circuit is shown in Fig.15.

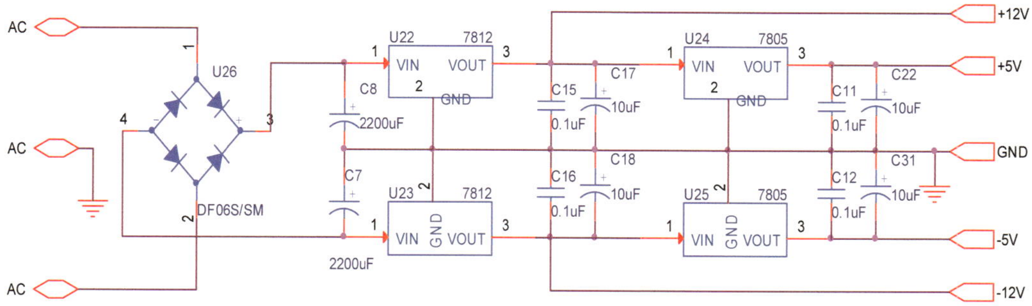

Fig. 15. Analog power circuit

4. LabVIEW virtual instrument design

The main thought of LabVIEW virtual instrument design is: LabVIEW virtual instrument recieves the pressure data of each sensor which sent from microcontroller by serial port, then the pressure data is transformed, arranged and filtered. At last, it is divided into four groups and each group of data represents the press state of head area, back area, buttocks area and crus area. The sensor signals in each area of mattress are shown in real time in different waveform chart, and then be saved in the corresponding file named by the user. Then LabVIEW calls the data saved in the excel file and analyzes them, if the point bearing the most in certain part does not change during the setting time, the system will recognize that the skin in this part has been pressed for a long time and it will easily cause bedsore, then the LabVIEW virtual instrument sends control signals to microcontroller and begins to alarm, microcontroller controls pump to massage this part of skin, its flow chart is shown in Fig.16.

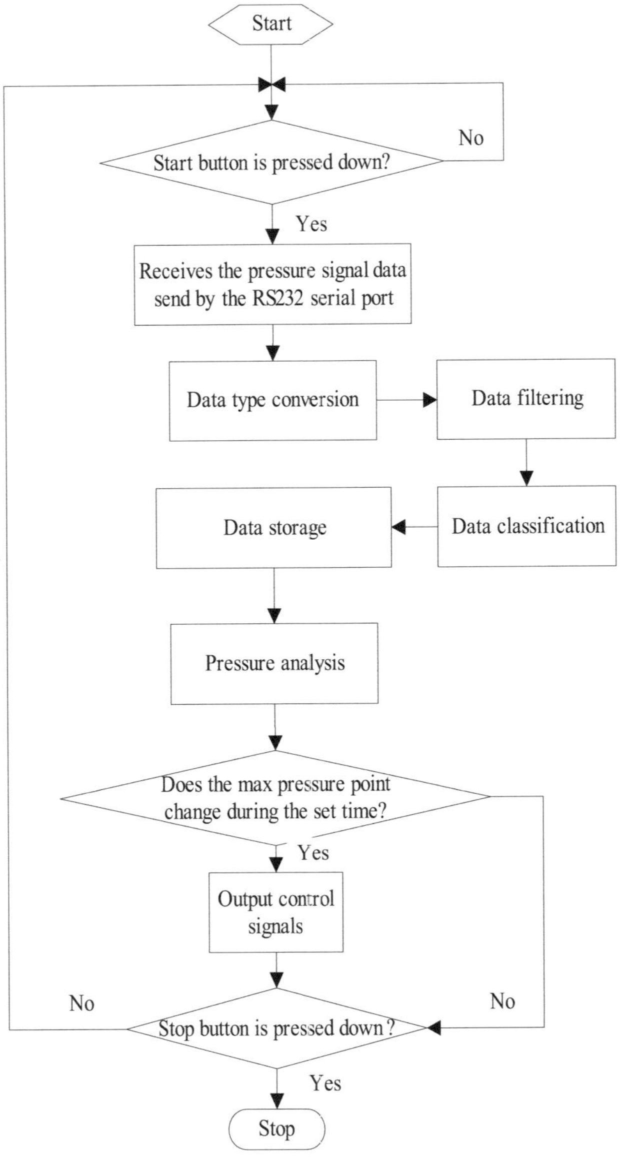

Fig. 16. LabVIEW main program flow chart

First, open National Instruments LabVIEW 2009 software, then choose "Empty Project" in the left side of the "Getting Started" window to build a new project, at last name the project with "Design of a Intelligent Bedsore Prevention and Treatment System".

4.1 Data receiving and storage

Data receiving and storage progam is composed with four parts: read serial port, data transformation and arrangment, data filtering and area saving, its concrete program block diagram is shown in Fig.17.

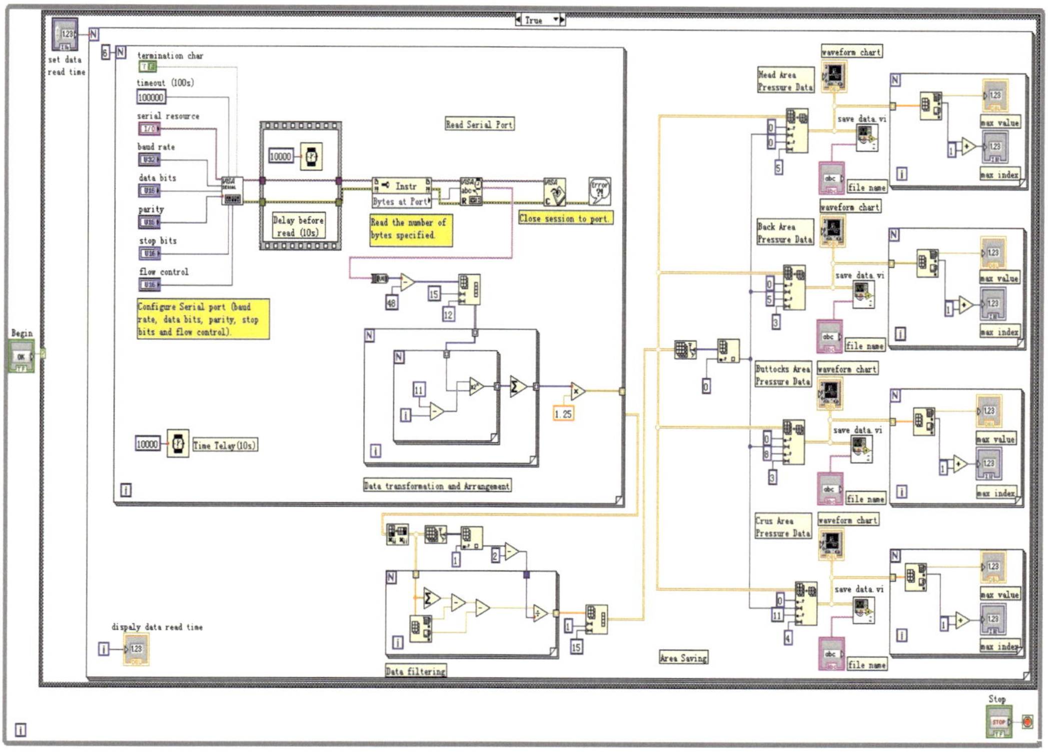

Fig. 17. Data read and storage program block diagram

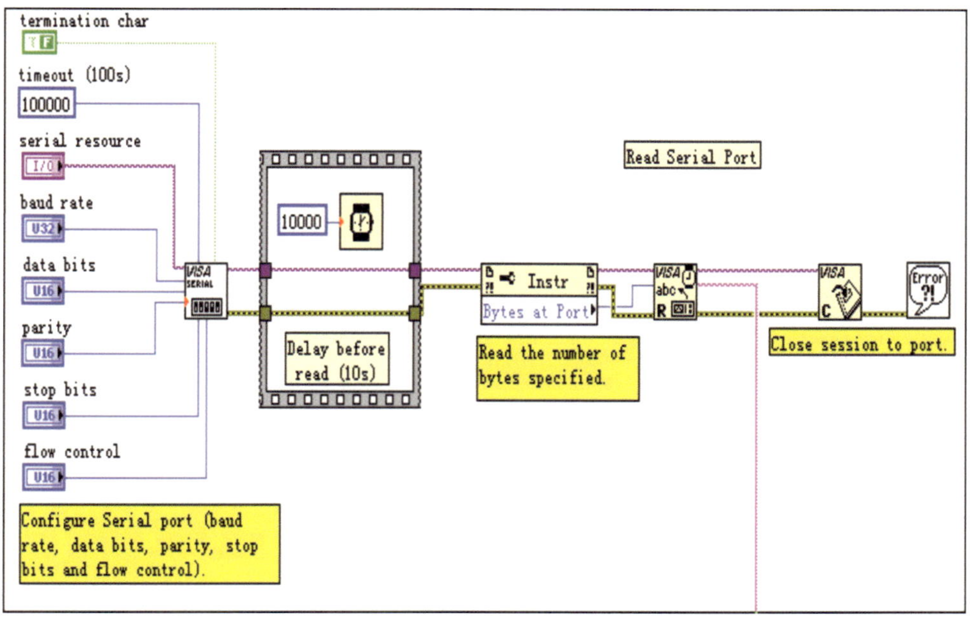

Fig. 18. Read serial port program block diagram

Concrete steps are as follows (Chen, 2007):

1. Build a new program in this project and name it with "data read and storage.vi".
2. Read serial port: the data communications are based on the RS232 serial port protocol. The serial port should be initialized before the data communications, the settings of serial port in the software and the hardware should be consistent, and its block diagram is shown in Fig.18. VISA Configure Serial Port VI is used to initializes the serial port, the parameters usually want to be configured are: baud rates, data bits, stop bits, flow control and so on. VISA Read Function is used to read the specified number of bytes from the serial port and return the data in read buffer, these functions are in the Instrument I/O | Serial Palette of the Functions Palette.
3. Data transformation and arrangement: in the LabVIEW virtual instrument, the type of data read from the serial port is binary string, so it should be converted to binary integer firstly, we use String To Byte Array Function to convert a string into an array of unsigned bytes, but each byte in the array has the ASCII value of the corresponding character in the string, so its value should decreases 48. All the converted sample data composes a binary one-dimension array with a length of 180n(12x15xn), we should transform it to a denary two-dimension array with fifteen columns and n rows, and the data in the same column is the sampled data of one sensor. Reshape Array Function is used to change a one-dimension array to a two-dimension array, after use this function, a one-dimension array with a length of 180 is changed to a two-dimension array with 12 columns and 15 rows. Then we should convert the binary data to the denary, change the binary data to decimal data in each row accoring to the binary to decimal conversion formula. After series of data transformation and arrangement, the data is transformed into a denary two-dimension array with n rows and 15 columns. But the data is not the pressure data we need at last, it is the data after A/D conversion, the relation between this data and the real pressure data is linear, so the data should be multiplied by a factor, the value of the factor is related to measurement circuit and A/D conversion circuit. Data transformation and arragement block diagram is shown in Fig.19.

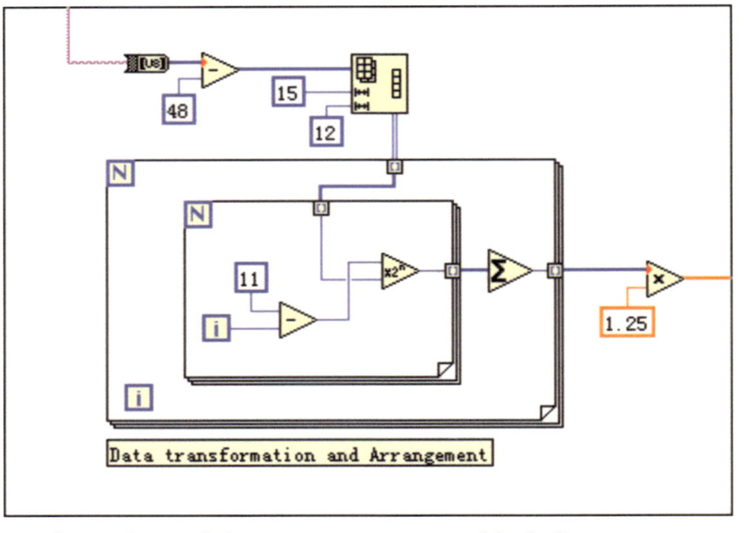

Fig. 19. Data transformation and Arrangement program block diagram

4. Data filtering: data transmission errors and data loss is likely to occur during the RS232 serial communications, so the data need to be filtered. The main thought of data filtering is: LabVIEW virtual instrument recieves a group of data which sent by the RS232 serial port every 10 seconds, so it will receive 6 groups of data in a minute. Removing the maximum and minimum values of the 6 groups, the average value of the remaining 4 groups is thought as the pressure data in one minute, its block diagram is shown in Fig.20.

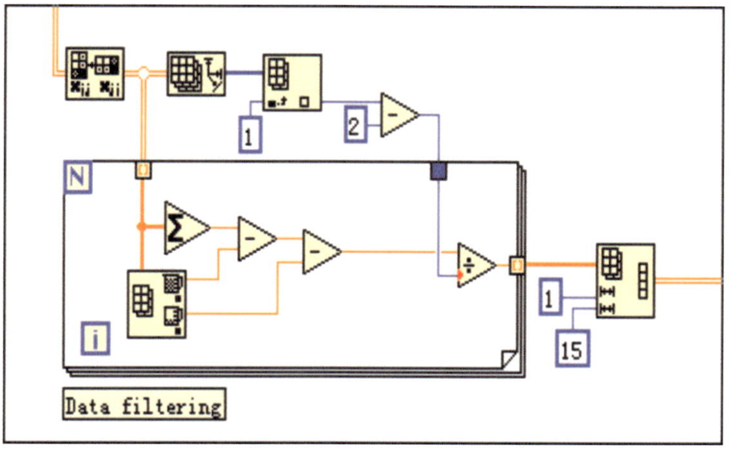

Fig. 20. Data filtering program block diagram

5. Area Saving: because the pressure analysis in each area is only relative to the measured pressure signals in the areas, the sensor signals can be saved by areas to different files. The column number of the array in each file is the same to the number of sensors in the corresponding area. That is to say, the two-dimension array will be divided into four new arrays with the row number invariable. We use Array Subset Function to divide the array, after using this function, 1~5 columns, 6~8 columns, 9~11 columns and 12~15 columns of the array will form 4 new arrays with the row number invariable. This 4 new arrays are pressure data of sensors in head area, back area, buttocks area and crus area. The sensor signals in each area of the mattress can be shown in real time in different waveform chart. Array Max & Min Function is used to show the maximal pressure of the area and the sensor number is under the maximal pressure, the program block diagram is shown in Fig.21.

4.2 Data storage

In Fig.21, the 'save data. vi' block is a LabVIEW subroutine, its function is to save the new two-dimension array of each area, which block diagram is shown in Fig.22. The pressure signals in each area will be saved into four different excel files. Write To Spreadsheet File VI is used to save the data into excel files, the intraday two-dimension array in each area can be save by entering the corresponding file name in the front panel of the subroutine, save path is "d:\file\(date)(file name).xls".

Concrete steps are as follows:

1. Build a new program in the project, and name it with "data storage.vi";
2. Draw program block diagram is shown in Fig.22;

3. Edit icon and connector. Double click the icon in the upper right corner and edit it, right-click the icon pane in the front panel and choose "Show Connector" in the shortcut menu. And then connect the controls in the front panel with the terminal of the connector. One input terminal should be connected to the array which needs to be saved, the other input terminal should be connected to the file name which wants to be saved.
4. Save this VI file, so we can use it next time.

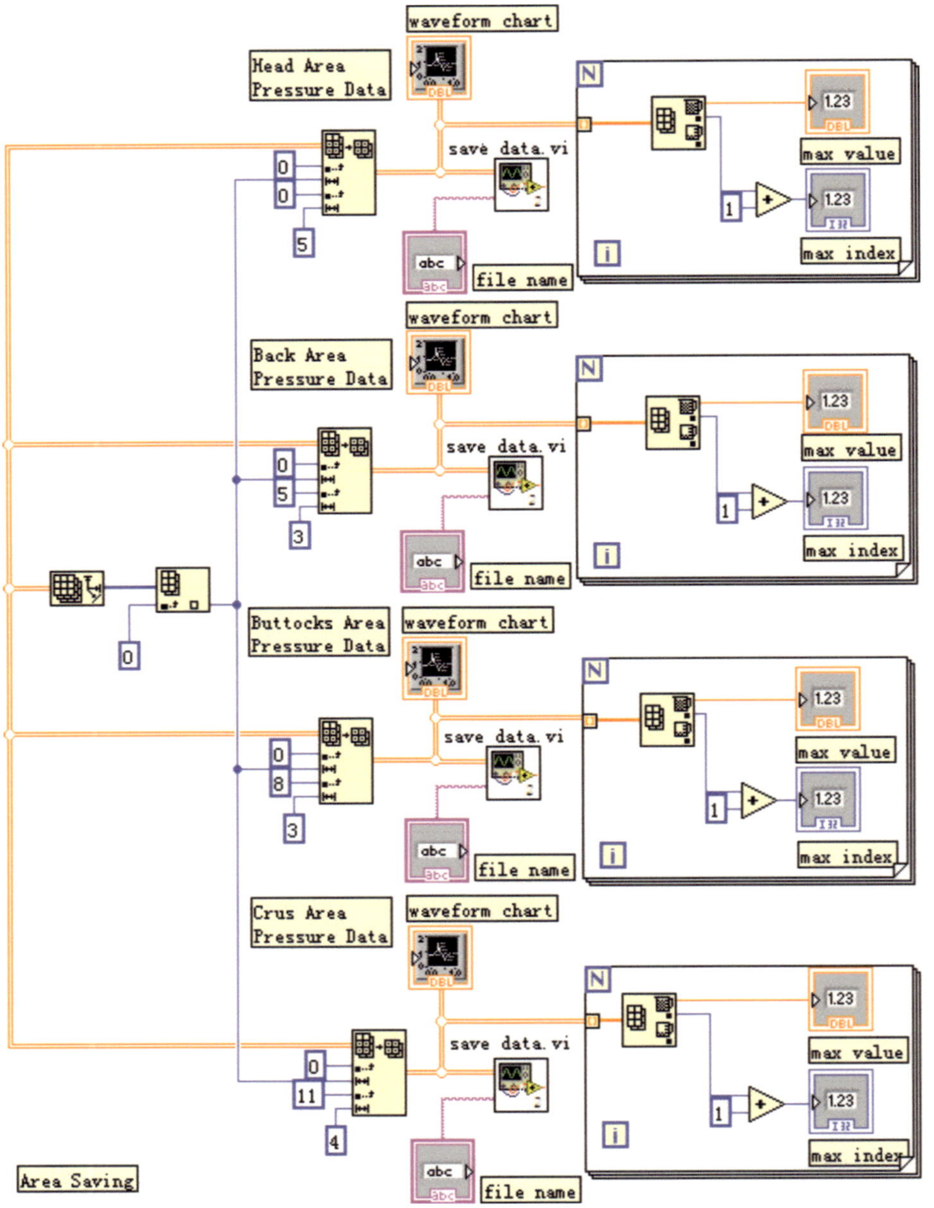

Fig. 21. Area saving program block diagram

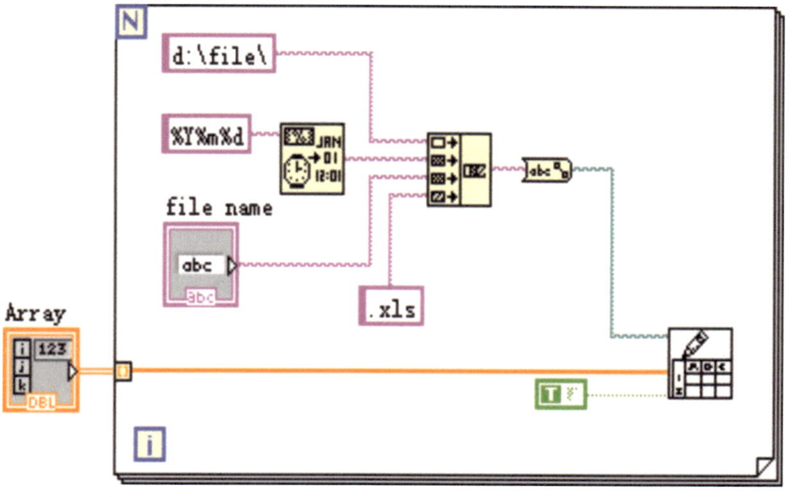

Fig. 22. Data storage block

4.3 Pressure analysis in each area

The press state of each area is got by comparing and analyzing the saved pressure data. The pressure analysis of the single area can be taken as an independent LabVIEW subroutine, the concrete program block diagram is shown in Fig.23.

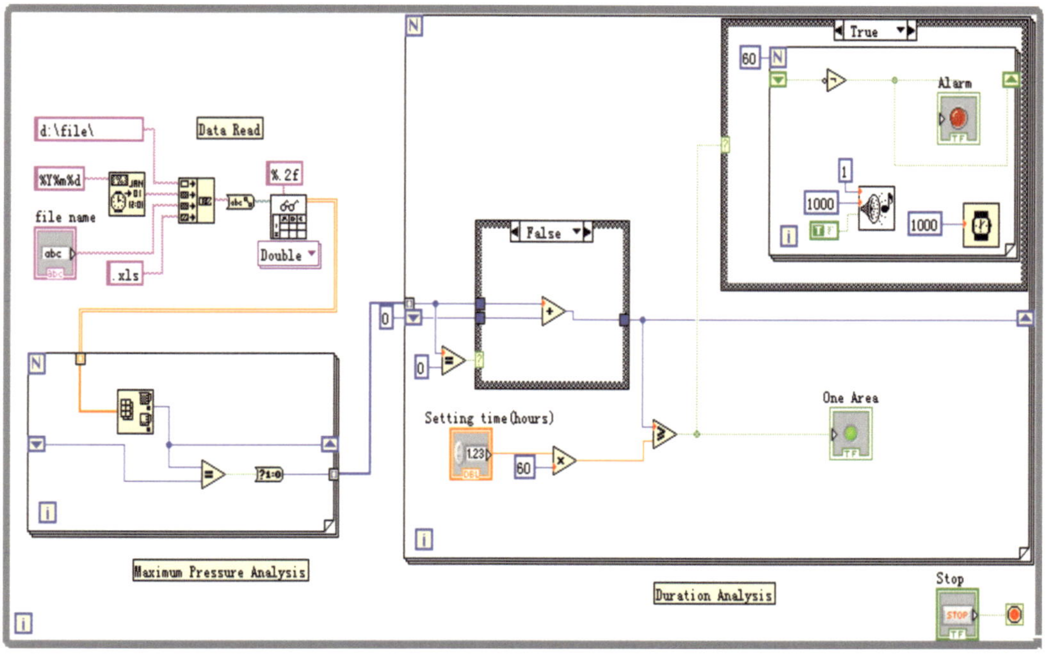

Fig. 23. Pressure analysis program block diagram

The point under the biggest pressure in the certain area of mattress can be got by comparing the corresponding data in this area. The maximum value in a row is the maximal pressure of the area at the certain time and the position of the maximal value can show the sensor which is under the maximal pressure. If the point bearing the most in certain part does not change during the set time, the system will recognize that the skin in this part has been pressed for a long time and need to be massaged. Otherwise, the system will recognize that the main bearing point in this area has been changed and this area do not need to be massage during the time (Zhou, 2008).

The maximum duration under pressure in each part of human body is different, because the maximum pressure in each part is different. In addition, the weight of patient is always different, thus the maximum duration should be set according to the characteristic of the patient and the specific part. If the sensor signals are set to be sampled every 10 seconds and stored every 1 minute, the maximum duration is set to be x hours. Then when the maximum values in all the seriate 60x rows are in the same column, it can be concluded that there is no move in this area during the x hours. The LabVIEW instrument send relevant signals to the microcontroller according to the analysis result, then the pump of certain area will be controlled to run (Yang, 2007).

Concrete steps are as follows:

1. Build a new program in the project, and name it with "pressure analysis.vi".
2. Data read: its block diagram is shown in Fig.24. Read From Spreadsheet File VI is used to read the saved pressure data files, and then output a double-precision two dimension array, the file path is "d:\file\(time)(file name).xls".

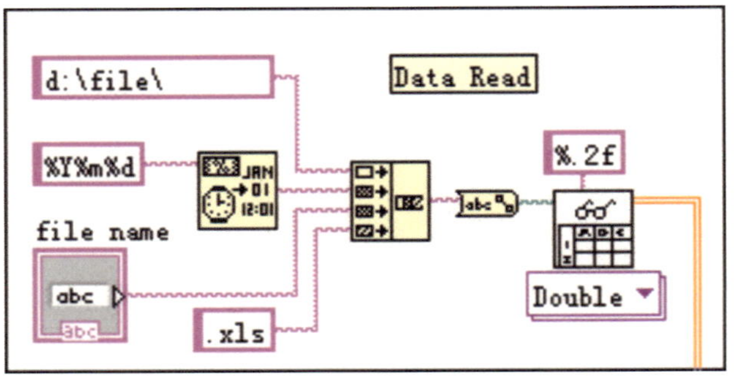

Fig. 24. Data Read program block diagram

3. Maximum pressure analysis: The array of pressure data can be read row by row, Array Max & Min Function is used to find the position of the maximal value in this row, then compare it with the position of maximal value in last row, if they are same, it will output Boolean variable '1', its program block diagram is shown in Fig.25.
4. Duration Analysis: its program block diagram is shown in Fig.26, if the position of the maximal value in this row is same to the position of the maximal value in last row, the value of register variable will increase 1. If the value of the register variable is larger than the setting time, it will output display signals and control signals, and it will begin to alarm.

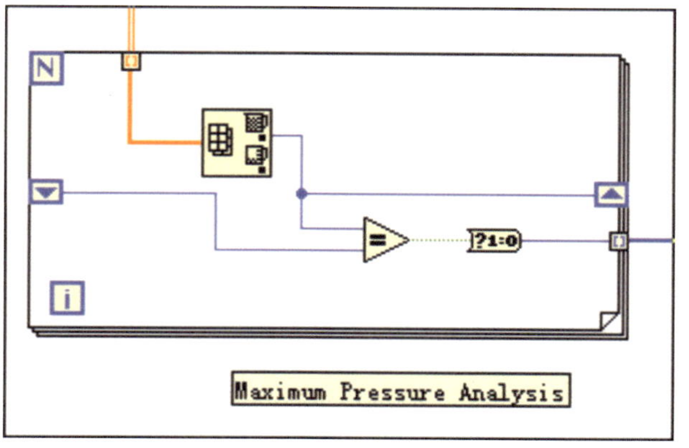

Fig. 25. Maximum Pressure Analysis block diagram

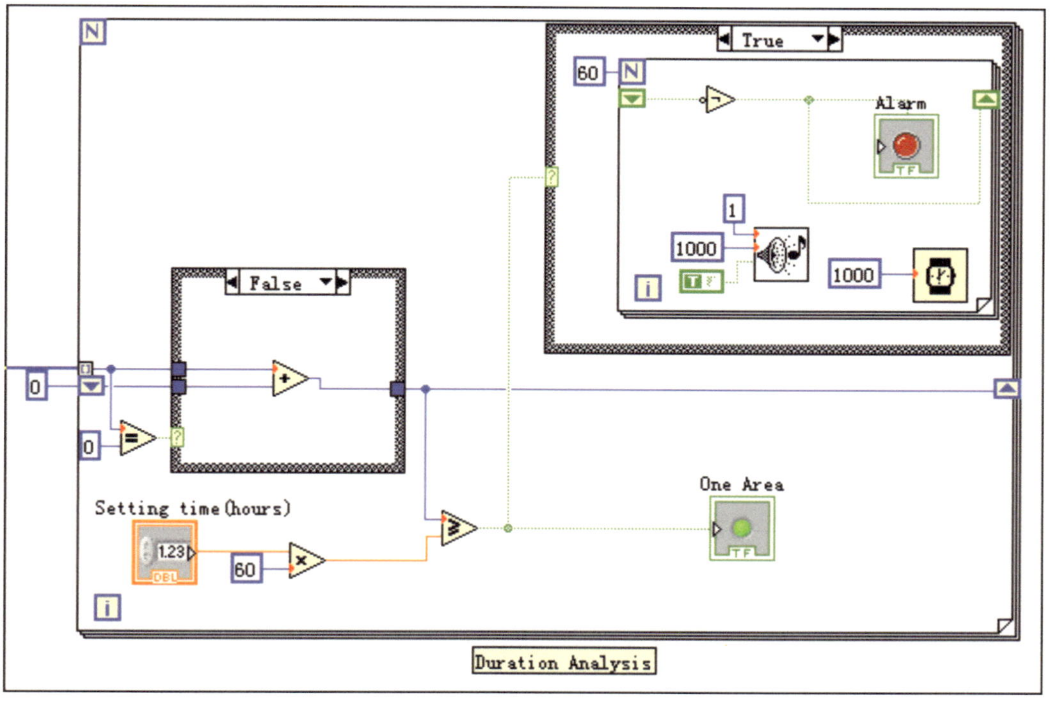

Fig. 26. Duration analysis program block diagram

4.4 Control signals sending

We will send a 4 bytes string to microcontroller according to the result of pressure analysis in each area, each byte of the string indicates wheather the pump in this area begin to run, for example, a string of "0011" indicates that the pumps in buttocks area and crus area will begin to run, its diagram is shown in Fig.27.

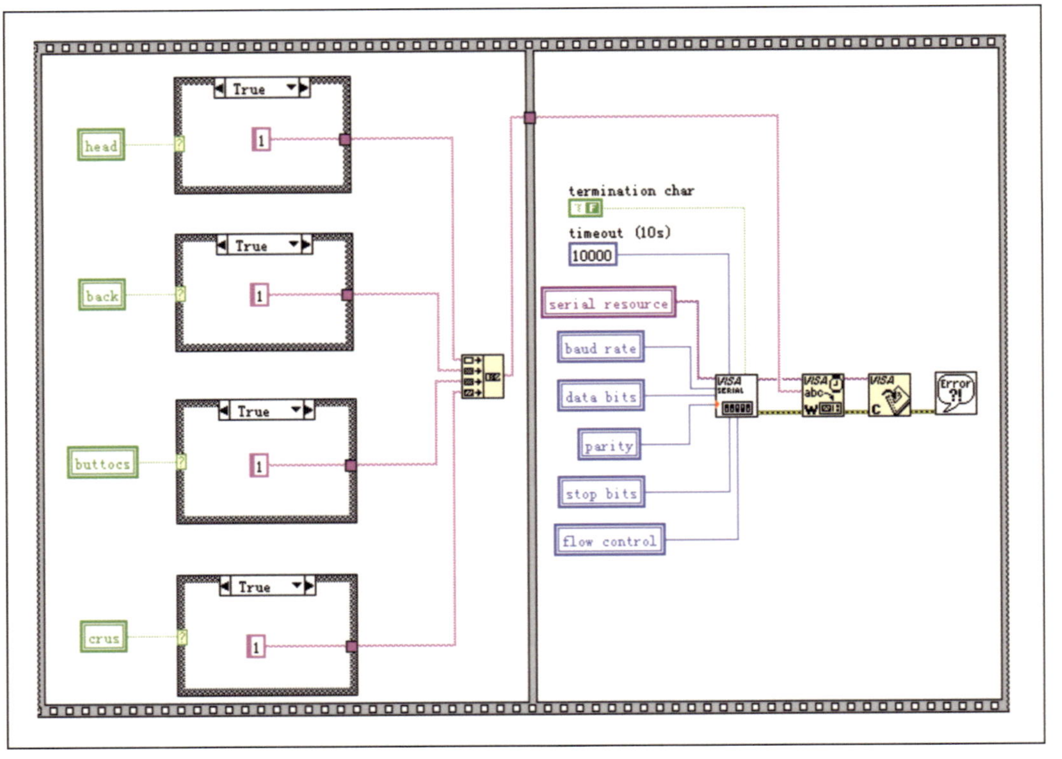

Fig. 27. Control signals sending block diagram

4.5 Instrument interface and function verification

The designed instrument interface is shown in Fig.28.The sensor signals in each area of the mattress are shown in real time in different waveform chart, and then be saved in the corresponding file named by the user. Saved pressure data file of different area is shown in Fig.29. The maximum duration under pressure of each area can be set by doctor. The alarming is visual and the status of different areas can be shown.

The system is set as in Fig.28, the signals in the waveform chart of buttocks area shows that the point bearing the most in this area has been changed during the past two hours, so there is no alarm. Alarm in the head area and the back area occurred after 3 hours, because the signals in these areas changed slowly during the time. Although the point bearing the most in crus area does not change after 3 hours, but its duration is less than the setting time (4 hours), so there is no alarm in this area either, its waveform chart is shown in Fig.30.

5. Conclusion

By analyzing the multi-channel sensor signals, the human body areas that need to be massaged can be recognized automatically. The system is designed considering the practicality, and it can make the patients having a better rest, so that the purpose of the bedsore prevention has been achieved. For the function of LabVIEW virtual instrument is easy to extend, we can perfect the system gradually in the clinic experiments.

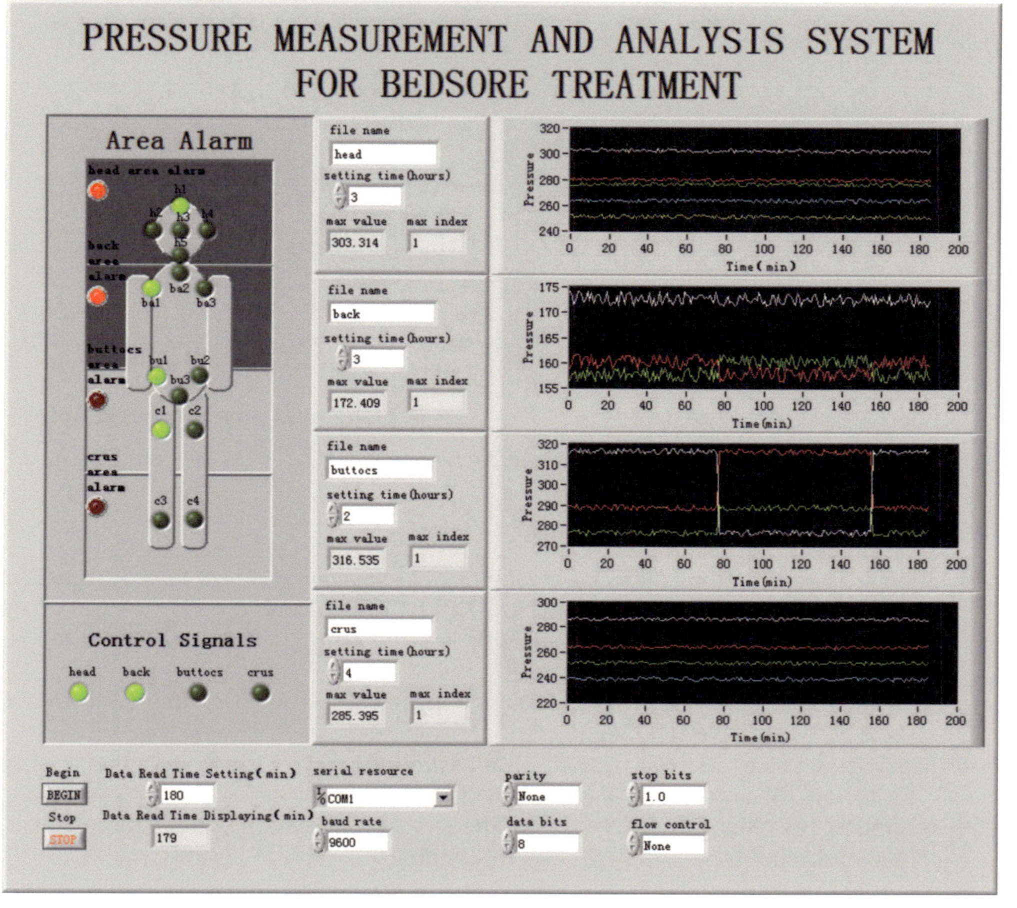

Fig. 28. Instrument interface

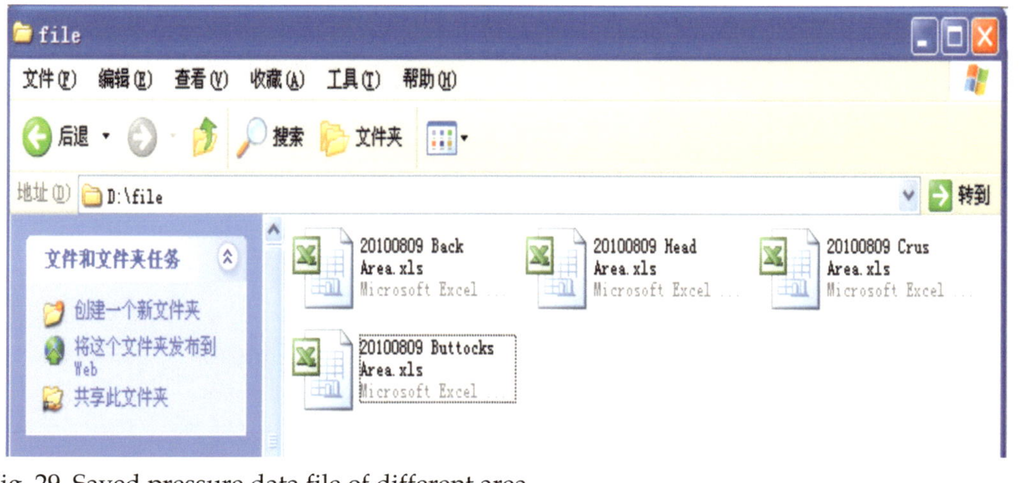

Fig. 29. Saved pressure data file of different area

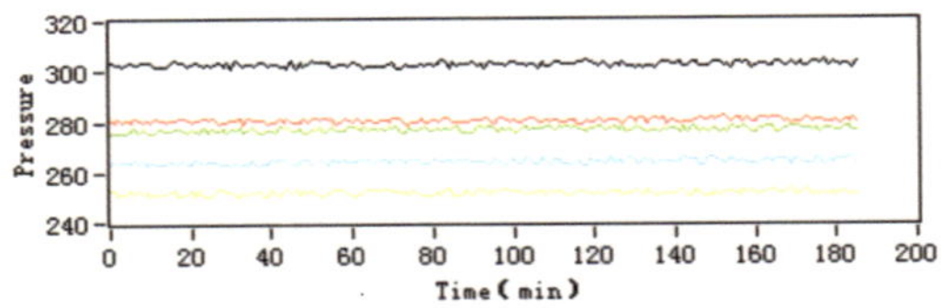

(a) Head area pressure waveform

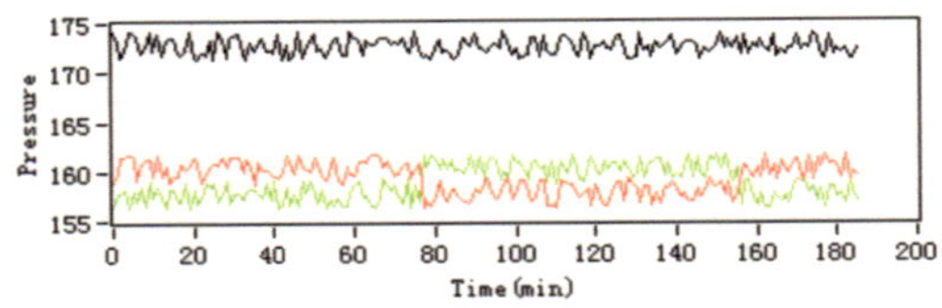

(b) Back area pressure waveform

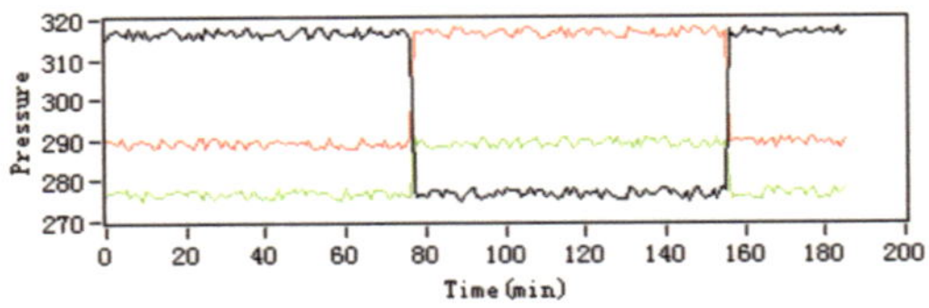

(c) Buttocs area pressure waveform

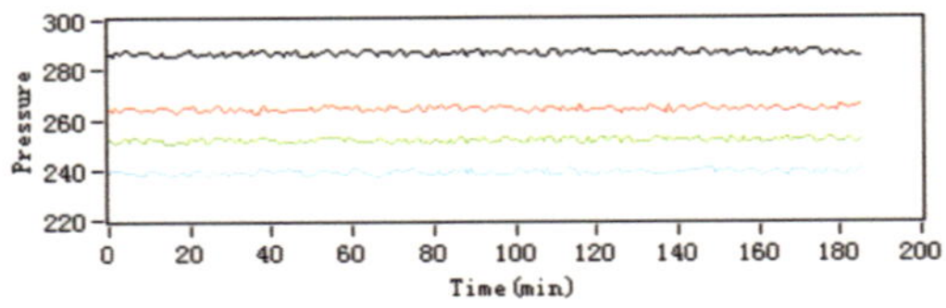

(d) Crus area pressure waveform

Fig. 30. Waveform chart of pressure signals in each area

6. References

Chen Xihui. & Zhang Yinhong. (2007). *LabVIEW 8.20 Programming Design from Introduction to Master*, Tsinghua University Press, 978-7-302-15230-9, Beijing

Hu Hancai. (2003). *Microcontroller Theory and Interface Technology*, Tsinghua University Press, 7-302-07737-1, Beijing

Yang Leping et al. (2007). *LabVIEW Advanced Programming Design*, Tsinghua University Press, 978-7-302-15674-1, Beijing

Zhou Runjing & Hao Xiaoxia. (2008). *Multisim&LabVIEW Virtual Instrument Design Technology*, Buaapress, 978-7-81124-319-2, Beijing

Zhou Runjing & Hao Xiaoxia. (2009). *Sensor and Detection Technology*, Publishing House of Electronics Industry, 978-7-121-08530-7, Beijing

Part 4

LabVIEW in the Educational Domain

12

Web Based Real Time Laboratory Applications of Analog and Digital Communication Courses with LabVIEW Access

Aynur AKAR and Ayse YAYLA
Marmara University
Turkey

1. Introduction

Engineering education has a big importance in development of technologies. For this purpose, various methods have been developed to improve learning processes. The technological researches and developments provide new concepts in education [5]. Especially internet facilities present new approaches and methods to design virtual and real time laboratory applications for education purposes. Laboratory work is an important part of the engineering course, in which the students can make practice of what they learned in the classes, which helps them to reinforce the learning of the concepts [10].
Facilities of the laboratories in educational institutions are generally insufficient when the number of students is considered. Implementation of a laboratory to meet the requirements has a very high price.
Because of using intensively software and minimum hardware, virtual laboratories (VL) that can be controlled remotely as a real time have become alternative to the traditional laboratories. In these laboratories, students can access to the experiments without time and ocation limitations [6]. In the virtual laboratory, students can set up parameters of experiments from a remote location and repeat the experiments, as they need.
LabVIEW program is one of the high level programming languages that is preferred in this study to perform VL applications. LabVIEW software provides an active and controllable interface for test, measurement, instrument control, data processing and data analysis applications [3]. By using LabVIEW program, both virtual instruments can be designed and the devices can be controlled via GPIB, RS232 or VXI interface and web based applications that users can access via internet can be performed. On the basis of LabVIEW program properties, a VL has been setup to provide an environment for both physical experiments and simulations [4].
There are many web based virtual laboratory examples in the literature and some of them can be found on the following. In [2], power electronics experiment is programmed in a remotely controlled laboratory. It is a real power electronics experiment conducted in the laboratory but remotely control and monitoring by web based tools. In [1], it presents a new web based virtual laboratory on a frequency modulation experiment for the teaching of an undergraduate course on communication principles in the National University of Singapore (NUS). It enables students to have a natural hands-on experience of using an expensive

spectrum analyzer on a one-to-one basis and provides a solution for distant engineering education. In [7], a virtual laboratory that offers different aspects of instruments and circuits is described for Electrical and Electronics teaching. This laboratory is based upon the use of LabVIEW program. In [8], a web based platform for distance learning is performed. The platform is used in the course "Electrical Measurements" at Faculty of Electrical Engineering in Zagreb, Croatia. In [9], a web-based laboratory in a distance course on automatic control in the Department of Computer Sciences and Automatic Control of the Spanish University of Distance Learning (UNED) is described.

This study describes a web based real time virtual laboratory that its purpose is to provide a tool to be used as a teaching aid in analog and digital communications course. We present a web based VL on Amplitude Modulation (AM, with carried, double side and signal side band), Pulse Code Modulation (PCM), and base band digital modulation techniques such as Amplitude Shift Keying (ASK), Frequency Shift Keying (FSK) and Phase Shift Keying (PSK) experiments are designed. For performing the above experiments in an efficient way, theoretical concepts and the procedures of real time and virtual applications related to experiments are given on the web page that is designed by using Microsoft Visual Studio 2005 and also to conduct and perform the experiments; the user only needs to install LabVIEW Run Time Engine that is placed on the user input page. In our virtual laboratory, HP 3632A DC Power supply and HP 34970A Digital Multimeter devices are controlled via GPIB interface.

In Section II, the typical user interfaces including web site of the study and LabVIEW control panels that have been installed into the web site are described. Section III describes the hardware and software system architecture and finally, conclusions are drawn in Section IV.

2. User interface

2.1 Control panels

In this virtual laboratory, both computer-simulated and real time applications have been performed but only the front panels of real time applications have been presented in this paper. In Figure 1, Q=32 a=1 PCM front panel is shown. Similarly, in Figure 2, AM front panel and in Figure 3, FSK front panel is shown. The front panels are called user interfaces and they have been designed as realistic as possible. The front panels of these applications that contain two sections such as control buttons on the left and input-output waveforms of the experiments on the right are designed in a simple and intelligible structure.

In these applications, the frequency of sample impulses (PCM) and carrier frequencies (ASK, FSK, PSK, AM) is changed as virtual and the frequency of message signals is changed as real time by using control buttons. So students can change the message signals in real time via voltage controlled circuit (VCO) by controlling the connected devices (HP 3632 A DC Power Supply). Also in the front panels, there are five types of signals such as sinusoidal, square, triangle, saw tooth and random on the message signal part. In addition to this, the front panels display message signal, sample impulses, carrier signals as input and AM modulated signal, PCM code sequence, ASK, FSK, PSK signals as output. The experiments can be stopped at any time by pressing stop button located at the bottom of the left side of the front panel. In order to start up the application, these graphs and control buttons must be connected in the proper form in the block diagram. These diagrams will be explained in the hardware and software section.

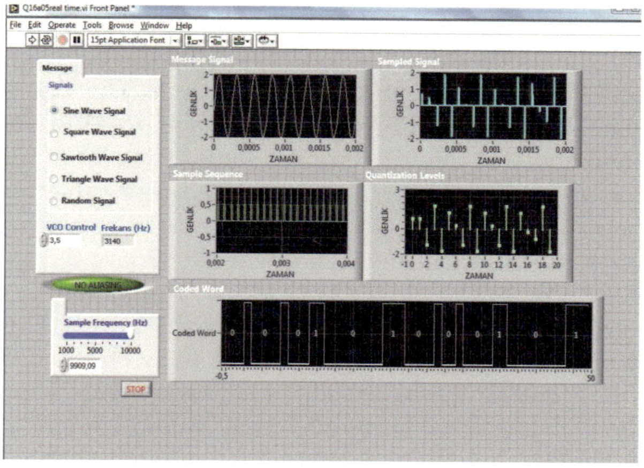

Fig. 1. PCM Front Panel (Q=32, a=1)

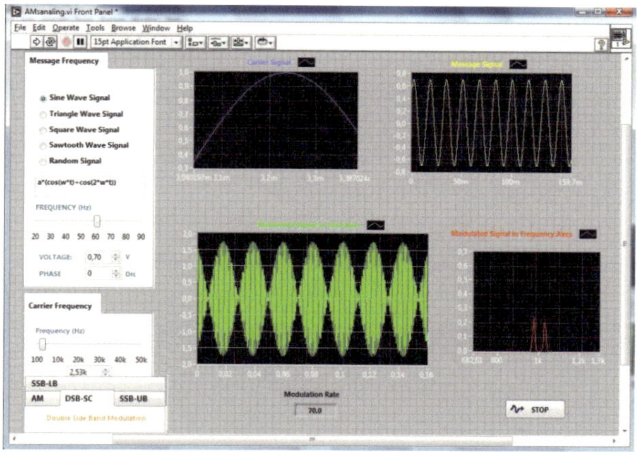

Fig. 2. AM Front Panel

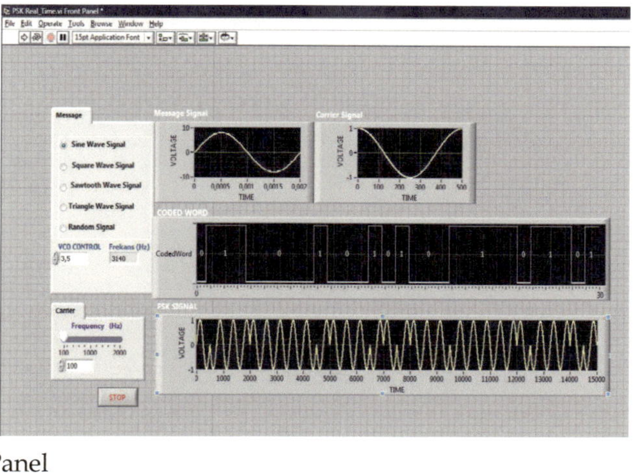

Fig. 3. PSK Front Panel

2.2 Web site

In this study, a web site is designed to perform Analog and Digital Communication experiments and increase the efficiency of these experiments. The web site is designed both in Turkish and English languages. The web site contains the theoretical information of experiments and virtual and real time experiment steps. The aim of these web pages is to give some information about experiment. Any interested user can access these documents freely and install them without logging on, at the same time without interrupting the experiment. To conduct and perform the experiment, students need to have web browser and LabVIEW Run Time Engine.

The web site is designed in accordance with Microsoft Internet Explorer. In real time applications, because of controlling the devices as well, the web site is designed in order to allow only one user to access at the same time. Microsoft Visual Studio 2005 program is used for designing the web site and Microsoft Access is used for user account registration. National Instruments has developed Dynamic Link Library (DLL) that is a function library to control the LabVIEW applications from different programming languages (Visual Basic, C++, C#) dynamically. Through this DLL, virtual instruments developed in LabVIEW program can be integrated into the .NET applications easily. Many functions and methods presented in DLL have been used in our designed web site [11]. On the designed home page, there can be seen if there is any user in the system or not and if there is a user in the system, the experiment which the user is performing (real time or simulation) can be seen as well. In Figure 4, the home page of web site is shown. The necessary steps for conducting and performing the experiment are given as follows:

- Students can choose the experiment from the buttons
- Username and password for authentication is requested from the user when the user clicks to the experiment link.

Fig. 4. Home Page

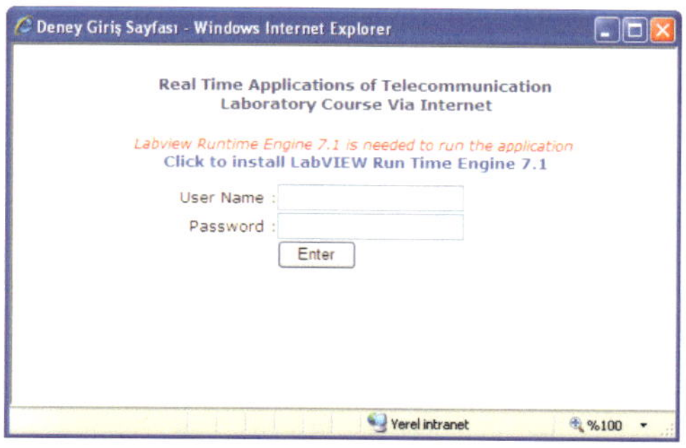

Fig. 5. Application Input Page

- After a successful log on to the session, the user interface for controlling the instruments and performing the experiment will appear.
- Students can now change the experiment parameters such as the control voltage of VCO circuit to get message frequency, sampling frequency and carrier frequency and obtain the results.
- While the student is performing the experiment, teacher may only observe the experiment simultaneously. During the session, if the student changes the parameters of the experiment, the teacher can only watch these changes and also student and teacher can communicate with each other via the chat platform developed in the web application.
- Students are allocated with 15 minutes and the session can be terminated by the user any time or after a default time limit of 15 minutes. When the student finishes the experiment, the message "The student finished the experiment" is shown on the teacher web page.

Because of the fact that, students are able to perform the device control in the experiment as well, the web site allows to access only one student at the time. In order to add or erase experiments, update the current experiments and disable / enable the system, an administrator page is designed in web site as shown in Figure 6.When the system is

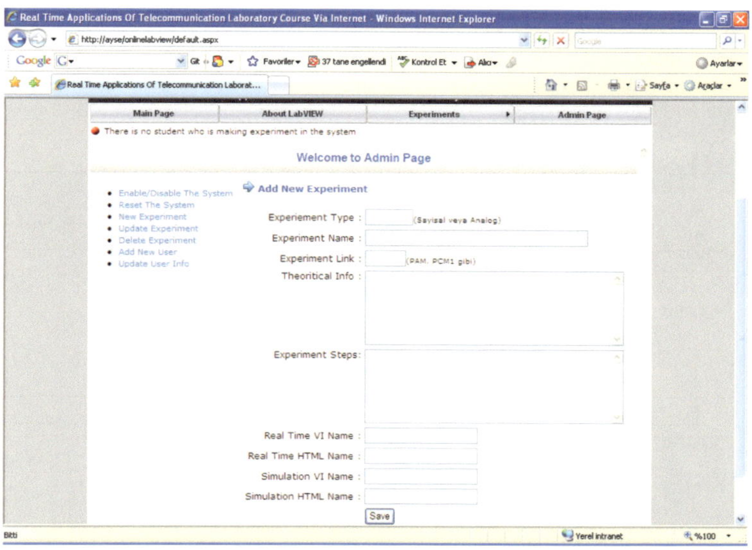

Fig. 6. Administrator Page

deactivated by the system manager (generally teacher), nobody can access the experiments. If somebody wants to access the experiments at this time, "Because of deactivating the system, you can not access the experiments" message is shown. When the system is deactivated, the student can only access the other pages such as LabVIEW information, experiment menus.

3. System architecture

3.1 Hardware system

The hardware system and its components of the real time Analog and Digital Communication experiments are shown in Figure 7.

In this hardware structure, HP3632A DC power supply and HP 34970A digital multimeter devices have GPIB card and are connected to server PC through GPIB card and cables. LabVIEW is adopted to implement local instrument control. On the basis of the GPIB address assigned to the instrument, the commands are transferred through the GPIB card and cable to the corresponding instrument which implements the commands and executes the actions. Laboratory PC which includes GPIB and Ethernet interfaces is called as a server PC and communicate as a full duplex form with digital multimeter and DC power supply.

By using Voltage Controlled Oscillator (VCO) as shown in Figure 8, message signal has been obtained for experiments. The input signal of VCO is controlled by the HP3632A DC power supply with GPIB and the output signal of VCO circuit is measured with HP 34970A digital multimeter and then sent back to the Laboratory PC through the GPIB. This measured signal is applied to the system as a message frequency.

VCO circuit converts the voltage between 3,5 to 5,5V to the frequency between 1,6 to 11 kHz. With the designed VCO circuit, the message signal of real time PCM experiment and carrier signals of ASK, PSK and FSK experiments are get. In Figure 9, the set of the instrument located in a standard laboratory is shown.

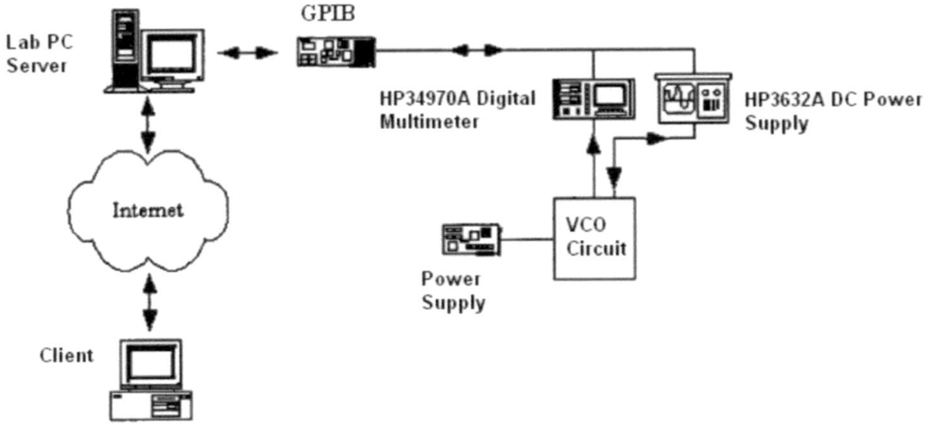

Fig. 7. Hardware Structure of Application

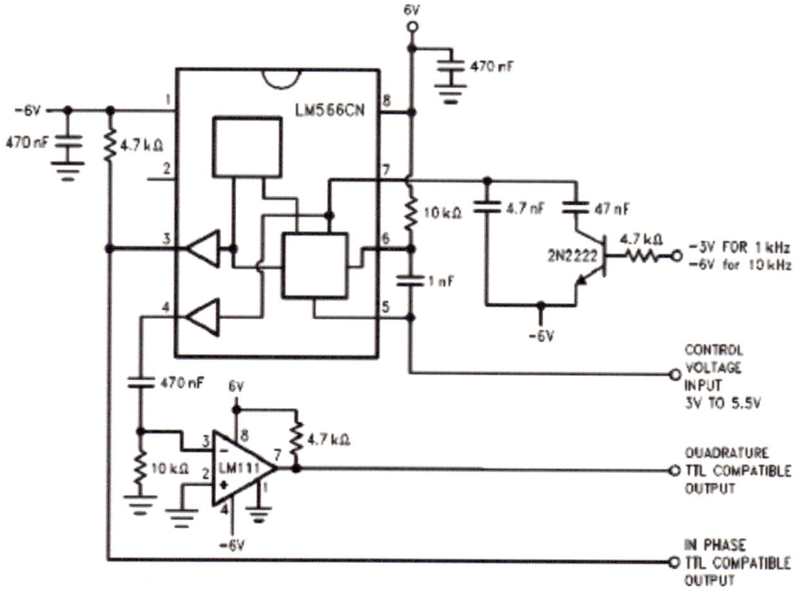

Fig. 8. VCO Circuit

Fig. 9. Laboratory Appearance of Application

3.2 Block diagram

The block diagrams are the main part of the experiments. Connections between the VI's, analog I/O are implemented under LabVIEW using the G programming language. Also programs are verified by using Formula node in the block diagram. In Figure 10, as an example, the block diagram of PCM experiment is shown.

A block diagram of the PCM experiment contains four sections. In the first section, by using signal generation VI's, the message and sampling frequency are generated. Then a program is written in Formula Node to select sample values In the third section, in Formula node, a program is developed to allocate levels to the infinite range of amplitude of sample values of the analog signal using uniform quantization operator. This program is carried out by using quantization parameters (quantization step size a=1 and a=0,5, the quantization levels Q=8, 16, 32).

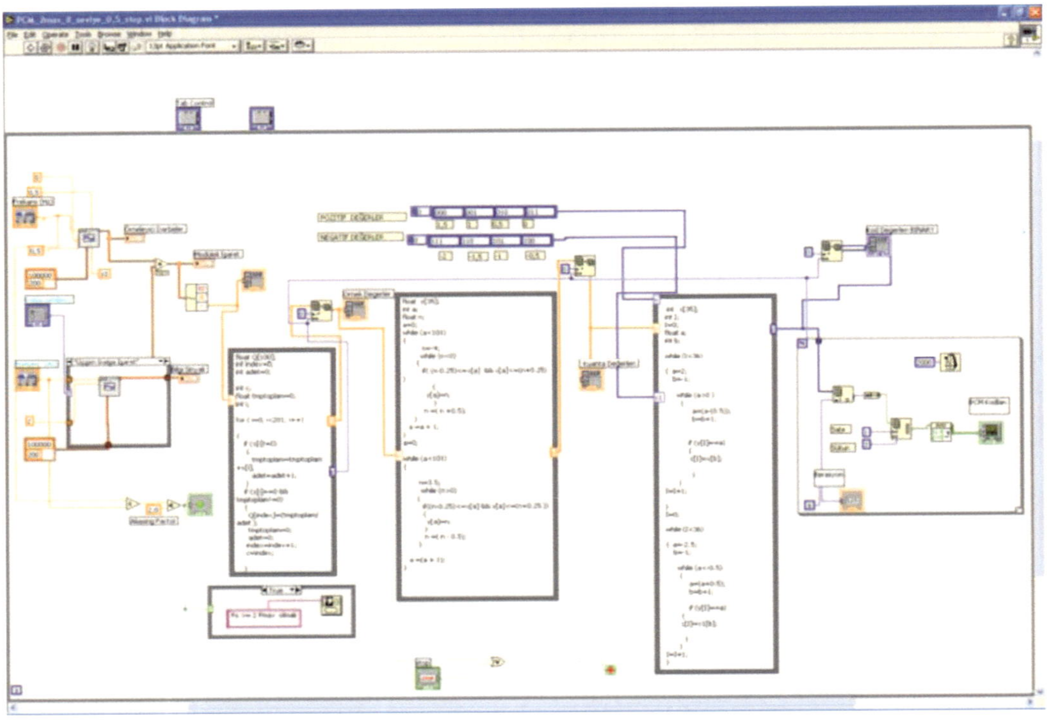

Fig. 10. PCM Block Diagram Structure (Q=32, a=1)

In the last section, encoding operation is performed by developing a program in Formula Node. In this step, each quantization level is expressed in a code. According to number of quantization levels, code word length (n) is selected 3, 4, 5 bits. n bits (0,1) binary code words are converted to Binary- Non-Return to Zero (B-NRZ) pulse sequences to transmit. For the other experiments, similar block diagrams are developed.

According to digital source data (0 and 1), in ASK experiment the amplitude of carrier signal, in FSK experiment the frequency of carrier signal and in PSK experiment the phase (0, π) of carrier signal is changed.

Each of three experiments uses PCM experiment digital signals as digital source data. This means that, source is the digital output of analog signal. Consequently, by changing the analog message, the student can get the digital source data that is converted analog to digital. The modulated signals are received by developing structures for each of them.

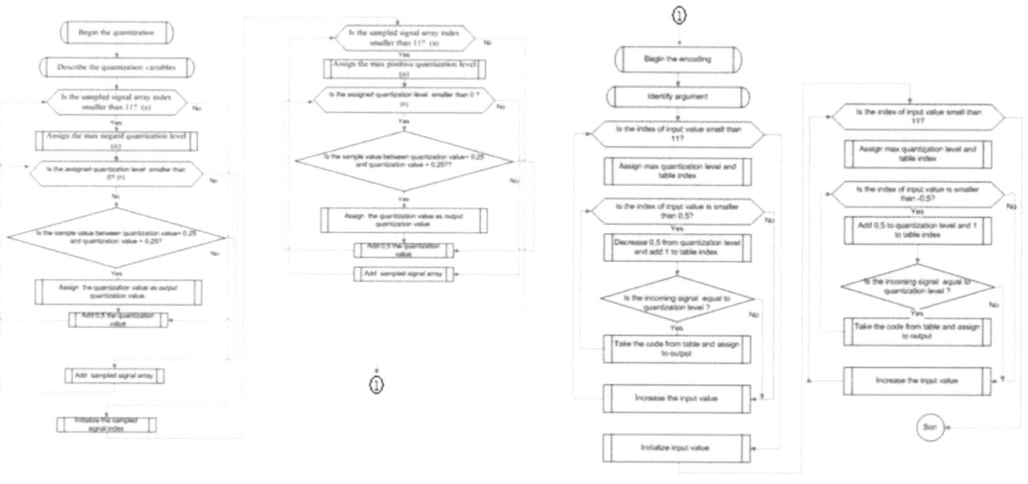

Fig. 11. PCM Block Diagram Algorithm (Q=32, a=1)

4. Conclusion

In this study, for supporting laboratory applications of students, a general methodology has been presented to create real time and virtual experiments of Analog and Digital Communication courses. And also this study supports effective and complete learning and provides a solution for distant technical engineering education. The aim of these experiments is to study the frequency spectra of AM, DSB, SSB modulated signals and time spectra of PCM, ASK, FSK, PSK signal forms according to input parameters. These experiments are designed based on theoretical knowledge.
Various experiments corresponding to modulation techniques have been designed under LabVIEW program to real time and virtual applications. Hereafter, it is planned on to develop the demodulation applications of these experiments. This methodology can also be extended to other communication system techniques. Users can access the virtual laboratory in Marmara University campus.

5. References

Ko, C.C.; Chen, B.M.; Han, J.; Hu, S.; Ramakrishnan, V.; Cheng, C.D.; Zhuang, Y.& Chen, J. (2001).A Web-Based Virtual Laboratory on a Frequency Modulation Experiment. *IEEE Transactions on Systems Man.and Cybernetics*, pp 295-303,

Cheng, K.W.E.; Chan, C.L.; Cheung, N.C.; Sutanto, D.(2002).Virtual Laboratory Development for Teaching Power Electronics. *Institute of Electrical and Electronics Engineers*, pp. 461-466,

Higa, M.L.; Tawy, D.M.; Lord,S.M.;(2002). An Introduction to Labview Exercise for An Electronics Class. *32nd ASEE/IEEE Frontiers in Education Conference*

LabVIEW Manual , National Instruments, 2005

Basher, H. A.; Isa, S. A.;(2006). On - campus an Online Virtual Laboratory Experiments with LabVIEW. *Southeast Conference*, pp. 325-330,

Basher, H. A.; Isa, S. A.; Henini, M. A.; (2004). Virtual Laboratory for Electrical Circuit Course. *IEEE Southeast on 2004 Conference*, pp. 330-334,2004

Xiaoyan, C.; Xiaodong, Z.& Xi, C.; (2005). A Virtual Laboratory for Electrical and Electronics Teaching. *IEEE International Symposium on Microwave, Antenna, Propagation and EMC Technologies for Wireless Communications Proceedings*, pp. 491-495, 2004

Jurèeviæ, M.; Malariæ, R.& Šala, A.; (2006). Web Based Platform for Distance Training On Electrical Measurements Course. *Measurement Science Review*, pp.36-39,

Dormido, S.; Vargas, H.; Sánchez, J.; Duro, N.; Dormido, R.; Canto, S.D.& Esquembre, F.; (2007). Using Web based laboratories for Control Engineering Education. *International Conference on Engineering Education*

Salzmann, Ch.; Gillet, D.&Huguenin, P.; (2000). Introduction to Realtime Control using LabVIEW with an Application to Distance Learning, *International Journal of Engineering Education* ,pp. 255- 272,

National Instruments. (2002) Distance- Learning Remote Laboratories using LabVIEW. Available:http:///one.ni.com/devzone/conceptd.nsf/webmain/7BD0B01FCF3CF61A86256B510059F0FB/$File/WP223 .pdf

13

LabVIEW Remote Lab

Aurel Gontean and Roland Szabó
"Politehnica" University of Timişoara
România

1. Introduction

LabVIEW is a quite interesting programming language, and despite its odd first impression is very powerful. We remember when we started to use it for the first time it was somehow strange to me, we thought what this, a graphical programming language? For the first contact whit this language, LabVIEW somehow hides its power, this could be due to fact that for the first contact everyone tries the simulation part. A usual first application would be to generate a sine wave to a graph. Unfortunately, this won't really impress a user.
All LabVIEW field engineers nightmare is to know that the users think that LabVIEW is a simulation environment. Their main job is to erase that from the users mind. Of course it has a very strong simulation part, but the main target is the real hardware controlling.
If we think put of the box a little, we will realize that if LabVIEW hides its power, that means is very simple to use, but if we think about the big amount of software and hardware National instruments make, we will see that it's quite an extraordinary programming language.
To make a short count, we can see that only LabVIEW 2009 with Modules, Toolkits and Device Drivers are 3 DVDs in compressed kit version. If we consider that in other hand we have NI Multisim circuit design suite, LabWindows/CVI C programming language for instruments and Measurement Studio LabVIEW style buttons add-on for Microsoft Visual Studio, then we can imagine that engineers National Instruments create a lot of software.
In hardware area we can just say that they have a lot of stuff, and if they don't have am equipment, then another company has it and LabVIEW has the driver for that equipment. Sometimes the diver is made by the National Instruments engineers, sometimes is made by third party vendors, but my only concern is to work, and they mostly do. A useful section in the www.ni.com webpage is the IDNET (Instrument Driver Network), where you can find the LabVIEW and LabWindows/CVI drivers for almost any equipment. You just have to search here: www.ni.com/devzone/idnet. A good instruments vendor would be Agilent Technologies; we can say that it's very hard to find equipments from Agilent without LabVIEW or LabWindows/CVI driver.
This way we can easily say that LabVIEW it's much more than MATLAB Simulink in color. LabVIEW has a strong programming part, despite its simple appearance, if we go deeply in some specific area, like NI Vision or CompactRIO, then things will start to get quite complex and complicated. But knowing that this is complicated in LabVIEW, if we think to do the same thing without LabVIEW, in another programming language, it could be almost impossible, for a reduced number of engineers, in a short amount of time.
In LabVIEW it's possible, almost everything is possible.

We would like to correct the sentence above; some things are possible only indirectly. Some extra programming in needed, but after all an engineer can do what he planned.

2. Tips and tricks in LabVIEW

As we said not everything can be done directly, some of them need some extra programming. We are not really sure why they did not include it in the LabVIEW package; maybe they had a good reason. On forums is really hard to find a solution for these problems, this way we will present a few common and useful tips and trick that we was forced to develop, because we needed them during my projects.

2.1 Very long HEX String to ASCII Conversion

We shall show a method in LabVIEW how to convert a very long HEX string to ASCII.
This could be useful if we want to analyze memory dumps or binary files, which are mostly in HEX, but to be interpretable, we need to convert it in some form, which we can understand, and mostly we convert it in ASCII.
As we can see in Fig. 1. the program is working.

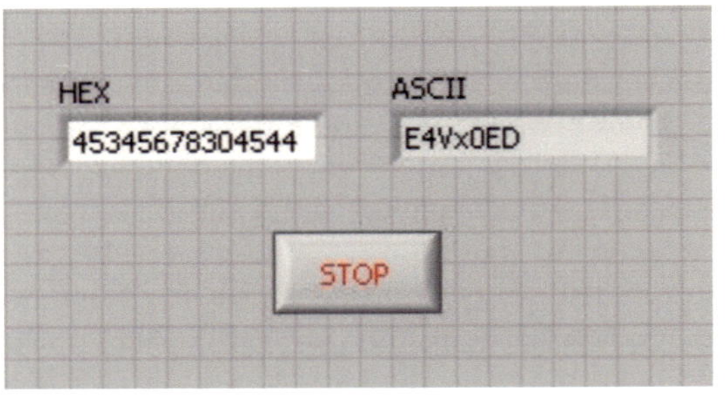

Fig. 1. HEX to ASCII Front Panel.

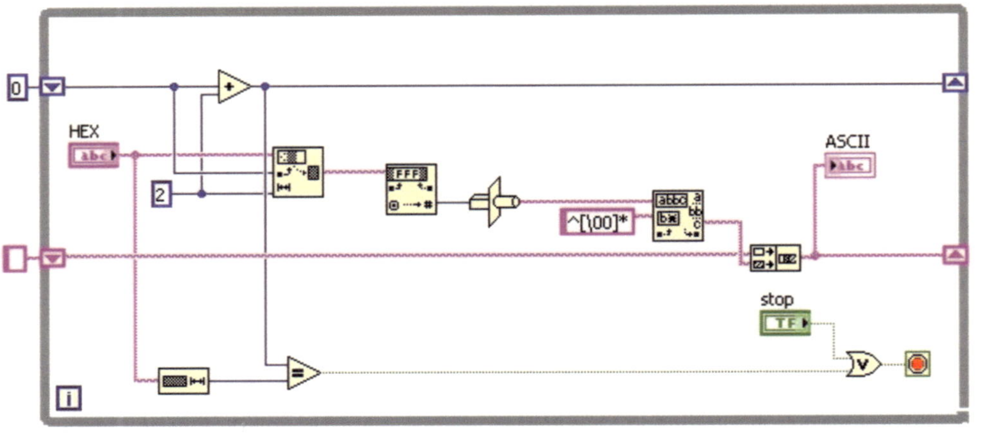

Fig. 2. HEX to ASCII Block Diagram.

In Fig. 2. we have the solution for the problem. First of all we have to enter a very long HEX string. With the String Subset VI we have to fragment the string into groups with 2 HEX numbers (8 bits). The first Shift Register with 0 initialization will always increase the fragmentation index with 2, this way we will reach at the end minus 2 (n-2) of the HEX word. There is a condition too, if we reach at the end of the HEX string to exist the While loop. From String Subset we convert the HEX string to number, the number is converted to ASCII with the Type Cast VI. For some strange reason the Type Cast VI puts an ASCII space before the converted ASCII character, this space is a \00 type space, so this will have to be deleted, it's deleted with the Match Pattern VI using the ^[\00]* command and wired to the after substring output (after the \00), and we will obtain the good converted ASCII value. This value will be concatenated with the following strings using the second Shift Register with the empty string initialization.

2.2 Very long ASCII to HEX string conversion

If we made the HEX to ASCII conversion, than we have to do the reverse operation too. In LabVIEW ASCII to HEX the conversion is not that simple. Unfortunately there is no VI which will do the job, so the user has to make his own VI. On possible method will be presented next.
In Fig. 3. we can see the working program.

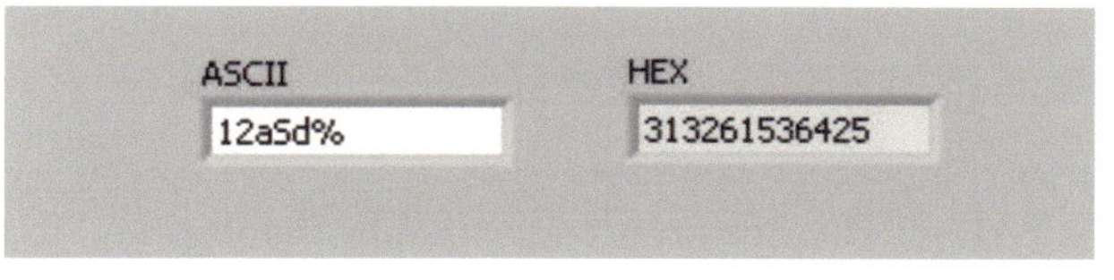

Fig. 3. ASCII to HEX Front Panel.

In Fig. 4. We have the ASCII input, which will be converted in a number, with byte data type. Byte is more than enough, because we have a total of 128 ASCII characters, in the other hand in LabVIEW there is no ASCII string to number conversion in with other data type, so this is our only solution. The numbers are converted into HEX with the length of 2 for each HEX number. The string to number conversion makes an array, this way the HEX values will be an array of HEX string with the length of 2. We want to make a long HEX string, not an array of strings. We made a For loop with the number of iteration equal to the length of the HEX array. We indexed the array and with the use of Shift Registers we concatenated it into a long HEX string.

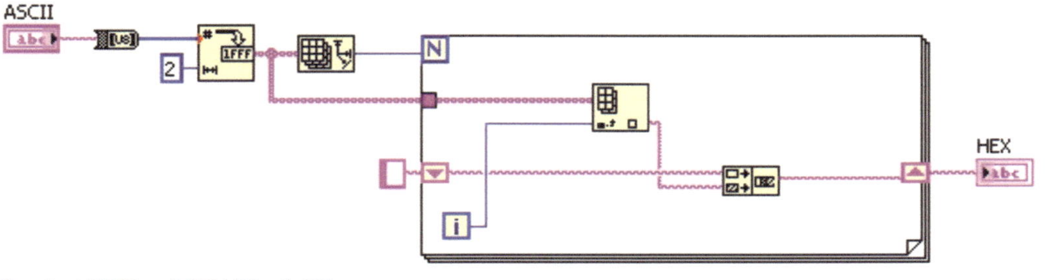

Fig. 4. ASCII to HEX Block Diagram.

2.3 Creating a toggle button from a push button

This application would be useful when we want to have an LED light to be ON, for very short impulses, like the sound of claps of falling coins, otherwise we would see only a LED blink and we would have to be very attentive. The idea would be to keep the signal on "1" logic for a longer period with shift registers. There could be many variants, but the hardest variant will be presented, the one where after the first "1" logic the light is ON and after the second "1" logic the light is OFF. For the Button the "Latch When Released" Mechanical Action was used, so it's a push-button.

As we can see the program's name is Button Latch (Fig. 5.), we need a latch to keep the LED ON after only one impulse and to turn the LED OFF after the second.

Fig. 5. Button Latch Front Panel.

In Fig. 6. we can see that Shift Registers were used. As we can see the initialization value for the Shift Registers is FALSE. The Button is connected to the Implies VI, which computes an OR logic between the negated x (first) input and y (second) input. In case of Button press, we will have FALSE in x input and FALSE in y input, so FALSE output, this means that from the Select VI the FALSE output is activated, which has an input of inverted FALSE (which is TRUE), so the LED will be ON.

If the Button is pressed again, then we will have FALSE in x input and FALSE at y input of the Implies VI, so at the Implies function will have FALSE output. The input of the second Shift Register will be TRUE, because before this the LED in ON. With the FALSE Implies VI we activate the inverted TRUE (which is FALSE), so the LED will be OFF.

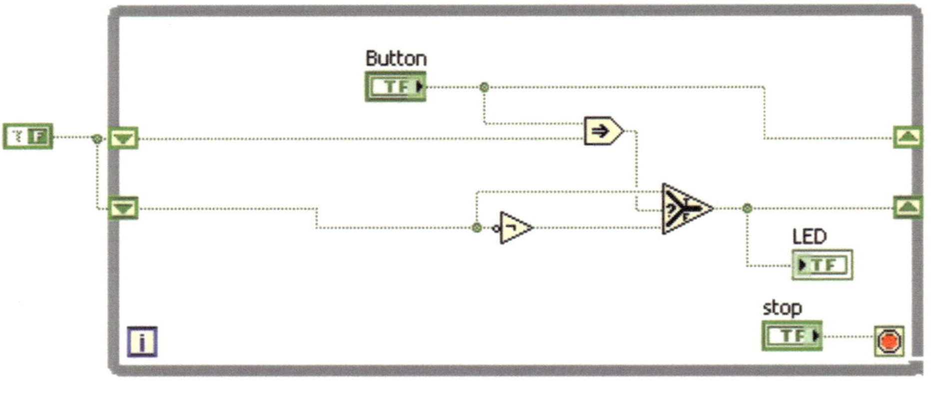

Fig. 6. Button Latch Block Diagram.

2.4 Append file (Write to file line by line)

Surprisingly in LabVIEW we can't find a simple method to append a file. If a program writes to a file for the second time, it will overwrite the previous data. This is what we want to avoid, when we want to make complex logs or even when we want to save the parameters of a program during execution. This program is useful when we make some moves, like mouse, joystick moves, and we want to save the coordinates into a file and maybe the file will be closed an opened in the program more times. We can create programs to move robotic arms with mouse, or to save the specific parameters of measuring equipments.
Fig. 7. shows that after multiple runs of the program, the previous text is not erased.

Fig. 7. Text File with Appended Text.

In Fig. 8. we have the standard dataflow of the programming with the settings and the writing to the file, between the opening/creating and closing the file. At the end it's good to put a Simple Error Handler. The file opening/creating VI is set to open or create and a certain path is given to it. The file setting VI is set to have an offset with the length of 0, and is set to write at the end of the file. The writing VI has an input with a text which is concatenated with a new line constant, this way after any running of the program we will have the appended text in a new line, keeping the old information.

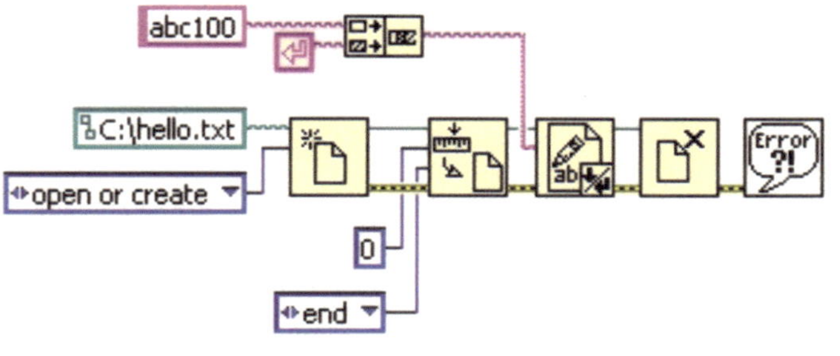

Fig. 8. Text Append Block Diagram.

2.5 Create an arbitrary signal

As we know LabVIEW has a lot of built in signals, but it's impossible to have any arbitrary signal. It has the possibility to create arbitrary signals, but we have found it not really flexible in some situations. It has an arbitrary signal creator with Express VIs, but we always avoid using them, because you can have more control over traditional VIs. The chosen

signal was the trapezoidal signal, which is mostly used when controlling motors. Nobody wants a square pattern for the motors acceleration. In cars, in lifts the motor usually accelerates in a trapezoidal pattern.
As we can see in Fig. 9., the program is working. The hardest part is configuring the parameters. The parameters are configured using equation (1).

$$\begin{cases} N_p \cdot U_{minr} = A - U_0 \\ N_p \cdot U_{minf} = A - U_0 \end{cases} \tag{1}$$

Where N_p is the number of points; U_{minr},U_{minf} are the minimal voltages for rise and fall; A is the amplitude of the signal; U_0 is the start voltage. In our case it will be: 0,0003 * 10000 = 5 – 2, this way we created the trapezoidal signal.

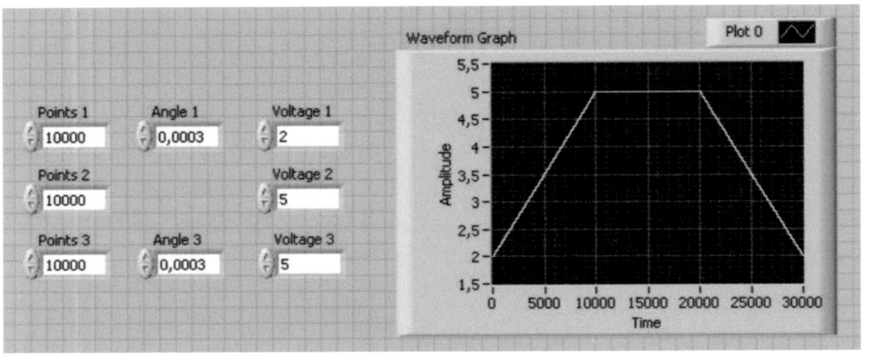

Fig. 9. Trapezoidal Signal Front Panel.

The Block Diagram (Fig. 10.) it is not so complicated, the main thing is the idea to build arrays of rising edge, continuous part and falling edge. The building of the arrays is made with For loops, shift registers and the exit from the loops is made with enable indexing, which is by default at For loops. Maybe the hardest part is the building of the array, which builds three 1D arrays intro one 1D array. Normally LabVIEW makes the built array in multidimensional array, but we need a 1D array, because we want one single signal. This can be done by changing the enable indexing to disable indexing and then change it back to enable indexing again at the exit from the For loop of the horizontal signal.

3. Virtual instruments for the PXI chassis

Our LabVIEW remote lab has 6 PXI experiments working and controllable trough a web browser.

3.1 Transfer characteristic of a NAND gate

The first experiment makes the transfer characteristic of a gate; we made it for a NAND gate. In Fig. 11. we can see the block schematics of the transfer characteristics of the NAND gate.
We generate a rising ramp signal at the NAND gates one input and supply a constant voltage to the other input and measure the voltage at the output, this way we have the transfer characteristics of the gate.

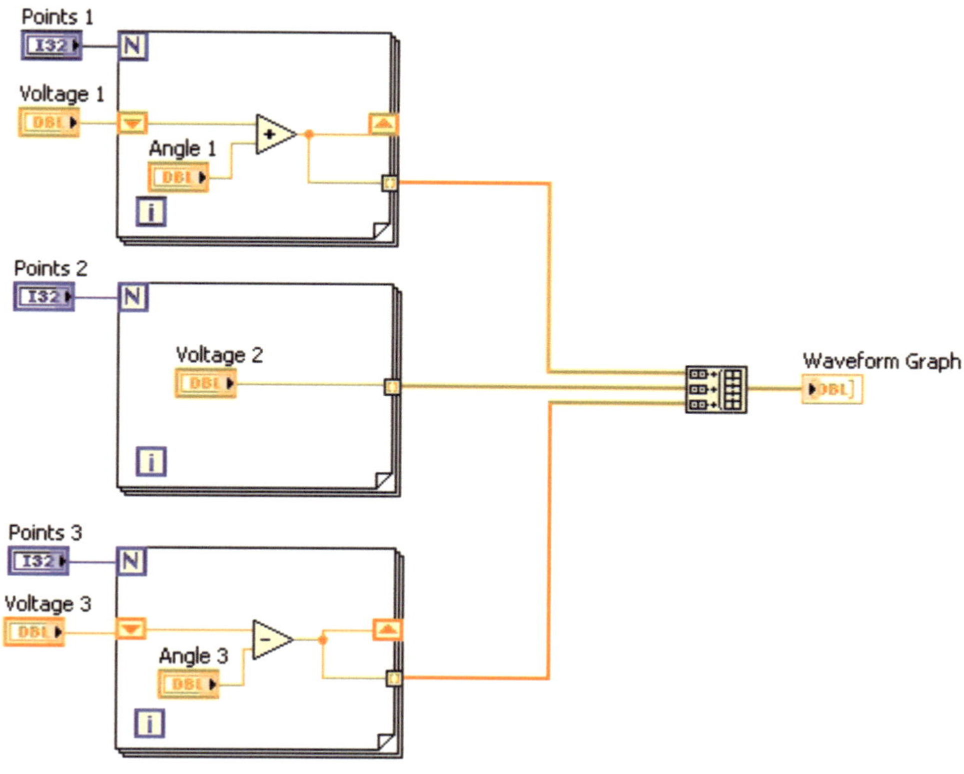

Fig. 10. Trapezoidal Signal Block Diagram.

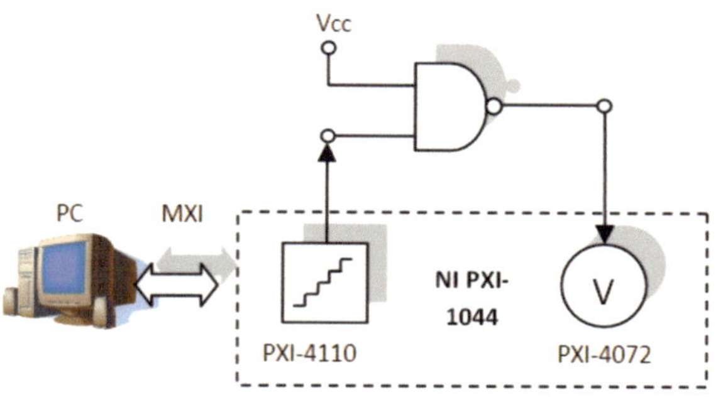

Fig. 11. Block Schematics of the Experimental Setup.

The transfer characteristic is the input voltage as a function of the output voltage like shown in equation (2).

$$U_{out} = f(U_{in}) \quad (2)$$

In Fig. 12. We can see the experimental setup of the NAND gate on a PCB with protection and connectors for accessing. The used NAND gate is integrated in a 74ACT00 IC.
The used NI equipment for this experiment was the NI PXI-4110 power supply and the NI PXI-4072 digital multimeter.

Fig. 12. NAND Gate with PCB.

In Fig. 13. we can see the Front Panel of the experiment.
As we can see we have the digital multimeter (DMM) configuration with reference ID, a range at 5 V and resolution at 6½ digits. We have two channels (0 and 1) of the power supply activated with the current limit set to 100 mA and a slider to set the voltage level from 0 - 4 V. The most important part is the XY Graph where we see the actual transfer characteristic of the gate, we have also indicators of the temporary value on both axes of the graph. We have also cursors to measure certain values.
As we can see is not so complicated to program, the hardest part is maybe that we use traditional NI acquisition cards, not the newer DAQ cards.
In Fig. 14. We have the Block Diagram of the program.
All the instruments are programmed in this pattern, first we have to create the channel and after it close it. Between these two VIs we have the configuration or acquisition and generation. Mostly we have the creation, configuration and closing outside the loop and the acquisition or generation part in the loop.
In out experiment we first create the channel for the DMM and than configure its range ad digits. After it we will create the power supply's channel we configure the voltage and current for the first channel and enable the output, after we will do the same or the other channel. For channel 1 we will measure the output voltage. We will measure the voltage with the multimeter at the output of the NAND gate. Finally we will close an reset the two equipments.
We can remark that LabVIEW uses the read expression for acquisitioning and the write expression for generation, this way the used icons for the VI are mostly a pair of glasses for reading and a pencil for writing.

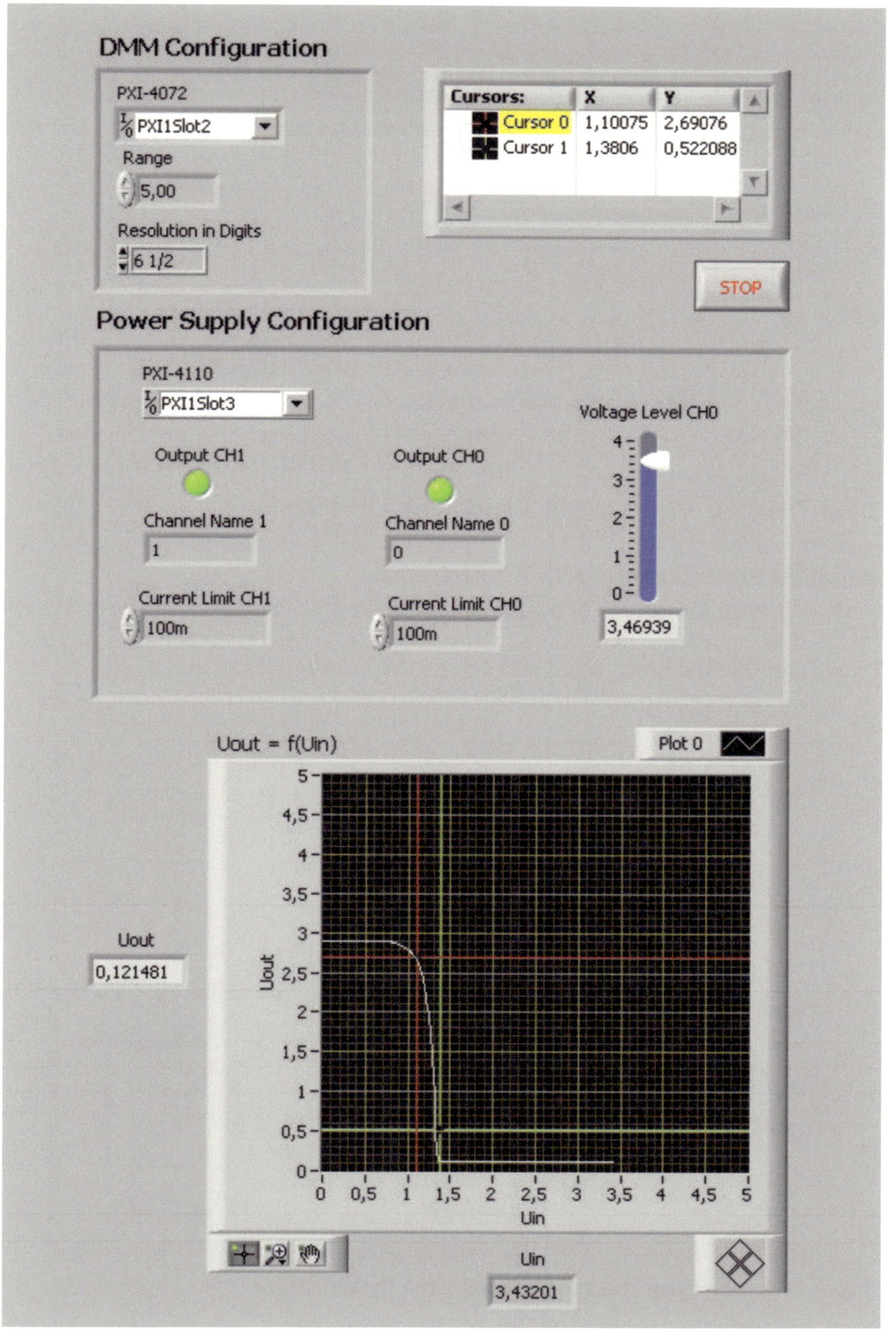

Fig. 13. Front Panel of the Transfer Characteristic Program.

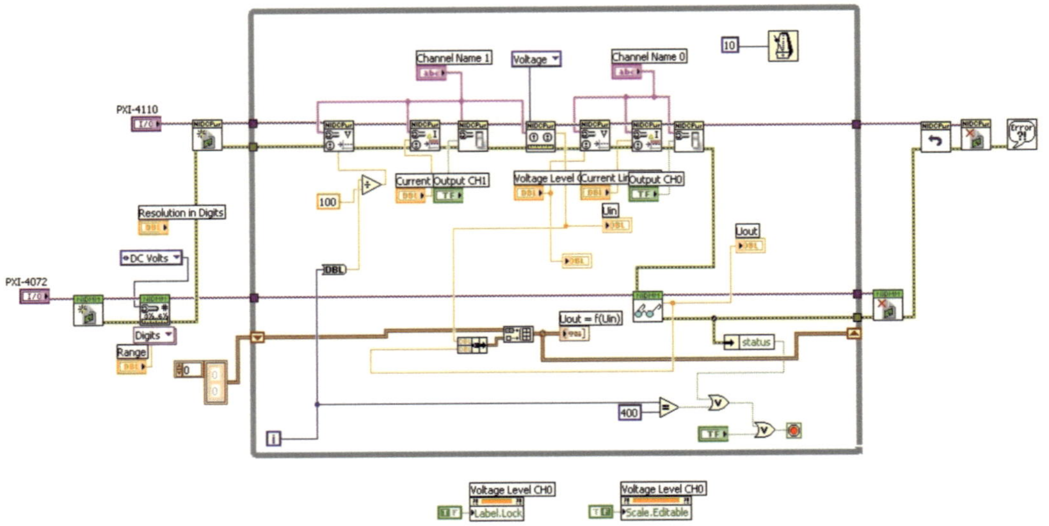

Fig. 14. Block Diagram of the Transfer Characteristic Program.

3.2 Propagation time measuring for a NAND Gate

This experiment uses the same 74ACT00 NAND gate, but measures the gate's propagation time.

In Fig. 15. we can see the block schematics of the experimental setup.

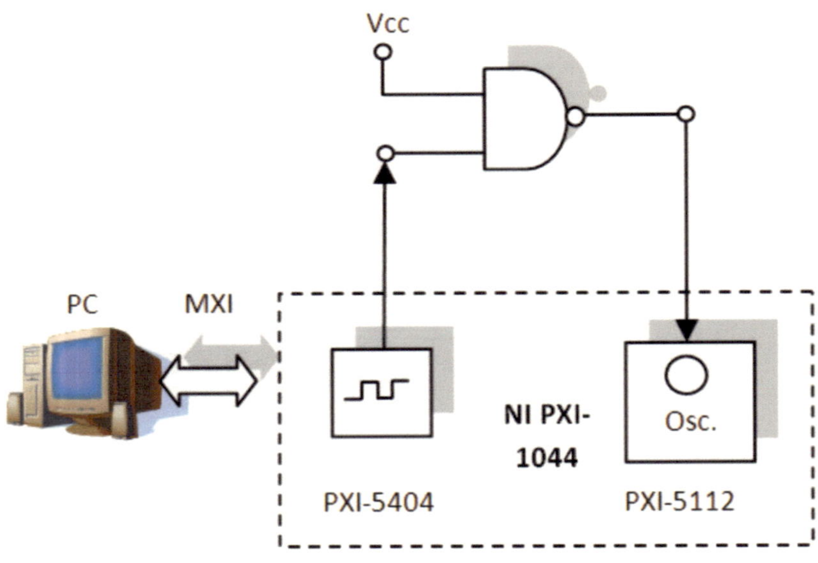

Fig. 15. Block schematics for the propagation time measuring.

We generate a square waveform to the gate's one input with a signal generator and measure its output with an oscilloscope.

The propagation time is given by the formula from equation (3).

$$t_p = \frac{t_{pHL} + t_{pLH}}{2} \qquad (3)$$

In the standard TTL gate's case t_{pLH} = 12 ns and t_{pHL} = 8 ns, so tp = 10 ns.

The experimental setup can be seen on Fig. 12. The setup is on the same PCB as for the transfer characteristic.

The used NI equipments are NI PXI-4110 power supply, the NI PXI-5112 oscilloscope and the NI PXI-5412 signal generator.

In Fig. 16. we can see the Front Panel of the experiment.

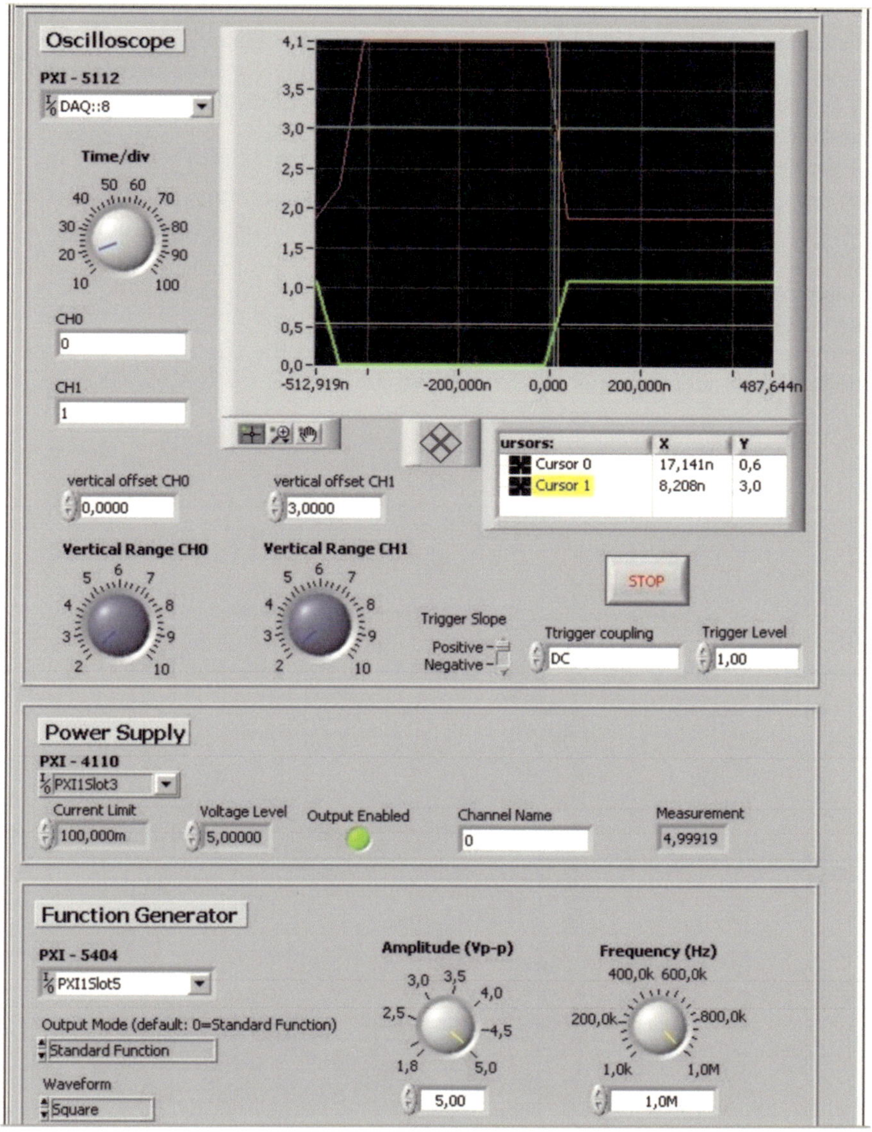

Fig. 16. Front Panel of the Transfer Characteristic Program.

As we can see we have the configuration of the oscilloscope, the power supply and the function generator.
The oscilloscope has a configured resource ID and the Time/div setting. It has also both channels activated with 0 V offset for channel 0 and 3 V offset for channel 1 and Volts/div (Vertical Range) dial. It also has some triggering configurations like slope on positive, DC coupling and 1 V level. We have the both graphs (input and output of the NAND gate) on the waveform graph and cursors to measure the propagation time.
The power supply has a basic configuration just for supplying current to the IC. It has resource ID, current limit to 100 mA, 5 V voltage level, output enabled indicator, an indicator showing 0 as the selected channel, and a measurement of the output of the activated channel.
The function generator has resource indicator, the settings for output mode, which is on standard, square waveform type, and the setting for amplitude, which is at 5 V and the setting for frequency, which is at 1 MHz.
In Fig. 17. we can see the Block Diagram of the program.
As we can see we have the initialization for the function generator, the setting of the output mode, the amplitude and frequency setting, the enabling of the output and the starting of the generation.
The oscilloscope is initialized and has standard initialization.
Finally the power supply is initialized.
We enter in the While loop. We configure the voltage and the current of the power supply; we enable its output and measure the output voltage.

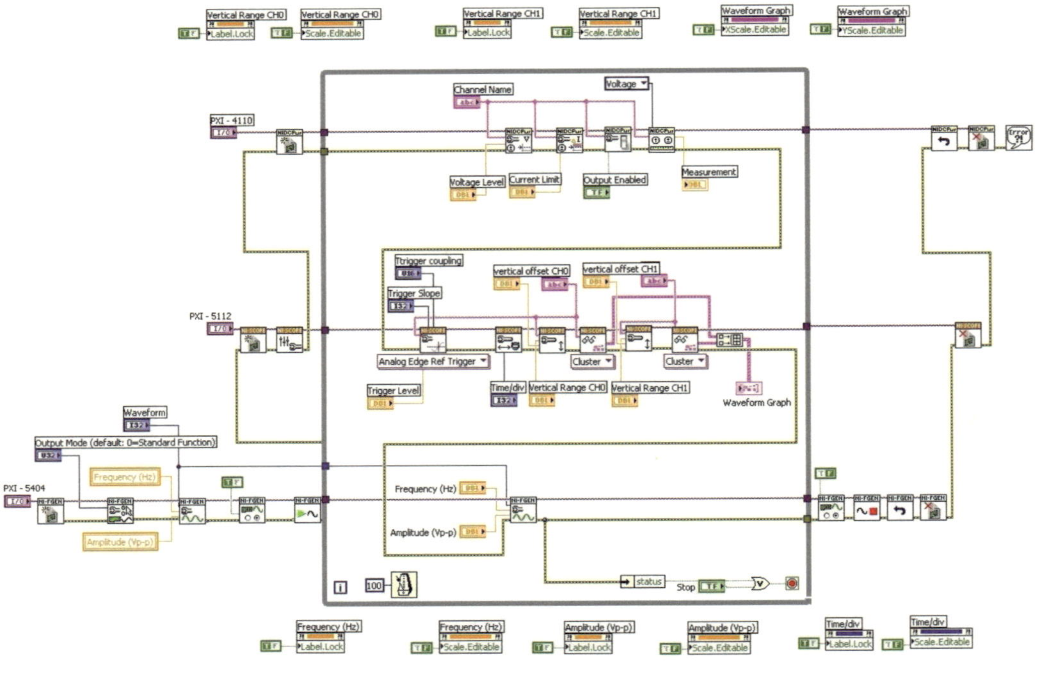

Fig. 17. Block Diagram of the Transfer Characteristic Program.

We continue to the oscilloscope, we configure the trigger settings, the timing settings. After we make the settings for the vertical range and start the readings of the values for representing on the graph both of the channels (0 and 1). We unite the two channels with a Build Array and output it on a Waveform Graph.
For the function generator we can control the frequency and amplitude during the program execution, this way we have it inside the loop too.
When we exit the loop we disabled the output, we stopped the generation we resettled the device. Finally we close the function generator, the oscilloscope, we reset and close the power supply and end the whole execution with a simple error handler to have the error messages in case if something goes wrong.

3.3 Duty cycle analyzer

The duty cycle analyzer experiment has a more complicated setup. We have the 33250A signal generator from Agilent and the NI PXI-6541 logic analyzer from National Instruments.
In Fig. 18. We have the block schematics. We have the Agilent signal generator, which generates a square signal to the Duty Cycle Analyzer. The signal is generated in the logic control and in the PLL. The signal that exists the PLL will be entering in a counter and after I in a display module. The signal is gathered with a logic analyzer from National Instruments and shown on a graph.

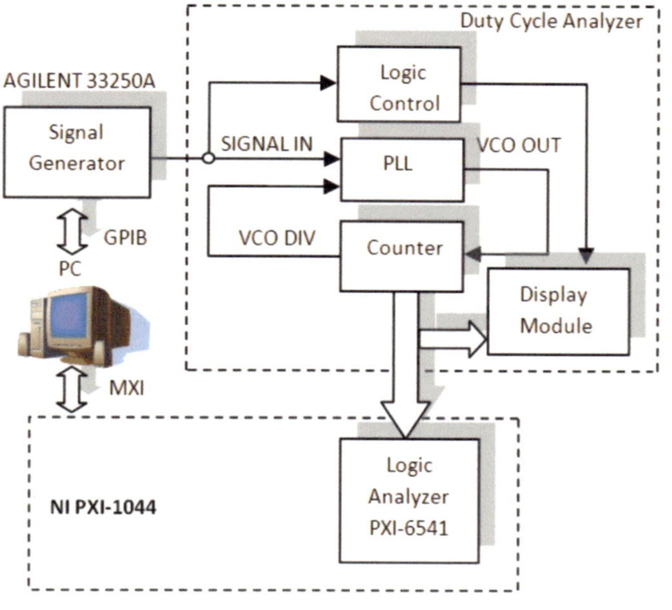

Fig. 18. Block Schematics of the Logic Analyzer Experiment.

We have also an external circuit which can be seen on Fig. 19. This external circuit is a duty cycle analyzer on which 14 different signals are analyzed with the experiment. The circuit has more modules like a logic control, a PLL and a counter and the duty cycle of the square signal is shown on the dual digit seven segment displays.

Fig. 19. Experimental Setup of the Logic Analyzer Experiment.

In Fig. 20. we can see the front panel of the Duty Cycle Analyzer program.
For the logic analyzer we have a resource ID, 14 activated channels, and the clock rate at 300 kHz and 10000 acquired samples.
For the Agilent signal generator we have resource ID, square waveform type, 100 Hz for frequency, 5 V amplitude, 25 % duty cycle, 0 V offset. The first signal (Clk) represents the duty cycle. The second signal (VCO_Out) is the representation of the PLL. The third signal (VCO_Div) is one input for the PLL. Q0 - Q7 is the counter part. Mst_QA, LD_Dcd, Mst_nQ represent logic levels for testing purposes.

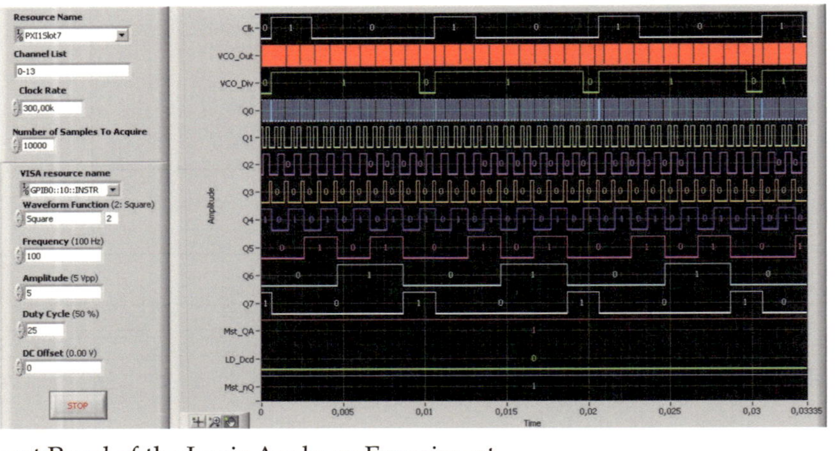

Fig. 20. Front Panel of the Logic Analyzer Experiment.

In Fig. 21. we have the block diagram of the experiment.
We have the initialization of the logic analyzer. In a while loop we have the configuring of the channels, settings of the clock, setting of the buffer (Number of Samples To Acquire) and finally we represent the data.
The Agilent signal generator is initialized, the amplitude, frequency, offset and waveform type is configured. We continue with the duty cycle is configuration, the output is enabling

and at the end we close the signal generator. Finally the logic analyzer is closed too, and the program is ended with a simple error handler.

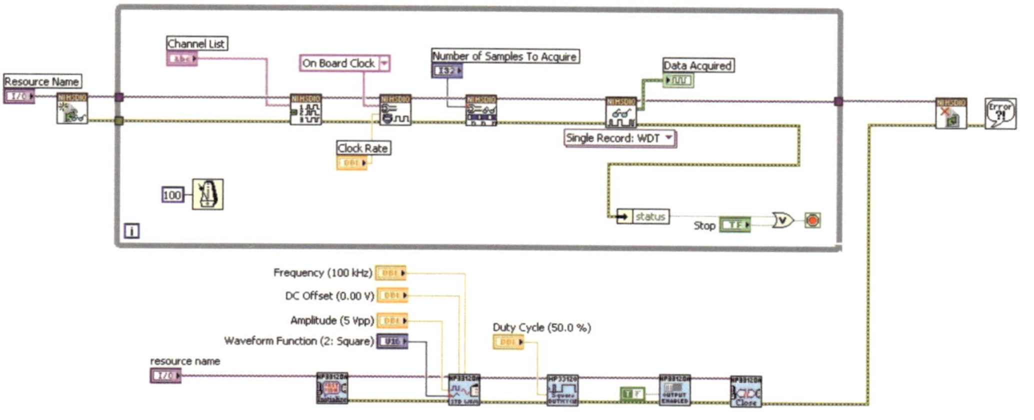

Fig. 21. Block Diagram of the Logic Analyzer Experiment.

3.4 Simple motor control

In Fig. 22. we can see the Block Diagram of the experiment.

This experiment uses only PXI instruments and thee PICDEM Mechatronics board from Microchip for amplifying and PID control. We have the NI PXI-6115 as the signal generator which generates a trapezoidal signal using the method presented in paragraph 2.5. The signal is amplified for the motors with the PICDEM Mechatroncis board; this board has also an implemented PID algorithm. The motor has a disk with slots, which rotates between an optocoupler pair, similar to and old mouse with ball. The signal from the optocoupler is sent in a signal; amplifying and conditioning circuit. The output signal is sent to the NI PXI-6608 counter and with a simple formula the RPM is calculated. The signal that the optcoupler reads should be similar to the generated signal, in our case both trapezoids should look the same.

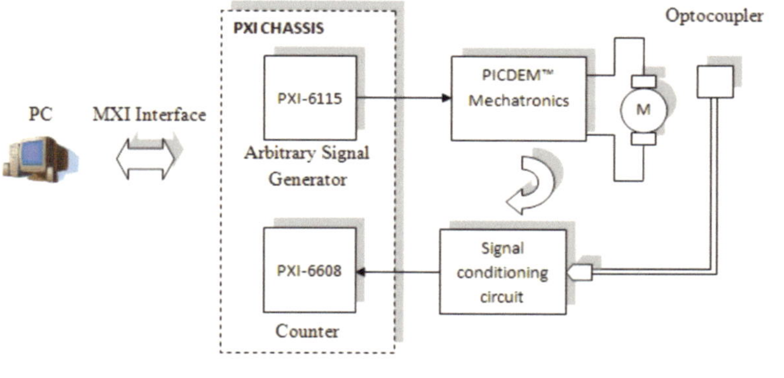

Fig. 22. Block Schematics of the Simple Motor Control Program.

In Fig. 23. we can se the PICDEM Mechatronics board and the motor with the disk with two slots.

Fig. 23. Experimental Setup of the Simple Motor Control Program.

In Fig. 24. we have the Front Panel of the program in LabVIEW with the trapezoidal signal generation on Waveform Graph and the RPM readings represented on Waveform Graph 2. The signal generation method is similar to the method presented in paragraph 2.5.

In the upper part of the Front Panel we have the signal generation configuration, where we have the resource ID of the signal generation DAQ and the minimum value a t 0 V and the maximum value at 5 V.

The second part of the Front Panel is the counter configuration with resource ID, rising edge, minim frequency at 100 KHz and maximum frequency at 1 MHz, 100 samples per

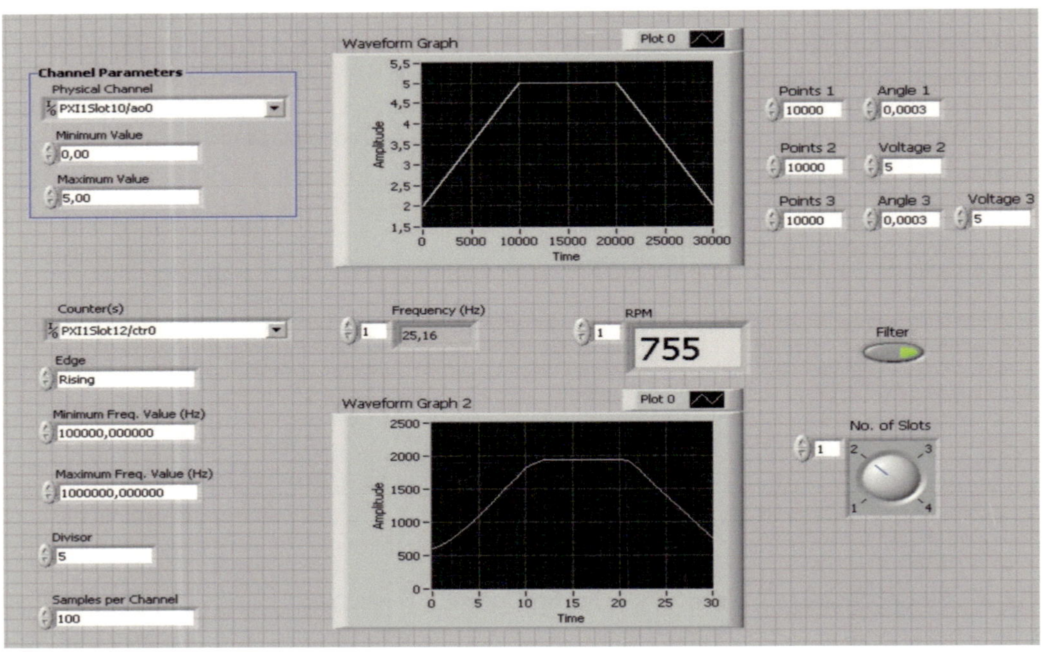

Fig. 24. Front Panel of the Simple Motor Control Program.

channel and the sampling divisor is 5. We have also indicators for frequency and RPM. We have also a median filter which can be deactivated with a button and we have a slot setting dial, which must be set to be equal with the number of slots of the disk present on the motor. This should be correctly set to calculate the RPM.

In Fig. 25. we can see the Block Diagram of the program. We have two parallel while loops. The first loop is for the trapezoidal signal generation. We have first the creation of the channel, after we have the start of the generation process. Next we enter the While loop, we have here the trapezoidal signal creation similar to paragraph 2.5. This is the method how a signal is generated by a DAQ board; we provide the numbers (samples) of the signal and the use the write signal VI, which has the icon with the pencil. After we exit the loop with closing the instrument (delete task) and we finish the program with the simple error handler.

The second loop is for the counter configuration. We have channel creation for the counter, the timing settings (sample configuration), the start of the execution continues, followed by the signal reading, which is filtered and with a specific formula we calculate the RPM and represent it on a Waveform Graph.

Equation (4) shows how to calculate the RPM from the frequency.

$$RPM = \frac{f}{N_s} \cdot 60s \tag{4}$$

Finally we close the instrument and we handle errors. We put everything in the loop to be controllable during execution.

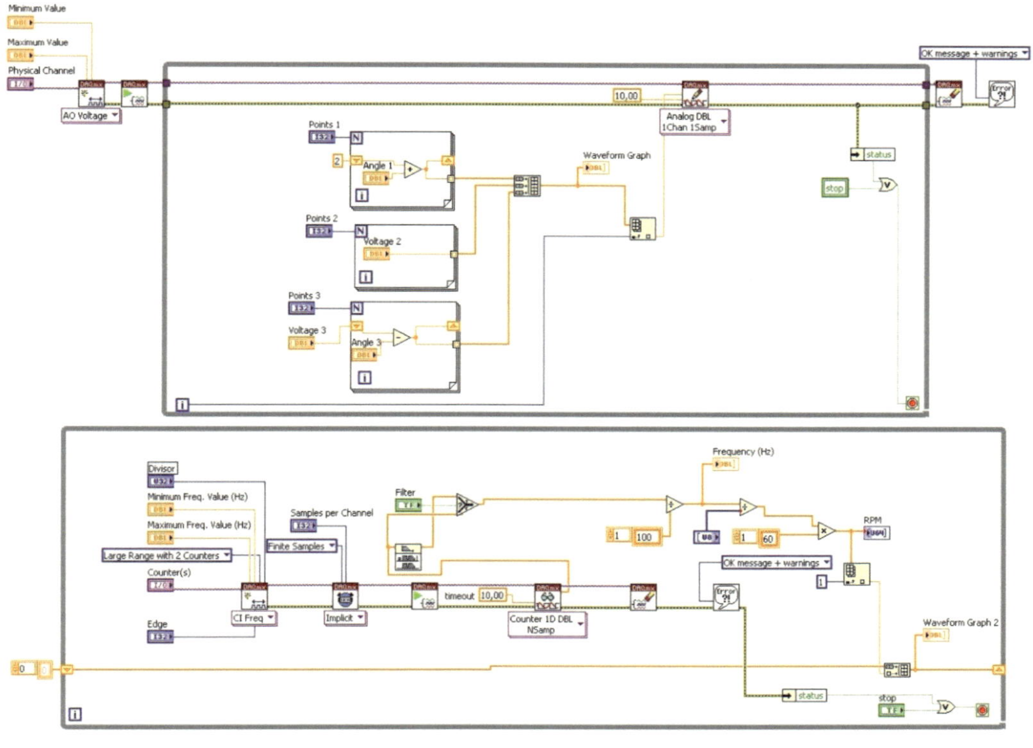

Fig. 25. Block Diagram of the Simple Motor Control Program.

3.5 Simple temperature measuring

In Fig. 26. we can see the setup for the temperature measurement. We have an LM35 centigrade sensor and an NI USB-6251 acquisition board. We also made the experiment with the NI USB-6009 smaller acquisition board and worked very well. The idea of this experiment is to measure voltage given from the temperature sensor and with the formula from the datasheet we convert the voltage to temperature.

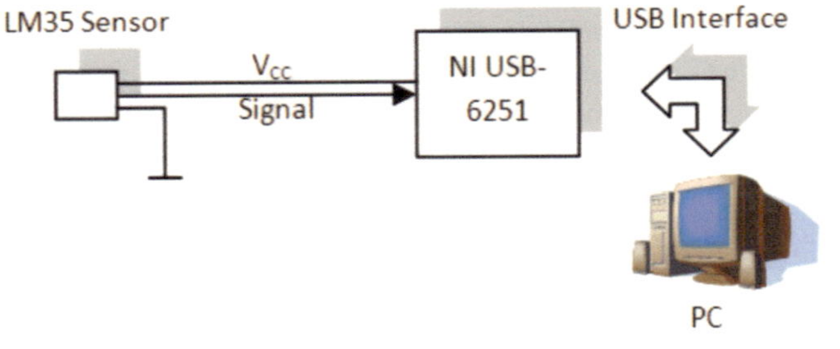

Fig. 26. Block Schematics of the Simple Temperature Measuring.

In Fig. 27. we have the Front Panel of the program. We have resource ID, timing rate at 1 and the actual temperature shown on an indicator and on a Waveform Graph.

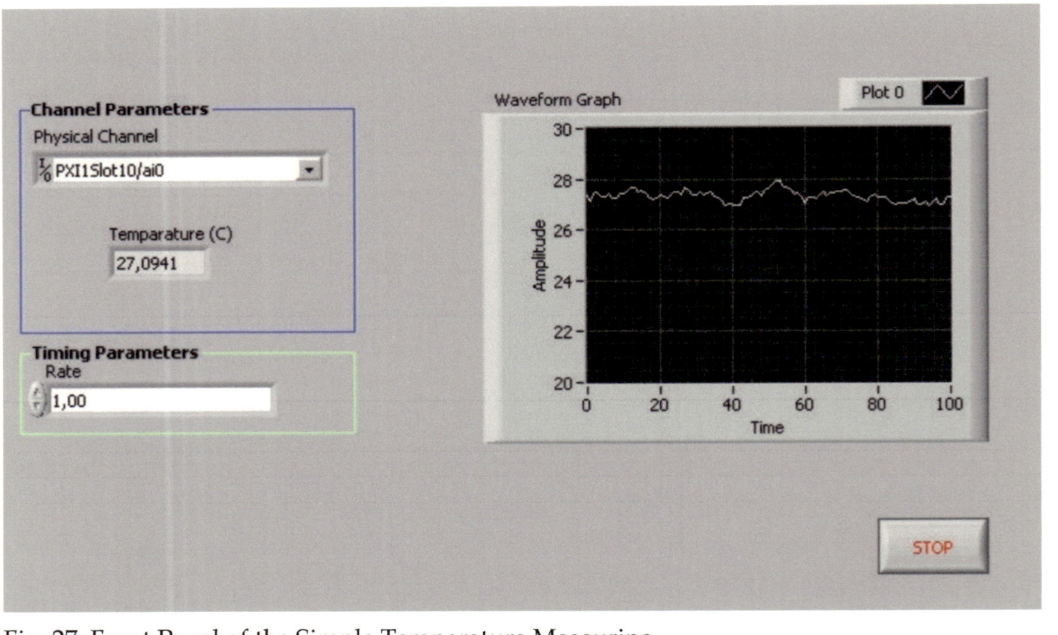

Fig. 27. Front Panel of the Simple Temperature Measuring.

In Fig. 28. we have Block Diagram of the program. We start with the channel creation, the setting of the timing (samples) and the start of the process. We enter in the While loop, here we have the reading of the samples and some mean value calculation over 10 samples. The temperature at the output of the LM35 centigrade sensor is its output voltage multiplied by 100. Finally we close the instrument and handle errors.

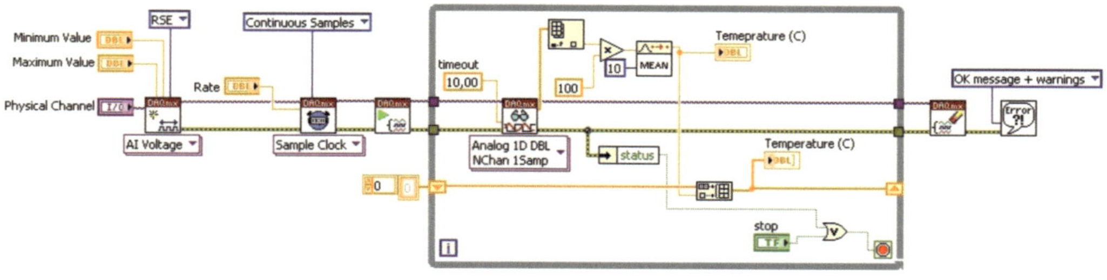

Fig. 28. Bock Diagram of the Simple Temperature Measuring.

3.6 Power supply testing

This experiment represents a more complex functional test. If we have many samples it's not the best solution. For many samples graphs are not indicated, but for only one sample this is the best test. With a graphs we can see really if the power supply is working.

The signal is generated with an Agilent 33250A function generator and the input and output signals are viewed using an NI PXI-5112 oscilloscope (Fig. 29.)

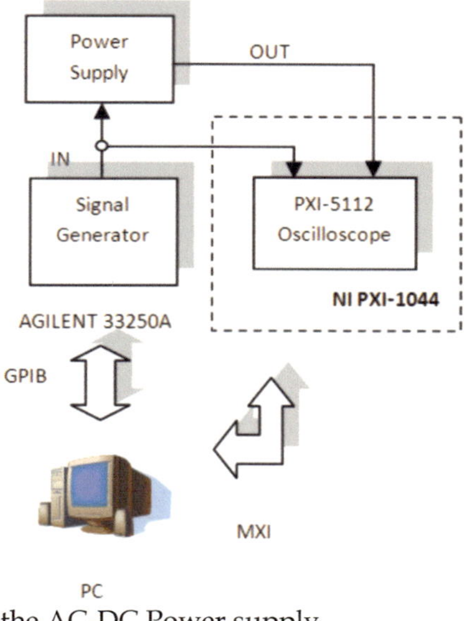

Fig. 29. Block Schematics of the AC-DC Power supply.

In Fig. 30. we can see the AC-DC power supply.

Fig. 30. Power Supply.

In Fig. 31. we have the Front Panel of the Agilent 33250A signal generator. As we can see we have resource ID, the waveform type is sine wave, the frequency 100 kHz, the offset is 0 V and the amplitude is 5 V.

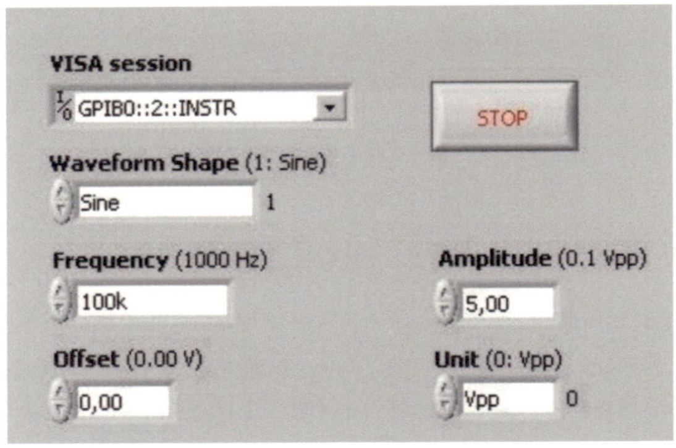

Fig. 31. Front Panel for the Agilent 33250A Function / Arbitrary Waveform Generator.

In Fig. 32. we can see the Front Panel of the oscilloscope application. We can see the resource ID of the oscilloscope and the horizontal adjust dial. We have two channels activated with two graphs and two vertical adjust dials. The first graph represents the input AC signal and the second graph represents the output DC signal. From this graphs we ca see that the power supply works correctly and we have an AC - DC power supply.

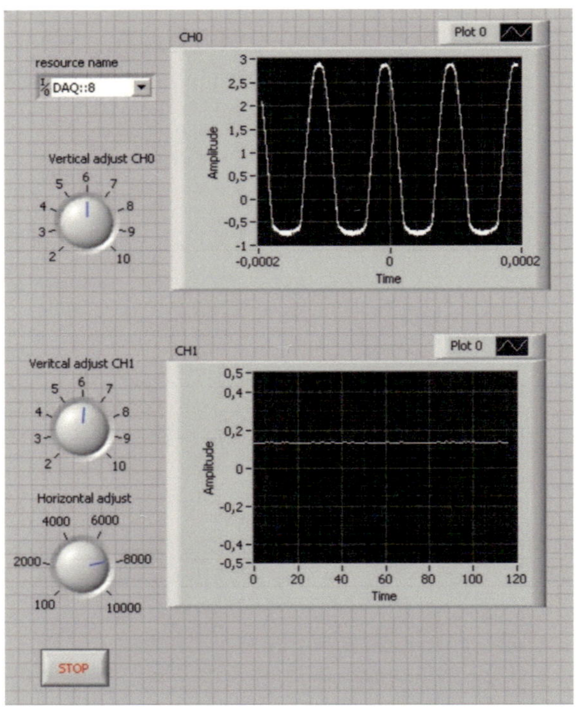

Fig. 32. Font Panel for the Power Supply Testing with Oscilloscope.

In Fig. 33. we have the 33250A Agilent signal generator programming. We have between the initialization and closing a While loop. In the loop we have the waveform configuration VI and the output enable VI.

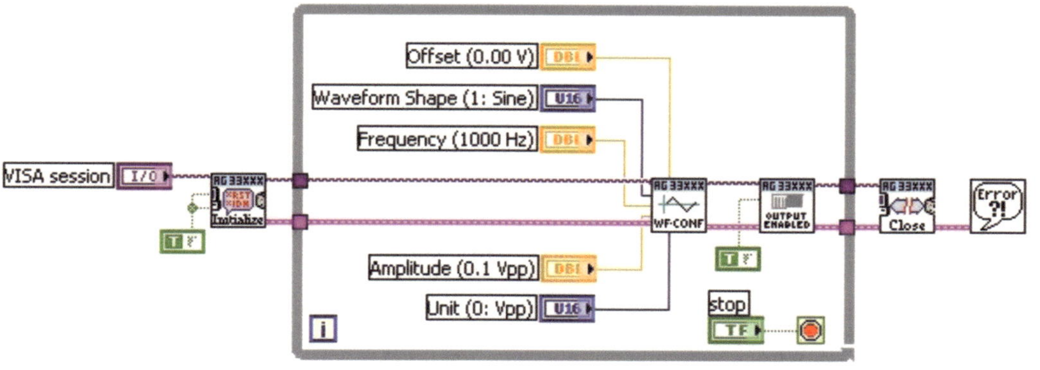

Fig. 33. Block Diagram for the Agilent 33250A Function / Arbitrary Waveform Generator.

In Fig. 34. we have the Block Diagram of the oscilloscope application.
We start with the channel creation. We enter in the while loop. We have some timing settings for the horizontal adjust and the vertical adjust and readings for the both activated channels (channel 0 and channel 1). We put a Bessel filter to the output signal of the voltage supply. When we exit from the while loop we close the instrument and handle errors.

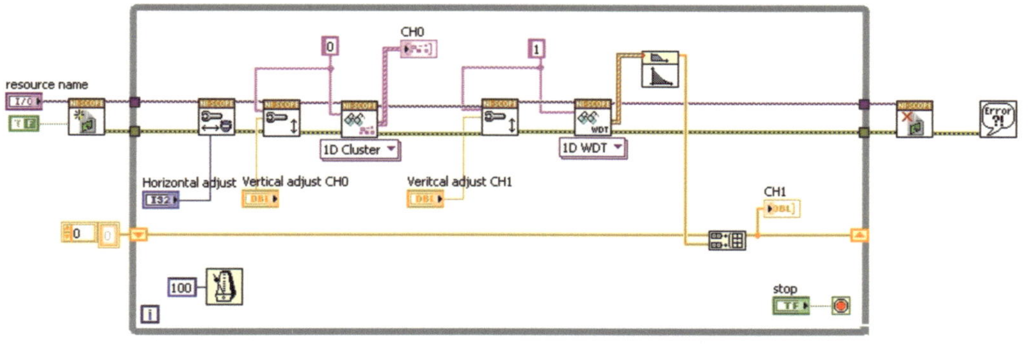

Fig. 34. Block Diagram for the Power Supply.

4. Virtual instruments for the CompactRIO chassis

4.1 Advanced motor control

In Fig. 35. we can see, we used both the PXI and the CompactRIO chassis. The trapezoidal signal is generated with the NI PXI-4110 Power Supply. The signal then is amplified with the NI 9505 H - bridge. The CompactRIO is programmed to make a PID loop too. The motor is connected to NI 9505 H - bridge. The motor has a disk with 100 slots, which rotates between an optocoupler pair.
The optocoupler is connected to the counter to read the frequency and calculate the RPM.

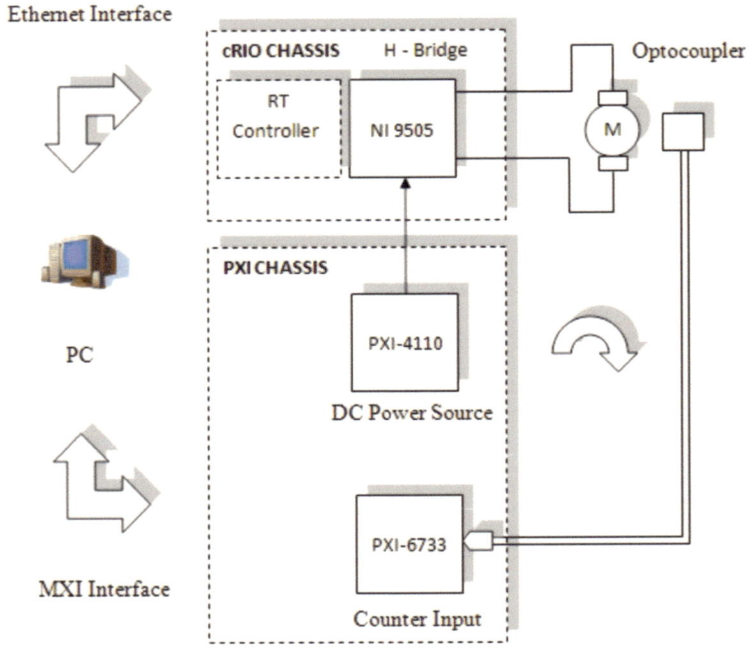

Fig. 35. Block Schematics of the Advanced Motor Control.

In Fig. 36. we can see the experimental setup with the motor and the CompactRIO.

Fig. 36. Experimental Setup of the Advanced Motor Control.

In Fig. 37. we can see the front panel of the signal generation program, which is similar to the program presented in paragraph 3.4. The trapezoid generation uses the method presented in paragraph 2.5. In the signal generation program the NI PXI-4110 power supply is used. In the Front Panel we have the resource ID, channel 1 is activated, the current limit is set to 100 mA and the voltage is measured at the output of the power supply.

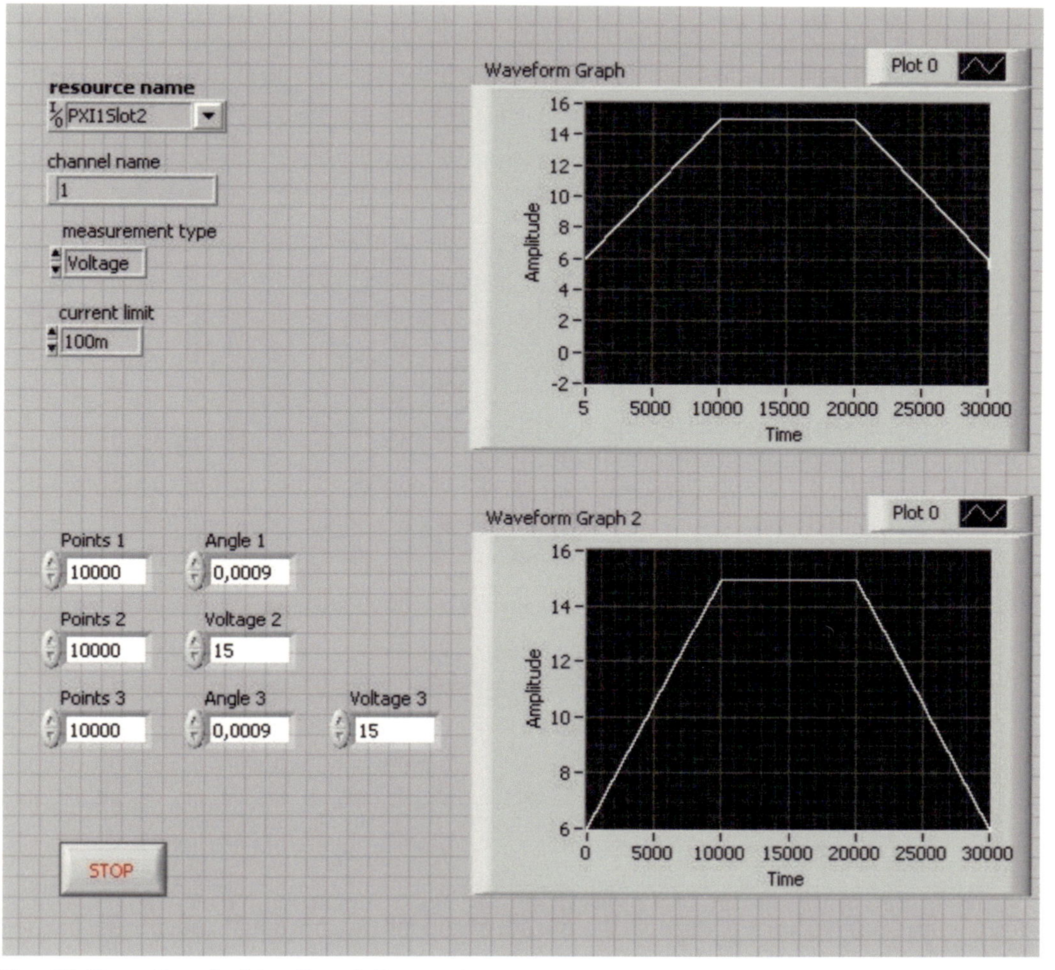

Fig. 37. Front Panel of the Signal Generation.

In Fig. 38. we have the RPM reading program. We have resource ID, rising edge, minimum frequency set to 100 kHz and maximum set to 1 MHz, 100 samples acquisitioned at the channel and the sampling divisor set to 5. We have put indicator for frequency and RPM and a Waveform Graph to represent the RPM. This graph should be similar to the generated signal.

In Fig. 39. we have the Front Panel of the FPGA programming. We have a lot of controls and indicators, which are use to control some functions of the NI 9505 H - bridge, which are also shown on the card with some LEDs. We have Enable Drive, Disable Drive and Enable Emergency-Stop. We show the status of the Drive, the Drive Fault and the Overtemperature Fault, the supply current (Vsup Present) present and the presents of the analog input's trigger (AI Trigger). We have the Current Loop Rate set to 50 µs, this rate is the rate of the PID loop. We have the PID parameters: 350 for the proportional gain, 300 for the integral gain and 5500 for the derivative gain. We have a current setpoint at a negative value (in our case -16) this for rotating the motor in one direction, if it's positive the motor rotates in other

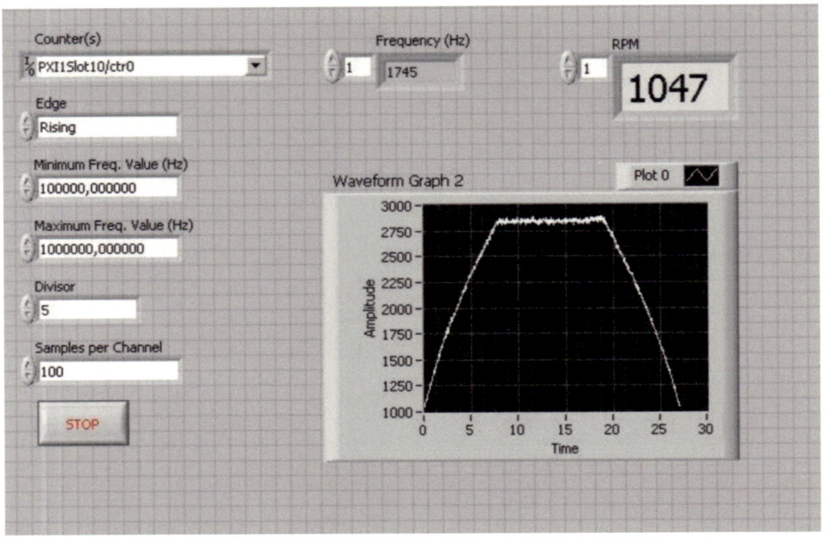

Fig. 38. Front Panel of the RPM Reading.

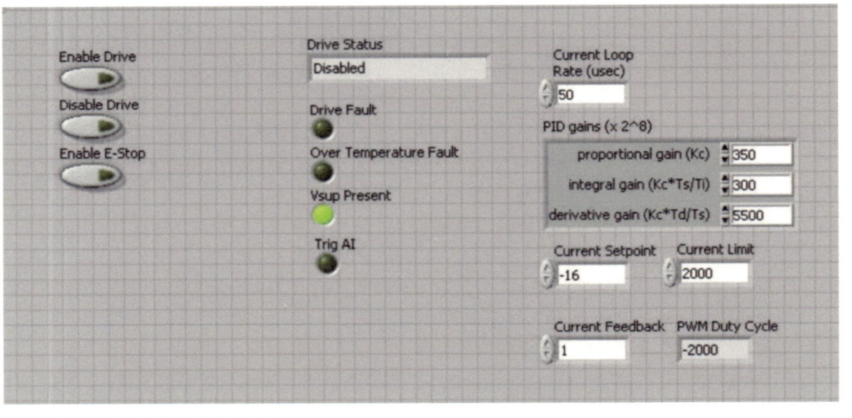

Fig. 39. Front Panel of the FPGA Part.

direction. We limit the current at a certain value (in our case 2000) and we set current feedback to 1, after we read the PWM Duty Cycle. The PWM Duty Cycle has the same sign as the Current Setpoint, this way to show the direction of the motor rotation. The Front Panel is almost the same with this one for all Block Diagrams which will be presented next.

In Fig. 40. we can see the Block Diagram of the trapeze generation program. This program is similar to the first While loop from Fig. 25., but it's made with a power supply, not a DAQ. The trapeze is generated with the method presented in paragraph 2.5.

The programming starts with channel creation. After entering in the While loop we set the voltage. Here is connected the trapezoidal signal. After we set the current, we enable output and we measure the voltage at the power supply's ports. When we exit from the While loop, we disable output and close the instrument.

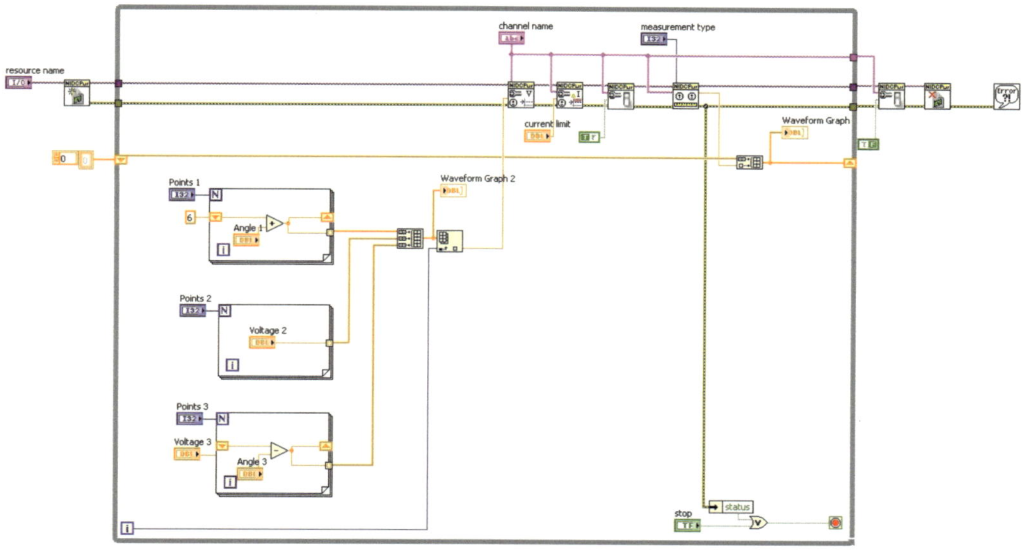

Fig. 40. Block Diagram of Trapeze Generation with Power Supply.

In Fig. 41. we have the RPM reading Block Diagram, which is same with the second While loop from Fig. 25.

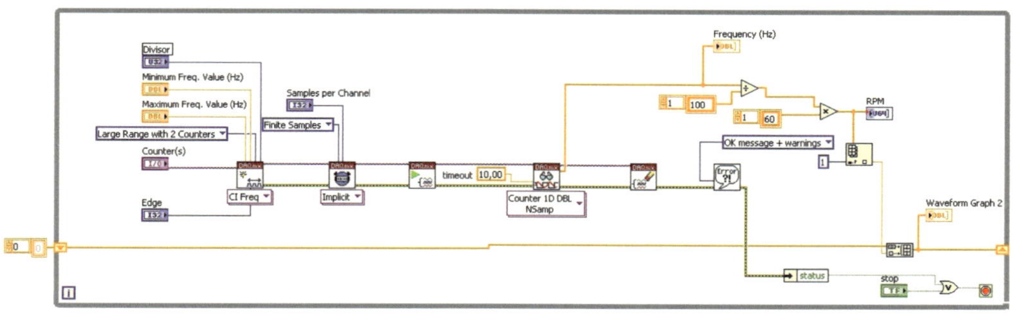

Fig. 41. RPM Reading Block Diagram.

In Fig. 42. we can see the we have a big While loop with all the controls used in the FPGA part and called by the Real-Time controller. At the left part we have loaded the FPGA part and at the output we closed it and we handle errors.

In Fig. 43. we have the block Diagram of the networked real-time host. This VI is made copying the VI form Fig. 41. and adding global variables to send the data trough network to the Windows host. We have the global variables also before of the FPGA part loading for initialization.

In Fig. 44. we have the Windows host with the same global variables as in the networked real-time host, but mirrored. This means if in the networked real-time host we had a control in the windows host we have indicator and vice-versa. We can imagine an invisible line between the global variables with the same name starting from the control to the indicator.

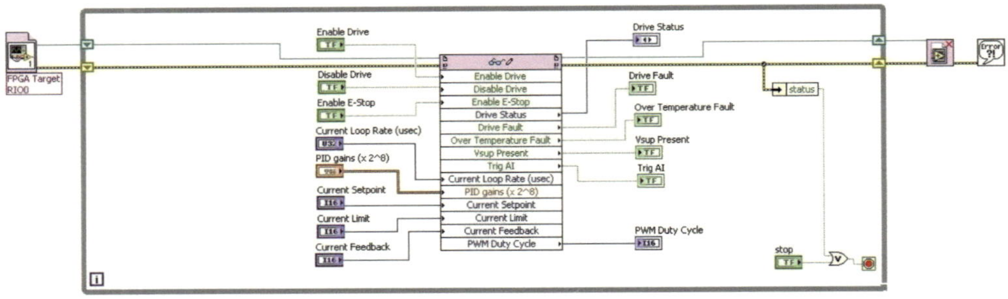

Fig. 42. Block Diagram of the Real-Time Host.

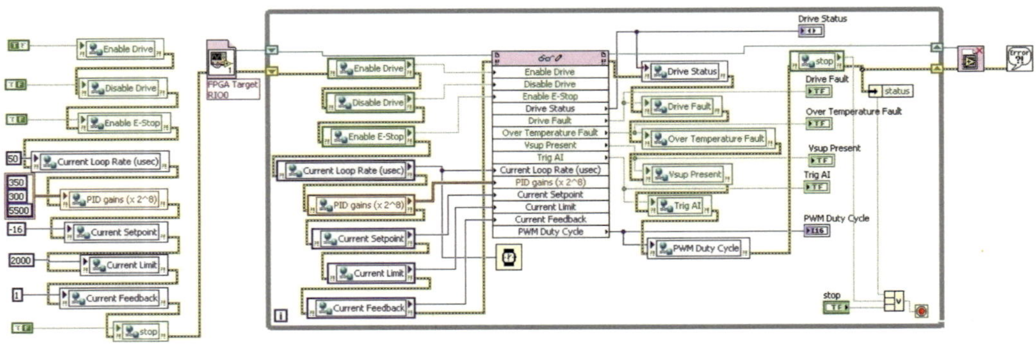

Fig. 43. Block Diagram of the Networked Real-Time Host.

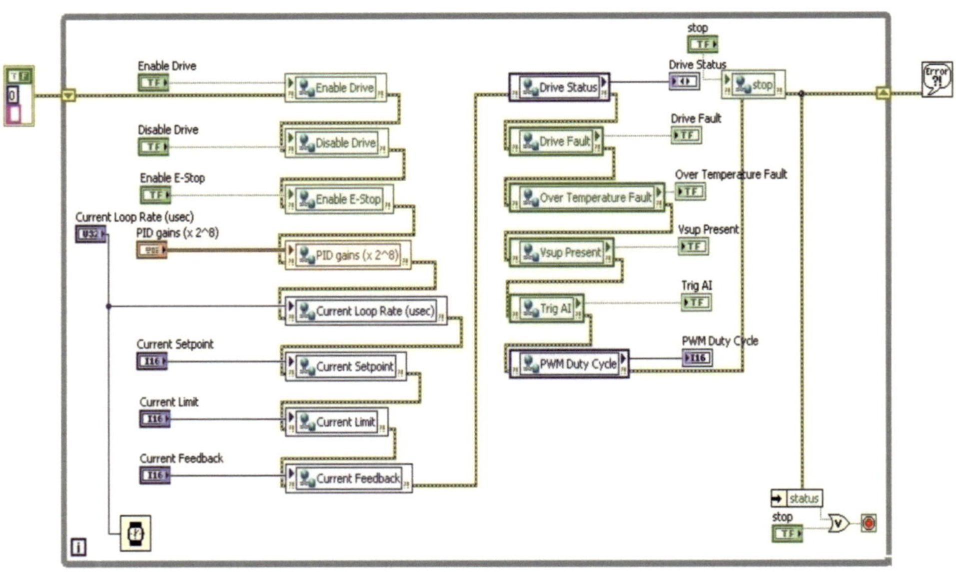

Fig. 44. Block Diagram of the Windows Host.

global variables communicates not only between different VIs on the same computer, but between VIs on different computers, connected via networks cables if they are in the same subnet.

4.2 Advanced temperature measuring

In Fig. 45. we can see the block schematics of the experiment.

We have the LM35 centigrade sensor connected to the NI 9201 analog input C series module which is connected to a CompactRIO. The CompactRIO is connected via Ethernet interface to the PC.

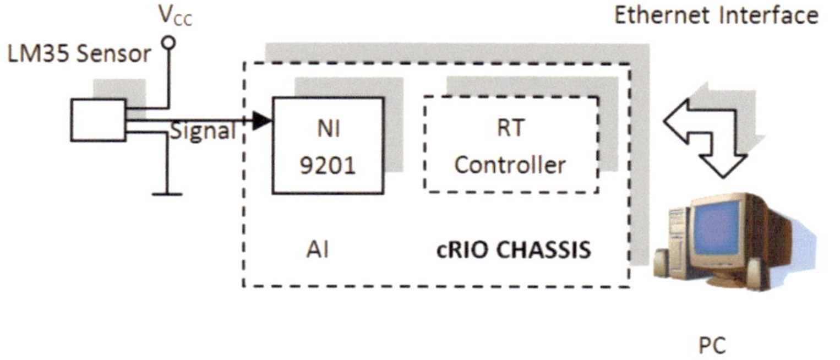

Fig. 45. Block Schematics of the Advanced Temperature Measuring.

In Fig. 46. we have the Front Panel of the FPGA part. We have only raw data collected here; we just measure the voltage in mV with the NI 9201 analog input module. We ca set the loop timing and we visualize errors.

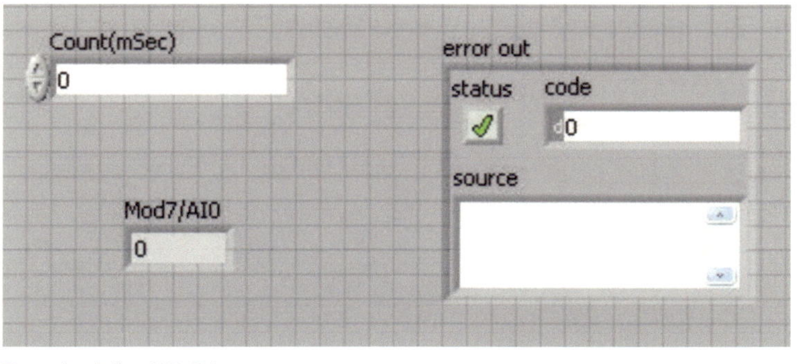

Fig. 46. Front Panel of the FPGA part.

In Fig. 47. we have the Front Panel of the networked real-time host part. Here we have the voltage converted in temperature in °C, we visualize errors and we display the log of the temperature o both Waveform Graph and Chart. Here we ca see a big log of the temperature over one day when turning the air conditioning system OFF and ON.

In Fig. 48. we can see the Front Panel of the Windows host part. We have here a special stop button (Stop Windows GUI). With this button we can stop only the windows part of the program, the temperature acquisition will continue on the real-time system. We have indicator for the Temperature and we have a Waveform Chart for graph. We have c dial control for the sample interval in ms.

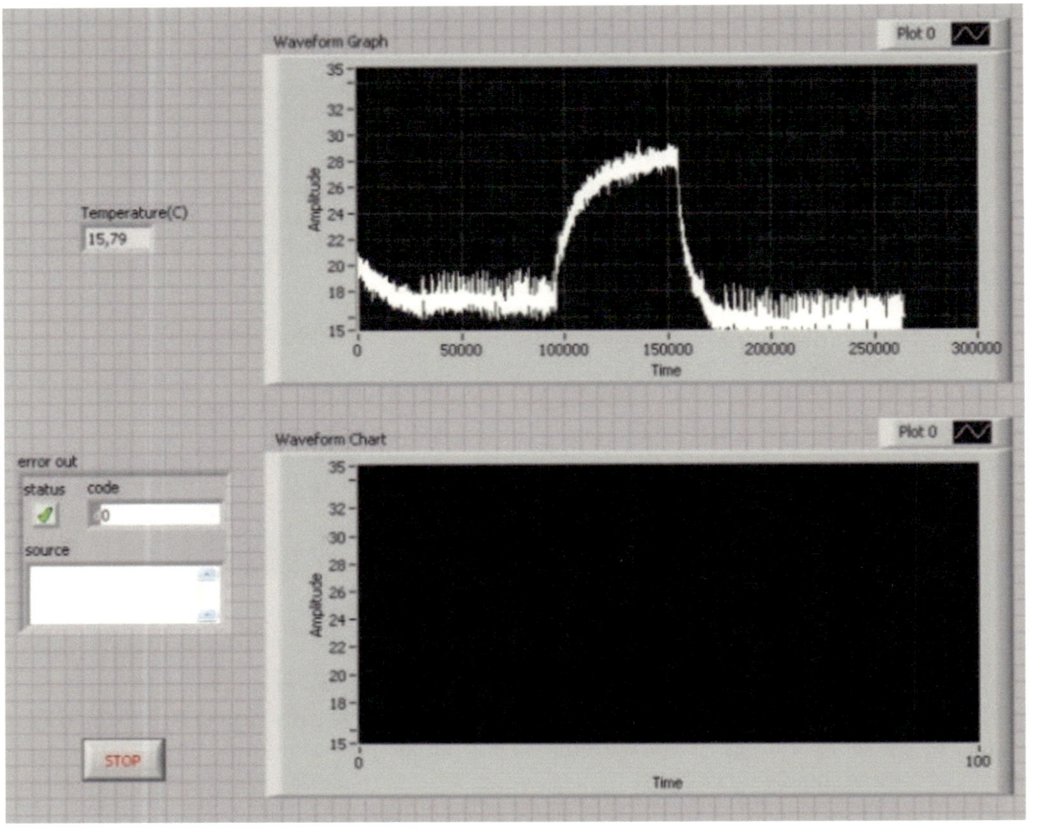

Fig. 47. Front Panel of the Networked Real-Time Host.

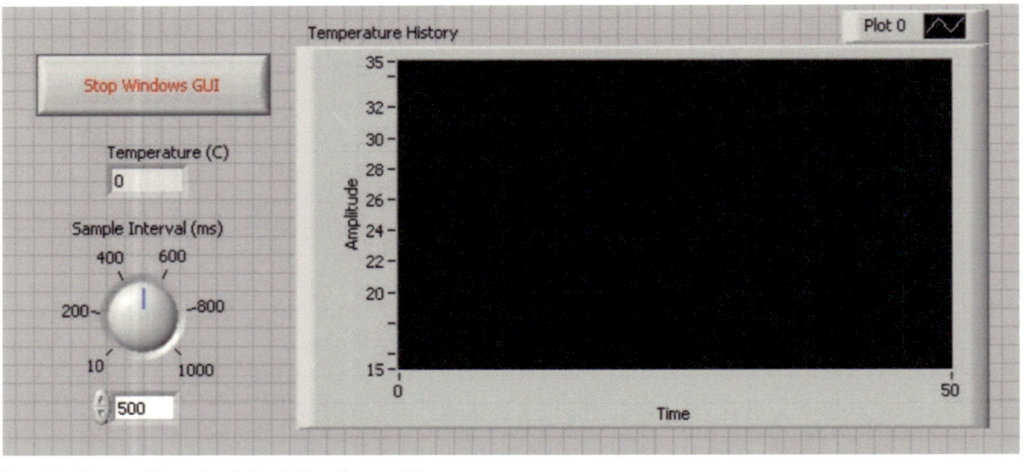

Fig. 48. Front Panel of the Windows Host.

In Fig. 49. we have the block diagram of the FPGA part. We have While loop and a Flat Sequence with some special FPGA timing and the acquisition with the FPGA node.

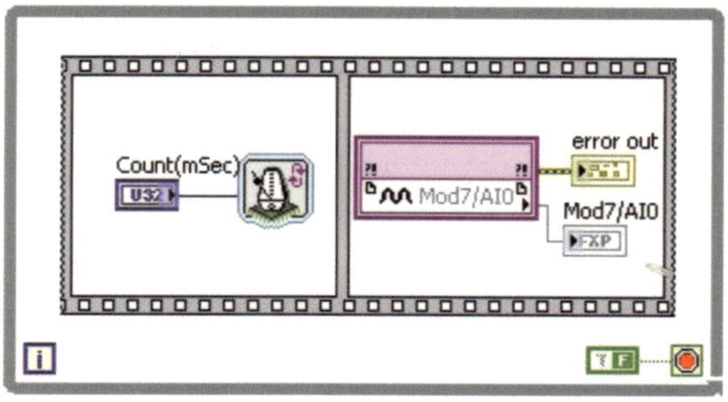

Fig. 49. Block Diagram of the FPGA part.

In Fig. 50. we can see the Block Diagram of the real-time host part. We have the FPGA program loaded in the real-time host (FPGA Target RIO0). We have a while loop with the used variables, the conversion from voltage to temperature in °C with multiplying with 100, a mean of 100 values. After the exit from the While loop we have the closing of the FPGA program loaded in the real-time host and the handling of errors.

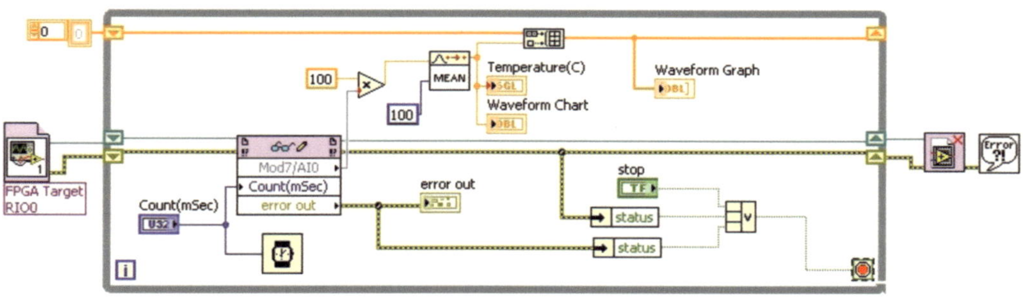

Fig. 50. Block Diagram of the Real-Time Host.

In Fig. 51. We have the Block Diagram of the networked real-time host, which is the copy of the real-time host plus the adding of the global variables to the controls and indicators.

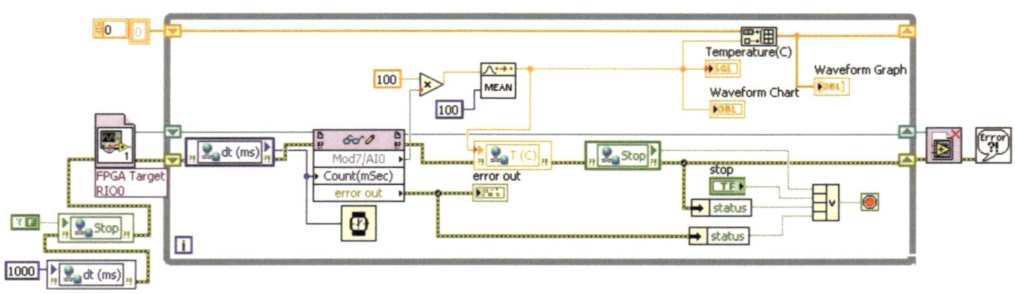

Fig. 51. Block Diagram of the Networked Real-Time Host.

In Fig. 52. we have the Block Diagram of the Windows host, which has the global variables as the mirror image of the networked real-time host. This means where we have control, we will have indicator and vice-versa. We can imagine an invisible line, connection between these global variables. These lines transport the data between the two VIs via Ethernet. The data is sent from the networked real-time host, but there is also feedback from the Widows host.

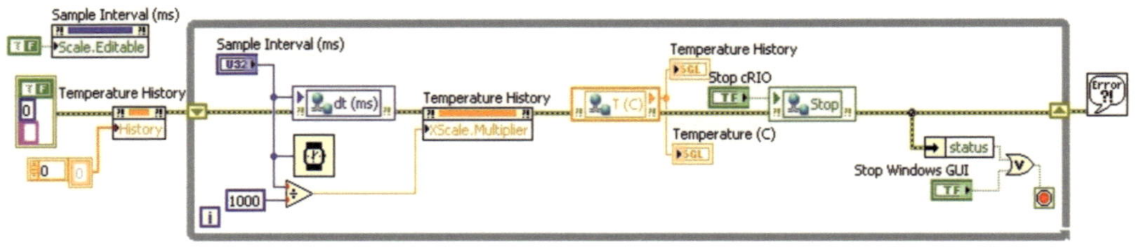

Fig. 52. Block Diagram of the Windows Host.

5. Conclusion

LabVIEW is a very complete programming language. We could say that if assembly is a first level programming language and C is a second level programming language, than LabVIEW should be a third level programming language. LabVIEW is graphical and has a lot of implemented blocks, as they say; you don't have to invent the wheel again. This concept makes programming really fast and could reduce very much an engineer's work.
As we could see in paragraph 2., LabVIEW has a lot of block, but not enough. It hasn't got everything that is needed. In paragraph 2. we presented only 7 programming tricks that we made and we thought that should be important to know. We are sure that are much more tricks in this programming language. We encountered and solved much more programming problems, but we decided not to present those tricks, because, they are not so general. After all LabVIEW is a very complex programming language, but there is place for more.
After the tricks we presented 6 applications made with the PXI industrial system and 2 applications made with CompactRIO. They have similarities; some of them are made with both of the PXI and ComapctRIO platforms. The applications were made for didactical purposes and for publishing them on the LabVIEW Remote Lab. All the applications are published and accessible from the http://plst.etc.upt.ro address with a user name and password.

6. References

Antonovičs U. & Priednieks Ē. (2006). Interactive Learning Tools for Electrical Engineering and Electronics Course, *Electronics and Electrical Engineering*, ISSN 1392-1215 - Kaunas Technologija, No. 7(71), pp. 29–34, 2006.

Auer, M.E. & Gallent, W. (2000) The Remote Electronic Lab as a Part of the Telelearning Concept at the Carinthia Tech Institute, *Proceedings of the ICL2000, Villach/Austria*, 2000.

Garbus, R.U.; Aguirre, I.J.O.; Sanchez, R.C. & Pureco, O.R. (2006). Virtual Remote Lab for Control Practic, *Electronics, Robotics and Automotive Mechanics Conference*, vol. 2, pp. 361-366, 2006.

Gontean, A.; Lie, I. & Szabó, R. (2009 a). LabVIEW powered remote lab, *Design and Technology of Electronics Packages, (SIITME) 2009 15th International Symposium*, pp. 335-340, Gyula, Hungary, September , 2009.

Gontean, A.; Lie, I. & Szabó, R. (2009 b). Using a Low Cost Programmable Power Supply for Automated Testing, *Design and Technology of Electronics Packages, (SIITME) 2009 15th International Symposium*, pp. 341-346, Gyula, Hungary, September , 2009.

Gontean A. & Szabó R. (2009 a). Remote temperature measurement with and without FPGA, *TELFOR 2009 – 17th Telecommunications Forum*, pp. 775-778, Belgrade, Serbia, November, 2009.

Gontean A. & Szabó R. (2009 b). Comparison between PIC and CompactRIO remote motor control, *TELFOR 2009 – 17th Telecommunications Forum*, pp. 747-750, Belgrade, Serbia, November, 2009.

Grober, S.; Vetter, M.; Eckert, B. & Jodl, H.-J. (2007). Experimenting from a distance – remotely controlled laboratory, *Eur. J. Phys.*, vol. 28, pp. 127-141, 2007.

Hercog, D.; Gergic, B. & Matko, V. (2005). Remote Lab for Electric Drives, *Industrial Electronics – ISIE 2005 Proceedings of the IEEE International Symposium*, vol. 4. pp. 1685-1690, 2005.

Khalil, A.; Hasna, M.; Benammar, M.; Chaabane, M. & Ben Amar, C. (2009). Development of a remote lab for electrical engineering program, *Signals, Circuits and Systems (SCS) – 3rd International Conference*, pp. 1-5, 2009.

Mihela Lascu (2007). *Advanced programming techniques in LabVIEW*, Politehnica Publishing House, Timişoara, 2007.

*** National Instruments (2008). *LabVIEW™ Data Acquisition and Signal Conditioning Exercises*, 2008.

*** National Instruments (2008). *Data Acquisition and Signal Conditioning – Course Manual*, 2008.

*** National Instruments (2007). *LabVIEW™ Basics II: Development – Course Manual*, 2007.

*** National Instruments (2007). *LabVIEW™ Basics I: Introduction – Course Manual*, 2007.

*** National Instruments (2008). *CompactRIO™ and LabVIEW™ Development Fundamentals – Course Manual*, 2008.

Paladini, S.; da Silva, J.B.; Alves, G.R.; Fischer, B.R. & da Mota Alves, J.B. (2008). Using Remote Lab Networks to Provide Support to Public Secondary School Education Level, *Computational Science and Engineering Workshops – CSEWORKSHOPS '08 11th IEEE International Conference*, pp. 275-280, 2008.

Szabó, R.; Gontean, A. & Lie, I. (2010). Sound Based Coin Recognition and Clapper, *MENDEL '10 – 16th International Conference on Soft Computing*, pp. 509-516, Brno, Czech Republic, June, 2010.

Szabó, R.; Gontean, A.; Lie, I. & Băbăiţă, M. (2009). Oscilloscope Control with PC, NAUN 2010 – *International Journal of Computers and Communications*, pp. 33-40, Issue 3, Volume 3, September, 2010.

Uran, S.; Hercog, D. & Jezernik; K., (2006). Remote Lab Experiment RC Oscillator for Learning of Control, *International Journal of Online Engineering*, vol. 2, no. 4, pp. 1-8, 2006.